Fathering Your Father

*The Zen of Fabrication
in Tang Buddhism*

Alan Cole

UNIVERSITY OF CALIFORNIA PRESS
Berkeley · Los Angeles · London

University of California Press, one of the most
distinguished university presses in the United States,
enriches lives around the world by advancing scholarship in the humanities, social sciences, and natural
sciences. Its activities are supported by the UC Press
Foundation and by philanthropic contributions from
individuals and institutions. For more information,
visit www.ucpress.edu.

University of California Press
Berkeley and Los Angeles, California

University of California Press, Ltd.
London, England

Library of Congress Cataloging-in-Publication Data
Cole, Alan, 1964–.
    Fathering your father : the Zen of fabrication in
Tang Buddhism / Alan Cole.
        p.   cm.
    Includes bibliographical references and index.
    ISBN 978-0-520-25484-8 (cloth, alk. paper)
    ISBN 978-0-520-25485-5 (pbk., alk. paper)
    1. Zen Buddhism—China—History.   I. Title.
BQ9262.5.C65   2009
294.3'9270951—dc22   2008026040

Manufactured in the United States of America
16 15 14 13 12 11 10 09 08 07
10 9 8 7 6 5 4 3 2 1

This book is printed on Natures Book, which
contains 50% post-consumer waste and meets the
minimum requirements of ANSI/NISO Z39.48–1992
(R 1997) (Permanence of Paper).

A

Philip E. Lilienthal

BOOK

The publisher gratefully acknowledges the generous support of the Philip E. Lilienthal Asian Studies Endowment Fund of the University of California Press Foundation, which was established by a major gift from Sally Lilienthal.

Fathering Your Father

This book is dedicated to Friedrich Nietzsche

Almost all the problems of philosophy once again pose the same form of question as they did two thousand years ago: how can something originate in its opposite, for example rationality in irrationality, the sentient in the dead, logic in unlogic, disinterested contemplation in covetous desire, living for others in egoism, truth in error?

Nietzsche, Human, All Too Human (1)

The significance of language for the evolution of culture lies in this, that mankind set up in language a separate world beside the other world, a place it took to be so firmly set that, standing upon it, it could lift the rest of the world off its hinges and make itself master of it.

Nietzsche, Human, All Too Human (11)

Contents

Preface

This book is an attempt to rethink the history of early Chan (Zen) in a manner closer to what I take to be a History of Religions approach—trying to figure out how and why certain forms of religiosity took shape the way they did instead of assuming that it was just religious experience that made religion.[1] While several revisionist histories of Chan and Zen have been published in the past twenty-some years, these histories continue to read early Chan texts—the seventh- and eighth-century genealogies that chronicle the "descendants" of Bodhidharma (n.d.)—as basically the effect of new forms of religious experience in China. Hence, though it has been widely admitted that the Bodhidharma genealogies are unreliable for a range of historical details, this has not shaken the assumption that behind these texts there is nothing less than a budding Chan School made of real teachers, their innovative teachings, and their faithful disciples. As this book attempts to prove, this assumption of simplicity and innocence at the beginning of Chan does rather poorly at the task of explaining how these texts were pieced together and why their contents

---

1. I should note that this definition of History of Religions is quite at odds with the ahistorical and *völkisch* agenda supplied by Mircea Eliade and others in the 1950s and 1960s when the term *History of Religions* took hold in academia. For discussion of this vexed moment in Religious Studies, see Ivan Strenski's *Four Theories of Myth in Twentieth-Century History*, chaps. 4–5. For more specific indictments of Eliade's fascist past and its implications for evaluating his academic work, see Alexandra Laignel-Lavastine's *Cioran, Eliade, Ionesco*; Daniel Dubuisson's *Impostures et psuedo-science*; and Florin Turcanu's *Mircea Eliade*.

seem designed to accomplish a range of tasks far from simply depicting a new style of Buddhist practice. Thus, in place of the "religion first, texts second" approach, this book argues that these texts were written for reasons that have little to do with Buddhist practice, or new forms of enlightened wisdom, or "orthodoxy," and much more to do with politics, property, and, perhaps most importantly, a newfound enthusiasm for claiming to own the totality of the Buddhist tradition. Hence, I believe that what we have come to call Chan was really an accidental creation, not born from men-with-truth and their trusty historians, but rather from a wavering cycle of writing and rewriting narratives that hoped to convincingly demonstrate the new ownership of the fullness of the Buddhist tradition in China.

Unlike many arguments in academia, the differences between my approach and the previous explanations of Chan are substantial, with important consequences for how we think about medieval Chan and its modern forms in East Asia and the Occident. Similarly, deciding where one stands in this debate likely will have lasting implications for how one thinks, in general, about the production of truth in religion. I would wager that few readers will be able to put this book down without asking a series of troubling questions about what the Chan tradition was originally all about and what this tells us about the way humans, medieval and modern, relate to truth, authority, and perfection. And, as the uncomfortable reflexivity in the title *Fathering Your Father* suggests, figuring out the mechanics involved in the "birth of Chan" will involve addressing several forms of ingenuity and bad faith in the conception of the perfect "truth-fathers."

To offer an analogy for my approach, I take the early genealogical texts that explain how perfect Buddhism got lodged in certain Chinese men of the seventh and eighth centuries to be like wedding photos entered in a yearly competition at the local county fair in which the winner, as decided by a panel of judges, takes home $500. If membership on the panel of judges is stable, then over the years various assumptions about what makes a winning wedding photo will emerge, and competitive photographers will do their best to understand these past decisions and prepare their photos accordingly. They will do so *not* with a commitment to rendering the Real of any particular wedding in its most lifelike form but rather by imagining what will most likely appeal to the judges' taste in wedding photos, given past successes. Not surprisingly, then, each year the photos will likely show shared thematic assumptions and, similarly, seek to enhance elements that the photographers perceived to be winning angles. For instance, certain moments in the ceremony will be regularly selected, just as certain compositions will be relied on to generate a set of moods and meanings. Of course, once in a while a daring photographer will step outside these accepted clichés and try a new look or theme. Naturally, if this new presentation wins the day, then next year's photos likely will reflect an awareness that a new winning thematic has entered the repertoire.

And, somewhat ironically, one of the stylistic choices that might emerge from this cycle of competition is a set of techniques for making the photos look as lifelike as possible. Thus, the photographers in this contest might end up competing by developing techniques to make their photos look less like art and more like "simple" presentations of the Real of the wedding, and yet this, too, would be an extension of their art and an effect of the county fair's selection process. That is, hiding the competitive quality of the art could very likely become part of the competition since that would, presumably, enhance the charm of the art. Consequently, the key to understanding any particular photo requires placing it in its formatting historical matrix, with particular attention paid to the set of intersubjective expectations regarding quality wedding photos that the photographers and judges shared, however imperfectly. In short, any particular photo in this series isn't about the wedding; it is about the competition.

In light of this analogy, previous discussions of early Chan texts have been staring at these photos (texts) trying to step *into* these scenes to figure out who was doing what at that moment in history when the photos were snapped. Thus, with the goal being to pierce the glossy surface of the photo to get at the Real of wedding day events, each photo is demoted to being no more than a transparent and irrelevant medium, and certainly not a highly worked "canvas," dominated by the artist's calculations and the web of desire and competition surrounding the county fair. For my part, instead of trying to look "through" these photos (texts) to the supposed Real behind them, I will linger on their surfaces to clarify their art and artifice and to see how these art forms developed over time through forces that were *completely* outside of the photo and certainly far from the wedding day details, because in many cases there appears not to have been a wedding at all as the photographer dressed his friends up to pose for the perfect shot. In brief, I will be arguing that we have not been reading these texts in the right register, and we have thus ignored or underestimated the formatting function of the county fair competition and consequently misunderstood the *art of competition,* in both senses of the phrase.

Moreover, in addition to pointing out how calculating and conniving these works are as literary gambits, my approach will show that it is not just the historical "facts" about various masters that have been thoroughly manipulated for polemic reasons but that key elements in Chan discourse that are deemed more philosophical and "practice-oriented"—such as sudden enlightenment, inherent buddhahood, and the all-natural master—are also best understood as slave-pistons in various motors of competition. For instance, sudden enlightenment, in league with innate enlightenment, appears to have been seized upon not for its philosophic plenitude, or basic "psychological" reality, but rather because it handily accomplished a number of crucial narrative tasks that I will point out in the chapters to come. In short, the form and function of truth in these texts will at every turn seem to have been conditioned by the politics of writing about truth and its ownership. Thus, I will be arguing that truth is as truth does, with truth being the stubby little tail that the dog of polemics vigorously wags.

To give another analogy that highlights what is at stake in shifting to this style of reading, consider preparing a study of the American sitcom, *Happy Days.* Following previous styles of Chan Studies, the researcher would begin to write the history of Fonzie and the other figures in the Cunningham family as though one could watch the 1970s show and gather information about their supposed lives in the 1950s. Put this way, the drawbacks of such an approach are obvious. And, presumably, once one fully accepted *Happy Days* as a fictional presentation designed to whet the appetite of 1970s American viewers hungry for a range of nostalgias, any effort to read the sitcom's particulars apart from their narrative functions would be abandoned. In this light, reading *Happy Days* well would require a foray into several sectors of American history, including Cold War anxieties, the expanding nexus of twentieth-century media and advertising, and burgeoning uncertainty over race, class, and gender—along with an appreciation for the long track of sitcoms that predated *Happy Days,* such as *Leave It to Beaver.* Keeping an eye on a similar range of cultural, historical, governmental, and media forces in Tang China is exactly what I hope to do in giving close readings of the early texts that contributed most to the formation of the Chan tradition.

In fact, the case of Fonzie is particularly germane to a discussion of Chan, since Fonzie, like many Chan masters, is presented as a node of resistance to State-sponsored normalcy, even though he lives and breathes within a media form—prime-time TV—completely involved in State-approved projects. Thus, Fonzie, as the tight-jeaned, leather-jacketed centerpiece of *Happy Days,* presents a titillating foil to the perfectly wallpapered middle-class Cunningham household, but he does so within a set of stylized idioms that never stray far from well-coded American civility, even as they celebrate Italian and working-class virility. Thus, despite his rebel image, Fonzie represents the full domestication of resistance: his predilection for physical gestures over logical discourse, his disregard for formal education, his magical ability to fix things such as jukeboxes with gentle but knowing violence, and his general savoir-vivre in the end are but slightly tangy condiments designed to accompany well-cooked TV dinners. Clearly, at the base of Fonzie's quaint "antinomianism" is a reliably attractive nugget of *coolness:* a natural unflappability that marks him as one above the masses, aligns him with mystical forces drawn from beyond the stifling confines of middle-class suburbia, and, most importantly, distinguishes him as a kind of "Absolute Master"—one for whom the brutal economies of life, whether symbolic, sexual, or economic, never encroach on his comfortable freedom and general jouissance. Actually, setting out on this brief excursion into American "cool" is well worth the trouble since we will see that Chan writers, too, over decades and centuries gradually developed a very parallel kind of Chan "cool," which, like Fonzie's, flourished in the zones defined by the State, the literati, and the aristocracy.

One more historiographical thing needs to be mentioned here at the beginning: it is altogether clear to me that this book covers only a sector of the relevant textual, epigraphical, artistic, and architectural evidence for early Chan. Aware of my limits, I have focused on two things: (1) reframing the historical narrative in a way that seems most in line with the evidence as we currently have it; and (2) providing close readings of the pivotal texts that I believe were most involved in generating Chan-styled discourse between 600 and 750. This does not mean, however, that I am claiming that I have covered all the pieces of the story—I haven't—but I am sure that we cannot build a satisfactory history of Chan without first revising the basic narrative that we have been relying on to make sense of these texts and the historical realities that produced them. It is just this task that I have taken to be the guiding arc of this book, knowing that in time many adjustments and improvements will have to be made to the history that I am creating here.

Acknowledgments

I would like to thank a number of people who made this book possible. First, I want to express my enduring appreciation for my graduate adviser, T. Griffith Foulk—for the early guidance he gave me in graduate school, for his creative and independent-minded scholarship on the Chan tradition, for his no-nonsense approach to historiography, and for his clear prose. Back in the early 1990s, at the University of Michigan, during a rather difficult time for both of us, I saw in him a stubborn and principled courage that I hadn't seen in anyone in academia before; the impact of those days hasn't worn off. I hope he finds here at least some small compensation for the efforts he made on my behalf.

Also crucial at the University of Michigan was the encouragement of Robert Sharf, who, for a semester in 1988, and with no particular incentive in view, took it upon himself to offer me weekly tutorials in reading early Chan texts. Besides giving me a taste for these odd and difficult texts, Bob impressed me with his passion for clear thinking and his commitment to wide-ranging reading. I am grateful for his friendship and scholarly example.

The University of Michigan was also the place where I met the indomitable Brook Ziporyn, who, with humor and Hegel, made me rethink most of the assumptions that I had gathered around me in my previous twenty-five years. It was in the late eighties, during brutally cold afternoons, that we developed an addiction to samurai-style racquetball in a gym overheated to the point of inducing giddiness, and when, on the walks home, we began what I think we both take to be a lifelong debate about everything. This book, like the last one, couldn't have been written without his help, his resistance, and his presence, real and/or/maybe metaphysical.

Once installed at Lewis & Clark College in 1994, I have been encouraged and educated by a number of colleagues whom I would like to thank. Susan Glosser taught me a lot about maintaining humor and integrity in the bewildering maze of "institutionalized education"; Paul Powers instilled in me a deeper appreciation for the measured response and reminded me of the long-term benefits of listening to Johnny Cash; Rob Kugler, as my department chair, encouraged and advised me in an altogether productive and vivifying way; Kurt Fosso demonstrated, with irrefutable clarity and mathematical regularity, that smarts and playfulness can coexist and that Wordsworth, Monty Python, and John Lennon aren't necessarily odd bedfellows; Ben Westervelt reminded me, with occasional references to *The Year of Living Dangerously,* of the vanity of most human pursuits; and Stephen Weeks was my model for that fine blend of steady patience and vigorous focus that still recognizes the value of the well-chosen throwaway line. Lewis & Clark College was also kind in granting me a Luce Foundation Fellowship in summer 2005, which helped support the final stages of editing. And I benefited from my earlier sabbatical, in 2001, during which I wrote and rewrote the bulk of this book. I also owe warm thanks to Aline Letrou for leasing me her apartment in Paris in 1999 and 2005; not only is it a very good apartment, but I really appreciated having a sense of home away from home. I am also grateful to Stephanie Ranes for her friendship, for her humor, and for arranging my stay at her family's home in Vaux, France, in 2001. My "New York friends," Angela Zito and Stuart Lachs, have, in their different ways, done much to mentor me and to keep me hopeful, and for that, I am very appreciative. Likewise, the two outside readers for the University of California Press—Timothy H. Barrett and Elizabeth Morrison—did their best to improve the text, and I am grateful for their comments and criticisms. For giving me years of encouragement, I will be forever indebted to Reed Malcolm, acquisitions editor at the Press: I really couldn't have finished this project without his calming and inspiring advice. Also, Sheila Berg and Cindy Fulton were very painstaking in editing and producing the book, and for that I am very thankful.

Besides my colleagues and friends, I owe a rather immense, perhaps even monstrous, debt to Lewis & Clark students who, for the past decade, have been asking me thoughtful questions that bounce from details in Chan texts to ethical issues implicit in framing any kind of historical argument to the existential implications of thinking about truth-in-history in such a critical mode. I am quite sure I would not have persevered with this project if I hadn't seen, year after year, how taken twenty-year-olds are with questions of truth, innocence, and integrity.

Finally, my proofing assistant Roger Motis was kind, patient, funny, and very hardworking, making the grueling months of July and August 2008 a whole lot more bearable.

CHAPTER I

Healthy Skepticism, and a Field Theory for the Emergence of Chan Literature

PART ONE: THE ART OF ZEN

In the wake of twentieth-century popular and scholarly writings, Chan (Zen) typically appears as a charming and inscrutable mix of Buddhist wisdom and sagely ease. Moreover, it is regularly associated with a kind of *über*-authenticity: Chan is completely Buddhist and yet unfettered by tradition, basking, so it seems, in the sunshine of being the religion beyond religion, with a truth that uniquely transcends right and wrong and a philosophy that, conveniently, has only ineffable tenets. And yet when we look closely at the history of Chan, and its gradual emergence in Tang dynasty (618–907) literature, we see a very different and troubling profile—troubling, that is, for those who like to think of religion and politics as separate activities, and imagine that truth, and the literature that purveys it, comes from truth and not a host of other less inspiring sources.

Elements that we have come to call Chan first began emerging in the seventh and eighth centuries in a series of aggressive and shifting lineage "histories" intent on claiming that the total truth of the Indian Buddhist tradition had recently come to China, where it was perfectly lodged in the bodies of contemporaneous Chinese men. And by "perfectly lodged in the bodies . . . ," I mean that the imported Indian truth was imagined to fuse completely with the Chinese masters in a manner that annulled the anxieties of importing truth from afar and trans-

I

formed these men into full-fledged masters of tradition—buddhas, in other words. In arguing for this immaculate transmission of truth, it was claimed that the totality of the Indian Buddhist tradition had been miraculously "zapped" into the being of these men. Of course, once the unthinkable vastness of tradition had supposedly become the very stuff of these men, the texts then turned to explain how the totality of tradition could be extracted from them in order to feed those hungry for the fullness of tradition. Put this way, one can see how magical the arrangement was from the beginning—hence the verb *zap*.

In trying to demonstrate the successful arrival of the fullness of the Indian Buddhist tradition, the emphasis in these early genealogies is not on meditation or insouciant off-the-cuff lines that might prove the mastery of tradition but rather on presenting sober historical accounts explaining why certain men, generally eminent men with court connections, should be regarded as buddhas or buddha-like, due to having inherited, directly and in a genealogical manner, the Buddha's wisdom. Thus, Chan—and at that time these genealogies did not yet bear that name or have the distinction of being a school, sect, or branch of Buddhism—was primarily a discourse dedicated to three agendas: (1) fetishizing the truth-of-tradition into a compact and transmittable form, whether a text, a robe, a poem, or simply a Thing-which-can-be-transmitted; and, then, (2) setting up convincing formats and rules for controlling that private ownership of the truth-of-tradition such that it would be restricted to a very small group of leading monks, yet offered, in a partial way, to the public and court whose recognition and patronage were sought; and, finally, (3) presenting these rather audacious claims in a rhetorical framework that made these prior two agendas appear natural, innocent, and unconstructed, and therefore acceptable.

Thus, if we can set aside the image of the delightfully quixotic and confidently rude Chan master—so carefully refined through centuries of writing and rewriting—to return to the earliest and often awkward efforts to create Chinese buddhas, we can start to appreciate how complicated this style of Buddhist discourse was as it sought to own tradition in a new and audacious manner that would refigure the landscape of religious authority in Tang China. To consider the origins of Chan in this manner, four interlocking questions will be useful. First, the question of genre: How, exactly, were these genealogical texts designed to interact with the reading public and draw them into recognizing these men as buddhas, or buddha-like? Second, the question of genre development: How were these narratives remanufactured and modified

over time, and under what external forces? That is, as the genealogists borrowed from one another, why were some literary techniques
advanced while others were discarded? Third, the question of content:
What relationship do these texts bear to the men and their teachings
described in these texts? If the particular content assigned to a deceased
master shifts dramatically each time his "history" is represented, what
exactly is the content of his content? This question becomes more irk-
some when we see how frequently accounts of the past masters were
stitched together with documents drawn from other eras that previously
had nothing to do with the genealogy or the figures in it. Apparently,
the Chan genealogies were written with frequent trips to the dustbin
of history from whence random, but useful, items were retrieved and
inserted into "living" genealogies to accomplish various narrative tasks.
And, fourth, the question of politics: How should we assess the social
and political forces outside the texts that seem, in many cases, to have
"written" the interior of the texts, even if that quasi-authorial hand of
realpolitik remains an unadmitted element in the mix.

Part and parcel with the above questions regarding genre and
genre development is the intersubjective nature of these texts — a
crucial dynamic that has been overlooked in previous studies. Thus,
I argue, and it seems obvious once it is pointed out, that these texts
were not only public texts designed for the Other's consumption, but
were conceived and circulated within the understanding that claims
to own tradition work only when the Other is convinced. Naturally,
then, these texts need to be read, if we are to read critically, as works
formatted by the authors' sense for what the Other wanted to hear
about truth — wedding photos for the county fair, according to the
analogy in the preface. In this light, the presentation of the internal
truth-experience of the master would be largely dictated by a sense
for how that depiction would play out in the public sphere. Similarly,
given this dialectic, it seems fair to assume that the master's experience
would be created in line with the author's sense of public expectations,
expectations that were based on how similar "experiences" had been
cataloged in previous literary statements.[1] In short, those realities "outside" of the text — in particular, the literary record and the trove of

---

1. The problem of "experience" in Buddhist texts, especially meditative works, has
been treated by Robert Sharf in his "Buddhist Modernism and the Rhetoric of Meditative
Experience." For reflections on Tang-era writing about the self and authenticity, see
Stephen Owen's "The Self's Perfect Mirror."

"public memory"—need to be recognized as crucial for the writing of not just the inside of the text but the "insides" of the masters who inhabit these texts.[2]

Thus, besides appreciating the density of literary precedents at play in any particular claim to own tradition, we also have to admit that if these texts were really written in this competitive fashion—and I will be doing my best to show that this is the case—then they really are not about any master's particular experience of truth. Instead, the account of the master represents the crystallization of a particular historian's participation in the dense literary tradition to which *he,* the historian, belonged. Ironically, then, claims to own the perfect form of human experience took shape around these newly manufactured Chinese buddhas in a manner that was fully human in the sense of being a cultural and literary product but also fully divorced from any particular human's experience since it was stitched together from a range of prior cultural statements in what I call a "Frankenstein" method of giving birth to the master.

Though a "Frankenstein" approach to building images of the perfect Chinese man-buddha suggests that seams and bolts would be all too visible—and they were at times—it is also true that smoothing over just those joints and sutures was something that authors worked at. In fact, in getting the master to look as lifelike and put-together as possible, authors also seem to have realized the value of a kind of literary self-negation whereby the texts displaying the masters were designed to evaporate in the reader's imagination, leaving just the alluring residue of the supposedly real-life master. In other words, to best cloak the way that historians "fathered" the masters was to work with a kind of disappearing literature that hid the life-giving powers of the historians while also giving the reader the impression of gazing beyond culture, literature, history, and politics—that is, all things human—to peer directly into the transcendent Real of human nature, as manifest in the master qua buddha. Of course, this doesn't mean that Chan's "lens of literature" really is invisible but rather that it got good at hiding in plain

2. Dale S. Wright has argued for the importance of language in Chan and Zen, and yet in taking enlightenment as a real thing, and assuming that Chan/Zen discourse is fundamentally intent on conveying enlightenment, he shies away from the more difficult issues surrounding language's role in seducing readers with the images of such entities as truth and enlightenment. He argues, "The rationale for their intense focus [on language] was simply that nothing was thought to have greater potential to awaken the mind than the rhetorical excursions of the great Zen masters." See his *Philosophical Meditations on Zen Buddhism,* 83.

sight. Thus, in contradistinction to kitsch, which is recognizable as the pathetic and somewhat lovable failure to disappear as an aesthetic, the Chan aesthetic comes into its own when it draws the reader into looking *through it* while ignoring the tools and tropes of engagement that allow for just this kind of penetration. In this sense, Chan literature works like a paper funnel: it wraps around itself to produce an opening through which elements can be usefully poured as they avoid the constraining walls that make that opening what it is. How this literary aesthetic then contributed to a growing desire for truth-beyond-culture and how this desire provoked, ironically, the production and consumption of new forms of literature will be ongoing issues in the chapters to come.

In thinking about the construction of these perfect truth-fathers, we should also recognize that these genealogists seem to have been addressing the basic angst that any tradition has to face: How to generate convincing images of truth, legitimacy, value, and order in the eyes of the public and the powers that be and then move this constellation forward in time in a reliable manner. Once framed in this manner, Chan appears as the unintended consequence of repeated attempts to generate images of a perfect and static past that, despite its thrilling distance from the present, is, nonetheless, also fully available in the present. Of course, here we bump into the difficult matter of assessing to what degree a religion is about itself in the sense of organizing its content in forms that can "live" in time and space, in a reliably reproductive manner. Thus, that which at first appears to be about human experience turns out to be, at the very least, heavily inflected by these macro-level issues regarding the structural reproduction of meaning.[3] Actually, insofar as Chan was largely shaped by basic Chinese notions of patriarchal reproduction, we should expect that, just as filial piety is about the reproduction of filial piety, so, too, is Chan a system designed to transmit itself, with its own being or essence defined, first and foremost, by just this need for self-transmission.[4] In short, and it takes a

---

3. In thinking about the "life" and "needs" of religious systems, I have been influenced by Louis Althusser's work, in particular, "Ideology and Ideological State Apparatuses."

4. As I have written elsewhere, there is a stunning circularity to the ethics of filial piety: "You receive the law from your father and that law is about how to receive the law, and other inheritances, from your father. Thus, the *content* of filial piety is largely about maintaining the *form* in which it arrives, is practiced, and then repeated. This structure in which form and content twine around each other needs to be considered more closely within appreciation for the Chinese proclivity for making ethics wrap around time and reproduction." This passage is taken from my review of *Filial Piety in Chinese Thought and History*.

shift toward something like "meme theory" to appreciate this, Chan's whole premise of the pure transmission of total tradition can't be separated from what we might call the "biology of religious traditions," which demands that meaning be centralized, substantialized, and set on tracks to run from the past into the present and future.[5] Those with more devotion to tradition will no doubt cry "foul" whenever someone asks about the structural forces shaping meaning—fearing, correctly, that to do so will ruin the transcendental quality of religious discourse and practice—and yet I would argue that we have fallen away from an essential element in the History of Religions if we duck a call to address these structural pressures inherent in the reproduction of a meaning system, that is, tradition. Likewise, we lose the specific "Chineseness" of Chan if we remove the Bodhidharma genealogies from the larger sphere of Chinese "historiography," which seems to have a marked penchant for just this practice of ancestor invention.[6]

Truth in Advertising

Besides wondering about the play of structure and content in genealogies, it is probably already obvious that I will be treating the Bodhidharma genealogies as thoroughly selfish works (in the sense of the "selfish gene") in which discussions of truth and enlightenment are inseparable from concerns over power, property, and prestige. Grounds for taking such a suspicious view of Chan's origins derive from the discovery of a significant number of mutually contradictory eighth-century genealogies that, at the beginning of the twentieth century, were taken from a sealed temple cache located in Dunhuang, an oasis town in western China. In the decades that followed this find, it slowly became clear that the genealogies of truth that modern representatives of Chan and Zen cling to are rather late, and clearly much reworked, versions of earlier efforts to write truth into the bodies of particular Chinese men. That the trove of the Dunhuang texts represents an embarrassing time capsule against which later versions of Chan genealogy can be

5. A good essay could be written exploring how far Richard Dawkins's theory of memes might work in explaining the success of Chan genealogies. For Dawkins's early formulation of meme theory, see *The Selfish Gene*. For an attempt to apply meme theory to cultural inventions, see J. M. Balkin's *Cultural Software*.

6. For pre-Buddhist modes of inventing ancestors, see Mark Csikszentmihalyi and Michael Nylan, "Constructing Lineages and Inventing Traditions through Exemplary Figures in Early China." For nineteenth- and twentieth-century styles of re-creating the past, see Michael Szonyi, *Practicing Kinship*.

measured is, however, only part of the problem. Presumably, if it were only a case of too many "true" accounts of truth's descent in time, then apologists could simply content themselves with the belief that their version of truth's history was as true as any other out there, and leave it at that.

However, the Dunhuang "scandal" opened up two other more interesting issues. First, the plethora of legitimacy-seeking genealogies found at Dunhuang casts a long shadow on the very act of seeking legitimacy in this manner. That is, this eighth-century enthusiasm for claiming to have inherited the entirety of tradition from Bodhidharma now looks like it gave rise to a minor cottage industry that busily produced these sumptuous pedigrees. And, second, seeing in these genealogies a track of repeating literary gestures that seek to create and manipulate the image of truth-beyond-writing—whether in the form of sudden enlightenment or illiterate perfection or silent meditation—makes it hard to avoid the conclusion that the eighth century was a time when Chinese Buddhists learned new ways to write about truth and tradition, and did so in a manner that was fully conscious of itself and of the need to cloak these writing skills with a focus on the opposite: the perfect masters who somehow held ineffable truth apart from language, texts, and polemics.

To offer a slightly humorous analogy for the challenge that the Dunhuang texts present, imagine that you moved to a small town in Virginia, and once you became a regular at the corner bar, you began hearing from the locals how the town mayor was related to George Washington and that was why his tenure as mayor was so successful. That was interesting enough, but then one day when you ventured across town to another bar, you heard that it was actually the previous town mayor who was really Washington's descendant, a mayor who happened to be the bartender's cousin. Then, a short time later, when the campaign warmed up for the next mayor, it was widely rumored that the new figure contesting the incumbent mayor was, in fact, the one really related to George Washington. What would you do with all these stories about the connection between leadership in the present and some distant ancestor? And provided that you had a good liberal arts education, how would you think about the political economy of this town where clearly the assumption of leadership is connected to recycling a genealogy that was fixed in reference to Washington, yet also flexible enough to be redirected as necessary? In this situation, the question, Which mayor really was related to George

Washington? probably isn't going to be very telling. Much more informative will be questions such as: Why did this town start talking about its mayors in this genealogical fashion? Or, how does this claim about a prestigious past set up certain fantasies about politics in the present? And, more theoretically, what should we make of a discourse focused on patriarchal inheritance in which paternal continuity as a silent, antilanguage Real, works well to bolster and direct other kinds of language?

A Question of Precedent

The paradigm shift that I am advocating here, though new in some respects, is not without substantial precedents that come in five forms. Forty years ago, Philip Yampolsky, in his classic study, *The Platform Sūtra of the Sixth Patriarch*, mentioned in several places his impression that much of the genealogical material in this text had been worked over for various purposes.[7] Though this appraisal did not prompt him to shift his style of reading—he still treated the *Platform Sūtra* as reflective of real events and conversations—nonetheless, his comments, along with his framing of the history of Chan's histories, were important steps leading to other shifts that would come to Chan Studies. I should add, too, that Yampolsky's work relied to a large degree on the work of Yanagida Seizan, who, perhaps more than anyone, did a truly amazing amount of work editing, publishing, and translating the Dunhuang material after World War II, work that I and all others in the field have benefited from, even if we don't share his nostalgic views of the emergence of early Chan.[8]

Then, in the 1980s and 1990s, Bernard Faure advanced a number of interesting and provocative arguments about how power, symbolic or otherwise, structured Chan discourse. Though I follow some of Faure's reasoning, and like him have benefited in particular from Pierre Bourdieu's work, my approach is different in three ways. First, I will be working more closely with the structure and details of these texts,

7. See his *The Platform Sūtra of the Sixth Patriarch,* esp. 4, 14.
8. For Yanagida's views on what these early genealogies give us, see "Passion for Zen," esp. 7, where he argues that these early Chan texts, discovered at Dunhuang and in previously overlooked Korean sources, represent a breath of fresh air before the tradition was compromised: "One can say that through the texts from Dunhuang and Korea we could hear the fresh voice of Zen Buddhism when it was still young." Later in this same paragraph he speaks of these early Chan texts reflecting Bodhidharma as a figure "in living dialogue between India and China."

with a particular focus on narrative and its implications for judging the content of these texts. Faure, though he started out in the text-critical mode, tends in his more interpretive works to reify Chan above and beyond the details of any Chan text without giving due attention to the particular agendas of each of these texts. Thus, to support his characterization of early Chan as marginal and antinomian, he offers chosen passages, often drawn fairly randomly from disparate texts and eras, to support this position, without giving a fuller account of the arc and function of the narratives that held these passages. My approach will be, as much as possible, to close read these texts in order to gradually build arguments about their form and content in which the medium and the message aren't so easily separable.

Second, Faure regularly treats Chan discourse without considering intersubjectivity. That is, Faure, even in his groundbreaking essay, published in 1986, "Bodhidharma as Textual and Religious Paradigm," doesn't delve into the role of fabrication, seduction, and calculated narrative strategies in Chan, and tends, like Yampolsky, to imagine that these texts can be read for their real honest-to-goodness doctrines, even though Faure will on occasion pull away from these assumptions and critique just such a reading gesture. What one senses in many of Faure's writings is that he is quite at odds with himself as he insists on various methodological insights, yet hesitates in carrying through on what those insights require in terms of reading and interpretation.

This leads to the third difference: Faure's tendency to nostalgia. Despite his evocation of a number of useful critical approaches, some of which are specifically aimed at combating nostalgia, Faure's writing remains, in my opinion, colored by the nostalgic hope of mining Chan for material that is philosophically relevant in the present and, in particular, relevant to post-1968 attempts to speak back to orthodoxy from the supposed innocence of the periphery. For instance, in the early chapters of *The Rhetoric of Immediacy*, his comments bounce from critiquing the whole fantasy of lineage, with its pretensions to stable orthodoxy, to still assuming a kind of innocence for the origin of Chan, an innocence that came to an end once it was brought within the sphere of the political. For instance, within the space of five pages, Faure draws attention to Derrida's critique of the fantasy of pure origins (25) and yet still describes the history of early Chan as one in which "there was a shift from the open ambiguity of the early teachings to the rather sterile dichotomies of 'orthodox' Chan" (21). And, slightly later, "once Chan became the Buddhist orthodoxy, it had to surrender its independence and become part of the imperial administration."[9] In this unstable argument, it is hard to see how the Derridean discussion did much to revise the basic contours of Faure's history of Chan. Too, I would argue that Faure's use of the term *orthodoxy* has little value in describing Tang-era Chan since, in fact, orthodoxy in the basic sense of commitment to a particular defining content of tradition was precisely what no author cared about. That is, it is hard to see how having one's version of the truth-fathers accepted, however temporarily, would reflect a "will to orthodoxy," just as it seems unlikely to read these texts hoping to learn about their authors' commitments to any particular version of doxa or content. Thus, it would appear that even Faure's attempt to critique Chan with the postmodern luminaries has lodged within it a kind of nostalgia for content and the supposed innocence of discourse that arrives from the periphery. For instance, it is hard to accept Faure's claim that the paradigm of gradual versus sudden enlightenment is the essential motor of invention in the evolution of Chan textuality, an assumption that privileges doctrinal and/or experiential content over political pressures, narrative exigencies, or the demands of the "biology of tradition" and that doesn't hold up when the cycle of genealogies is read more carefully.[10] In short, though Faure often asks good questions and brings to the field a wealth of theoretical perspective, he has never settled on a reading strategy that could explain how and why these genealogies were written, or how we ought to treat the content in them.[11]

The third important precedent for this study is the work of John

9. See his *The Rhetoric of Immediacy,* 21; similarly, Faure claims that Chan started as a heretical reaction against orthodoxy but then became codified as the new orthodoxy: "On the one hand, Chan can be seen as a reaction against what was perceived as a Buddhist *trahison des clercs* (in both senses of clerics and intellectuals). On the other hand, Chan turned into a 'tamed heresy' " (17).

10. For comments reflecting Faure's assumption that argument over sudden vs. gradual enlightenment is the key to understanding Chan, see, for instance, *The Rhetoric of Immediacy,* 4: "The gradual/sudden paradigm, which functions as the matrix of the Chan/Zen tradition . . ." Chapter 2 of *The Rhetoric of Immediacy* follows in this vein and is dedicated to reading the Chan tradition along the axis of sudden and gradual enlightenment.

11. Faure seems to be aware of these contradictions and lapses in coherency; in *The Rhetoric of Immediacy,* and other publications, he spends time justifying his self-contradictory approach by claiming that he is simply echoing tradition's ambiguity and multivalence; for instance, see 6–9. But is it wise to have one's reading strategy match the "target material," even if this were feasible? For instance, should we adopt a "humble hermeneutic" in reading Christian material if it is assumed that humbleness is the nature of human subjectivity as it is constructed in Christianity?

McRae, who, for the past twenty-some years, has written extensively on these early Chan texts and has, with increasing clarity, questioned how we ought to read them. However, like Faure, even in his more critical moments McRae doesn't jump out of the paradigm of treating these works as basically reliable. Thus, for instance, though he opens his promisingly titled *Seeing through Zen* with rules for doubting various lineage claims (part of "McRae's Rules of Zen Studies"), the narrative that he constructs for the emergence of early Chan still follows the format that each of these texts creates for itself: Chan master Y was exceedingly brilliant and had some particular ideas that he got from Chan master X and then gave to Chan master Z, and because these ideas were so good and truthful, a community of believers formed around this lineage, and practices concomitant with these truths emerged, such as "encounter dialogues," which McRae takes to be the real essence of Chan and Zen.[12] Besides relying on these texts to hook together a seamless flow of early Chan in which it is real ideas, practices, and masters-leading-congregations that matter, he moves too quickly from textual claims to historical realities. Thus, throughout *Seeing through Zen*, McRae still ends up assuming, without a clear debate about why this is a good assumption, that it was the masters who made the tradition and not their clever historians, even though he regularly points out how unreliable these texts are for gauging what anyone actually might have been doing.

As for the fourth important precedent, the past twenty years have seen the publication of detailed studies of a number of Buddhist texts and teachers in the early Tang. For instance, work on Zhiyi (532–97) and Guanding (561–632) by Chen Jinhua, Elizabeth Morrison, Leslie Penkower, and Kōichi Shinohara has given the field of Chan Studies excellent material to think about the longer tracks of genealogical writing in the seventh and eighth centuries. Without their careful contributions to this period of Buddhist writing, I wouldn't have been able to frame this book as I have. Similarly, Jamie Hubbard's fine study of the Sect of the Three Levels, with its prominent Chan-looking leader,

---

12. For a recent version of his narrative for early Chan, see his *Seeing through Zen;* for his insistence that with the emergence of "encounter dialogue" Chan came into its own, see 18–19: "An event of overwhelming significance takes place in the 'middle Chan' phase: the emergence of 'encounter dialogue,' the idiosyncratic manner in which Chan masters are depicted in dialogue with their students. . . . [T]his is when Chan appears to have become really Chan, when Chan masters seem to have really behaved like Chan masters."

Xinxing (540–94), contributed much to my sense of repeating motifs in the early Tang.

Last, the most important of the five precedents that have shaped this book is the work of T. Griffith Foulk. Much of what I take for granted in my approach to reading Chan comes from my graduate studies with Foulk at the University of Michigan in the late 1980s and early 1990s. Foulk, in his 1987 dissertation, argued that Tang-era Chan could not be read through Song-era documents since the Song authors clearly made up much of the Tang material.[13] Foulk's approach gave me a sense for authorial creativity in Chan writing, along with an appreciation for Chan's close court connections in the construction and dissemination of histories of truth. Equally important, Foulk's more recent work, such as his "The Koan: The Form and Function of Koan Literature," shows a keen interest in understanding the cycle of writing and rewriting Chan material as later authors continued to develop literary techniques to perpetuate control over truth and authority.[14] Though I won't be addressing koans or Song-period Chan, Foulk's research figures prominently in the conception and articulation of this book's arguments, as it does in most current work on Chan.

Next to these five precedents, I should also point out that in the years that I have been working on this book, other scholars have been contributing to the discussion and have, likewise, been interested, in different ways, in adopting a more literary approach to the material and addressing political matters as well. Thus, this book, though not necessarily in agreement with the findings of these scholars, can be profitably read against the work of Wendi Adamek, Timothy H. Barrett, Jeffrey Broughton, John Jorgensen, Mario Poceski, Albert Welter, and Dale S. Wright, all of whom have taken up issues in early Chan and offered a range of interesting positions. Pointing out our various differences regarding interpretation and historiography would take another book, but I have nonetheless tried throughout this book to point the reader to their arguments and perspectives.

I mention these precedents to give a sense for the evolution of the field of Chan Studies and to remind the reader that academic writing develops under discourse rules that likely parallel those determining

---

13. For a more accessible overview of Foulk's position on Chan, see his "Myth, Ritual, and Monastic Practice in Sung Ch'an Buddhism."

14. Foulk's essay on the koan is in Steve Heine and Dale S. Wright, eds., *The Kōan: Texts and Contexts in Zen Buddhism.*

early Chan writing. That is, modern academics also have their county fair competitions and seductively fashion their "photos" in accord with a sense for what might win the day and, likewise, borrow heavily from precedents that seem to have worked in the past. Thus, no surprise that this book's effort to refigure the historical narrative for thinking about early Chan comes out of the work of many previous scholars, as well as the contributions of current colleagues, who provided the material for many of these arguments *and* the intellectual context that made me think that these arguments would be at least partially accepted. Whether the model I offer here succeeds in holding together the disparate historical and literary facts remains to be seen, but I hope that, nonetheless, the basic reading strategies that I present here will be interesting and useful for further discussions.

A Genealogy of Genealogies

To construct a history of the Bodhidharma genealogies, I think it best to begin with a review of literary efforts to win and control leadership roles during the Sui (589–618) and early Tang. At this critical juncture when China was reunified after several hundred years of intermittent civil war, figures such as Xinxing and Zhiyi were put forward as particularly attractive Buddhist leaders. Thus, though they are not normally counted as precursors to early Chan, from the wider perspective of a history of polemics they appear essential to this study as they present early literary efforts to organize Buddhist authority. The genealogies of Zhiyi are especially relevant because they seem to have directly influenced the early Chan writers. Thus, after this introductory chapter in which I discuss my reading strategies, chapter 2 delves into the way Zhiyi and Xinxing were constructed as quasi-buddhas for the newly unified Sui empire.

Chapter 3 takes up the question of Shaolin Monastery and its complicated legal problems under the Tang dynasty. This history of litigation will be the backdrop for reading that crucial stele written for master Faru (d. 689), in which Shaolin presents itself as the preeminent Buddhist institution by claiming that Faru descended directly from the Buddha, via Bodhidharma. This short narrative, which turns the biography of Faru into a history of true-Buddhism-in-China, complete with the trope of sudden enlightenment, seems to have set off the following cycle of writing and rewriting Bodhidharma genealogies during the early part of the eighth century.

Chapter 4 analyzes Du Fei's (n.d.) appropriation of the Faru biography in his *Record of the Transmission of the Dharma Jewel (Chuan fabao ji)*, a text that marks the birth of the genre of the free-floating genealogical claim. Chapter 5 turns to a close reading of what appears to have been a slightly later appropriation of the Bodhidharma legacy by the prince Jingjue (b. 683?), who proclaimed his own enlightenment and wrote the *History of the Masters and Disciples of the Laṇkāvatāra Sūtra (Lengqie shizi ji)* as proof of his inheritance. Chapter 6 considers the complex literature associated with Shenhui (d. 758), literature that reveals the solidification of a number of themes, even as part of it reveals the ferocity with which genealogical disputation could be conducted. In the conclusion, I address what it means to read Chan sources in this critical manner and what we might take away from this study as we think about the human love affair with transcendental truth.

Though the design of this book is itself linear and genealogical, I need to clarify that the actual mode by which these various texts influence each other is a good bit more tangled. Thus, for instance, though text D might appear to have been written partly as a response to text C, it likely knew text A and B, and thus text A's influence on D isn't simply through the chain of A>B>C>D but also directly A>D and indirectly from A>B>D. This isn't so troubling to think through, but things get worse when text E is written knowing A and D, seeing what D took from A, and then deforming content from A again but in a manner mediated by seeing what D did to A. Or, more specifically, if the author of text E read D and then returns to A, his appropriation of A has to be seen as partly determined by his reading of D's reading of A. Of course, then when the author of text F picks up the ball, all this further densifies. Oddly enough, what we will see repeatedly is that direct borrowing is fairly traceable, since authors seem to have wished to borrow the cachet of prior statements even as they twisted them in new and unprecedented ways. Hence, there is regularly a problem of surplus vestiges in these texts, with text D incorporating more of text A than it really needed, and then text E shaves down its borrowing from text A but inadvertently picks up elements from text D that it does not exactly need or want.

Mahāyāna Writing and the Genesis of This Book

In tracking this cycle of competitive lineages, we should not lose sight of the fact that the buddha lineages were also designed to undermine the Indian sūtras.[15] Clearly once the fathering of truth-fathers had been accepted, the value of the sūtras was diminished since a living buddha was now on hand who, besides having the advantage of being available for giving up-to-date commentary, spoke Chinese instead of a distant Indic language. Of course, in accomplishing this subversion of the sūtra genre, Chan authors relied rather heavily on the form and content of the sūtras, and this invites speculation on the long-term vicissitudes of Mahāyāna rhetoric. For instance, when we look closely at the early genealogies, we will see that there was a steady, if experimental, effort to create a *literature* that was dedicated to delivering the supposed *orality* of Chinese buddhas. This unsteady Chinese literary-orality was designed specifically to replace the preeminence of the literary-oralilty of the Indic sūtras, even as it clearly borrowed sūtra content. Thus, as usual, the past was overcome only by reorganizing the elements of the past in a manner that mimicked that past even as it rendered it less essential.

In this struggle between imported and native literary genres, there is also an equally interesting struggle between sūtras and monasteries. The Mahāyāna sūtras that were best loved by Tang readers generally belong to what could be called the category of "promiscuous literature," with sūtras such as the *Lotus Sūtra*, the *Diamond Sūtra,* or the *Vimalakīrtinirdeśa* offering the totality of tradition to anyone who would read them with devotion. Hence, by offering the reader a "cult of the text," this style of Mahāyāna sūtra does not rely directly on monastic forms of authority since the texts simply ask to be read, copied, worshiped, and passed on.[16] Bodhidharma genealogies, on the other hand, are dedicated to lodging the totality of tradition in particular Chinese men's bodies, and, in other cases, in particular Chinese monasteries. Thus, and painting in broad strokes, if certain Indian Mahāyāna texts—such as the *Lotus Sūtra* and the *Diamond Sūtra*—were dedicated to taking tradition *out* of the monasteries, then Chan rhetoric was intent on putting it back into the monasteries, or the men who inhabited those monasteries. It was, in fact, in the hope of making sense of these longer arcs in Buddhist rhetoric that I set out to write this book after treating the literary forms of several Mahāyāna sūtras in *Text as Father.*

---

15. For a different account of the role of sūtras in the later Chan rhetoric, especially that of Mazu, see Mario Poceski's "*Mazu yulu* and the Creation of the Chan Record of Sayings."
16. For more discussion of these matters, see my *Text as Father.*

PART TWO: THE ORIGIN OF A THEORY OF ORIGINS

The first thing to notice in making sense of early Chan literature is that for about four hundred years, from the end of the second century to the end of the sixth, authority and sanctity in Chinese Buddhism appear not to have been articulated in "spiritual" genealogies. Though one can find lineages or intimations of lineages in some encyclopedias and prefaces to translations, as far as I know they were not used to present contemporaneous Chinese Buddhists as buddha-like figures.[17] This situation changed significantly when in the seventh century there appeared several high-profile claims that the essence of the Buddhist tradition flowed down exclusive "family lines" into particular Chinese Buddhist leaders who were now presented as buddha-like. Though these seventh-century claims regularly recycled elements of earlier protolineage material, they still represent a fundamental shift in the use and meaning of Buddhist lineages because they transformed the earlier material into a more potent and commanding form of religious discourse. Similarly, presenting these new lineages began to take on a life of its own as authors broke free of previous genres, such as the encyclopedia entry, the sūtra preface, or the funeral stele, and, by the beginning of the eighth century, began working up an entirely new Chinese Buddhist genre: the freestanding genealogy of truth.

Dynasty Shifts and Moments of Weakness

When we return these genealogies to their historical settings, we see a number of dynamics tugging them into existence, such as those moments when the State seems to have been insecure in its symbolic standing and sought Buddhist help to construct legitimacy for itself. At these "hot" moments in the dialectic, the State may have even invited Buddhist authors to inflate their own cosmic prestige in order to be able to more impressively confer legitimacy on the throne—to be the State's Big Other, in other words.[18] At the very least, it seems that for

17. For a careful and comprehensive survey of pre-Song Buddhist lineages, see Elizabeth Morrison's "Ancestors, Authority, and History," 1–92.

18. I am using the Lacanian term *Big Other* in a slightly idiosyncratic fashion. For my purposes, it refers to a site of legitimacy—such as King Aśoka or the Indian Buddha or Bodhidharma—that is taken up for the purposes of establishing the identity and

brief moments the State was particularly generous, saying, in effect, "We, the State, are prepared to recognize your new claims to own tradition in order that you, quickly, give us what we need: your formal recognition, an act that will require that you take it upon yourself to speak for all Buddhists, all Chinese, and, in fact, the entire cosmos." In time, once the newly enthroned dynasty begins to widen its net of support, and accrues a kind of legitimacy simply from having held the throne for some time, the quid pro quo deal tendered to the Buddhists likely will become less generous.

Given the structure of these exchanges, it shouldn't be surprising that it was during these hot spots of dynastic upheaval that the more inventive genealogies were written. Two factors seem essential for explaining this. First, dynasty changes were particularly unstable moments, not simply because the newly enthroned State was symbolically weak, but also because the various structures linking the prior dynasty to Buddhist systems of recognition were plowed under. Consequently, with the arrival of a new political dynasty, Buddhism likely would also undergo a "dynasty" shift as the previously established conduits of power—the stable connection of certain Buddhists to State power—were reconfigured. Thus, though Buddhism as a whole would be relied on to deliver legitimacy, the actual agents and structures for delivering that mana would, in principle, have to be renegotiated. In fact, at times this open-field competition was so freewheeling, for example, during Empress Wu's reign (690–705), that we need something like a "peacock theory" for describing the interaction, with the throne as the female peacock, evaluating the parade of vari-

---

legitimization of the one who has selected this very Big Other. In short, one selects a Big Other in order to ratify the "self" that one wants to be and, equally important, wants to be known as. The "Big" in "Big Other" signifies that this is an Other that is supposedly preexistent and somehow outside the dialectic of self-other recognitions, and it is precisely with that image of independence from intersubjectivity that such a figure can best be enslaved into the task of granting recognition. In the case above, it is the Sui throne that was looking among Buddhist sources for a Big Other, but the relations were often reversed since various Buddhist genealogists often looked to the throne to play this role. In a basic sense, the entire cycle of Bodhidharma genealogies can be read as a sequence of attempts to find more workable Big Others for various Chinese Buddhist leaders. And, once we see that Big Others were hungrily stolen from prior claimants who had slotted particular Big Others into their own pedigrees, then we have more reason to think of early Chan genealogies in Lacanian terms in which desire and recognition are negotiated by recycling past recognitions, hoping to thereby win the desire of the Other. Wendi Adamek also uses "the Other" for the State in the Buddhist-State relationship; see her *The Mystique of Transmission*, 98 ff.

ous male peacocks displaying their lustrous plumages.[19] This model is particularly useful because it expresses not only the interplay between the throne and the Buddhists but also the competition between the various Buddhist "suitors."[20]

The second factor crucial for explaining the surge in genealogical innovation at the time of dynasty shifts has to do with another aspect of the law in China. Though China has a remarkably long history of maintaining a solid core of imperial law, with some continuity even back to the Qin dynasty (221–206), the advent of a new dynasty apparently was cause for Buddhist anxiety over the issues of landownership and monkly privilege. That is, the newly installed dynasty often decreed that the Buddhist monasteries had to surrender their land, or their precious metals, or defrock large numbers of monks so that they would again pay taxes and make themselves available for corvée labor. Consequently, the arrival of a new dynasty was seen as a time when Buddhists might in effect be asked to reapply for the right to maintain control over their lands and valuables, rights that though sanctified by the previous dynasty would now be up for renegotiation. Just this anxiety seems to have spurred Shaolin Monastery's political efforts in the seventh and eighth centuries, in particular, its effort to create a lineage for itself that explained why it was the unique site of the most perfect form of Buddhism.

Bourdieu and the Pricey Economy of Buddhist Genealogies

To get a clearer sense of these rough-and-tumble struggles to own the Buddhist tradition and to be a suitable Big Other to the throne, I would like to introduce a reading strategy that is somewhat parallel to Pierre Bourdieu's reading of the art world of modern France, as he presented it in his 1977 essay, "The Production of Belief: Contribution to an Economy of Symbolic Goods."[21] As the title promises, Bourdieu wanted to explore the complex workings of the field of cul-

---

19. For a survey of Empress Wu's efforts to find legitimizing spokespersons, see Richard W. L. Guisso, *Wu Tse-t'ien and the Politics of Legitimation in T'ang China*, esp. chap. 4.

20. I should add that Empress Wu also regularly looked to various representatives from the Daoist tradition to provide useful sources of legitimacy. For a survey of her Daoist-oriented activities, see Timothy H. Barrett, *Taoism under the T'ang*, 40–45.

21. For an English translation of this essay, see Pierre Bourdieu, *The Field of Cultural Production*, 74–111, esp. 74–86. For a more involved discussion of the interplay of literary invention and politics, see Bourdieu, *Les règles de l'art*.

tural production that directs the world of art. His essay is useful for writing a history of Chan for three reasons. First, he is committed to an interpretive framework in which the interior, or content, of a piece of art/literature is to be read in a multidirectional manner. The content of art or literature is to be seen *not* as sui generis or isolatable from surrounding mercantile and symbolic economies. Second, Bourdieu is interested in understanding the production of images of innocence and disinterest, images that he argues belong to the world of art in all its economic and competitive aspects. Hence, Bourdieu insists that the various vectors in the production and marketing of art are regularly mediated through conduits of disavowal or negation. No surprise, then, that we get phrases such as "Art for art's sake" floating around in thickly contested and thoroughly capitalized art scenes. In short, a key component in organizing the economy of art, on both the monetary and symbolic levels, is the construction of belief in a zone of artistic freedom and integrity that somehow rides above and beyond the cutthroat world of art dealers. Hence, the myth of the artistic genius who supposedly remains impervious to the Real of art's economy, even as this construction of innocence is crucial to just that economy. By insisting on this play of levels and negation, Bourdieu describes how art takes on the pristine image of value-beyond-any-economy but does so *precisely to better participate in the money economy.*

And, third, Bourdieu offers a useful paradigm for thinking about fields of contention, as he describes how artists jockey to collect, control, and perpetuate whatever cachets of value and connection they may have won. Thus, Bourdieu builds up a model for the "taking of positions" on the field of art production in which the pressures and pulls on artistic work arrive not only from the other side, the economic side, but also from one's competitors. In defining this side of art production, the work of other artists either can be seen as a vehicle to piggyback on, in the event that the work of the Other has been recognized as value, or it can be positioned as a stepping-stone—an essential element in the construction of new art, but whose presence has use only insofar as it is negated and surpassed.

To get an idea of how this kind of competition might have worked in Sui/Tang China, below I first offer a general model for the external discourse pressures, and then a more limited model for struggles between competing genealogists.

A Mountain of Symbolic Power:
The State and the Shape of Buddhist Genealogies

If we imagine the field of Tang-era society as a topographical map in the form of one mountain of symbolic power—provided by the State apparatus—then, ringing the highest central peak, we ought to imagine several smaller sister peaks that are located on the flanks of the central mountain. These secondary peaks represent a range of institutionalized forms of cultural, social, and economic power, including the "big" aristocratic families, the literary tradition and its representatives, the budding education system, the Confucian ritual tradition, the emerging Daoist clergy, and, of course, the Buddhist establishment. In setting up this thought experiment, I am suggesting that insofar as elevation equals distinction, power, and privilege, sites of elevation were dispersed in a variety of institutions and cultural practices, yet were grouped around the State in a pattern of symbiotic support that nonetheless included competition and intrigue.[22]

In terms of the interactions that took place on this crowded field, it appears that there was a gradual homogenization in which differences were minimized in favor of securing shared interests. And, given the complexities of such multivariable engagement, we might expect that any particular author on this field would pitch his discourse in such a manner that it would be efficacious on several fronts. Hence, an effort would be most likely to succeed when it struck a balance by piggybacking on the proven themes-of-success of prior contestants, even as it treated other themes and contestants as stepping-stones. In view of these pressures, we shouldn't be surprised to note that biographies of Buddhist masters, aggressive though they were, were also written on the basis of widely shared assumptions about generic Chinese values. Jumping a bit ahead for effect, while this model might seem ungainly for the moment, it will certainly pay its way as we try to understand the profiles of Chinese buddhas that emerged by the middle Tang in which their images appear Frankensteinesque—stitched together from elements drawn from a vast array of previously established forms of symbolic capital.

---

22. This thought experiment is loosely based on Bourdieu's notion of contentious cultural production; for more details on his position, see his "The Field of Cultural Production, or: The Economic World Reversed."

Passage from India and the Innocence of Time Past

Unacknowledged in my above mountain analogy is the major problem that Buddhism's origin in India presented for medieval Chinese Buddhists. This problem took two forms. First, Buddhism as an import was always vulnerable to chauvinist and xenophobic rhetoric based on the assumption that good things could only be Chinese things, and thus Buddhism as an Indian creation was basically a barbarian entity to be discarded along with all the products of other undercivilized places. This vulnerability played out in important ways as Chinese authors sought ways to negotiate Buddhism's foreignness. For instance, it can't be happenstance that Chinese origins for perfect Buddhism were established in figures like Huineng who achieved enlightenment on his own, more or less, and whose contact with the lineage from India does little more than confirm what he had already owned through his basic Chineseness (see chapter 6). This dynamic also seems responsible for the way Chinese Buddhist masters were regularly depicted as Laozi look-alikes.

The second form of the India problem had to do with explaining how the geographic, linguistic, and cultural divide between India and China was overcome. On one level, this gap between China and India, or more exactly, the Buddha's India, played out in a variety of theories regarding transmission, theories that were put forward to create a workable bridge between the two cultures. On another level, this anxiety over transmission and interpretation was addressed by slowly making the need for transmission disappear. That is, though the genealogies were clearly intent on explaining how perfect Buddhism came to China, the success that the genealogies won for themselves meant that India became less and less important for articulating truth and legitimacy. Thus, once genealogists started producing Chinese buddhas, there was little point in returning, via texts and travels, to India. Oddly enough, then, theories explaining the genealogical descent of tradition from India became the most secure way for talking about Chinese things.

In publicizing these new, exquisite identities for the Chinese masters, the genealogies had to produce, in their narratives, convincing images of other figures recognizing the masters in just this manner. Ironically, then, though the genealogies promised to deliver the most sublime point of view from which to view the Real and the essence of tradition, they would in fact need to spend considerable time creating and presenting to the reader other reliable spokespersons viewing and ratifying the owners of that sublime viewpoint. Of course, this sets up the awkward situation of trying to get the reader to look, correctly, at other figures in the narrative looking correctly at the Chan masters, all in order that the reader can conclude that he is getting an unobstructed vision of the truth-fathers.[23] Thus, in the promise of offering a vision of the visionaries, we see several layers of mediation just in the way that Roland Barthes's delightful essay explains how the Eiffel Tower works as a relay between seeing, being seen, and, in a certain sense, seeing seeing itself.[24]

In producing this sensation of seeing, it was clearly useful to claim that the genealogy was innocently produced according to the motto "History for history's sake." Thus, the aggressive desire of the genealogist to claim ownership of the totality of tradition was smoothed over by making the genealogy look suitably historical, and therefore desirable precisely in its own supposed lack of desire for the reader's desire. That is, the genealogy as history appears attractive for its supposedly factual, noncompetitive representation that, like the genealogy itself that trails off into the distant past, appears to originate beyond current polemical struggles and arrives in the present only through an interest in maintaining its reservoir of value for future readers. As long as the content of the genealogy manages to look like it was "written" by the deeds of the past that it describes, it will appear above suspicion. Or in other words, as long as it seems as though real history wrote this particular history, everything will be fine. Consequently, the early genealogies worked to give the impression of being above the fray of polemics so as to incorporate (in all three meanings of the word: somaticize, include, and organize)

---

23. As a useful point of comparison, the Gospel of Mark can be read in just such a manner: Jesus is presented as the essence of tradition—due to his genealogical relationship to God—and consequently he is the quintessential place to look in order to see what was wrong with "imperfect" tradition, as embodied in the purity laws, established ethics, written literature, and priestly privileges of Jewish tradition—and yet much of the narrative is dedicated to presenting a host of characters, from the voice of Heaven to John the Baptist to the long list of those cured of diseases to the Roman centurion, all looking at Jesus and identifying him as the Son of God and thus the fullest form of tradition. In short, the gospel works around just this relay structure that offers the reader the perfect seeing of perfect seeing, and does so all the more convincingly by doing it "silently," that is, as an unannounced narrative ploy in which narrating Jesus' identity as Son of God disappears into the supposed "history" of others realizing that reality to be a prenarrative truth.

24. For an English translation of this essay, see Barthes, "The Eiffel Tower."

an aggressive transcendence that was successful precisely because it appeared on the back of that supposedly unmanufactured kernel of truth that couldn't possibly be accused of competitiveness since, after all, it came from another time zone and, better still, was simply true.

Instant Family and the Sudden Making of a Master

These various forms of innocence culminate in the figure of suddenness, a figure that works much as "artistic genius" does in Bourdieu's account of the French art world. In Tang China, suddenness, whatever its resonances in the literature before and after this period, was positioned in a number of these early genealogies as the way to control inclusion in the lineages as this suddenness explained how one was magically zapped into the family of truth-fathers. Obviously, suddenness put an especially brutal end to any discussion of techniques for inclusion in the lineage, techniques such as meditation or asceticism that might allow *anyone* into the lineage through their adoption of potentially efficacious means. Read in this light, terms such as *sudden enlightenment (dunwu)* or *sudden entrance (dunru)* were deployed due to concerns over identity and inclusion in the lineage, not with regard to new kinds of knowledge and experience. Thus, instead of assuming that these texts were born of human experience, and the wish to convey that experience, I believe it better to see that the category of suddenness has more to do with the binary nature of identity and the structural demands of lineage combat. One is a master or not; there are no half-masters, just as there are no half-kings, and thus movement between ordinary identity and buddha-identity cannot be gradual.

Actually, in the wake of this fundamental separation between masters and the masses that the genealogies effected, there are suddennesses offered to the masses, but these are secondary suddennesses, often associated with more minor concerns such as "sudden precepts." The two forms of suddenness can be clearly distinguished in that the masters never give their supporters the *right to give authenticity,* and thus, somewhat like drone bees, the recipients remain forever dependent on the source of the gift, conserved at the center of the hive. Hence, suddenness appears as a key element in establishing the public narration of a family that owns truth, a family that, like all families, preserves its boundaries by making permission to traverse that dividing boundary a gift that can only be given by those already within its limits.[25]

Simply Wonderful

With suddenness read in this manner, we ought also to reconsider the trope of the "simple" Chan master since it is clear that many of these narratives are able to delight in the simple master—and, at times, a country-bumpkin-buddha—precisely due to the narrative flexibility offered by the concept of suddenness. With each new master, regardless of his social status or real life history, zapped into his new station as this generation's reigning buddha, to speak of any other causality in the production of his identity would ruin the transcendent identity that is being organized for him. Thus, sudden enlightenment acts as a replacement for all normal ways to produce status and authority—whether through study, ethics, intelligence, or practice—and consequently allows the narrative to play up the masters' innocence and simplicity. Thus, by making enlightenment arrive suddenly and usually through the agency of the previous master, what need could a master-to-be have for study, practice, court recognition, or even familiarity with Buddhism?

In addition to the useful link between simplicity and suddenness, authors seem to have realized that they could enhance desire for these figures by casting this sudden-simplicity in the vein of very old Chinese notions of "profound simplicity" as found in the *Daode jing* and the *Zhuangzi,* two texts that were often mentioned or referenced in these genealogies. In fact, close reading a number of important Chan biographies—Hongren's and Huineng's, in particular—with a focus on this fusion of simplicity, suddenness, and lack of ambition opens up a number of interesting perspectives regarding the production of desire *for* these masters produced by voiding them of human desires and, in some cases, voiding them of any kind of recognizable human "interior." Actually, the way these narratives celebrate these one-dimensional figures suggests that we ought to read the desirelessness of the master as part of an attempt to purify desire-producing discourses with their opposite—the desireless and utterly simple master.[26]

---

25. Faure is right to point out the connection between doctrines of sudden achievement and the creation of elite masters, especially in terms developed by Derrida and Bourdieu; see his *The Rhetoric of Immediacy,* 38.

26. For more discussion of competitive simplicity, see my "Simplicity for the Sophisticated."

In this sense, the interior of the narrative, focused as it is on the chain of desireless patriarchs, serves as an alibi for the frame of the narrative, which is intent on evoking desire for these masters. The two must work in tandem, with form and content essentially doing each other's work, even as they pose as separate, unrelated entities: a narrative of desire works by narrating desireless men who can only be who they are supposed to be once the narrative of desire works on the reader. Hence, it is not shocking to find that the richest fantasy in these texts is that the masters contained in the narrative are not only free of language's constraints, especially written language, but also exist in spaces of subjectivity completely liberated from constraining exchanges with others. In economic terms, the text creates a field of exchange wherein "buying into the system" is induced through desire for a figure that appears lodged completely beyond the system and beyond exchange, even as that fantasy of separation and purity is produced by the system and positioned to drive the system of exchange. In short, the image of the end of intersubjectivity and exchange becomes the greatest incentive to engage in intersubjectivity and other related exchanges; or, in other terms, "art for art's sake" as proclaimed by art dealers.

Kingmakers and Other Types of Readers

Missing in previous readings of these genealogical texts is an account of the role that the reader is expected to play in the ideological exchange that these texts demand.[27] As outlined above, the reader must be seduced into accepting the lineage as historically real, or the text fails at its fundamental task, which is to privatize enlightenment and then display it to the desirous public. In any of the genealogical texts, enlightenment is no longer a public possibility available to the smart or the diligent, even when some texts delight in recounting the success of some extraordinary "commoner-to-master" story, as in the case of Huineng. Similarly, enlightenment is no longer distributed in varying degrees in the various schools in China. Instead, it is in the bodies of certain masters and nowhere else, with all other Buddhists resoundingly criticized for this or that fault, or, failing specific lapses, at least the fault of not having received the gift of being in the lineage.

---

27. Faure does mention in passing that the master's status is a function of social definitions but doesn't explore this theoretical angle in terms of close reading a genealogical narrative; see his *The Rhetoric of Immediacy*, 22–23.

As all this implies, the installation of truth in a private family has rather profound implications for the reader's relationship to truth, which, if the narrative is believed, must now be mediated by means of the text and/or the representatives of the lineage of truth-fathers that it has created. However, the process of privatizing enlightenment is not simply a one-way street, with the texts stealing truth away from more public sites like sūtras, rituals, and all the other masters-lacking-genealogies. Instead, the public needs to cooperate with the texts for the "thieving" to actually occur. I explore this dialectic below, but for now let me note that the transfer of truth into the lineage is finalized only when those outside the lineage desire the lineage for what it "has." Thus, ironically, the lineage that reproduces itself via the "internal" gift of enlightenment from master to disciple is itself fulfilled by the "gift" of belief from those outside the lineage, who, in typical intersubjective form, are in charge of turning ordinary men into masters, even as they overlook their own role of kingmaker in the exchange.

This cycle of recognition may sound unduly complicated at first, but I believe we have to say that in a genealogical assertion of truth-through-family-belongingness, the private ownership of truth can only be secured when non–family members see the family as it wishes to be seen. Thus, privatizing truth-claims ironically exist in and through the Other, an Other who, as reader and observer, must be made to look *into* the lineage and see therein a fullness of truth and authority that appears to predate the language that both constructed that presence-of-truth and drew in the public vision to confirm that presence. Or, in other terms, the potency of the master can only fructify in his chosen disciple(s) in the narrative when that narrative of transmission fructifies in the reader who participates in "fathering the father" once he believes that fathers are fathering replicas of themselves behind the narrative and not simply in it.

Moreover, the genealogy's essential dependence on the reader is cloaked with a kind of solicitude from the lineage texts that regularly promises to take care of the public. Thus, though the gift of enlightenment moves forward in time, privately from master to master in these texts, there are also many promises of a partial sharing of this universal good with the public, promises that come with the rider that no other local being/institution can "serve" the population like this one; naturally these promises to share publicly the patrimony naturally only come in the wake of privatizing enlightenment in the first place. Obviously, if the lineage members did not have what everyone wanted, how could they offer it up? Of course, the prior moment of exchange—when the public verified and legitimized the lineage—is left unspoken, making the gift from the lineage look sublimely disinterested and benevolent. In fact, the master's generosity is often likened to an "echo" in many Tang texts where he is presented as one who responds reliably and selflessly to the needs of the populace who, of course, can only be thusly served if they first serve up faith in the reality of truth in the lineage and its supposed automatic benevolence. Ironically, then, by internalizing a doctrine of an external patriarchy that reproduces itself with pure truth, the reader has estranged himself from exactly what the lineage promises to give back to him—truth and final family belongingness.

SAMENESS AND HYPER-SAMENESS:
WHY NOBODY DOES IT BETTER

Intersecting this basic two-tier system produced by founding a truth-family separate from its adoring audience is the language of universal buddhahood, which also often comes under the rubric of a family connection—buddha-nature, buddha-seed, and son of the buddha. Misunderstanding how these two families fit together has been the basis for naive comments about Chan as democratic and egalitarian.[28] Though Chan texts might assert that all beings are repositories for an internal buddha or have the buddha-seed or lineage within themselves, only the patriarchs supposedly have actualized this nascent identity. More importantly, the lineage texts claim that their patriarchal conduit is the only source or tool for actualizing the ubiquitous universal buddha-nature, which otherwise would languish as an altogether inaccessible reality. In short, inclusion in the basic, universal family identity of buddha-nature is not simply a happy birthright but rather the basis of congenital incompletion and self-alienation since one is required to rely on the specific family of actualized buddhas qua masters who are unique in their capacity to complete, and verify, everyone else's "innate" identity.

Given the constraints of family logic, it should be clear that the claim to have the right to give identity back to the text's audience means

---

28. A history of Buddhist funerals shows clearly how the Chan system relied on a two-tier system of death to institutionalize the gap between masters and everyone else; for more discussion, see my "Upside Down/Right Side Up."

that the gift can never really be given since, despite the promise of inclusion, one is never quite in the truth-family. Or, as argued above, this rhetoric imposes the rule that one only really has one's identity when one is sanctioned with the power to give identity to others. The logic of the situation is that the aggressive ideology intent on securing enlightenment in a sealed patriline cannot, without annihilating its reason for being, ever give back what it took away from the public. To see the truth-father in the lineage, then, is to see oneself as a quasi-son who is paradoxically vaguely family to the lineage by natural "birth" but also strictly excluded from it on the grounds of not having been "reborn" into the lineage as the next master-father. In a classic Catch-22 arrangement, you learn of your rightful patrimony from a source that, once accepted as a legitimate speaker for the reality of your patrimony, will forever prevent you from owning what they just said you actually own.[29]

Thinking more broadly about the issue of refathering Buddhists, it seems fair to say that the genealogies of the seventh and eighth centuries adopted the basic trope of Buddhist fathers and sons as found, for instance, in the *Lotus Sūtra* but relocated that trope in historical time, with the notable effect that the *lineage* now reproduces Buddhist sons, instead of the sūtra. Similarly, it would seem that this genealogical rhetoric took Mahāyāna rhetorics that speak of the internal split between hidden buddhahood and sullied sentient beingness, as found in the *Tathāgatagarbha Sūtra* or the *Laṅkāvatāra Sūtra,* and expanded them into a whole sociology of difference such that masters of the lineage were just those sentient beings who have folded themselves completely into the true "half" of their given identities and offer themselves up as objects of devotion for others to emulate, again with the caveat that the texts explaining this reality will not, in the absence of contact with the lineage, advance one toward this goal.[30] In short, we have the familiar function of desire in religious literature in which total closure in truth and goodness is shown to the reader even as the very form of that demonstration serves to produce an unbridgeable gap between the reader and his own closure with truth, along with the blindness

29. A dual-family structure seems to be at work in the Christian tradition as well. In the Pauline letters and the Gospels, it is belief in the completely unique sonship of Jesus that becomes the gateway for a parallel kind of kinship with God that nonetheless is always second to Jesus' primal kinship that made the secondary kinship possible.

30. For more discussion of this problem of the rhetoric of the internal buddha, see my *Text as Father,* chap. 5.

of not seeing how that seeing was constructed by means of language, presentation, and alienation.

Though the Chan genealogies work at producing just this exciting gap between the reading public and the master, this phenomenon has been largely left out of modern critical studies. The essential problem in this oversight is that we have always taken Chan to be about masters, not noticing that the masters were presented to the reader to be desired. Clearly, these texts were for the reading public—they certainly were not for the masters themselves, who were usually dead before their buddha-stature was created—and thus they have to be read as conduits conjoining the sublime icon of the master and the ordinary reader, who, in his fantasy-vision of the textualized hero, wishes to be by the master's side, or quite literally in his family. To fail to interpret these texts in this manner would be like reading or watching advertisements and thinking that they were about the products and not about the relationship between the viewer and the products, a relationship that is designed to produce future exchanges and fidelities. It is just this function of genealogical literature as a conduit that draws the eyes of the desirous reader to the advertised master that I hope to recover in the following discussions.

With these general comments and perspectives in view, let us turn to consider how two Sui-era masters—Zhiyi and Xinxing—were created as buddha-like figures.

CHAPTER 2

The State of Enlightenment

The Empire of Truth in Zhiyi's Legacy and
Xinxing's Sect of the Three Levels

INTRO: PATTERNS AND GESTURES

A sensible history of the "birth" of Chinese buddhas ought to begin with two particularly important Buddhist leaders from the sixth century—Zhiyi and Xinxing. Though quite different in style and focus, both masters gained wide renown and were recognized by the court as powerful Buddhist leaders. Similarly, at different junctures in their careers, including their posthumous careers, both were treated as quasi-buddhas around whom, it was hoped, the entire cloak of Chinese Buddhism could be wrapped. Thus, clarifying their careers sets a benchmark for recognizing, in pre-Tang sources, Chinese enthusiasm for constructing icons of perfect Buddhism apart from the mass of Mahāyāna sūtras imported from India.

In the case of Zhiyi, it was primarily through the writings of his disciple Guanding that he was turned into a buddha-like figure in a manner that was largely unprecedented in the history of Chinese Buddhism. As several other scholars have noted, after Zhiyi died, Guanding audaciously created and distributed several contradictory genealogies for his master that worked to enhance his legacy and to render that legacy useful for a number of projects that Guanding pursued in the first half of the seventh century. In reviewing Guanding's writing, it will become evident that it needs to be set at the beginning of an account of Chan genealogies, since it seems that early Chan writers borrowed both form and content from Guanding's different narrative strategies and, similarly, inherited a number of discourse "logics" from him. In short, as Linda Penkower has concluded, it is worth arguing that Guanding is essentially the father of Chinese Buddhist genealogy, and thus we would do well to pay close attention to his rhetorical inventions and the external social forces that likely motivated them.[1]

Xinxing is equally relevant to this inquiry, since he, too, became the focus of an attempt to recast Chinese Buddhism's relationship to India by concentrating the totality of tradition in his own person. Xinxing, with startling levels of success, assumed the identity of a uniquely gifted bodhisattva who declared that no other Chinese Buddhist had the right to read or interpret Buddhist scripture and that, instead, Chinese Buddhists ought to focus on silent regimes of meditation and repentance, and accept as definitive Xinxing's idiosyncratic interpretation of tradition. Thus, though Xinxing and his followers, who went under the banner of the Teachings of the Three Levels (Sanjie jiao), would be formally banned as heretics at times throughout the seventh and eighth centuries, the structuring of Xinxing's identity seems to have important resonances with early Chan writing, especially in terms of centralizing tradition in a single man and then slotting followers into subservient roles defined by meditation and repentance. Though I do not assume any direct transmission of content from the Xinxing movement to early Chan writing, I do think there is much to be gained from seeing the figure of Xinxing as a semisuccessful attempt to make something like a Chinese buddha, an attempt that likely influenced Chan writers who pursued similar goals decades later.[2]

While arguing for Guanding's influence on later genealogical writing won't raise eyebrows, including Xinxing as a pivotal figure in Chan's "prehistory" may appear controversial, so let me offer four specific reasons why this is a good idea and then several more general reasons for good measure.[3] First, his legacy was strong enough that his biography was included in the meditation (chan) section of Daoxuan's (596–667) Encyclopedia of Eminent Monks II (Xu gaoseng zhuan),

---

1. For this assessment of Guanding's role in the invention of Buddhist genealogy, see Linda Penkower, "In the Beginning . . . Guanding (561–632) and the Creation of Early Tiantai," esp. 246–48.

2. I first suggested some kind of continuity between the Sect of the Three Levels and early Chan in my review of Jamie Hubbard's Absolute Delusion, Perfect Buddhahood.

3. I am happy to note that Adamek includes a discussion of Xinxing in building a background for understanding eighth-century Chan; see her Mystique of Transmission, 120–28.

which functioned as a crucial "Who's Who in Chinese Buddhism" and from which Chan writers drew regularly.[4] Thus, a genealogist leafing through Daoxuan's entries on meditation masters would have seen the entry for Xinxing sitting not too far from Bodhidharma's or Huike's and thus not thought to exclude him, as we have in modern studies of Chan, from the matrix of potentially useful material. Second, on the field of politics Xinxing's legacy seems to have produced enduring effects, since after his death his supporters appeared significant enough to warrant imperial censure—in 600 under Sui Wendi, then in 695 and 699 under Empress Wu, and yet again in 713, 721, and 725 under Emperor Xuanzong.[5] Of course, these later suppressions were right in the midst of one of the most creative times for writing Chan genealogies, and thus we have reason to believe that Xinxing's legacy was very much in the air during this period. Third, Xinxing was ancestrized in the mid-seventh century by Tanglin, in his *Record of Miraculous Retribution (Ming baoji)*, where he presented a proto-lineage for Xinxing.[6] Last, and this seems important for structural reasons, the sect of the Teachings of the Three Levels, while espousing a universal doctrine of innate buddhahood designed to overcome all sectarian differences, ended up creating a Buddhism-within-Buddhism. Thus, by resituating the totality of Buddhism in their master and then in a "mini" form in each follower, Xinxing's rhetoric of universality translated into a new form of sectarianism. In fact, this sectarianism was so pronounced that the Sect of the Three Levels succeeded in winning the right to set up its own special living quarters within established Buddhist monasteries, identified as separate cloisters *(bie zhong)*.[7] Just this tension between sectarianism and a rhetoric of universalism will reappear in Chan efforts to define their own Buddhist identity and to establish a visible institutional basis for themselves.

In more general terms, the best reason for including Xinxing in an account of China's efforts to produce a Chinese buddha is Xinxing's

---

4. Xinxing's biography is found in Daoxuan's *Encyclopedia*, in the Taisho, T.50.559c–560b. "Taisho" refers to the most common version of the Chinese Buddhist canon, the *Taishō shinshū daizōkyō*. Volume, page, register (a, b, c), and line will be cited in that order. For discussion of Daoxuan's text and sources, see Hubbard's *Absolute Delusion, Perfect Buddhahood*, 4–5.

5. For more discussion of these suppressions and their motivations see Hubbard, *Absolute Delusion, Perfect Buddhahood*, 190–222; for a different analysis that I find insightful, see Mark Edward Lewis, "The Suppression of the Three Stages Sect," esp. 226–32.

6. For a translation, see Donald Gjerston, *Miraculous Retribution*, 157–60.

7. Hubbard notes this in *Absolute Delusion, Perfect Buddhahood*, 10.

radical reconstruction of Chinese Buddhism around his own author-ity. Thus, Xinxing represents a good example of creating an "absolute master" who supposedly held tradition in a manner that upset two main structures that had hitherto been responsible for defining Chinese Buddhism: the priest-laity divide and the India-China divide. Both these fundamental structures were recast once Xinxing, and those around him, claimed that Xinxing *the man* was more important than all other Chinese monks and, equally stunning, that he was more important than all other Buddhist literature and the Indian origins from whence that literature derived. In effect, Xinxing was created not simply to collect tradition as it was known in the sixth century but also to break the back of the reigning Buddhist institutional hierarchy and the stan-dard practice of receiving tradition through reading Mahāyāna sūtras imported from India. Of course, just these two characteristics define Chan as well, so there are good reasons to gain at least a little familiar-ity with Xinxing and his Sect of the Three Levels.

Actually, there are other parallels between Xinxing's movement and early Chan. For instance, Xinxing advocated a kind of sudden teaching *(dunjiao)* for his followers that was conjoined with a course of medita-tion and self-discipline oddly directed at the laity, who were encour-aged to pursue this monkly training even though there was never any expectation that advancement could be won by these means. Thus, even though Xinxing insisted on an unbridgeable gulf between himself and his followers, he also preached a seductive ideology for building com-munity in which his followers, though sometimes referred to as "mute sheep-monks" *(ya yang seng),* were consoled within their permanent secondary status by an emphasis on their inherent buddhahood.[8] This twofold structure in which an image of unique and inaccessible Buddhist leadership was displayed to the public in conjunction with appealing pronouncements of universal buddhahood would reappear as a domi-nant theme in Chan literature, just as the allure of "sudden teachings" and the mysteries of meditation would be advanced as part of an attrac-tive package designed to promote this two-tier structure of legitimacy.

Equally interesting, given later developments in Chan literature, Xinxing's overcoming of tradition was cast as the negation of normal monastic identity. Hence, in the middle of his career he renounced

---

8. For the term *mute sheep-monks,* see Lewis, "The Suppression of the Three Stages Sect," 223; see also Hubbard, *Absolute Delusion, Perfect Buddhahood,* 89–91, 146 n. 66.

his robes and monk status, making clear that his authority was no longer dependent on the legitimizing functions normally provided by official Buddhist structures. And, again like later Chan narratives, Xinxing's overcoming of official religious authority was strengthened by adding a touch of naturalism, a naturalism apparently designed to make Xinxing appear humble and close to the earth and the peasants. Thus, Xinxing supposedly took up manual labor, which presumably relocated him in a zone of perfection that was at the peak of the Buddhist symbolic order and somehow beyond it, too, since he also occupied the position of a laborer.[9] Arguably, then, Xinxing's perfection was constructed in a way that included the top and the bottom of the symbolic order, just as the biographies of the Chan masters Hongren and Huineng would.

In short, given the fruitful life that parallel rhetorical strategies would have in the centuries to come, ignoring Xinxing in a history of the reconstruction of Chinese Buddhist authority would be like excluding the American Revolution from a history of the French Revolution. The point isn't that there was direct "transmission" from one revolution to the other but rather that the facts of the American Revolution were, in one form or another, quite well known by the various contending factions in Paris during the 1780s and 1790s and thus served as an important point of reference for French authors and activists. In effect, including Xinxing's legacy within the framework of early Chan genealogical writing means leaving a genealogical model of historical influence and shifting toward a more holistic model of causality in which influence is understood to work in a multiform manner that has various layers of efficacy and directness.

I should add here, too, that unlike the later chapters, which will be built around close readings of early Chan genealogies, this chapter is more reliant on the analyses of other scholars who, in the past decade, have made significant contributions to understanding Sui-era Buddhism.

SUI BUDDHISM

To understand efforts to buddhify Zhiyi and Xinxing in the early part of the seventh century, we should begin by recognizing the

9. For the context of this gesture, see Hubbard, *Absolute Delusion, Perfect Buddhahood,* 8; and for more reflections on Xinxing's efforts to humble himself with simplicity and self-mortification, 24–27.

overall intensity of the State's involvement in Buddhist affairs under the Sui dynasty. Since the insightful work of Arthur Wright in the 1950s, we have had good reason to see that the Sui dynasty was unusually interested in putting Buddhism to work in State-building enterprises. This engagement with Buddhism, at the clear expense of Confucianism and Daoism, appears in several forms, ranging from the first Sui emperor Sui Wendi's personal piety—presumably due to being raised by a Buddhist nun and then marrying an especially pious wife—to a series of governmental policies that relied on the Buddhist clergy. While a close examination of this interesting moment in Chinese Buddhism is beyond the scope of this book, to build a useful context for evaluating the emergence of Buddhist genealogies, we need to keep track of four types of Buddhist-court interaction.

First, both Sui emperors, Wendi (r. 581–604) and Yangdi (604–18), selected monks whom they judged especially gifted and granted them honors, gifts, and institutional prominence. Zhiyi is certainly to be included in this set of honored monks, but the list is fairly long, and in the discussions to follow it has to be kept in mind that the Sui court negotiated relations with a number of eminent monks. More exactly, the Sui emperors, apparently in their insecurity over ousting the prior dynasties, sought to build support for themselves through several Buddhist channels and were rather "promiscuous" in developing special relations with one prominent monk and then moving on to another as soon as they saw fit. This intense, if furtive, imperial enthusiasm for such relations suggests that this moment in Chinese Buddhist history, like the later reign of Empress Wu (690–705), represents a hot spot when symbolic and institutional creativity emerged in more than ordinary abundance.

Part of the Sui's support of elite monks was manifest in creating an elite body of clergy who were referred to as the Great Virtuous Ones (Dade).[10] Evidence of this budding institution of court-sanctioned Buddhist luminaries first shows up with the mention of three Dade monks relied on to perform evening vespers for the emperor and his wife in the 580s.[11] Slightly later sources from the Tang speak of groups

10. For discussion of previous imperial structures for regulating the Buddhists, see Stanley Weinstein, *Buddhism under the T'ang*, 9–11.

11. Arthur Wright mentions this group of *Dade* monks in "The Formation of Sui Ideology, 581–604," 78.

of six, ten, or thirty *Dade* monks chosen and supported by the court and housed in the capital at Luoyang.[12] Though it is not clear how the Dade title and its attendant institutions worked in the Sui, nonetheless, it seems that the title already represented a nascent form of State-sponsored Buddhist authority that was designed to organize hierarchy in the Buddhist order and facilitate mutual recognition between court and clergy. Presumably in conjunction with this effort, the first Sui emperor, Sui Wendi, founded a large State-sponsored monastery, the Monastery of Meditation *(Chanding si)*, which was to be staffed by one hundred twenty elite monks and seems to have been built to be the leading monastery for the nation.[13]

Second, Sui Wendi thrice organized massive relic distributions, which, as Chen Jinhua has pointed out, were designed to use Buddhism as a tool for developing and sanctifying center-periphery relations throughout the Chinese empire.[14] Thus, in 601, 602, and 604 Sui Wendi ordered the Buddhist monks to distribute recently "rediscovered" relics of the Indian Buddha Śākyamuni to each of the thirty provinces and to construct pagodas there to house them.[15] The edicts promulgated on these occasions make abundantly clear that Sui Wendi hoped that the distribution of tangible representations of pure Buddhist essence—in the form of the Buddha's remains—would prove useful in drawing his dynasty, Buddhism, and the populace into a harmonious whole.[16]

Third, as an essential component of the relic distributions, Sui Wendi articulated his imperial authority as an echo of the Indian model of kingship, known in China through the translation of the "histories" of the first great Buddhist king, Aśoka, who unified India in the first half of the third century B.C.E. Promoting this rhyme scheme was particu-

12. For brief mention of these groups, see Chen, *Monks and Monarchs, Kinship and Kingship,* 17, 63; for fuller discussion, see his "A Holy Alliance." See also Antonino Forte's excellent essay on the *Dade* monks, "Daitoku."

13. For details of this monastery, see Chen, *Monks and Monarchs,* 6–10. I should add that I am not convinced by Chen's assessment that this monastery, with the word *Chan* in its title, is directly related to early Chan. I would resist such a direct link as one of the most important aspects of Chan writing is the overhauling of the meaning and implications of the word *Chan,* and thus we can't take its mere presence to signify the later Chan tradition. Too, there is no evidence that this monastery made use of the Bodhidharma "histories" or other genealogies—the hallmarks of early Chan—all of which seem to have been invented later.

14. For details and discussion of this policy, see Chen, *Monks and Monarchs,* 51 ff.

15. For more details, see Chen, *Monks and Monarchs,* 63 ff.

16. For a translation of the edict most associated with this first wave of relic distribution, see Chen, *Monks and Monarchs,* 54 ff.

larly attractive since Aśoka was represented in Chinese Buddhist documents as a "universal monarch," a *cakravartin,* who ruled successfully with the aid of Buddhist cosmic powers and with the support of his devoted Buddhist populace. As Wright put it, "The figure of Aśoka, as enshrined in Buddhist legend, had a persistent appeal for [Sui] Wendi in his effort to build a peaceful and united empire under an all-powerful divinely sanctioned emperor."[17] Thus, Sui Wendi, at least in this zone of ideological effort, settled on King Aśoka to be the Big Other to the Sui dynasty, a Big Other who, though far beyond the borders of China and eight hundred years in the past, still was expected to provide a sanctifying precedent.[18]

Fourth, completely in keeping with long-standing Chinese strategies for legitimizing a dynasty, both Sui emperors sought out reports of miracles that confirmed both the legitimacy of their reigns and their ongoing ability to marshal cosmic forces in the work of leading the nation.[19] In these efforts, the standard procedure was, first, the discovery of an item such as an urn or stone, often with writing on it, which was then brought to the attention of the court and trusted to speak for some greater reality—usually the Dao and/or Heaven. What is unusual about the Sui reliance on such talking icons was that the search for these confirming miracle items was often organized by Buddhists; moreover, they were often harvested from Buddhist power sources, such as the distributed relics, or, as discussed below, from Zhiyi's remains. Thus, in league with linking the Sui rulers to King Aśoka, these miraculous finds were counted as part of a conversation between Sui rulers, Buddhist leaders, and the deep structures of power and legitimacy in the universe.[20]

In fact, though I have separated these efforts of the Sui rulers into four categories, they were in fact quite intertwined. Thus, for example, *Dade* monks apparently led the relic distribution, an effort that was explicitly designed to mimic King Aśoka's relic distribution, as described in several popular accounts of his life, with these efforts

17. For more discussion of Sui Wendi's attempt to cast himself as a *cakravartin,* see Wright, "The Formation of Sui Ideology," 98 ff.

18. Erik Zürcher notes that this gesture to look to Aśoka as a paradigmatic international ruler, and to likewise search for his relics in China, was widespread in pre-Sui eras. For his comments, see *The Buddhist Conquest of China,* 277–80.

19. For a discussion of imperial efforts to search for omens and portents during the Sui and early Tang, see Howard Wechsler, *Offerings of Jade and Silk,* chaps. 2–4.

20. For Wright's comments on the nature of this conversation, see "The Formation of Sui Ideology," 102.

organized to harvest a host of miracle confirmations.[21] Most important for establishing a background of State-Buddhist interactions is recognizing that these public dramas emerged within a triangle of engagements in which the State reached out to Buddhism to produce a Big Other, here in the form of King Aśoka and the budding institution of *Dade* monks, in order to confirm the dynasty's legitimacy in the eyes of the populace.

In the Sui's construction of this triangular conversation, though *many* monks would be singled out at various times to play important roles vis-à-vis the court, including Zhiyi and Xinxing, none seemed to have been accorded a dominant and lasting form of power and prestige on the scale of King Aśoka. For instance, though Chen Jinhua has shown that the monk Tanqian (542–607) was intimately involved in orchestrating the three relic distributions, he never seems to have been taken up by the court as a Big Other. Similarly, the monks invited into the ranks of the *Dade* monks, though winning recognition and institutional benefits, never seem to have raised themselves up to engage the throne as fully endowed Big Others. Instead, the Sui emperors seem to have treated the various *Dade* monks as intermediaries who were charged with the task of arranging symbolic relations between the Sui dynasty and older, weightier forms of authority, as imagined in the figures of King Aśoka and the Buddha Śākyamuni.

It was in the midst of the Sui's intensive and wide-ranging engagement with Buddhist elites that Guanding began his various attempts to create his master Zhiyi as a fully qualified Big Other to the State. Perhaps without realizing the import of his actions, Guanding set in motion a trend in which the court was asked to look no further than to its own native monks for a full-fledged Big Other who could offer legitimacy in as thorough a manner as the relics of the Indian Buddha or the precedent of King Aśoka. Though Guanding's various efforts were less than successful, his initial reconstruction of Zhiyi's identity in the first decade of the seventh century marks a crucial turning point in Chinese Buddhist hagiography; henceforth Chinese authors seem to have become more comfortable promoting Chinese masters as buddha-like, or as descendants of the Buddha.

Of course, in promoting Zhiyi as a quasi-buddha, Guanding was

21. For an edict mentioning the role of the *Dade* monks in relic distribution, see Chen, *Monks and Monarchs,* 61; and for the various accounts of Aśoka that served as templates for Sui Wendi's actions, see 75–76.

reconstructing an important leg of the triangle defined by the State, the populace, and Buddhism, even as he was also negotiating the transference of Real Buddhism from India to China. In arranging for a full form of real Buddhism to be lodged in a contemporary Chinese monk, Guanding had to concern himself with two interlocking problems. First, he had to convincingly explain tradition's exclusive presence in Zhiyi—that is, how it got there in the first place while all his contemporaries had failed to receive it. Second, he had to install that legacy of pure tradition in a form that could be controlled and moved forward in time. In fact, we will see that Guanding experimented with several narratives explaining why Zhiyi, as a buddha replica, should be worshiped as the font of tradition, even as Guanding also experimented with several techniques for holding that cachet of buddhaness in various items: Zhiyi's mind, body, monastery, and chosen text—the *Mohezhiguan*. Naturally, too, Guanding put considerable effort into making this reconstruction of Zhiyi look authentic and untainted by greed or sectarianism.

Before more closely considering Guanding's writing, it is worth reviewing several details about Zhiyi. First, Zhiyi was, and still is, recognized as one of the most impressive Buddhist intellectuals of all time. Anyone familiar with even a section of his oeuvre cannot help but be awed by his breadth of learning, his powerful intellect, and his clear writing. In the late sixth century he had been recognized as an eminent master by the Chen court that ruled southern China before it was overrun by the Sui.[22] Then, as the Northern Chinese forces that would found the Sui dynasty sought to unify the country in the 580s, the Sui prince of Jin made sustained efforts to build a relationship with Zhiyi, presumably in the hope that such a friendship would facilitate the unification of the empire. Reading Zhiyi's life, and especially his final years, in light of these political developments is not a new idea, and even in the 1950s Wright gave us good reasons for seeing Zhiyi entangled in the Sui effort to unify the nation. What has only come to light recently is how complicated matters turned once the empire was unified in 589. More specifically, the prince of Jin, who would soon inherit the throne, came to see Zhiyi less as a quilting point for seducing the South into accepting Sui leadership and more as an icon of

22. For details on Zhiyi as something of a National Master under the Chen dynasty, see Chen Jinhua, *Making and Remaking History*, 58. A similar category had been employed slightly earlier in the sixth century; see Chen, *Monks and Monarchs*, 154.

legitimacy that could provide the prince of Jin with supernatural signs to legitimize his own newly won imperial identity.

In this emerging dialectic between the prince of Jin, Zhiyi, and the Buddhist community that sought to maintain Zhiyi's legacy, the crucial event was the death of Zhiyi in 597. As he was dying, Zhiyi had requested, and won, a written promise from the prince of Jin that a monastery be built for him at the base of Mount Tiantai, in the coastal region of what is now Zhejiang. This promised monastery was in fact completed in 601. At first, the monastery had simply been named Tiantai Monastery, but this name would change with the change of rulers at court. In 600 the prince of Jin was promoted to crown prince (he was Sui Wendi's second son), and then with the death of his father in 604, he was crowned the second Sui emperor, Sui Yangdi. Then, in 605, based on dreams and miracles that spoke of Zhiyi's relationship to the Sui rulers, dreams and miracles that Guanding and the monks of Tiantai Monastery had reported to the throne, the new Sui emperor came to visit the area and officially had the title of the monastery changed to Nation Purified *(Guo qing),* a title that supposedly Zhiyi had dreamed of years before—before the new Sui dynasty had come to power and certainly before it became clear that the prince of Jin would supersede his older brother and take the throne.[23]

In making sense of this drawn-out conversation between the prince of Jin and the monks at Tiantai Monastery, we should note that in the letters that were exchanged with the court over the eight-year period from 597 to 605, there is a steady effort to foster a very special relationship that brought together Zhiyi's legacy, the newly built monastery, and the recently established Sui dynasty, with special emphasis on the rise of the prince of Jin. Not surprisingly, Guanding's first genealogical writings date from this period (between 601 and 605, to

---

23. For discussion of the meaning of the monastery's new title, see Kōichi Shinohara, "Guanding's Biography of Zhiyi, the Fourth Chinese Patriarch of the Tiantai Tradition," 105. Shinohara translates the monastery's name as "Temple That Purifies the State," but given that the explanation of the title in the *One Hundred Letters* clarifies that the completion of the temple will coincide with the unification and pacification of the state ("when the temple is completed, the State will be pure [peaceful?]," 105), I think there are good reasons to put it in the past tense: "Nation Purified Monastery." A later gloss on the temple's name in Daoxuan's biography of Zhiyi also suggests that it be read in the past tense: "When the state is purified *(guo qing shi),* the three areas will be unified into one. A nobleman will then build a temple for the Meditation Master [Zhiyi], and temple buildings will fill the whole mountain" (Shinohara, "Guanding's Biography of Zhiyi," 132).

be more exact) when in two different texts Guanding sought to direct Zhiyi's legacy for maximum symbolic effect on the new rulers and for increasing the prestige of the newly built monastery at Tiantai. In short, the shift in dynasty, the newly crowned emperor, and the recent death of Zhiyi provided the occasion and the motivation for building up a genealogy of Buddhist truth that could stand as a suitably Big Other to the throne and provide it with the urgently needed legitimacy.

ALL THE KING'S MEN: PHASE ONE OF GUANDING'S WRITING

In the first decade of the seventh century, Guanding involved himself in two major writing projects. The first was the *One Hundred Letters from Nation Purified Monastery (Guoqing bailu)*. This text, which another monk had been working on until he died, was basically a collection of Zhiyi's correspondence with the officials and rulers of the recently collapsed Chen dynasty and then the newly established Sui dynasty. After the rise of the Sui dynasty in 581, many of the letters are to and from the prince of Jin. More telling for understanding this collection, and Guanding's reconstruction of his master, are twenty-some letters that were written in the time after Zhiyi's death, letters that were exchanged between the Sui court and the monastic community newly established at Mount Tiantai.

While the earlier portion of the one hundred letters, written to and from Zhiyi, are rather varied in their interests, the letters written after his death have a tighter focus. For instance, right after Zhiyi died, Guanding began delivering letters to the prince of Jin that included testimonials from monks explaining how Zhiyi had predicted the building of their temple by a powerful prince and how the completion of their monastery would reflect the consolidation of the new dynasty. In letter 69, written soon after Zhiyi's death, Guanding details how the monks of the monastery remembered Zhiyi saying, "If we locate the foundation of the temple, a 'prince' *(wang)* will build a temple. Minor monks like you cannot arrange for the building of the temple. Someone else who is powerful will accomplish it. Unfortunately, I will not be able to see the completion of the building."[24] Here, the goal seems to have been

---

24. Translated in Shinohara, "Guanding's Biography of Zhiyi," 100.

to ensure that the monastery will be built by flattering the prince and giving him good cause to fulfill his side of the bargain.

However, we should not overlook the important fact that the report also positions Zhiyi as one who knows the deeper narrative for both the throne and this particular monastery and that, obviously, they are intertwined.[25] Read this way, the report makes Zhiyi into a kind of political seer, with the monastery positioned as visible proof of this prearranged set of relationships that gain their legitimacy in a twofold manner: (1) the establishment of the Sui dynasty and Nation Purified Monastery were cosmically predestined realities and therefore, de facto, legitimate; and (2) Zhiyi, as the privileged and precocious "reader" of these cosmically ordained events, sanctified both institutions—the Sui dynasty and Nation Purified Monastery—precisely in his knowledge of them and, by implication, because he, too, had a place in that deep structure of the cosmos.

Once the monastery was finished in 601, the letters to court shift emphasis away from the building project and begin to highlight miracles in which the legitimacy of the Sui dynasty was affirmed, usually by way of a spectral Zhiyi who regularly showed up to offer Delphic commentary on the fortune of the empire. Presumably, in this fashion Guanding and the other monks at Tiantai Monastery hoped to convince the prince that this monastery would facilitate his task of stabilizing the still-uncertain dynasty. Of course, too, these letters insist that Zhiyi, though now deceased for five years, was still quite able to uphold his side of this three-way conversation with the monks of Nation Purified Monastery and with the newly recognized crown prince. The success of this writing campaign is evident in letters from the throne ordering the monks at Nation Purified Monastery to open Zhiyi's grave (twice) in the hope of producing more miracles and making closer contact with his postmortem presence.

In sum, reading these letters and noting their shifting agendas, it seems hard to avoid the conclusion that Guanding and the other monks worked to generate around Zhiyi an aura of deep and abiding Buddhist legitimacy that was designed first and foremost to support their effort to be a suitable Big Other for the young and uncertain Sui Yangdi.

---

25. In terms of assessing the level of bad faith here, we ought to notice, as Shinohara points out, that this claim was clearly post facto and contradicted earlier written statements by Zhiyi. See "Guanding's Biography of Zhiyi," 100.

ZHIYI'S BIOGRAPHY

In 605, the prince of Jin, now enthroned as Emperor Sui Yangdi, decided to make a trip to the south to pay the monks of Nation Purified Monastery a visit. In letters announcing his arrival, or rather his virtual arrival as he seems to have gone only as far as Jiangdu, he called for a biography *(xingzhuang)* of Zhiyi to be drawn up so that it could be circulated nationally and then used as the basis for cutting a stele at the monastery.[26] Kōichi Shinohara speculates that this biography was to replace interest in Zhiyi's grave site.[27] This seems reasonable as the biography, or at least the later version that has survived, was structured to include accounts of a variety of the State-supporting miracles that, once grouped around the life of Zhiyi, were then to be broadcast around the nation.[28] In short, by requesting a biography of Zhiyi, Emperor Sui Yangdi seems intent on turning Zhiyi's life into a mirror that would reflect the legitimacy and power of the Sui dynasty. The task of writing this biography fell to Guanding, a choice that probably reflects his leadership role in writing the letters to court after Zhiyi's death.

If we assume that the surviving biography of Zhiyi, by Guanding, is the same as the biography mentioned in the letters exchanged with the emperor, and this is a pretty good bet, then what is striking about it is that Guanding clearly set out to create the impression that Zhiyi was, after a fashion, a king, too.[29] For instance, early in the *Biography* Guanding invents the story that at Zhiyi's conception a voice announced to his mother, "Because of karmic connections of previous lives, you will be entrusted with a king *[wangdao]*."[30] Besides recounting what this unidentified voice predicted for Zhiyi and that the birth was marked by auspicious magical light, Guanding added, for good measure, the detail

---

26. This plan appears first mentioned in letter 86; see Shinohara, "Guanding's Biography of Zhiyi," 104.

27. For evidence that Sui Yangdi hoped that miracles relating to his rule would be found at the opening of Zhiyi's tomb, see Shinohara, "Guanding's Biography of Zhiyi," 104–6.

28. That the biography was designed to function in this manner seems clear in letter 91; see Shinohara, "Guanding's Biography of Zhiyi," 108. Guanding's surviving biography of Zhiyi, *Sui Tiantai dashi Zhizhe dashi biezhuan,* is printed in the Taisho, T.50.191a–198a.

29. For Shinohara's discussion of this assumption regarding the equivalence of the *xingzhuang* mentioned in the *One Hundred Letters* and the surviving *Sui Tiantai dashi Zhizhe dashi biezhuan,* see his "Guanding's Biography of Zhiyi," 107–8.

30. Translation from Shinohara, "Guanding's Biography of Zhiyi," 118; T.50.191b.4.

that Zhiyi was born with double pupils as sage-kings are supposed to be.[31] Then, instead of simply displaying Zhiyi's postmortem penchant for producing miracles indicative of the Sui's legitimacy, as he had in the previous letters sent to the throne, the biography also contains an involved account of Zhiyi as a member of a protolineage (considered below), a claim that Guanding used to make Zhiyi appear as an unusually authentic monk who received and commanded the entirety of tradition. Thus, in the dialectic between monk and emperor, Guanding generated a narrative of Zhiyi's identity that dovetailed with contemporaneous State agendas, even as he used this occasion to reconstruct Zhiyi's identity as the king of Chinese Buddhism. In this sense, Zhiyi's identity, in the hands of Guanding, ought to be read as an epiphenomenon of this exchange, with Zhiyi dressed up as a miraculous sage-king to look like a suitably grand Big Other to Sui Yangdi. Though we will never know whether Guanding would have inflated Zhiyi's status even if this State-sponsored opportunity to broadcast his master's identity around the empire had not appeared, it is clear that it was only in this context and not in the earlier letters that Guanding drew up a history for Zhiyi that presented him as the veritable king of Buddhism.

To clarify why the inflation of Zhiyi's identity was likely the natural result of these exchanges with the throne, imagine that Guanding had not invented Zhiyi in this manner. With Zhiyi as but *another* important scholar and adept among the many in China, how could he function as a mirror for Sui Yangdi and the Sui dynasty? How useful would all his miracles be to the State if there were equally valid spokespersons elsewhere in the kingdom who could be consulted and who might offer varying assessments of the situation? Put this way, it seems clear that it was precisely because the emperor needed to be ratified as the single site of political authority that he needed Zhiyi to be seen as the king of Buddhism who could grant that legitimacy through his unique control over the symbolic domain of the Buddhist tradition. Thus, it was the State's need to write its own deep history of the present that led it to search out so enthusiastically any religious spokesperson—dead or alive—who could ratify its place in history and in the cosmos. And, since this history of the State was essentially genealogical, we shouldn't

31. Ibid., 118; T.50.191b.8. The idea that kings have dual pupils is found in the *Book of History (Shiji)*; see Shinohara, "Guanding's Biography of Zhiyi," 130 n. 3, for more details. Double pupils for kings was mentioned in a text much closer to Guanding's writing moment—Mouzi's *Lihuo lun*, which likely was written in the fifth century; for the passage, see John P. Keenan, *How Master Mou Removes Our Doubts*, 82.

be surprised to see how Guanding, in time, turned to the genealogical model in order to inscribe Zhiyi in a comparably compelling deep history so that he could more ably account for the legitimacy of the State's genealogy. In short, I think we can see here good evidence of a kind of metastasis of genealogy in which the State's need to lodge itself in some larger temporal matrix requires an Other who can vouch for this deeper reality of the State, and who, himself, needs a parallel kind of transtemporal identity to make that assessment of the State seem true and not the function of current politics, and certainly not the effect of an extended quid pro quo exchange with the State.

Two stories from Guanding's biography of Zhiyi exemplify his effort to give Zhiyi this deeper, transtemporal identity and to raise him above his contemporaries. The first is an account of Zhiyi's tutelage under the monk Huisi (515–77), who seems, in fact, to have been Zhiyi's teacher in the 560s.[32] Early on in the biography Guanding has Huisi say to Zhiyi, "In the past both of us were at Vulture Peak and heard the *Lotus Sūtra* preached by the Buddha together. Impelled by the power of karma from previous lifetimes you now have come to me so that we are together again."[33] In this audacious historical claim, Zhiyi's relationship to his Chinese master Huisi is recast as a relationship established under the Buddha, in India, and at the glorious moment that the *Lotus Sūtra* was preached. Of course, recounting this deep past produces a lineage of sorts since Huisi's instruction of Zhiyi in the sixth century is cast as a duplication of a parallel time in the past, in India, when they supposedly were disciples of the Buddha, directly receiving from him the *Lotus Sūtra*.

Moreover, in setting up this rhyme scheme it would seem that Guanding has portrayed Huisi and Zhiyi's relationship in a manner that replays the *Lotus Sūtra*'s initial chapter, in which Mañjuśrī explains to Maitreya that even though Maitreya cannot remember his past lifetimes, Mañjuśrī can, and knows that Maitreya has already received the *Lotus Sūtra* directly from the Buddha many times in the past.[34] Thus, Guanding appears to be repeating the *Lotus Sūtra*'s own legitimizing technique in order to locate Huisi and Zhiyi at the heart of tradition. In relying on this narrative template from the *Lotus Sūtra*, Guanding has

32. For a study of Huisi, see Paul Magnin, *La vie et l'oeuvre de Huisi (515–577)*.
33. See Shinohara, "Guanding's Biography of Zhiyi," 119; T.50.191c.14 ff.
34. For more discussion of this narrative strategy in the *Lotus Sūtra*, see chap. 2 of my *Text as Father*.

for the moment no need to construct a more historically visible lineage that would deliver the Buddha's essence to Zhiyi in sixth-century China. In effect, the logic of this rhyme rests on the the power of karma and Huisi's memory of this perfect past and does not need any other force or logic to build a bridge from the past into the present. Actually, recognizing Guanding's recycling of this logic from the *Lotus Sūtra* suggests that the narrative of Zhiyi's life is taking its *form* from the active pull of political pressures—the need to have a deep genealogy to vouch for the State-directed miracles—while its *content* is being supplied by recycling both the cachet of the *Lotus Sūtra* and the logics it used to legitimize itself. Thus, the contemporaneous political situation led Guanding to refather Zhiyi with the *Lotus Sūtra,* which supplied the paternal "substance" to explain Zhiyi's relationship not just to his own master, Huisi, but also to the entire Buddhist tradition. That is, in making Zhiyi "rhyme" with the State, Guanding worked to get him to "rhyme" with the deepest forms of legitimacy in the Buddhist tradition.

Guanding's attempt to present Zhiyi as the essence of tradition takes a different turn later in the biography when he describes Zhiyi's special enlightenment. This vignette was clearly designed to replay the story of the Buddha's enlightenment, and thus again Guanding is working up Zhiyi's identity by making him rhyme with the foundational elements of the Buddhist tradition. In this case, Guanding sets the narrative on Mount Tiantai, where Zhiyi has supposedly entered deep into the forest and spends the night fending off demons.[35] At dawn, a supernatural monk *(shenseng)* shows up and says, "You have controlled and overcome enemies and can be said to be courageous. No one can pass these trials better than you did." This monk then confers on Zhiyi a special teaching of the "One Truth of Reality," concluding with this promise: "From now on, in your own spiritual cultivation and in your effort to help others, I will always be with you like a shadow or an echo."

As with the previous story regarding Huisi and the *Lotus Sūtra,* Guanding has infused Zhiyi's person with what would have been taken as a deeper and more immediate form of tradition. The value of this enhanced form of tradition is underscored in the narrative when the spectral monk explains that this version of tradition, handily titled "One Truth of Reality," was available only after Zhiyi passed a fright-

---

35. See Shinohara, "Guanding's Biography of Zhiyi," 121, for translation and discussion in which he, too, reads the narrative as full of allusions to the Buddha's enlightenment. The following two quotations are also from this source.

ful night tormented by demons. This transmission is made even more secure by then having this magical monk promise to be Zhiyi's spiritual double, a double who would henceforth accompany him in all that he does. In short, Guanding has gone beyond simply creating spokespersons to vouch for Zhiyi's legitimacy, such as Huisi and the unidentified voice that told Zhiyi's mother that he was to be a king, since now he is claiming that this magical monk will *reside* in Zhiyi's practice and in his engagements with others, leaving little doubt that while Zhiyi might appear as a Chinese Buddhist intellectual who lived and trained far from India and distant in time from the Buddha's era, he was in fact inhabited by a super-form of tradition that guided his every action. This was underscored when Guanding added the detail that this was a "foreign" *(fan)* supernatural monk, with the character *fan* being the same one used to designate India. In effect, then, this supernatural monk works as a perfect conveyor of tradition—a carrier of a kind of compressed lineage that moves tradition from India to Zhiyi, such that he is actually two people: himself and this supernatural monk who supposedly shared Zhiyi's body.

Though evidently designed to cast Zhiyi as a uniquely legitimate figure on the field of Chinese Buddhism, Shinohara believes, and I agree, that Guanding took some of these narrative elements from entries for other monks, as found in the first *Encyclopedia of Eminent Monks (Gaoseng zhuan)* by Huijiao (497–554), and rewrote them as though they were Zhiyi's own experiences.[36] Hence, in his effort to generate an image of Zhiyi as the font of tradition, Guanding dug up pieces of tradition that had been vaunted in the past and stitched them into an account of Zhiyi's life. Thus, ironically, Zhiyi's life, in Guanding's hands, has become the repository of tradition but only via this Frankenstein manner of scripting Zhiyi's life with elements drawn from the biographies of other monks. In short, with Guanding as the posthumous father, Zhiyi's life was fleshed out with the literature of tradition, a strategy that we need to keep in view if we are to understand the creation of the Chan masters.[37]

36. For Shinohara's account of this, see "Guanding's Biography of Zhiyi," 129–30.
37. There is another angle to this point: Shinohara points out that Guanding's emplotment of Zhiyi's life is largely defined by Zhiyi's interactions with sacred images. In this light, Zhiyi's life is again constructed as a kind of quilting point where various strains of the Buddhist literary and cultic tradition are woven into a singular whole. For Shinohara's discussion of this problem, see "Guanding's Biography of Zhiyi," 106–11, 136, 154.

One more thing to note about this version of Guanding's biography of Zhiyi. Besides including in Zhiyi's biography episodes from other monks' lives, Guanding mentioned that Zhiyi was the unique inheritor of a legacy of wisdom and meditation that he received from his teacher, Huisi, a legacy that supposedly derived from two monks, Buddhabhadra and Xuangao, both of whom lived at the beginning of the fifth century and were mentioned in the first *Encyclopedia of Eminent Monks*. Without specifying how this legacy was moved from the fifth to the sixth century, Guanding relies on accounts of these earlier eminent monks to inflate *and* ground Zhiyi's legitimacy by stating that their successful fusion of meditation and wisdom languished until it was revived by Huisi, who then passed it on to Zhiyi. Guanding writes, "Long ago Buddha *(badhra)* and Xuangao developed meditation *(ding)* and wisdom *(hui)* in tandem. Later, their [teachings] deteriorated and became like a one-wheeled [cart] and a single-winged [bird. So the situation remained] until it was righted by [Huisi of] Nanyue, and reached its prosperity here [with Zhiyi]."[38] That Guanding mentions these two monks as significant precedents to Huisi and Zhiyi in this biography written sometime around 605 is important, since in his final statement of Zhiyi's lineage, written before his death in 632, Guanding concocted another theory completely at odds with this version. In this later account, Guanding created a "new" master for Zhiyi's master, a certain Huiwen (n.d.), and claimed that it was this "grandfather" of Zhiyi's that had captured the total truth of Indian Buddhism and given it to Zhiyi's master, Huisi, who then gave it to Zhiyi. In short, Guanding did a fair amount of experimenting in organizing Zhiyi's lineage, inventing and dismissing Zhiyi's ancestors as he saw fit.

As a baseline set of conclusions we ought to agree that Zhiyi's identity, and the literature in which it was fabricated, emerged from a set of high-level exchanges between the throne and the monastery at Tiantai, first in the form of the *One Hundred Letters* and then in the imperially sponsored *Biography*. During this time, Guanding must have realized that the prince of Jin wanted to read his imperial destiny in the story of Zhiyi and Nation Purified Monastery, and thus Guanding went about portraying Zhiyi's mystical advance knowledge of the prince's imperial successes, thereby sanctifying the Prince's rights to rule and grounding

---

38. T.50.192c.21–33; translated by Penkower, "In the Beginning," 281; for Chen's discussion of this account of Zhiyi's masters, see *Making and Remaking History*, 20–21.

his dynasty in some cosmic reality that Zhiyi alone had access to. Along the way, Guanding turned Zhiyi into a king of Buddhism in order to satisfy the political needs of a particular prince newly, and perhaps in some eyes illegitimately, raised up to lead the empire. In sum, the State needed, temporarily, a law bigger than itself to confirm its own right to rule, and Guanding was prepared to write and rewrite history to meet this need and to make Zhiyi into a suitably large symbolic Other.

PHASE TWO: GUANDING'S PREFACE TO THE *MOHEZHIGUAN*

The next effort by Guanding to present Zhiyi as an ancestor who held the totality of tradition came in a preface that Guanding wrote to Zhiyi's masterpiece on meditation and insight, the *Mohezhiguan*. Having taken it upon himself to edit this massive work, Guanding prepared three different prefaces for it; in fact, for one hundred fifty years it seems that these three prefaces were in circulation, though only the final version has survived. Modern scholars have argued that, judging from various statements made by seventh- and eighth-century authors who commented on the *Mohezhiguan* and its various prefaces, what distinguishes the surviving preface from the other two is that it draws Guanding's new version of Zhiyi's genealogy out of the body of *Mohezhiguan* and presents it as an organizing element in the preface.[39] In fact, the surviving version, which was probably written closer to Guanding's death in 632, is basically structured in two parts: the first part is dedicated to telling the story of Zhiyi's lineage; the second is organized around clarifying the contents of the *Mohezhiguan*.[40]

In comparison with Guanding's Sui-era writing on Zhiyi's ancestors, the preface gives a very different picture. Now, though Zhiyi is

---

39. For discussion of this problem, see Penkower, "In the Beginning," 268 ff.

40. Penkower, "In the Beginning," 272 ff, argues for an earlier date for Guanding's first attempt to write this lineage into the preface to the *Mohezhiguan;* she also sees the preface as of a piece with Guanding's efforts to promote connections between the Sui rulers and Nation Purified Monastery. However, I believe that the preface was written after the fall of the Sui and after Guanding's exit from that monastery; this appears sensible because the preface takes up Zhiyi's legacy in a very different manner from the texts that Guanding wrote and edited in the period 600–607, when he worked hard to associate Zhiyi with Nation Purified Monastery and the fortunes of the Sui dynasty. For instance, outside of mentioning in passing that Zhiyi lived under the Sui, there is no effort in the preface to capitalize on those relationships that were so central to Guanding's earlier writing. Thus, it would seem that by the time the preface was written the Sui dynasty had collapsed.

still presented as the link back to the Buddha in India, Guanding has shifted strategies and explains that Zhiyi belonged to a lineage that descended from the Buddha in step-by-step fashion that is much more akin to a family genealogy. In fact, Guanding goes out of his way to list the names of the sixteen preceding masters, Indian and Chinese, who form that conduit of transmission that connects the Buddha to Zhiyi. Thus, whereas his earlier attempts to ancestrize Zhiyi as a king of Buddhism involved creating (1) doubles for Zhiyi and Huisi in a previous lifetime when the Buddha taught the *Lotus Sūtra* in India; (2) dream initiations at the hands of a supernatural foreign monk; and (3) a vague connection to the eminent fifth-century monks Xuangao and Buddhabhadra, in the preface Guanding settled on man-to-man transmission to explain, in a presumably more historically defendable manner, how the totality of tradition flowed down a line of men from the Buddha to Zhiyi.[41]

Actually, not only has the overall structure of Guanding's ancestral claims for Zhiyi changed, its destination has shifted as well. Whereas Guanding's earlier writing—especially at the end of the *One Hundred Letters*—worked to sink Zhiyi's legacy into Nation Purified Monastery, now the point is to show that Zhiyi's legacy resides in this text, the *Mohezhiguan*. As mentioned above, this shift to rewrite Zhiyi's legacy away from the Sui dynasty and Nation Purified Monastery presumably had everything to do with the dynasty's fall in 618.

While these shifts in strategy are important, a number of elements and gestures remain the same in Guanding's reconstruction of Zhiyi's identity. Most notable is Guanding's ongoing willingness to create Zhiyi's lineage by recycling and altering previously published material drawn from sources that had nothing to do with Zhiyi. For instance, in order to create that sequence of sixteen teachers linking Zhiyi to the Buddha, Guanding picked up a genealogy of twenty-four dharma masters from a text titled *The Account of the Causes and Conditions of Transmission of the Dharma-Treasury (Fu fazang yinyuan zhuan),*

---

41. Modern scholars, such as Penkower, often describe this form of transmission as "noncontinguous," because two ancestors, Nāgārjuna and Huiwen, aren't said to have met, with Huiwen simply reading Nāgārjuna's book, the *Mahāprajñāpāramitā Śastra (Dazhidu lun),* in order to receive the transmission. However, even with this mere book transmission holding the history together, it seems more sensible to see this "history" as intent on creating the image of continuity. The "noncontiguous" assessment seems to have derived from anti-Tiantai polemics that appeared centuries later. Certainly, with regard to Guanding's earlier attempts to ancestrize Zhiyi, this version is much more intent on presenting a contiguous form of transmission.

a work that appears to have been written in China in the fifth or sixth century.[42] This text develops in an awkward and long (six volumes) narrative the story of how the essence of Buddhism bumped down this track of masters, ultimately being received by the hapless Siṃha, the twenty-fourth master, whose head was cut off by an evil king, thereby ending the transmission of dharma. The point of writing this text seems to have been to warn Chinese rulers that they, in advancing anti-Buddhist policies, might cause the death of the dharma. That is, the text worked to fetishize tradition in this lineage in order to offer a jolting cautionary tale based on the following logic: kill a monk, and who knows, he might have been *the one* who had tradition, and now that he is dead, Buddhism is destroyed.

From this long and cumbersome narrative, Guanding pulled out the list of twenty-four dharma ancestors and explains, with some fina-gling, why the first thirteen ancestors are actually Zhiyi's ancestors and why they represented the Indian side of that conduit connecting the Buddha to Zhiyi.[43] Thus, as Elizabeth Morrison has argued, Guanding not only "adopts" these ancestors, he completely rewrites their basic

42. T.50.297. For discussion of this text, see Henri Maspero, "Sur la date et l'authenticité du Fou fa tsang yin yuan tchouan." More recently, Morrison has written an important analysis of the text and an excellent account of its place in the development of Chinese genealogical writing; see her "Contested Visions of the Buddhist Past and the Curious Fate of an Early Medieval Buddhist Text" and also the first two chapters of her dissertation, "Ancestors, Authority, and History," 1–92. Adamek has important infor-mation on the *Account;* see *The Mystique of Transmission,* 101–10. Unfortunately, Adamek's account of Guanding's multiple rewritings of Zhiyi's ancestors follows Penkower's argument that this schema in the preface represents a kind of discontinuity in the theory of transmission from the Buddha to Zhiyi (see *The Mystique of Transmission,* 110–14). The better argument is that Guanding was writing genealogies for Zhiyi that were progressively more intent on showing continuity between the Buddha and Zhiyi.

43. It seems likely that Guanding would have been drawn to this set of twenty-four masters after they had been installed in the Dazhusheng cave (modern-day Henan) in 589 by Lingyu (518–605); for more details, see the useful discussion in Adamek, *The Mystique of Transmission,* 101–4. The plot thickens when Adamek points out that this cave and its architect seem to have links to Xinxing and the Sect of the Three Levels (103). Also, it is worth noting that during Empress Wu's reign, this set of ancestors would be again recycled, though now counted as twenty-five, and installed at Longmen (104). Empress Wu's adoption of these patriarchs also suggests that we need to imagine a complex cycle of genealogical figures being swapped back and forth between the throne and Buddhist authors. In another eighty years this list of ancestors, slightly revised and lengthened, would be attached to the Bodhidharma lineage and put forward as the basis of all future Chan and Zen claims to authenticity. Adamek also points out that even as Chan authors were taking hold of this set of masters, two other "schools"—the Yogācāra School and the Zhenyan School of Amoghavajra—latched on to this list, giving, again, the sense of how ancestors were selected and employed willy-nilly for various projects.

raison d'être so that the entire tale is no longer a dire warning about the end of Buddhism but instead a comforting account of perfect Buddhism coming to China and finding its way into Zhiyi's person.[44] In order to attach Zhiyi to this borrowed lineage, Guanding simply claimed that though the lineage of the twenty-four masters did extend to the luckless Siṃha, it had in fact sprouted a branch during the time of the thirteenth patriarch, Nāgārjuna. This hitherto unknown collateral segment of the lineage was generated when Nāgārjuna supposedly wrote a text, the *Mahāprajñāpāramitā Śāstra*, which, when it came to China, brought Huiwen into total enlightenment, thereby effecting an immaculate transmission of the essence of Indian Buddhism into a Chinese man. Then, according to Guanding's preface, Huiwen passed the lineage's legacy on to Huisi, who was also suddenly and totally enlightened. And, of course, Huisi then passed this enlightenment on to Zhiyi. By explaining how the essence of this lineage of the doomed track of twenty-four masters had slipped out before its demise, Guanding essentially hijacked the genealogy's payload in order to make it land on Zhiyi, thereby making it irrelevant if it was later snuffed out when Siṃha was executed.[45] Obviously, in appropriating this lineage and attaching it to Zhiyi and his master, Huisi, Guanding simply gathered up a previous effort to gather up tradition and rerouted it for his own ends.

And, just as Guanding adopted and rewrote the *Account* for his own purposes, the *Account*, too, appears to have been a forgery that expanded a previous list of five dharma masters that had been constructed for an altogether different purpose in several Indian works translated into Chinese, including the *Aśokāvadāna*.[46] Setting up these five (six, really) dharma masters (Mahākāśyapa, Ānanda/ Madhyāntika, Śāṇavāsa, Upagupta, Dhītika) as the initial link back to the Buddha, the authors of the *Account* simply added on nineteen

44. For her comments, see "Contested Visions of the Buddhist Past," 18–20.
45. Guanding's list of the twenty-four ancestors is slightly different from the one presented in the *Account*; for a translation of this section of the preface, see Neal Donner and Daniel B. Stevenson, *The Great Calming and Contemplation*, 101–3. For a useful table of the various rewritings of this list of twenty-four, see Yampolsky, *The Platform Sūtra of the Sixth Patriarch*, 8–9.
46. For a brief discussion of these five figures in India, see Étienne Lamotte, *History of Indian Buddhism*, 203. The five dharma-masters can be found in the second Chinese translation of the *Aśokāvadāna*, T.50.152c, and translated into English by Li Ronxi, in *The Biographical Scripture of King Aśoka*, 107–46. John S. Strong has translated the Sanskrit version of the *Aśokāvadāna*, which lacks this list of the five dharma-masters; see his *The Legend of King Aśoka*.

more masters, with some like Nāgārjuna and Aśvaghoṣa presumably chosen for name recognition and others simply made up to serve as placeholders. Especially interesting for judging later Chan "historiography," the *Account* then filled in biographic information for each of the first five dharma masters with material drawn from another text, the *Sarvāstivāda Vinaya*, presumably in an effort to make their lives and the *Account* look more historical.[47] Thus, the authors of the *Account* took the *form* of a lineage from one text—as defined by a list of names—and then stuffed it with biographic material from another unrelated work in the hope of producing a more convincing account of the history of truth as supposedly owned by this line of men. For the later nineteen figures whose biographies are not presented in the *Sarvāstivāda Vinaya*, the *Account* has little to say, except in the case of high-profile figures such as Nāgārjuna, for whom there was biographic material in other texts that the authors of the *Account* could draw on.[48] In short, the *Account* from which Guanding drew up Zhiyi's list of ancestors was itself an altogether contrived work that had created a conduit of perfect tradition to speak to a rather desperate political situation in the late fifth century.[49]

While plundering the *Account* to find Zhiyi a more convincing family of saints, Guanding shares a fundamental brotherhood with its authors since in fact what he has done to the *Account* is quite parallel to what the authors of the *Account* had done to *their* sources. In short, and this presages much of the genealogical writing in Chan, when Guanding went angling for ancestors for Zhiyi, he hooked a text that also had gone fishing for ancestors, even if for a very different purpose. Thus, while on the level of narrative Guanding completely destroys the logic of the *Account*, on the level of craftsmanship, in constructing a genealogy from borrowed sources he has, after a fashion, doffed his cap to the authors of the *Account* by doing to their work what they had done to their own sources. In short, here is early evidence of an unspoken

47. Morrison makes this point; see her "Contested Visions of the Buddhist Past," 4–8.

48. For promising research on the biographies of Nāgārjuna, Aśvaghoṣa, and Āryadeva, see Stuart Young's dissertation, "Conceiving the Indian Buddhist Patriarchs in China."

49. Adamek expresses "deep admiration" for the "drama of the Dharma brought to life" in the *Account*. Though I find this comment courageous, it remains a mystery to me why this text would warrant an "irony-free accolade." For her comments, see *The Mystique of Transmission*, 134.

genealogy of genealogists, in which the tricks of the trade are transmitted even as those author-to-author connections remain suppressed as
each new genealogist does his best to keep the reader's eye on the inside
of his genealogy in order to prevent the reader from seeing the new
genealogy's place in the sequence of genealogies and recognizing it as a
derivative of a derivative.

Despite Guanding's hope to keep his readers in the dark about
his narrative creativity, his literary efforts in the preface reveal an
intriguing phenomenon: Guanding took more of the lineage narrative from the *Account* than he needed. Though he only needed the
Account's lineage up to the thirteenth figure—Nāgārjuna—he in fact
recites the whole doomed lineage up to the twenty-fourth ancestor,
Siṃha. Thus, the ancestors that occupy the post-Nāgārjuna section
of the lineage, slots 14 through 24, linger in Guanding's preface as a
useless vestige limb, marking how an older skeletal form was covered
over with new flesh. However, I wonder if we might not be right in
imagining a good reason for this faithful, if useless, repetition of
the *form* of the *Account*'s history of the dharma. I imagine that in
terms of reader seduction, Guanding likely felt obliged to show the
lineage that he was hijacking in its fullest "original" form, as if to say
to his reader, "You remember that lineage of twenty-four ancestors,
right? Well, it *was* basically legitimate. It is just that the story goes
differently now." In effect, then, and we will see this in the Chan lineages, each author who thieves a lineage needs to maintain that prior
lineage's form and prestige—as a reliable body of building materials—even as he redesigns its content and final destination. Or, put
otherwise, though Guanding only wants the first thirteen ancestors,
all twenty-four need to be "visible" for the cachet of the *Account* to
be appropriated.

While the ancestors from the *Account* in slots 14 through 24 linger
awkwardly in Guanding's new narrative for Zhiyi's lineage, his own
previous literary attempts to construct Zhiyi's legitimacy are much less
in view and never appear as languishing vestiges. For instance, one
of the most striking things about Guanding's preface is that Nation
Purified Monastery, which Sui Yangdi had built for Zhiyi, isn't mentioned once. Though Guanding notes that Zhiyi was recognized by
Chen and Sui emperors, there is no mention of Zhiyi's close connection
to that monastery or all the splendid miracles that had, in Guanding's
earlier writings, tied Zhiyi's life to the Sui dynasty and that monastery.
Apparently, by the time the preface was written, Guanding still wanted

Zhiyi to be a kinglike figure but now had no use for the Sui dynasty or Nation Purified Monastery. Thus, with the lineage taken from the *Account,* conjoined with the claim that Zhiyi's two Chinese ancestors achieved enlightenment as an effect of that lineage, Guanding did for Zhiyi what he had been trying to do all along—turn him into the sole legitimate representative of Buddhism in China. Moreover, Guanding now directs the legacy of that lineage into an entirely new receptacle, the *Mohezhiguan,* the very text to which Guanding is attaching this preface.

Key here is the way in which this final form of Zhiyi's genealogy suppresses and occludes the history of events that led to the writing of this history. Thus, that thick matrix of political pressures and literary precedents is whisked from view as soon as one faithfully reads Guanding's preface and looks along the "spine" of the narrative from Zhiyi back down the track of the ancestors to the Buddha. In starker terms, it was unusually lucky—for modern historians, at least—that Guanding's earlier writings survived, allowing us to watch the gradual formulation of Zhiyi's genealogy and his quasi-buddha status. Consequently, we have the good fortune to be able to see the history of how Guanding went about writing Zhiyi's history.

It is also worth mentioning that in the case of Guanding, it wasn't the winners who wrote history but rather the historians who turned out to be the winners. Whether he personally arranged it or not, Guanding was soon seen as Zhiyi's only real successor in place of Zhiyue, who Zhiyi had appointed and who had managed Nation Purified Monastery until his death in 616. Thus, as I detail below, soon after Guanding's efforts to ancestrize his master's identity, Guanding's own disciples then slipped him into that newly generated lineage, claiming, against a number of previously published statements, that Guanding alone had inherited the essence and totality of Zhiyi. Arguably, then, not only did Guanding change the modes of claiming Buddhist authority in medieval China, he generated a kind of symbolic coinage that, once in circulation, seems to have maintained its value. In short, the historian of the master in time became a master, too, largely as the effect of historicizing his own master.

While sorting out what Guanding has done in his efforts to ancestrize Zhiyi reveals a lot about how genealogies were written during the early Tang, it is also the case that this list of twenty-four ancestors, as defined in the *Account,* reappeared in Chan genealogies from the mid- to late Tang, such as the *Platform Sūtra,* the *Lidai fabao ji,*

and the *Baolin zhuan,* in particular.[50] Actually, though these three
histories would, like Guanding's, be overcome and absorbed by later
genealogists during the Five Dynasty era and the early Song, it turns
out that this list of twenty-four ancestors would, with slight expansion, become the staple of later Chan and Zen writing, remaining in
place even in the modern era.[51] Thus, Guanding's reinvention of the
past in the early seventh century was to have a lively legacy down to
the present.

THE QUESTION OF HUIWEN

Examining Guanding's use, in the preface, of Huiwen as Zhiyi's "spiritual grandfather," suggests again that Guanding was rather unscrupu-
lous in rewriting history. As mentioned above, in the two genealogies
that Guanding wrote before the preface—the *One Hundred Letters*
and the *Biography*—Zhiyi is linked to Huisi, who seems to have been
a real historical character and, in fact, was Zhiyi's teacher. However,
in these earlier writings, there is no mention of Huiwen. In light of this
absence, the question has to be: If Huisi really had a master named
Huiwen, who was so important in establishing the lineage that Zhiyi
was to inherit, why did Guanding wait to mention him until this third
version of the lineage, a lineage that is completely at odds with the
previous two?[52] The most obvious answer is that, along with the other
ancestors that Guanding has dragged onstage, Huiwen wasn't at all
related to Zhiyi's existence and was simply included as a narrative
expedient.

In fact, there are good reasons to conclude that Huiwen never existed
and instead was created, ex nihilo, as a useful pivot in this new formulation of Zhiyi's lineage. Huiwen is not known in any contemporaneous
documents that survive, and apparently there was no funerary stele
that Daoxuan knew of to give him a biography in the *Encyclopedia
of Eminent Monks II.* In addition to these pieces of negative evidence,

50. For an overview of these various genealogies, see Yampolsky, *The Platform
Sūtra,* 8–9. For more up-to-date discussions, see Adamek, *The Mystique of Transmission,*
esp. chaps. 4, 5; see also Morrison, "Ancestors, Authority, and History," 70–75.

51. For discussion of this period of Chan genealogical writing, see Albert Welter,
"Lineage and Context in the *Patriarch's Hall Collection* and the *Transmission of the
Lamp.*"

52. Chen also points out the oddness of the late appearance of Huiwen in the account
of Zhiyi's past; see *Making and Remaking History,* 20–21.

let's look carefully at what Guanding says about Huiwen in the surviving preface:[53]

> Huisi studied under the Chan master Huiwen. During the reign of
> Gaozu (550–560) of the Northern Qi dynasty, the latter wandered alone
> through the region between the Yellow and Huai rivers, his approach
> to dharma unknown to his age. Indeed, people [daily] tread the earth
> and gaze at the heavens, yet have no idea of the earth's thickness nor
> heaven's loftiness. Huiwen's mental discipline was exclusively based on
> the *Mahāprajñāpāramitā Śāstra (Dazhidu lun)* which was expounded by
> Nāgārjuna, the thirteenth patriarch in the line of those who transmitted
> the treasure of the dharma. It says in Zhiyi's *Treatise on Contemplating
> Mind,* "I entrust myself to the master Nāgārjuna." By this we can verify
> that Nāgārjuna is the founding ancestor *(gao zu)* [of our line].

Clearly, in Guanding's account of Huiwen's life, there are no details:
there is no mention of his family name, his birthplace, his main monastery, his teachers, and his place of death—all the standard elements in a
monk's biography. And yet, even with these glaring absences, Guanding
manages to historicize Huiwen by associating him with Emperor Gaozu,
presumably so that the reader could imagine that Huiwen was alive at
the right time to instruct Huisi. Similarly, by locating Huiwen somewhere in "the region between the Yellow and Huai rivers," which is
basically no different from saying "central China," Guanding has given
Huiwen's life a suitable, if highly nonspecific, locale. Furthermore,
and this tendency will be repeated in future genealogical fabrications,
Guanding creates an aura of secrecy around Huiwen, since though he
supposedly wandered widely, no one recognized him for who he was.
And again presaging Chan authors' techniques, Guanding wraps up
this package of vagueness with an allusion to the *Zuozhuan,* a widely
known non-Buddhist history from the Warring States period.

In drawing from the *Zuozhuan* for that line explaining people's
long-standing inability to recognize sages even when they meet them,
Guanding not only legitimizes his lack of details, but does so with a
passage from a work that would have brought to his discussion an air of
historicity and respectability. In short, when we look at this passage on
Huiwen, we learn nothing of substance about Huiwen, his life, or his
teaching, and instead learn simply that his greatness went unrecognized
and that this lack of recognition is to be understood via the *Zuozhuan*

---

53. Translation from Donner and Stevenson, *The Great Calming and Contemplation,*
106–7, with minor changes.

allusion, as simply the way things often go for sages. Presumably, then, it wasn't by accident that Guanding inserted the *Zuozhuan* quote here: its stolid cachet appears designed to compensate for the brash creation of Huiwen ex nihilo.

Three other details point toward Guanding's creation of Huiwen. First, there is no description of Huiwen interacting with his supposed student, Huisi. As noted above, Huiwen doesn't have a home monastery or any real locale, and thus Guanding says nothing about how, where, or why the two men might have met, elements that are usually of primary interest in the lives of eminent monks. Second, Huiwen's relationship to tradition is altogether different from Huisi's: Huisi is Huiwen's disciple and supposedly absorbs the totality of tradition from his master, man-to-man, while Huiwen doesn't have a teacher and instead gets the total-ity of tradition from his reading of the *Mahāprajñāpāramitā Śāstra*. Thus, if this account were based on real human experience, we can imagine Huiwen, in light of his success with the *Mahāprajñāpāramitā Śāstra*, saying to Huisi, "Please read this text if you want to receive the Buddhist tradition en toto—it worked for me."

Third, Guanding's explanation of Huisi's enlightenment is oddly multifaceted and quite different from Huiwen's reading of the *Mahāprajñāpāramitā Śāstra*. Guanding has Huisi's practice develop based on three disciplines: sūtra recitation, repentance, and medita-tion. In fact, these three practices are ones that Zhiyi recommended, and they are most likely listed as part of Huisi's repertoire to give the impression that what Zhiyi taught he actually learned from his master and that, of course, these teachings were what caused enlightenment along the way. The problem is that Guanding doesn't push this content back to Huiwen, giving no details about Huiwen's practice or teach-ing and simply noting that Huiwen's "mental disciple was exclusively based on the *Mahāprajñāpāramitā Śāstra*." These narrative incon-sistencies, in league with Guanding's track record of inventing and manipulating history, leave little doubt that Huiwen was Guanding's creation.

Standing back from this assessment of Guanding's writing, we ought to reconsider the claim that China is an unusually historically conscious culture, since it would seem that those in charge of the production and maintenance of history had a very complex relation-ship to its content. Thus, on the one hand, Guanding, like all literati, knows his various histories, as seen in his use of the line from the *Zuozhuan*. Too, by quoting from that text for effect, Guanding is most certainly expecting that future readers will know their histories as well. Similarly, by supplying the extra, post-Nāgārjuna ancestors from the *Account*—those in slots 14 through 24—that add nothing to his narrative other than to preserve the integrity of a previous list of ancestors, Guanding seems again to be expecting his readers to know that source and to bring those familiarities to bear in evaluating his own history. In effect, Guanding is densely involved in reading history, and he is counting on his readers to be likewise familiar with past histories in order to appreciate his new history. The problem, though, is that Guanding clearly isn't respecting the histories he is *reading,* or, if he is, this does not prevent him from rewriting these sources in the effort to present a new version of the past. And, more interesting, he is clearly not respecting the histories he is *writing,* since he keeps changing the story in a way that completely undercuts his previous accounts. It is just this ironic relationship to the past, and to past histories, that seems to have eluded previous discussions of Chinese Buddhist genealogists and that warrants careful reflection as we watch parallel gestures performed in text after text in the centuries that followed.

JIZANG AND THE PROBLEM OF ZHIYI'S "THOUGHT"

Some modern readers may think that I have read Guanding in an unduly harsh manner, or that I have unwisely imposed modern notions of historical veracity on a medieval situation that operated with looser notions of historicity. However, I believe that once more evidence is in view, it will be clear that my suspicious approach is warranted. Crucial for setting a sensible register in which to assess Guanding's writing is another embarrassing scandal regarding Zhiyi's legacy, which I explore briefly below and which again casts doubt on Guanding's good faith as a historian of truth and tradition. Equally important for deciding how to read these problems in Guanding's writing is evidence that Guanding's manipulations of history were recognized by later writers who sought either to create new narratives to vouch for those that they saw as too obviously corrupt or to extend these narratives in new, more audacious ways so as to make the original narratives more plausible.

As for this other scandal, Guanding is credited with collecting a variety of Zhiyi's lectures on different sūtras. One such famous work is Zhiyi's *Commentary on the Lotus Sūtra (Fahua wenju).* However, the provenance of the contents of this text has recently been shown to be rather complicated.[54] In 1985 Hirai Shun'ei published a groundbreaking study in which he showed that Guanding apparently "borrowed" a substantial amount of material from another monk, Jizang (549–623), in "recording" Zhiyi's lectures.[55] This might at first seem to be no more than a case of sloppiness or expediency. However, this borrowing has several layers. First, there are good reasons for thinking that Guanding and Jizang were competitors, at best, and more likely, enemies. Jizang was a famous monk at court, fully supported by both the Sui and Tang emperors, and installed on the "board" of the ten *Dade* monks after the transition to the Tang. Guanding, on the other hand, was never accorded these accolades and in fact seems to have been accused and tried for sorcery in 611 when he was at court. As Chen rightly assumes, this charge of sorcery would not have been brought unless Guanding was seen as a rival by the court-appointed monks.[56] In short, Guanding seems to be a monk on the periphery after those heady days when he was delivering the letters to court from Nation Purified Monastery. It would seem that several years after the interest in Zhiyi had cooled, his arrival at court wasn't welcomed by the court-appointed monks, and, as a consequence, they cooked up the sorcery charge that lead to Guanding's exile. Thus, that Guanding chose to borrow from Jizang's work seems either an attempt to steal the thunder of his rival or an effort to pad Zhiyi's position with content that Guanding knew had already proved successful at court.

This case of plagiarism certainly seems of a piece with Guanding's other inventive approaches to history and legitimacy, but it is especially interesting because later authors in the Tiantai sect appear to have been quite aware of what Guanding stole from Jizang. Consequently, and Chen Jinhua has done an excellent job of sorting through this material, later Tiantai writers concocted two new accounts of Jizang's identity in order to explain how Jizang's words got into Zhiyi's lectures.[57] In one version of the story Jizang is supposedly Guanding's disciple; in the other he is made into a disciple of Zhiyi. In either case the idea is to make it appear that it was *Jizang* who took material from Zhiyi,

54. In exploring this scandal, I am relying on Chen's fine historical sleuthing in *Making and Remaking History.*
55. See his *Hokke mongu no seiritsu ni kansuru kenkyū.* I owe this reference to Chen, *Making and Remaking History,* 155; and Penkower, "In the Beginning," 282 ff.
56. For Chen's assessment, see *Making and Remaking History,* 51–57.
57. For more details, see Chen, *Making and Remaking History,* chaps. 1, 4, 5.

either directly or from his disciple Guanding, and not the other way around. In coming to understand this aggressive reworking of history, we need to admit not only that these later Tiantai writers are rewriting their ancestors' lives and identities, but they seem to be doing so with the clear recognition that their ancestors—Guanding, at least—had rewritten the ancestors as well.

Lingering in the background is another interesting problem. As several scholars have pointed out, in several places Jizang's writings mention lineage structures and the need for master-disciple transmission in order to establish authentic and legitimate positions on the field of Buddhist disputation.[58] Though pursuing Jizang's notion of lineage will have to wait for another day, it is clear that Jizang (and his disciples) spoke of truth and legitimacy in language that was couched in the same lineage terms that Guanding would take up. Equally provocative in thinking about what Guanding might have borrowed from Jizang is the fact that Jizang seems to have held up the figure of Nāgārjuna as his own special ancestor. Hence, that Guanding's final version of Zhiyi's lineage of truth takes Nāgārjuna as the crucial Indian pivot appears all the more aggressive, and derivative, as Nāgārjuna had already been claimed by Guanding's rival in this game of truth-by-ancestors. Thus, Guanding's final construction of Zhiyi's truth-ancestors has to be seen as a rather well calculated narrative, linking together disparate items in a concerted effort to create Zhiyi as a Chinese buddha, even as he borrowed and subverted the claims, and points of pride, of the competition.

A MASTER HISTORIAN: GUANDING BECOMES ZHIYI'S SOLE HEIR

Soon after Guanding's death in 632, his followers, or at least those with an interest in being seen as such, wrote a funeral stele for him that then became the basis of Guanding's biography in Daoxuan's *Encyclopedia of Eminent Monks II*. Not surprising in light of the free-for-all attitude toward writing Buddhist history, this biography of Guanding significantly contradicts Guanding's brief autobiographical remarks found near the end of his commentary on the *Nirvana Sūtra*. Chen Jinhua

58. See Morrison, "Ancestors, Authority, and History," 26 ff; Penkower, "In the Beginning," 288; Chen, *Making and Remaking History*, 18; Timothy H. Barrett, "Kill the Patriarchs!" esp. 90; Dan Lusthaus, *Buddhist Phenomenology*, 387, 396.

pursues three separate kinds of invention in this version of Guanding's biography, but of particular interest for this discussion is the attempt to present Guanding as Zhiyi's singular disciple and to have the Sui emperor announce this in an edict. Thus, tucked in Guanding's biography in Daoxuan's *Encyclopedia of Eminent Monks II* we find:[59]

> Now that you, Chan master [Guanding], are the advanced disciple of Zhizhe [Zhiyi] and the person on whom the dharma-gate has relied, I am now sending an envoy to invite you [to come to the capital]. I hope that you will do me a great favor of accepting the invitation.

Thus, though the *One Hundred Letters* make clear that Zhiyi had chosen Zhiyue as his primary heir and leader of the community, this *Encyclopedia* entry omits reference to Zhiyue and instead inserts Guanding into that slot, granting him the unique position of being the one on whom tradition relied. Moreover, this passage performs that familiar gesture in which manhandling tradition is made acceptable through appealing to imperial voices who are made to recite Buddhist genealogical claims, a gesture that many later Chan texts will also turn to.

Using the emperor's voice to canonize this newly created link between Zhiyi and Guanding was supplemented with another audacious trope. As Chen points out, this biography also casts Guanding as Ānanda, the Buddha's cousin and attendant.[60] In adopting this trope, the authors of this narrative are making Zhiyi parallel in stature to the Buddha, even as they secure Guanding as a special and unique descendant of Zhiyi, just as Ānanda was the Buddha's special descendant. Besides the literary flourishes that hint at these specific claims, the biography explicitly identifies Guanding as the sole person who understood Zhiyi: "Furthermore, the eloquence of Zhizhe [Zhiyi], flowing like the clouds and pouring like the rain, was likened to the heavenly net or a necklace of precious stones. It was only Guanding who was able to uphold and comprehend [what was preached by him]."[61]

In addition, Chen has shown that this biography of Guanding was written by deforming details that were included in prior documents in order to lionize Guanding's identity. Thus, instead of assuming that the differing accounts of Guanding's life represent different sources, oral or otherwise, Chen argues that we are watching a process of

59. See Chen, *Making and Remaking History*, 47, with slight changes.
60. Ibid., 55.
61. Ibid., 55n. 63.

consciously rewriting prior material, an argument with which I am in full agreement. As Chen puts it, "The alarming discrepancies between some portions of Guanding's autobiography and his *Xu gaoseng zhuan* [Daoxuan's *Encyclopedia*] biography have alerted us to tremendous efforts made to glorify Guanding. Some *Xu gaoseng zhuan* passages analyzed above, which were either directly plucked from or rewritten on the basis of an inscription prepared for Guanding by his disciples, show clearly that Guanding's disciples tried to heighten Guanding's status."[62] Thus, unlike those who live by the sword, those who live by the.pen can keep on living, if they are lucky like Guanding and continue to grow in stature as their descendants pick up the pen of history to make the past what it needs to be.

It was in this climate of creatively rewriting the histories of newly found Chinese buddhas, or at least quasi-buddhas, that Shaolin Monastery would create its own set of ancestors in 690.[63] Before investigating the case of Shaolin, though, I want to close this chapter with a cursory review of Xinxing and the Sect of the Three Levels to show yet another seventh-century lineage effort and, more importantly, to highlight key discourse gestures that seem to function as antecedents for later genealogists.

XINXING (540–594): AN OVERVIEW

With the recent work of Jamie Hubbard and Mark Edward Lewis we have begun to appreciate how important Xinxing was, both during his life and in the centuries that followed. Though Xinxing would be ancestrized in the decades after his life and though he would have disciples with enough renown to warrant their own steles, I haven't yet found evidence that the genealogical side of his identity was particularly potent in defining the lineages found in early Chan.[64] On the other hand, Xinxing's teachings, as they have survived, reveal his form of Buddhism as an astute set of strategies for mediating the interface between India and China, between real Buddhism and evil Buddhism, and between Xinxing and the masses. Thus, with or without the direct transmission of content from Xinxing's teaching to early Chan authors,

---

62. Ibid., 55.

63. For a fuller account of lineage efforts in the pre-Faru period, see Morrison, "Ancestors, Authority, and History," chaps. 1, 2.

64. For epigraphic sources for Xinxing and his followers, see Jamie Hubbard, "Chinese Reliquary Inscriptions and the San-chieh-chiao."

Xinxing and his legacy offer a fine example of accomplishing all the symbolic work that Guanding and the Bodhidharma genealogies set out to do: to create images of perfect Buddhism in China.

Given the relative dearth of biographic details on Xinxing—his two surviving biographies, one in the *Miraculous Retribution (Ming bao ji)* and the other in Daoxuan's *Encyclopedia,* are short and very thin on early-life details—I will pick up the story of Xinxing's life in the 590s, when, after an apparently strong showing in the preceding decades, he was invited to court, under the auspices of Prime Minster Gao Jiong, who in fact gave him one of his personal residences for use as a monastery, Huadusi.[65] Actually, his successes appear on a scale larger than this since one of the biographies notes that five of the capital's monasteries were dedicated to Xinxing and his followers, who numbered roughly three hundred and seem to have thought of themselves as a group or community set apart from other Buddhists.

Though we do not know how the first Sui emperor, Sui Wendi, imagined Xinxing's role in Sui State-building enterprises, it is clear that Xinxing and his followers received imperial recognition. Once installed at the capital, the group appears to have grown in strength, though Xinxing soon died, in 594. The fate of his followers seems to have taken a nasty turn when Gao Jiong was deposed as prime minister in 599, an event that left the group vulnerable to an imperial injunction issued in 600 that forbade them the right to practice.[66] Of course, given Xinxing's insulting rhetoric that he alone was the valid spokesperson for tradition and his equally audacious effort to establish a separate Buddhist community of supposedly more authentic members, one can imagine that other leading Buddhists at the capital would have had little reason to support or accept Xinxing's followers, especially once their powerful patron had been deposed.[67] Still, throughout the seventh century and into the eighth, Xinxing's movement continued to attract imperial attention, both supportive and repressive, and nurtured an impressive following.

65. For Xinxing's biography and relevant sources, see Hubbard, *Absolute Delusion, Perfect Buddhahood,* 4–14.

66. For discussion of the politics of Gao Jiong's ouster and its likely impact on the Sect of the Three Levels, see Hubbard, *Absolute Delusion, Perfect Buddhahood,* 196–97.

67. Lewis has advanced the useful hypothesis that Xinxing's radical sectarianism was suppressed under the Sui and then later under Empress Wu precisely because both dynasties were interested in mobilizing a broad spectrum of Buddhist support for their reigns; for more discussion, see "The Suppression of the Three Stages Sect."

BEING TRADITION: XINXING'S POSITION

The place to begin analyzing the structure of Xinxing's doctrine is his notion that true Buddhism *only* resided in his teachings and the practices that he recommended. Accordingly, all other forms of Buddhist thought and practice were judged corrupt and harmful since they supposedly led to slandering the Buddha, a charge that Xinxing regularly leveled at his contemporaries. In effect, then, Xinxing's program had a rather vicious one-two punch: he first declared that all the efforts of the Other to practice Buddhism only further distanced one from success; and, conversely, he then declared that the only way to get close to authenticity was to submit to him and relinquish any sense of value that one might have gained from previous practices. That is, like the *Lotus Sūtra* and other Mahāyāna sūtras that he cited extensively, Xinxing first delivered a global indictment of Buddhism and then offered himself as the solution to the absolute failure that he identified in every other form of Buddhist practice.[68] Consequently, though Xinxing would prescribe specific practices for his followers, a large portion of his teachings were teachings *about* teachings—a kind of meta-review of legitimacy itself. Noting this meta-level of Xinxing's discourse is important because it locates his thought within the sphere of several Mahāyāna works that he favored, and it presages a variety of positions taken by later Chan authors.

Given the structure of this claim that only Xinxing's Buddhism was legitimate, it is not too surprising that Xinxing required his new members to convert *away* from contemporaneous forms of Chinese Buddhism. Not only did this requirement render normal Buddhism un-Buddhist, but it also resulted in new institutional forms. Thus, established Buddhist institutions were rejected in favor of new communities *(bu zhong)* of Xinxing's followers, which were explicitly described as separate groups *(yi bu)* that maintained a border between themselves and older forms of Buddhism.[69] While it makes sense to see the Xinxing movement relying on a standard form of Mahāyāna polemics, we shouldn't miss that a radical shift has occurred. A range of Mahāyāna texts tried to establish similar models for conversion,

---

68. For an account of how this dynamic works in the *Lotus Sūtra,* see my *Text as Father,* chaps. 2, 3.

69. See Hubbard, *Absolute Delusion, Perfect Buddhahood,* 16, for more discussion of these terms.

but they did little to prepare for the institutional enactment of these polemics. In fact, most of the Mahāyāna sūtras that work up this kind of conversion structure direct those desires for new Buddhist authenticity to the text itself, and offer the reader little more than the standard cult-of-the-text to ground this shift in religious identity. Xinxing's movement, on the other hand, represents a paradigm shift because this renovation of Buddhist identity isn't simply a faith-act produced in the reading moment, as it is in the cult-of-the-text, but rather plays out as a historical drama involved with other real-world elements, such as the monastic institution and the government. In short, whereas polemics such as one finds in the Lotus Sūtra remain largely about themselves—that is, "please convert to this text explaining the value of conversion, and agree to disparage all other forms of Buddhism"—in Xinxing's hands these rhetorics were redirected away from the cult-of-the-text in order to be attached to Xinxing and then brought to bear in refiguring the religious landscape that defined Chinese Buddhism.

To make conversion to his supposedly hyperorthodox form of Buddhism attractive and sensible, Xinxing advanced several interlocking agendas. The first, as just mentioned, was a thorough denunciation of current religious authorities. At first glance it would seem that Xinxing is simply basing his critique of Chinese Buddhism on the doctrine of the "end of the dharma" (mofa), a fairly popular notion at the time that imagined that in the centuries after the death of the Buddha there would come a time when human capabilities would be so diminished there would be little point in pursuing traditional practices.[70] Though Xinxing cites such theories regularly in his writing, he effectively shifts the import of this historical expectation so that it functions something like a sociology of the Other in which Xinxing claims to unerringly know real Buddhism when he sees it and, similarly, that real Buddhism isn't present in his fellow Buddhists. Thus, despite all the Buddhism that had been spilling into China in the previous five hundred years, Xinxing's indictment portrays the totality of that tradition as nothing more than a desert of failure. Precisely this structure of knowing-the-failure-of-the-Other will reappear in the Bodhidharma stories and in other early Chan literature, so it is important to clearly identify it here,

70. For an overview of Buddhist theories of the decline of the dharma, see Jan Nattier, Once upon a Future Time; for more discussion of Xinxing's notion of the "end of the dharma," see Hubbard, Absolute Delusion, Perfect Buddhahood, 76–94.

especially since Xinxing's position represents such a thoroughgoing version of it.

THE END OF READING: XINXING OVERCOMES THE SŪTRAS

Central to the denunciation of his contemporaries was Xinxing's claim that there was no value in reading Buddhist sūtras, a practice that was taken to be essential by most contemporaneous Buddhists. More precisely, he claimed that all sentient beings at this point in history, himself excluded, had absolutely no capacity to read and interpret Buddhist scripture correctly and thus belonged to that unfortunate "third level" *(san jie)*. Worse, according to Xinxing, when third-level beings attempt to read the sūtras, they only move farther from their goal of enlightenment. Equally alarming, Xinxing claimed that any form of textual exegesis would slander and abuse the buddhas, given the misinterpretations generated in such misguided readings. In short, though Xinxing himself was an avid reader of Mahāyāna literature and though he cited Mahāyāna sūtras to prove his point that Chinese Buddhists should stop reading sūtras, he essentially wrenched the imported Mahāyāna works out of the hands of his followers with the claim that correct reading was fundamentally impossible and that all interpretation was misguided and nefarious.

In place of the crucial connection that the sūtras had offered Chinese readers—with their cult-of-the-text promises that to read and accept them was to win the essence of Buddhism—Xinxing argued that real Buddhism was already in China. In fact, according to Xinxing, real Buddhism was already present in each and every person in the form of internal buddhahood, which he termed either "buddha-nature" *(foxing)* or "buddha-essence" *(fozong)*. Thus, with this perfect essence already on hand, there was no reason to rely on importing Buddhism through reading sūtras. To get at this internal form of pure Buddhism, Xinxing advocated meditation and the *dhūtaṅgas*—various forms of self-denial and asceticism, including begging (which had never caught on in China), silence, and the wearing of coarse robes.[71] In addition to these forms of practice, it seems that Xinxing, or at least his followers, advocated another kind of access to authentic tradition: one could make offerings to the huge storehouse, the "inexhaustible treasury"

---

71. For Xinxing's positions on practice, see Hubbard, *Absolute Delusion, Perfect Buddhahood*, 19–30.

(wujin zang) located at the capital, with the promise that such an offering would link the donor's karmic fate to Xinxing's, and since Xinxing was presented as a high-level bodhisattva destined for buddhahood, the gift was imagined to bring the donor to salvation in the future.[72]

Looking more closely at this polemic against reading sūtras, several points need to be underlined. First, it was with a new form of literature that Xinxing overcame the sūtras. Thus, though he was adamant about avoiding scriptural reading, he himself produced a body of literary works that were copied and circulated. In this gesture, we have an important precedent for a key element in Chan rhetoric in which scriptural reading is denounced and yet that very denunciation of sūtra literature launches a new Chinese genre of literature that effectively rivals and even replaces the sūtra precedent. Second, and equally predictive of Chan tropes, authority in Xinxing's writing is placed in a complicated relationship with the sūtras. Thus, as we have seen, to make his argument about the uselessness of reading sūtras, he quoted sūtras. Using the sūtras against themselves, however, was only possible by breaking up their basic mode of making meaning—the narrative. In particular, since the sūtras were designed to effect, in the linear reading experience, the conviction that the totality of Buddhism was present in the physical presence of the text itself, to cite select passages from these works ruined their overall strategy to redefine authentic Buddhism and deliver it to the reader.[73] Thus, all the mana that had been assumed to belong to the sūtras shifted from the original sūtra matrix into this newly designed literary container created by Xinxing.[74] This gesture of overcoming and recentering tradition through selecting and collecting sūtra quotes will be replayed in a number of early Chan texts, such as the *History of the Teachers and Disciples of the Laṅkāvatāra Sūtra,* the works of Shenhui, and the *Platform Sūtra.*

However, there is more here than a genre shift since the shift can only be accomplished with an authority on hand to vouch for moving authority from the sūtras into this new genre. Obviously, in the case of Xinxing, it was his authority based on his unique bodhisattva status

72. Hubbard discusses this in *Absolute Delusion, Perfect Buddhahood,* 168–80, esp. 174; see also 266–67.

73. For more discussion of narrative strategies in the Mahāyāna sūtras, see Hubbard, *Absolute Delusion, Perfect Buddhahood,* 48–50; also see my *Text as Father.*

74. For reflections on Xinxing's writing, see Hubbard, *Absolute Delusion, Perfect Buddhahood,* 11–12.

that supported this shift. The key is that his authority now appears as essentially "bigger" than the Buddha's voice, as found in the sūtras. Thus, though Xinxing relies on sūtra quotes to establish his position, his whole enterprise rests on his personal identity, a development that again presages what we will see in Chan. In sum, Xinxing took for himself the position of the absolute master who was large enough to rework tradition as he saw fit and to command respect for his position simply with the claim that he was tradition itself.

SWEETENING THE POT: INTERNAL BUDDHAHOOD FOR THE MASSES

What seems to have held all this together is Xinxing's insistence that all sentient beings were endowed with innate buddhahood. Hence, and I explore a parallel form of this more extensively in chapter 6 on Shenhui, it seems that Xinxing's radical self-aggrandizement and hijacking of tradition was inseparable from a rhetoric that located the essence of tradition in each sentient being. Thus, Xinxing's platform, while aggressively taking away the legitimacy of standard forms of tradition—texts and monasteries—offered his followers the idea that tradition, in its fullest form, was already lodged within their being.[75] With buddhahood already on the inside, what need could there be for reading, especially those long and difficult imported sūtras that were so often contradictory in their claims? Similarly, what need could there be for exegesis and analysis? Instead, Xinxing insisted that what all his followers needed to do was *practice,* and this meant a range of repentances, meditations, and self-denials. This package, too, will return in early Chan writings; in either setting, situating these practices for the masses seems to ride on the structure of an absolute master who takes it upon himself to explain to the masses that they, too, have the totality of tradition within themselves, but they don't have the rights or knowledge to get at the reality and thus need to rely on the master to mediate their relationship with themselves, truth, and tradition.

In creating this structure that claimed that the fullness of tradition was inside every being and yet only available via the master, it seems that Xinxing favored meditation as the practice most suitable

75. Hubbard gives ample evidence of the role of internal buddhahood in Xinxing's thought; see *Absolute Delusion, Perfect Buddhahood,* 99–122.

for enacting the logic of the situation. Thus, it seems clear from several surviving statements that he privileged meditation-for-the-masses, though it is less clear that he took meditation to be *his* chosen technique, even though he was given the title "Meditation Master" *(chanshi)*.[76] Thus, while previous forms of Chinese Buddhism had heralded a range of practices, including sūtra recitation, self-mortification, sūtra exegesis, and divination, Xinxing seems to have singled out meditation as particularly efficacious. As he wrote, "Seated meditation alone should be the foundation [of practice] for all the evil monks of the evil world after the Buddha's extinction."[77] Though throughout his writings he will insist on the value of keeping ethics, and on maintaining silence, meditation looms large as the most appropriate task for sentient beings, handicapped as they are as evil beings in this evil historical moment.

Advocating meditation for his benighted followers had obvious advantages within the constellation of Xinxing's ideology. For instance, since Xinxing was denying the value of reading sūtras, he was essentially revoking the possibility of importing Indian Buddhism because he certainly wasn't advocating trips to India or study with foreign monks. In league with Xinxing's privileging of internal buddhahood, meditation seems especially suitable as a practice because in meditation, content and tradition aren't imagined moving from the outside to the interior of the Chinese Buddhist as they would in reading or in discussions with foreign monks. Instead, meditation appears as a technique for mining what Xinxing insisted was already present: internal buddhahood. Also, with the focus on meditation, Xinxing found a way to speak of tradition's presence without ever having to assign it meaning or particulars. In effect, then, in Xinxing's Buddhism, the content of tradition has disappeared into a system of bouncing between the corners of a triangle defined as (1) the presence of internal buddhahood; (2) the singular absolute master who knows the reality of universal internal buddhahood and its ability to hold all of tradition; and (3) reasons for submitting to that master as the sole spokesperson for tradition, along with practices that reinforce that submission. Understanding how this triangle perfectly owns and redistributes tradition, while also solving

76. As Hubbard points out, in at least one personal statement Xinxing recounts that he had some early trouble with meditation, a comment that might simply be an act of humbleness but nonetheless is notable insofar as Xinxing is not claiming that he got his bodhisattva status through meditation; see *Absolute Delusion, Perfect Buddhahood,* 9.

77. Hubbard, *Absolute Delusion, Perfect Buddhahood,* 20.

the India-China divide and the hermeneutic nightmare that it engendered, is particularly useful since similar patterns will emerge in Chan texts.

MEDITATION YET TO BE MYSTIFIED

Though I believe we should see Xinxing's reconstruction of tradition as a relevant precursor to early Chan, we need to take stock of an important difference. In Xinxing's writing, meditation and the other repentance rituals appear as thoroughly practical realities, spoken of in direct, logical, and uninflected ways. Xinxing's writings on meditation do not veer off into jazzy colloquialisms or unthinkable conundrums, as they do in Chan. In fact, and this is crucial, though meditation is at the core of his instruction for his followers, Xinxing's writing does not suggest that he tried to deliver these instructions in a manner that would prove his authority with extravagant elocution or logic-defying pronouncements. In short, for Xinxing, Chan qua meditation still actually meant seated meditation, and it would only be in the decades to come that the term would slide off in many other directions, creating the basic problem that the Chan texts in the Tang actually had next to nothing to say about practicing meditation.[78]

Xinxing's straightforward discussions of meditation parallel Zhiyi's writings on the topic. Thus, for instance, Zhiyi's *Essentials of Practicing Meditation and Insight (Xiuxi zhiguan zuochan fayao)* presents exceedingly basic and even recipe-like discussions on meditation.[79] The reader is instructed how to organize his body, how to pay attention to his breath, what to do to keep his attention focused, and so on. The point is that for both Zhiyi and Xinxing, discussions of practice were still fundamentally practical and not rhetorical zones where the master *performed*. All this would change when later authors produced the image of Chan masters who, when they did speak of meditation, did so in wholly quixotic and beguiling ways, rarely if ever addressing practical concerns or offering useful advice to beginners. What this suggests is that the movement into what we call the Chan School involved, ironically, the movement away from meditation as a thinkable, discussable

78. This problem has been noted by Carl Bielefeldt in his "Tsung-tse's *Tso-Ch'an I* and the 'Secret' of Zen Meditation."

79. T.46.462–474. This text is also referred to as the *Xiao zhiguan.* For a translation, see Michael Saso, *Zen Is for Everyone.*

topic into a sublime Something that was written about not to instruct the disciple but to further aggrandize the master.

CONCLUSIONS

In considering the Sui figures Zhiyi and Xinxing, we have seen a variety of strategies for convincingly locating the totality of tradition in a single Chinese man—that is, early efforts to create something like a Chinese buddha. Along the way, we had ample reason to question how politics figured in these literary creations. Moreover, in the case of Guanding's various reconstructions of Zhiyi's ancestors, we saw important examples of creating authority by co-opting and refiguring lineages that had already been recognized as delivering legitimacy and tradition. Similarly, we saw in Guanding's writing a studied disregard for historical facts in the narration of perfect tradition's supposed past. Finally, in the case of Xinxing, we saw how fetishizing tradition in Xinxing's person allowed for denying meaning and value in the rest of tradition—whether literary or monastic—even as it also led to privileging meditation and belief in the internal buddha. As I argued at the outset of this chapter, there is much to be gained by seeing these two pre-Tang refigurations of tradition as providing a backdrop for the later Bodhidharma genealogists and for demonstrating a range of techniques and strategies in the Tang effort to create Chinese buddhas who perfectly owned the totality of tradition and overcame the India-China divide.

CHAPTER 3

Owning It

Shaolin Monastery's In-House Buddha

FRAMING AN ARGUMENT

In 690, the monks of Shaolin Monastery on Mount Song *(Songshan)* engraved a funerary biography for a certain master Faru (d. 689).[1] This biography is usually identified as the first Chan genealogy because the account of Faru slips away from chronicling his life and launches into a brief history of Buddhism—ranging from the Indian Buddha down to seventh-century China—in a literary gesture that would become the basic template for later Chan and Zen genealogies.[2] Key in this narrative, as in the later Chan and Zen genealogies, is the role of Bodhidharma, since he is the figure imagined crossing the divide between the two cultures and bringing perfect tradition to China. While it is true that Bodhidharma had been increasingly lionized in several other texts in the first half of the seventh century, the Faru biography marks the first

---

This chapter is based, in part, on a paper, "It's All in the Framing," I gave at the University of California, Berkeley, on March 17, 2002.

1. For a discussion of the stele's physical characteristics and a photograph of Faru's stupa, see Wen Yucheng, *Shaolin fanggu,* 99–100. Though I don't agree with Wen's narrative regarding the early events in Chan, his book provides useful material and makes clear that a detailed history of Shaolin Monastery is needed if we are to understand many key events in Tang Buddhism. A photo of a rubbing of the stele is provided by Yanagida Seizan at the front of his *Shoki Zenshū shiso no kenkyū.*

2. I will be reading Faru's biography as edited by Yanagida in *Shoki Zenshū shiso no kenkyū*

time that a freestanding narrative put Bodhidharma forward as the *unique* bridge connecting India to China and delivering the totality of the Buddha's enlightenment into the present.[3] Though Guanding had experimented with parallel strategies as he provided Zhiyi with different sets of tradition-delivering ancestors, he had not used Bodhidharma as the transcultural pivot, nor had he put his claims in a freestanding genealogical device. Thus, in terms of both form and content, the Faru biography represents a watershed for the literary project of generating "historical" images of the arrival of perfect Buddhism in China. And, I should add, this project is buoyed by the coincidence that Faru's name means something like "dharma-thusness."

Before reading Shaolin's narrative explaining Faru's inheritance of total tradition, we need to acknowledge that most of us come to this topic with a sense that Chan and Zen were always part of the Chinese or Japanese symbolic landscape and thus, in a certain sense, were never invented. Naturally, in assuming this "always already" nature of Chan and Zen, we miss the audacity of claiming ownership of the Buddhist tradition, especially when tradition was known to be somewhere else—in India and far in the past. If we sidestep this comforting nostalgia in which history is purified of its creativity, contingency, and angst, we get a chance not only to recover those stunningly innovative moments when these narratives were first crafted but also to appreciate the motivations that likely were behind these inventions. In shifting to this perspective, the key is to realize that the rhetorical devices that turned into Chan were developed, in part, to solve the basic problem of China's distance from India and the beloved Buddha. Thus, by implication, the Bodhidharma lineage claims were working from a perceived *lack of tradition and authenticity,* since obviously if Chinese Buddhists had been altogether confident in their sense of themselves as legitimate

3. Earlier, less developed stories about Bodhidharma's place in Buddhism had appeared in three places: (1) a random entry in *Record of the Buddhist Monasteries of Luoyang (Luoyang qielan ji)* of 547, where he is portrayed as a foreign monk who marvels at the beauty of a temple (for translation of this passage, see Jeffrey Broughton, *The Bodhidharma Anthology,* 54–55; John R. McRae, *The Northern School and the Formation of Early Ch'an Buddhism,* 16–17); (2) a brief biography from the early seventh century, attributed in the early eighth century to a monk named Tanlin, that was set as a preface to a text called the *Two Entrances and Four Practices* (Broughton, 8–9; McRae, 102–3); and (3) the biographic entries for Bodhidharma and Huike in Daoxuan's *Encyclopedia for Eminent Monks II* (Broughton, 57–63; McRae, 17–18, 21–24). However, none of these sources connected Bodhidharma to a grand arc of legitimacy that flowed from the Buddha into the present; and, obviously, none of these Bodhidharma stories was relied on to provide the basis for a whole narrative/text.

Buddhists, these claims of the new arrival of real Buddhism would be unnecessary and annoyingly redundant.

If we overlook the role that lack, uncertainty, and longing played in structuring these narratives and instead assume that the Chan tradition appeared due to a surplus of religiosity, then we will miss the logic of this writing moment. The obstacle here is that the reigning assumption has been that narratives of spiritual plentitude—the celebration of the arrival of total tradition—must reflect real plentitude. However, I think that in view of the evidence presented in the following chapters, the better assumption is that the Bodhidharma narratives are basically compensatory in nature. Moreover, and this is where matters get more interesting, it seems that Chan authors soon began to realize that this lack of a well-defined essence of Buddhism in China, once rightly held, could be turned into an unusually useful means for reinventing tradition and putting that form of tradition under local ownership.[4]

To put this situation in modern terms, Chinese writers in the Tang likely had the same structural problems that American Buddhists have when they try to present American Zen masters as fully authentic. The problem is that with their European names, their skin color, their hometowns, and their mother tongues, it is clear that these modern masters exist at a distance from what is taken to be the heart and hearth of tradition—East Asia. In short, there is a basic discomfort in claiming that the perfect There is really Here, and yet overcoming that divide is exactly what the category of the American master is designed to do. Though drawing this parallel between modern America and Tang China seems sensible, some Occidental partisans of Chan will have trouble imagining that their own blend of desire and anxiety regarding the distant font of tradition is not structurally different from that of the founders of Chan. In a certain sense, this is as it should be: the life of the Chan tradition relies on the living version of tradition imagining that the past version of tradition had perfectly solved all these problems of authenticity and legitimacy. And, arguably, it is just this imagined gap between the incompletion of tradition in the present and its assumed plentitude in the past that makes the Chan tradition viable and desirable. Or, more exactly, the Chan-Zen tradition rides on the hope of making the imperfect present come a little closer to the

---

4. Faure briefly discusses the role of lack in the generation of the Bodhidharma myths but in a somewhat difference sense; see his *The Rhetoric of Immediacy*, 16.

fantasized fullness of the past, and this fantasy falls apart if the past is imagined to have been fighting its own battle for authenticity.

When we consider how this kind of nostalgia works across cultural divides, we see something else interesting. For instance, we need to remember that though Zen *now* seems so thoroughly Japanese—thanks in part to the writing of D. T. Suzuki, who claimed to find Zen in the depths of the Japanese mind and language—the early Japanese masters such as Eisai (1141–1215) and Dōgen (1200–1253) felt obliged to prove their Chinese credentials to their Japanese audiences.[5] That is, for the founders of Japanese Zen, *the only good Zen was Chinese Chan*. Presumably, this fact is lost on American Zen enthusiasts who fail to see that their situation vis-à-vis Japan replays Zen's anxieties vis-à-vis Chan. Actually, this gap was at the base of Chan, too, since the early Chan writers had to finesse their claims of owning tradition around the basic assumption that real Buddhism was only found in India. In fact, I would suggest that at each historical juncture when supposedly perfect tradition is imported from "Beyond," the importer cannot see that even in the Beyond—in India, China, or Japan—authors and believers had their very own version of this problem-with-authenticity vis-à-vis whatever source they took to be the font of tradition.

Similarly, each importing culture overlooks the way that the desired culture-that-owns-tradition looks so enticing precisely because *it* found a convincing way to overcome just this problem. Consequently, it is worth considering that as Buddhism moved from India to China to Japan to America, there has been, at each stage, a growing sense of doubt and longing that was all the more intense because the preceding culture had suffered a version of the same doubt and had then compensated itself with a variety of theories explaining how perfect tradition had supposedly arrived, in toto, thereby simultaneously sealing off the angst of separation and making the next step of the migration all the more burdened with desire and doubt as the next culture looked on these compensatory inventions with envy and unease.

Given the power of modern nostalgia for Chan and Zen, and the blindness that it breeds, I would like to offer an analogy here that gets at the stunningly inventive nature of Faru's biography: imagine that one of the mega-churches outside of Washington, D.C., put up a

5. For a crucial perspective on this problem in Dōgen's life and writing, see Carl Bielefeldt, "Recarving the Dragon."

stele in their foyer explaining that one of its recently deceased ministers, named "Rev. Gospel," was a direct descendant of Jesus Christ
and that though he had lived quietly and unobstrusively, he had
nonetheless inherited Jesus' divine identity through a chain of inheritors—stretching back to first-century Jerusalem—thereby being no
less than a son of God and a full equal to Jesus. In this stele, it would
also be claimed that this narrative was not fabricated recently, since
Rev. Gospel and his five most recent predecessors had in fact been
recognized by the White House as Jesus-descendants and been given
the Presidential Seal of Approval, though no one in America seemed
to know of this fact. Moreover, the stele would claim that just before
he died, the church held a large revival meeting when Christians of all
stripes from around the nation came to hear Rev. Gospel preach the
gospel, an event that was initiated by all the guests recounting just
this very history of the Rev. Gospel's descent from Jesus, via the five
previous presidentially ratified Jesus-ministers. On closer inspection,
it would turn out these five earlier Jesus-ministers were mentioned in
a 1960s "Who's Who in American Christianity," in which very different information about their lives was presented, with a noticable
absence of any claims to their "Jesus-identity." Nonetheless, in one
of the entries—which clearly had been rewritten since the 1960s
in a reissued version of the encyclopedia—one could see the faint
glimmer of some sort of lineage, though even this mini-lineage didn't
line up with the account given by the mega-church. Despite the oddness of its claims, the stele closed out proudly announcing that Rev.
Gospel was buried behind the church with a portrait of Jesus hung
on his tomb.

This analogy, though not quite a perfect parallel for Shaolin's production of Faru's biography, is, nonetheless, pretty close and ought to
serve as a reference point for thinking about: (1) the audacity of the
Shaolin monks in making the claim to have recently had something like
a living buddha on-site; (2) the importance of the State as the supposed
guarantor of perfect religious identity, at least in the imagined world of
the narrative; and (3) the dubious way that past literature was recycled
and reworked in making lineage claims.

THE ANATOMY OF A REVOLUTION

John McRae, who has written the most about Faru in English, accepts
many of the basic claims of the narrative as found in Faru's stele at

Shaolin Monastery.[6] Thus, without arguing why he has chosen to read the biography as a reliable source, he assumes that the Shaolin stele records the life of a real master who "should be remembered as a significant figure in the history of Chan."[7] Moreover, McRae imagines that Hongren of East Mountain, Faru's putative master, according to the stele, transmitted some specific teachings and practices to Faru, which Faru then took to Shaolin Monastery, where this new form of religious practice won a large and dedicated following, as the stele also claims. McRae puts this reading of the stele within a larger historical narrative that explains that this early form of Chan—based on the teachings of Hongren and his master, Daoxin, and referred to as the East Mountain School—soon migrated to court at Luoyang, where it became a crucial part of what we have come, in the twentieth century, to call the Northern School of Chan.[8] In short, without any debate about how or why this text got written, McRae has assumed that the stele is a reliable indicator of those early historical moments when the Chan movement got under way. Similarly, McRae has chosen to write about Faru and this stele without reference to the complicated history of the seventh-century Shaolin Monastery, and thus the biography of Faru, though clearly an institutional product, has been torn from the reality of its writing moment.

For my part, though I am sure to be accused of looking for religion in all the wrong places, I am pretty sure that this assumption-of-innocence doesn't square with the evidence that we have and that once we gather up the relevant details there will be little enthusiasm for taking the Faru biography to be the effect of a straightforward and wholesome development of a new form of Chinese Buddhism, led by a buddha replica. To move to a more comprehensive reading of the text, and its place in Chinese history, I have decided to start with a series of questions that derive from specific pieces of evidence regarding Shaolin Monastery in the seventh and eighth centuries. Hence I ask the reader,

6. For McRae's comments, see *The Northern School*, 43–44, 85–86. Faure, too, makes similar assumptions; for a compact set of Faure's comments on Faru, see his *La volonté d'orthodoxie dans le bouddhisme chinois*, 34–35; and *Le bouddhisme Ch'an en mal d'histoire*, 58, 72–73, 166.

7. McRae, *The Northern School*, 44.

8. Thus, in *The Northern School*, 43, McRae opens his section on Faru by arguing, "The first of Hongren's disciples to make his mark in the Chinese capitals was Faru (638–89)." For a recent version of McRae's assumptions regarding the movement of Chan from Hongren at East Mountain to the "metropolitan Chan" of Luoyang, see his *Seeing through Zen*, 36 ff, 46 ff. Faure, at least in *The Will to Orthodoxy*, 4–5, presents a parallel history.

If you knew this about Shaolin Monastery, or about the year 690, or about the construction of the Faru narrative, would you still want to approach the text assuming it to be an honest and straightforward account of a historical reality, or would the boat of innocence begin to rock a little? And, then, at what point does the boat tip, plunging one into the murky waters of a writing agenda that is complex and far from the comforting assumption that the text is the simple account of a real master teaching Chan?

For starters, what might shift in our reading if we knew that at roughly the same time that Faru's biography was cut in stone, 690, the Shaolin monks also cut a copy of a letter written in 621 from Prince Li Shimin (later Emperor Taizong, r. 626–49) that explained why the monks had the right to be richly compensated for their role in helping, militarily, to establish the Tang dynasty?[9] In this letter, the prince writes, "Our appreciation on hearing of your deed was inexpressible, so the donation and the reward which we grant should be exceptional."[10] In fact, a large part of this letter speaks of the monks' valor in battle when they vanquished a Sui general, Wang Shichong, who had been occupying one of their landholdings, the Cypress Valley Estate *(baigu zhuang;* also referred to as Cypress Valley Fort, *baigu wu).*[11] The letter also mentions that the monks kidnapped the general's nephew. Besides reflecting on the audacity of putting this letter in public, a letter that might have raised serious questions about Shaolin's notion of Buddhist ethics, that the monks decided to recycle this letter some seventy years after it was written presumably had to do with political issues circa 690. So, an early orienting question ought to be: Was it simply happenstance that these two documents were selected to be cut in stone at about the same time? Certainly, with just this much evidence in view, one might rightly decide that there might not have been any connection.

But, then, what about the year 690? Was there something happening that would have led the monks of Shaolin to believe that it was a particularly urgent moment to claim that one of their recent members

9. This stele presenting the letter of 621 was found in 1980, and it has been deduced that it must have been cut roughly at the same time as the Faru stele. For the evidence and discussion, see Tonami Mamoru, *The Shaolin Monastery Stele on Mount Song,* 13–14; for a parallel assessment, see Meir Shahar, "Epigraphy, Buddhist Historiography, and Fighting Monks," esp. 25 n. 25.

10. Tonami, *The Shaolin Monastery Stele,* 12.

11. It is worth pointing out that Daoist monks supposedly also assisted the Tang armies and even marched with them. For discussion, see Wechsler, *Offerings of Jade and Silk,* 69.

was a quasi-buddha and at the same time remind everyone about their ownership of a large tract of land? In short, does the contemporaneous cutting of these two documents in stone represent a one-two punch made during a time when Shaolin Monastery's institutional integrity might have been seen as at risk? Readers familiar with Chinese history will know already that 690 was a tumultuous year: this was the year that Wu Zetian (the future Empress Wu) consolidated her political power and announced the new dynasty, the Zhou, with herself at the head. Thus, this was far from being a year like any other—it was one in which the foundations of Chinese society were thrown into question.

Then, with some sense that this would have been an especially delicate moment in Chinese politics, would our reading of the Faru biography shift if we knew that Shaolin had been in fairly regular conversation with the future Empress Wu in the years preceding 690?[12] What would shift in our reading of Faru's stele once we knew that in 683, the year Emperor Gaozong died, the Shaolin monks cut a stele explaining how they had in the 670s built a ten-story Maitreya pagoda for Wu Zetian and received her and the emperor, Gaozong, as guests?[13] In fact, this ten-story Maitreya pagoda was built, supposedly, so that Wu Zetian could make merit for her recently deceased mother. Hence, it would seem that Shaolin Monastery had become a site of considerable imperial interest.[14] In fact, that the monks built a Maitreya pagoda for Wu Zetian to mourn her mother is particularly interesting since in the 690s Wu Zetian claimed to *be* Maitreya, investing a lot of energy

12. For discussion of Empress Wu's involvement with Shaolin Monastery during this period, see Ogawa Takashi, "Shoki Zenshū keiseishi no ichi sokumen," esp. 311–16; Ogawa (313) cites Yoshikawa (see source below) for an important segment of his argument. Faure, though apparently trusting the stele's account of Faru's life, wonders if Empress Wu's visits had something to do with the arrival of Faru at Shaolin Monastery; see *Le bouddhisme Ch'an*, 58 n. 123.

13. For evidence of this building project and relevant source material, see Shahar, "Epigraphy, Buddhist Historiography, and Fighting Monks," 32 n. 50. This year, 683, was also the year that Emperor Gaozong and Wu Zetian came to the Mount Song area in anticipation of performing the *feng* and *shan* rites. This visit doesn't necessarily imply a direct connection with Shaolin Monastery, but it is worth keeping in mind. For more details, see Wechsler, *Offerings of Jade and Silk*, 188–89. Wechsler (192) also notes that Empress Wu came to Mount Song in 696 and performed the *feng* and *shan* rites.

14. For more discussion regarding the complications of building this Maitreya pagoda, see Wen, *Shaolin fanggu*, 87–90. In focusing on this work of generating images of legitimacy, it is easy to forget how much straightforward violence Empress Wu had to muster to take the reins of government. For a brief discussion of the civil war of 684 and her extermination of most of the Tang imperial family, see Weinstein, *Buddhism under the T'ang*, 40.

in finding Buddhist ways to prove this identity to the nation.[15] Thus, if we have reliable evidence that Shaolin Monastery was already in close conversation with the throne in the decades that preceded 690, wouldn't we be wise to see the Faru biography as part of a monastic-throne conversation, especially since the stele includes the claim that the throne had recognized Faru and his ancestral truth-fathers in just the way that Shaolin wanted?[16]

Then, would we be more apt to see a conjunction between the Faru biography and the imperial letter of 621 if a similar pairing was seen at a slightly later moment in Shaolin's history? As it turns out, a more distinct version of what I take to be a one-two punch was produced in 728 (actually, initated in 723) when, on a very large stele now called the Shaolin Monastery Stele, the Shaolin monks again cut Li Shimin's letter from 621, along with other legal documents clarifying their owner-ship of the Cypress Valley Estate, and on the same stone cut a history of the monastery designed to prove the monastery's preeminence and its special relationship to the throne.[17] In this history of 728, Faru is mentioned in passing, but he is now presented in the company of other eminent figures who basically bring the story into the "present."[18] That

15. For discussion of Empress Wu's efforts to get various elite Buddhist monks to support her claim to be Maitreya, see Antonino Forte, *Political Propaganda and Ideology in China at the End of the Seventh Century.*

16. It is also worth keeping in view that during Empress Wu's reign, statues repre-senting the twenty-five patriarchs of *Fu fazang jing* were cut in a cave at Longmen. For discussion and more sources, see Adamek, *The Mystique of Transmission,* 104 ff.

17. For discussion of the Shaolin Monastery Stele and its various agendas, as well as a translation of the stele, see Tonami, *The Shaolin Monastery Stele,* 32 ff. Forte (fore-word to Tomami, viii) and Herbert (preface to Tomami, xiii) share Tonami's view.

18. Moreover, the Shaolin Monastery Stele explains that in the Jinglong era (707–10), Shaolin was designated the exclusive site for producing the monks who sat on the board of the Ten Great Virtuous Ones *(Shi dade)*; see Tonami, *The Shaolin Monastery Stele,* 37. Tonami translates the passage as, "In the Jinglong period (707–10) it was decreed that at the Shaolin Monastery at the Central Mountain, ten positions of Great Virtue *(dade,* Chin. trans. of Sk. *bhadanta)* were to be set up. Whenever there was a vacancy in their number, [a monk] from within the monastery was to be picked to fill it." I think, however, that the phrase *Shi dade* in this passage needs to be taken to mean *the* imperially designated board of the Ten Great Virtuous Ones. It is only in this context of the national board now housed at Shaolin that concern over local staffing makes sense. Of course, whether or not this claim is historically accurate is hard to know. Thus, though the argument for the preeminence of the monastery in the Shaolin Monastery Stele is more institutionally developed and orchestrated to move forward in time than Faru's biography, in both there is a claim to uniqueness and a claim to be the functioning site of delivering perfect tradition. For passages in which the stele proclaims Shaolin's uniqueness, see Tonami: "Of all the numinous peaks within the seas, none matches Mount Song [Shaolin's locale] and of all the mountain sites where religion is practiced, this is the greatest monastery" (38).

a later moment of institutional writing so obviously linked land claims
with a narrative of imperially recognized institutional identity does not
require that 690 needs to be read in the same light, but it begins to
put in question how and why the Shaolin monks published important
"histories" of their monastery.

Like 690, the 720s were a time when, after the Tang had been rees-
tablished under Xuanzong (r. 712–49), the question of Buddhist landholdings was again an urgent one. As it turns out, in 724 the Shaolin
monks had the powerful minister Pei Cui (ca. 670–736) write this new
history of the monastery—the one to be cut in 728—with the explicit
hope that their uniqueness and preeminence would allow them to duck
a recently passed imperial edict of 722 that aimed at repossessing
monastic landholdings throughout the empire.[19] In short, some thirty-
five years after the Faru stele was cut, we see a more developed case of
claiming preeminence and imperial connections during a particularly
unstable historical moment. Similarly, we see that Shaolin monks were
fully capable of getting court officials as powerful as Pei Cui to act
on their behalf; they even got the emperor to write the calligraphy at
the top of this history and thereby joined it with two characters in
Taizong's hand, already present in the letter of 621. Knowing these
details regarding Shaolin's seventh- and eighth-century actions and
literary inventions, most readers would probably be ready to shift their
expectations to ask, Given how involved Shaolin Monastery was with
court at this time and given its history of claiming unique status as the

19. For evidence that this project was initially begun late in 723, see Tonami, *The
Shaolin Monastery Stele*, 18–19, 27. For the key lines in the stele explaining why the
history was written when it was, see 47–48, where Pei Cui's narrative clearly explains
that the goal is to guard Shaolin's landholdings against a recent imperial edict (722) that
was intent on reappropriating Buddhist and Daoist lands and giving them to "poor land-
less adult males." Pei Cui writes midway through the Shaolin stele:

> Recently, an enlightened decree ordered: "The landed estates of the Buddhist
> monasteries and Daoist temples of the empire are all to be confiscated." The
> present emperor, in consideration of the facts that the lands and mill of this
> monastery [Shaolin], the generous donation of his saintly predecessor [Taizong],
> for many a long year in the monastery's possession, cloaked in the bosom of
> the mountain and trailing a train of numinous traces, the dwelling of a host
> of immortals, surpassing the golden peaks of Rājagṛha, the abode of those of
> highest virtue, throwing into the shade King Aśoka's stupas, as a special favor,
> returned [the lands and mill] to the monastic community and did not include
> them in the official appropriation, for they had been alienated, in a pious gesture,
> from the domain of the state and graciously conferred upon the clergy. *Decidedly
> it was the case of "[this monastery's] fame exceeding all others in the lands, it is
> to be treated with special courtesy, setting it apart from all ordinary monasteries."*
> (36–37)

best monastery in China by writing self-promoting histories, how could we not read the Faru biography as part of this dense and convoluted conversation with court?

There are, in fact, other kinds of evidence that are equally troubling to an expectation of innocence in this narrative. For instance, what shifts in our reading expectations when we learn that basically next door to Shaolin Monastery, on Mount Gaosong (part of the larger Mount Song area), a Daoist monastery also produced a lineage for a resident master named Pan Shizheng (585–682) and his supposed disciple, Sima Chengzhen (647–735), and cut it in stone in 699?[20] Like Shaolin, this Daoist monastery had won the attention of both Emperor Gaozong and Wu Zetian (Empress Wu) and had been honored with several imperial visits between 676 and 683.[21] After Empress Wu assumed the throne, she apparently continued to patronize this monastery throughout the 690s. Figuring out the details of how these Daoist monks sought to create a genealogy of masters for themselves is beyond the scope of this book, but we ought to at least see that this Daoist monastery represents something of a double for Shaolin Monastery, a double in which we can see parallel political realities working out in parallel literary inventions.[22] In particular, it would seem that in either case, the genealogies were written, at least in part, in order to anchor previous and ongoing imperial recognition in a reproductive line of religious masters such that the monasteries could appear as larger-than-life entities able to legitimately conduct business with the throne, generation after genera-

20. For mention of Pan Shizheng's relations with Emperor Gaozong, see Weinstein, *Buddhism under the T'ang*, 36; and for sources of his biography, 161 n. 43.

21. For brief discussion of Mount Gaosong, its masters, its lineage claims, and its political activity, see Livia Kohn and Russell Kirkland, "Daoism in the T'ang (618–907)," esp. 342; for discussion of the seventh-century Daoist Master from Mount Gaosong, Pan Shizheng, who had extensive contact with Emperor Gaozong, see Russell Kirkland, "Ssu-ma-Ch'eng-chen and the Role of Taoism in Medieval Chinese Polity"; see also Timothy H. Barrett, "The Emergence of the Taoist Papacy in the T'ang Dynasty." Though not necessarily related to the monastery at Mount Gaosong, the case of the fifth-century Kou Qianzhi (K'ou Ch'ien-chih) is particularly relevant because it seems he lived on Mount Song, had close connections with the emperor, Taiwu, and received from him the title "Heavenly Master" *(tianshi)*, in part due to having received the fullness of the Daoist tradition in a mystical encounter with Laozi. For more discussion of this early example of the dialectic between a singular religious leader and the throne, see Richard B. Mather, "K'ou Ch'ien-chih and the Taoist Theocracy at the Northern Wei Court, 425–451"; see also Russell Kirkland, *Taoism*, 89, 92, 163.

22. For discussion of how Faru's lineage parallels the lineage of the Daoist monastery on Mount Gaosong, along with evidence of Shaolin Monastery's close connections with court and Empress Wu, see Yoshikawa Tadao, "Dōkyō no dōkei to zen no hōkei," esp. 20–21, for discussion of the stele of 699, which presents a genealogy for Daoist Master Pan Shizheng (585–682).

tion. In short, with a parallel Daoist genealogy taking form next door to Shaolin, the Faru biography seems best read as an older brother to this Daoist effort, born of the same matrix, and most likely taking shape through a kind of sibling rivalry.[23]

Even knowing this historical background, one might still hold out hope that the Faru biography should be read as a legitimate reflection of real religious events. And yet this hope will dim further once a close reading of the biography leaves little doubt that it is highly inventive, plays fast and loose with historical facts, and, most important, tries to cloak just this kind of literary invention. That is, the narrative reveals both crafty reworkings of prior material and an attempt to make those reworkings look innocent, which, as in the case of all alibis, simply means that the authors of the alibis were rather aware that they were producing an illicit account whose genesis and agendas needed to be shrouded.

Pushing the Faru narrative even further from a zone of reliability is the fact that it likely depended on a tangled account of master Fachong (587–665?) and his supposed relationship with Huike, as found in two places in Daoxuan's *Encyclopedia*. Here the problem is that the details of Fachong's life seem to have been created by giving him an entry in the appendix of the *Encyclopedia* that connected him to Huike and Huike's supposed master, Bodhidharma, and then rewriting the entry for Huike in order to make Fachong's post facto lineage claim look more legitimate.[24] Thus, put in question form, what happens to our confidence in the Faru biography when it seems that it picked up the recently invented Fachong lineage and reworked it in a manner that parallels the deformation that Fachong's genealogy had, clandestinely, wrought on its own sources a few decades earlier? In short, it would seem that Faru's biography borrowed from Fachong's

---

23. Of course, these years were ones in which Buddhist and Daoist competed with one another for imperially recognized preeminence. In 674, they were officially declared equal in importance, but in 691, Empress Wu made Buddhism the State religion; for an overview of the shifting fortunes of Buddhism and Daoism at court during this period, see Weinstein, *Buddhism under the T'ang*, 27–47.

24. For a partial translation of Fachong's biography in Daoxuan, see Faure, *The Will to Orthodoxy*, 146–47, 226 n. 2; Fachong's biography is found in an appendix to Daoxuan's *Encyclopedia*, T.50.666a; McRae discusses Fachong in *The Northern School*, 24–27, and provides a partial translation of his biography; Adamek deals briefly with Fachong in *The Mystique of Transmission*, 159–61. Hu Shi is the scholar who first pointed out that there was a connection between the biography of Fachong, added on after the first version of the *Encyclopedia* was made public in 645, and a strange, incongruent second layer in Huike's biography; see his "Leng-ch'ieh tsung k'ao," esp. 211 ff.

"life story" not only the elements for ancestrizing truth but also the audacity to do so.

Then, what will shift in our reading expectations when we see that the texts that borrowed from the Faru biography in the decades to follow, the ones that have been wrongly identified as Northern Chan, do so in a manner that is as dubious and cavalier as the way in which the Faru biography treated its textual precedents? When we see writers such as Du Fei and Jingjue pick up the Faru narrative and deform it to present other figures as the recipients of Bodhidharma's total truth, shouldn't we be ready to concede that these narratives represent a fairly coherent group of texts defined by a new mode of writing about Buddhist legitimacy that emerged through a complex process of recycling prior lineage claims? And, similarly, why would we cling to the model of innocence when a close reading of all these early Chan texts shows that they are far from being about practice, meditative experience, or religious community and instead are thinly veiled attempts to organize the ownership of the totality of tradition, and do so in terms that are borrowed from other authors involved in the same project?

I suggest that when we carefully put these various kinds of evidence in view, there isn't going to be much debate about leaving the old paradigm of innocence. There just isn't much sense in knowing all this and then continuing to believe that Chinese masters, with their new forms of practice and wisdom, invented Chan. Clearly something much more complicated happened—something that will take a good bit of theorizing to clarify because it will have to account for a variety of discourse pressures that range from the economic, the political, and the legal to the literary, and so on, but most importantly will have to remain cognizant of the Chinese tradition of inventively writing history for political reasons.

On this note, it is also worth mentioning that this suspicious framing of the early Buddhist lineages again seems sensible if we keep in mind that the seventh century was a time when elites and court figures appear to have had a particular interest in creating lineages and then rewriting them as needed. For instance, in 632, as the Tang dynasty sought to shore up its legitimacy and push back the power of the established big families, a board of genealogies was created to rewrite Chinese history to show that the Tang family, surnamed Li, was in fact the genealogical frontrunner among the various big families.[25] Similarly, once Wu

25. For Taizong's interest in writing and rewriting genealogies, see Howard J. Wechsler, "T'ai-tsung (reign 626–49) the Consolidator," esp. 212–13.

Zetian began to take the reins of government, she, too, had the genealogies rewritten (twice!) to favor her family.[26] And, of course, all this
genealogical ingenuity seems quite of a piece with what Guanding was
capable of in the early seventh century. In sum, assuming that genealogical "histories" are reliable documents seems most unwise when a
fuller picture of seventh-century Chinese "historiography" emerges.

The challenge, then, is twofold. First, we need to construct a narrative to explain the emergence of these Bodhidharma genealogies that
stays close to the facts as we have them. Second, we need to reflect on
what such a revised history of "early Chan" might tell us about how
truth and the image of perfect tradition were invented and made available in Tang China.

INNOCENCE IN THE MAKING:
AN OVERVIEW OF THE FARU BIOGRAPHY

Faru's biography of 690 opens with some brief details about his name,
birthplace, and initial study with master Ming. Then we learn that
master Ming, in the first major action in the narrative, sent Faru off
to study with master Hongren, telling him simply that Hongren had
a meditation of sorts, a "samādhi." Once in front of Hongren, Faru
bowed, and then Hongren suddenly caused Faru to enter into total
truth. After a florid description of Faru's new understanding of the
"secret meaning of the Buddha" *(fo miyi),* the narrative breaks off to
explain how Hongren had the totality of tradition in his possession
and thus was able, "due to past karmic connections," to give it to Faru.
To make this claim about Hongren's ownership of tradition appear
plausible, the narrative leaves China to briefly sketch a lineage of truth
holders in India—Ānanda, Madhyāntika, and Śāṇavāsa—that supposedly descended directly from the Buddha.

Then, without any explanation, the narrative jumps from these
three contemporaries of the Buddha to explain that Bodhidharma also
owned the totality of tradition and brought it to China and gave it to
Huike, who gave it to Sengcan, who gave it to Daoxin, who finally gave
it to Hongren. This genealogical information is provided in a mini-

---

26. For Empress Wu's interest in genealogical revisions, see Denis Twitchett and
Howard J. Wechsler, "Kao-tsung (reign 649–83) and the Empress Wu," 260–61. For a
more involved discussion of Tang-era historiography, see Denis Twichett, *The Writing of
Official History under the Tang.*

malist fashion, without dates or places or any other supporting details save for two explicit textual citations. The first is a quotation from a fifth-century text, the preface to *Dharmatrāta's Meditation Sūtra*, by Huiyuan (334–416), that explains the Buddha's transmission of an esoteric form of Buddhism to Ānanda and its secretive maintenance, generation after generation thereafter.[27] The second citation is more vague; the narrative simply says, "A history *[zhuan]* says," and then provides a skeleton outline of Bodhidharma's lineage in China: Bodhidharma "entered into the Wei [dynasty], and transmitted to [Hui] Ke, Ke to [Seng] Can, Can transmitted to [Dao] Xin, Xin transmitted to [Hong] Ren, Ren transmitted to [Fa] Ru."

After this vague track of past transmission is explained, the narrative returns to Faru's life to explain that after being zapped into total truth, Faru served Hongren on East Mountain in Huangmei for sixteen years, leaving only after Hongren died. Then, after some years of traveling, Faru ultimately ended up at Shaolin Monastery, where he lived incognito for three years before being recognized as a master. Finally, in the only visible activity ascribed to Faru in the narrative, he hosts an amazingly successful teaching session that supposedly brought together numerous monks of the nation whom he led into the realm of truth in a magical moment. This moment is described with a flurry of quotes from Buddhist sūtras and Confucian classics and seems designed to prove to the reader that Faru was a buddha-like figure who could manifest perfect tradition and whose absolute mastery was recognized by a nationwide body of clergy.

In line with the narrative's overall concern to demonstrate "public proof" of Faru's private inheritance, the first thing that this audience of national monks does is recount, as a unified chorus, the reality of Faru's place in the lineage. The stele informs us that, once gathered at Shaolin Monastery:

> Everyone said, "Beginning from the Wei [dynasty] up until the Tang [dynasty] there have been five generations of imperial representatives *(di dai)*, who covered nearly two hundred years—[during these years] someone has always come forth to define the virtue of the age. All of them bestowed upon us, the descendants, the legacy of the peerless great jewel *(wushang dabao)*."

---

27. For discussion of Huiyuan's preface, see McRae, *The Northern School,* 80–82. For a careful review of the preface as used in several different texts, see Morrison, "Ancestors, Authority, and History," chaps. 1, 2.

With these lines inserted into the mouths of this adoring audience, the author leaves little doubt that he wants the reader to see Faru just as these monks supposedly saw him: he was this generation's wondrous representative of the Buddhist tradition, imperially sanctioned, standing in line with the five similarly sanctioned masters of the past—presumably Bodhidharma, Huike, Sengcan, Daoxin, and Hongreng—and thus most able to tender tradition and truth to those who were in attendance. Even without, for the moment, taking into account the numerous literary allusions made in this passage, I suggest that the best way to begin thinking about the whole Faru narrative is to appreciate how the author has made this chorus of monks identify Faru in just the same manner that the prior parts of the narrative sought to do: Faru is the perfect scion of tradition, and this is because he is the most recent representative in the imperially ratified lineage of five Chinese masters that stretches back some two hundred years.

Of course, one might think that the text is simply representing what these monks actually said on this particular day, but this is an unwise assumption. In addition to their convenient choruslike articulation and their perfectly chosen literary allusions, the main problem with their group statement is that there is no evidence that this schema of "five generations of imperial representatives" was anywhere known before the Faru stele was cut. In fact, when any of these five figures, from Bodhidharma to Hongren, were discussed in previous documents, there was no mention that they were "imperial representatives." Presumably, if these figures had been imperially recognized in any way, earlier writers would have been more than eager to note this in their biographies.

Likewise, there is also the problem of how these monks from around the empire found out about Faru's identity and the history of his five predecessors. Given that the narrative has emphasized Faru's underground identity—he even supposedly lived clandestinely at Shaolin Monastery—it is far from clear how it would have become nationally known. More pointedly, we could ask, When, and how, exactly was Hongren or Faru recognized as such a singular master by the throne? Certainly, the narrative has left those events totally unexplained. Similarly, we shouldn't overlook that the author has waited until just this moment in the narrative to give Faru this imperially recognized identity: nothing in the account of Hongren or the transmission moment from Hongren to Faru hinted at the political side of Faru's master-identity, though clearly it is of paramount concern in the narrative. In fact, by postponing labeling Faru in this manner, it is as though the narrative has been preparing *the reader* for this announcement and not simply recording a fact.

In brief, it seems that behind the narrative there was a concerted authorial effort to make this lineage claim of five imperially recognized masters look preexistent, and *not* the effect of the narrative itself. Thus, the text creates the sense that its history of tradition was not an invention at all and instead was the effect of a prior historical reality that all the monks in the nation knew and accepted *apart* from this narrative and were eager to endorse once they were brought onstage. Thus, the Faru biography, like many of the Mahāyāna sūtras that it quotes, creates supposedly reliable spokespersons who appear external to the narrative—these monks from around the nation—and who repeat the narrative's most basic agenda and endorse it, without appearing to be literary creations designed to perform just this function. In light of this gesture in which the narrative doubles itself *in the effort to prove that it has nothing to prove,* we ought to read this text expecting to find several layers of cleverness at play as it seeks to lay claim to ultimate authority in a convincing and innocent-looking manner.

In fact, if we look closer at this moment in the biography, two other things are rather striking. First, the passage is combining Buddhist and imperial modes of endorsing the singular master of the nation. Thus, Faru's new identity as the absolute master of China is the result of both Hongren's gift and the throne's supposed support of this line of "imperial representatives." And yet the narrative only explains Hongren's gift of enlightenment, with no mention of how the State functioned in this crucial moment of transferring Buddhist legitimacy. Pushing on this issue, it would seem that the narrative has created two new institutions: (1) the singular, popelike master who is to be understood as a buddha replica; and 2) a new function of the State that understands its role in granting this buddha-identity, generation after generation. Of course, neither of these institutions seems to have existed before this "history" of Faru was written.

The Faru biography closes out by claiming that soon after the magical teaching event, Faru died in a series of incidents narrated to mimic elements of the Buddha's last moments. Faru was then supposedly buried, and the stele bearing his biography was cut in stone soon thereafter. Like the death sequence, everything about this postmortem care seems designed to heighten his prestige and to liken him to the Buddha—the monks supposedly went so far as to hang a portrait of the Buddha on

Faru's stupa.[28] Thus, Faru's life story, brief as it is, appears as part of a larger set of institutional actions dedicated to creating a perfect representative of the Buddhist tradition in seventh-century China, and then presenting that image of perfect Buddhism to the public in funerary architecture and in this narrative cut in stone.

In the decades that followed, Faru's biography was appropriated and rewritten several times by figures either at court or with important court connections. Thus, though the narrative is dedicated to bringing the totality of tradition from India and sinking it into Shaolin Monastery, it quickly slipped out of this holding pattern and was used for a variety of other purposes. In seeing the profusion of copycat texts that appear after the Faru biography, we probably ought to conclude that this newly constructed narrative was viewed as an attractive and convincing way to claim legitimacy. Of course, this evaluation of the narrative might have only really occurred after the first copycat text was successfully put in circulation, that is, that moment when the potential of the Faru biography was seized on and repositioned in a way that demonstrated what could be done with it. Moreover, given the nonchalance with which the historical details of the Faru narrative were rewritten, we ought to suspect that from the beginning of this cycle of copycat works, no one was concerned with preserving some kernel of historically legitimate material.

Ironically, then, in rewriting the past, as the eighth-century genealogists so clearly did, there was little concern with the past as it might have been known from more reliable sources. Instead, the past was but a donkey to dress up with bells and scarves and put before the cart-of-the-present to pull in the direction of a desired future. Thus, I think it best to assume that the Faru biography was seen for what it was: a power grab based on a clever, but not too well hidden, reconstruction of Buddhist (and State) history. Hence, though it may surprise my colleagues to hear this, I think the Faru narrative was read in the eighth century in the register that I am reading it in—a commanding claim to own tradition, produced in the guise of an innocent biography. Moreover, if this text was the touchstone for the early genealogies, then we have to admit that the founding impetus

---

28. For discussion of portraits in Tang Chan, see Wendi Adamek, "Imagining the Portrait of a Chan Master"; for a more wide-ranging account of portraits in Chan, see T. Griffith Foulk and Robert H. Sharf, "The Ritual Use of Portraiture in Medieval China."

of Chan is not in a master or a meditation or a truth but rather in an envious and cavalier attitude toward Shaolin's claim to own the fullness of tradition, an attitude that produced more of itself and opened the door not only to a long series of mutually contradictory genealogical claims but also to a Wild West approach to the writing of the history of how perfect Buddhism came to medieval China. When we see the extravagant inventions of later writers, we will have more reason to suspect that the extravagance of the Faru biography was clearly recognized for what it was and that, in effect, it became a legitimizing template for writing illegitimate history to prove one's legitimacy.

To give additional substance to the above arguments, the rest of this chapter provides a more detailed history of Shaolin and then a close reading of the Faru biography.

SHAOLIN MONASTERY: THE BASICS

Supposedly built by Emperor Xiaowen (r. 471–99) for the Indian monk Buddhabhadra at the end of the fifth century, Shaolin Monastery was the site of translation work and the home monastery for several other eminent monks throughout the sixth century, though the details on this period are sketchy.[29] The monastery also enjoyed good relations with the State under the Sui rulers, with Sui Wendi bestowing on Shaolin the fort-town, Cypress Valley Estate, which lay between the Shaolin temple on Mount Song and the city of Luoyang.[30] Owning this estate and its fortified town, and thereby effectively controlling the southeastern entrance to the capital, was a happenstance of history that seems to have influenced much of what happened to Shaolin in the seventh century.

The story of Shaolin took a dramatic turn in 621, when, despite having enjoyed Sui patronage, the Shaolin monks sided with the advancing Tang armies and apparently helped sack a Sui general and

---

29. The following summary of Shaolin's travails in the seventh century relies heavily on Shahar's excellent article, "Epigraphy, Buddhist Historiography, and Fighting Monks."

For some details on Buddhabhadra and the founding of Shaolin Monastery, see Paul Pelliot, "Notes sur quelques artistes des Six Dynasties et des T'ang," esp. 245–64, where he translates Buddhabhadra's biography from Daoxuan's *Encyclopedia*, T.50.551a, and then argues, convincingly, that Buddhabhadra (Fotuo) was also referred to as Batuo, which helps solve some of the confusion around the figures associated with the origins of the monastery.

30. Shahar, "Epigraphy, Buddhist Historiography, and Fighting Monks," 21.

his forces who had occupied the Cypress Valley Estate in the previous year of fighting. In what appears to have been fairly serious combat, the Shaolin monks overcame the general and his forces. Presumably, this course of action was motivated by the desire to recover their land from the Sui general and by their hope of ingratiating themselves with the Tang forces who appeared poised to win the war. Thus, the Shaolin monks started the seventh century turning to violence in an effort to maintain their hold on the estate and to stake their future with the incoming dynasty. Their choices paid off, and as a reward for their military exploits, the incoming crown prince of the Tang dynasty, Li Shimin (crowned Taizong in 626, after he murdered his older brother), wrote them a formal letter in 621 acknowledging their exploits and thanking them.[31] Included in this letter is a vague line that they should receive, as a consequence of their contribution to the Tang dynasty, a "fixed income." However, it would be a good number of years before the Shaolin monks formalized the recovery of their estate.

And here we ought to pause to take stock of this unexpected situation. The Shaolin monks proved themselves ready and willing to fight, and presumably kill, in order to hold their property. They decided in favor of these actions based on their estimation of who would likely win the civil war and lead the country, siding with the Tang forces once they had judged that the Sui was moribund. Of course, this is a bit shocking if one holds to the idea that Buddhist monks simply practice meditation, read sūtras, and sweep the courtyard. However, it is even more shocking to remember that the Shaolin monks had Li Shimin's letter cut in stone circa 690 and 728 and set on their grounds, thereby not only formally "publishing" their martial exploits but also endorsing Li Shimin's account of these events in which the destiny of Buddhism and the monastery were judged inseparable from dynastic fortunes. To get a sense of the dialogue between the State and the monastery, consider a section of Meir Shahar's translation of Li Shimin's letter from 621, as found on the stele of 728:[32]

> To: The Cypress Valley Fort Shaolin Monastery's dean and abbot, and their disciples, as well as to the military and civil leaders, officers, common people and the rest.

---

31. For more details on Li Shimin's violent ascendency, see Howard J. Wechsler, "The Founding of the T'ang Dynasty," esp. 186–87.
32. Shahar, "Epigraphy, Buddhist Historiography, and Fighting Monks," 22–24, with minor changes.

Recently, there has been chaos under heaven. Nowhere in the land is there a lord, and the world is falling apart. The Way of the Three Vehicles (that is, Buddhism) is declining. This has caused the Jambudvipa Continent to disintegrate. Warhorses sweep through the land. The Central Kingdom [China] is boiling, and the devils are all contending.

This court (that is, the Tang dynasty) has received the heavenly omens of government. It upholds the correct Buddhist truth *(di)*. Riding the phoenix and turning the wheel, it glorifies the Great Treasure [of the Buddhist faith]. Therefore, virtue will reach the common folk, and education will instruct the monastic community. Thus, the people will enjoy the grace of release from suffering, and all will be favored with the benefits of the other shore [i.e., nirvana].

Wang Shichong [the Sui general] usurped another's position. He dared oppose the heavenly principles. He coveted the Dharma-Realm (the Cypress Valley Estate). He acted recklessly, disregarding the laws of karma.

Now, the winds of virtue are blowing far, and the beacon of wisdom is glowing near. The Buddhist eightfold path is being opened, and throughout the land the Buddhist sanctuaries are being restored. Shaolin's Master of the Law *(fa shi),* together with the other monks, deeply comprehended the changing circumstances and adapted to them. The monks immediately realized which action would yield the Buddhist fruit, and they succeeded in drawing [up] an excellent plan. Together, they returned to the blessed land. They captured that evil bastard (Wang's nephew, Renze), and they cleansed the Pure Land *(jing tu).* The results of their respectful observance and expressed loyalty have become known at court. Their way of attainment and self-cultivation adds further glory to their Buddhist temple.

We heard [of Shaolin's contribution] with pleasure and appreciation. It surpasses imagination and words. The monastery should be supported, and its monks generously rewarded. Regardless of changing circumstances, the monastery should be provided with fixed income.

Among the fascinating elements in this letter, we ought to appreciate the irony of Li Shimin recounting Shaolin monks' catastrophic breach of Buddhist ethics as a particularly good Buddhist deed. Thus not only does this episode show the brass-knuckled Buddhist approach to maintaining monastic land but it also begins to mark out a register for understanding what kind of language was used in both stating facts and dressing those facts up in legitimate-looking phraseology, phraseology that Buddhist authors would also use in extending their side of the dialogue with the State.

This letter from Li Shimin recognizing Shaolin monks' contribution, however, wasn't the end of their troubles. The monastery was shut down in 622 for two years, apparently because its lands were thought

to be illegally held.[33] Then in 625, presumably after more negotiation, Li Shimin formally redonated the Cypress Valley Estate to the
monastery.[34] This fracas with the State, however, was only one wing
of the Shaolin monks' problems, since, despite holding this letter of
625 reconfirming their rights to the estate, they were soon sued by
local authorities—county officials from Dengfeng—who apparently
doubted the authenticity of the imperial letter of 625 and the account of
their martial exploits.[35] Thus, the county officials launched a full investigation, taking depositions from the monks involved in the assault on
the Sui general and weighing their testimonies in a manner not unlike
modern criminal investigations. This side of their legal troubles took
years to resolve; it wasn't until 632 that the monastery seems to have
cleared its ownership of this estate in the eyes of national and local
authorities.[36]

Two things are noteworthy in these legal battles. First, it is clear that
conceptions of historical accuracy were rather developed at the time.
The Dengfeng county officials, whatever their motivations for pressing
the case against Shaolin Monastery, sought to build a dossier of statements and facts to assess the reality of the overall narrative that Shaolin
had generated. Thus, when we think about seventh-century genealogists' manipulation of historical sources, we should not imagine that
medieval writers and thinkers were not sensitive to very clear notions of
historicity, or that they did not have rather sophisticated techniques for
checking stories and triangulating evidence. Second, that the Dengfeng
officials doubted the monks so thoroughly in the first place is interesting. Was it simply that these officials were vigorously attempting to
take the monastery's land, or was it that these officials were quite used
to the lengths that the Shaolin monks would go to in order to guard and
increase their holdings? Of course, suspecting the monks of fraud and
fabrication in order to regain their land would have been a small charge
given their evident willingness to engage in combat and kidnapping.

Understanding the struggle over this estate has to be put in the context of a nationwide struggle between the throne and the monasteries.
For instance, on the day after Li Shimin first took Luoyang in 621, he
passed an edict shutting down all the Buddhist monasteries in the city

33. Ibid., 25–26.
34. Ibid., 26.
35. Ibid., 27–29.
36. For the text and translation of these legal documents, see Tonami, *The Shaolin
Monastery Stele,* 20–28.

and allowed only sixty clergy in the city.[37] Shahar argues that these draconian measures taken in the capital also rippled out and worried monastics in rural settings. Similarly, the first Tang emperor, Gaozu, decreed in 625 that there should be only one Buddhist and Daoist temple in each prefecture, thereby effectively undermining the legitimacy of all the other monasteries and putting their property in legal limbo.[38] Luckily for both the Buddhists and the Daoists, this order was quickly reversed with the enthronement of the next emperor, Taizong (Li Shimin), in the following year, though this reversal has to be seen in the context of his earlier actions to clear the Buddhist clergy out of Luoyang. Clearly, then, this sequence of events shows how tenuous Buddhist landownership was in this period.

In more general terms, it seems clear that Shaolin monks, if they did not know this already, would have had good cause throughout the seventh and eighth centuries to know how very fickle imperial rulings on Buddhist landholdings could be and would have come to see that their fate as an institution depended on maintaining good relations with the court by steadily reminding the emperors of their past exploits. More exactly, they would have had good reason to see that it wasn't enough simply to be another good monastery but that in gaining some preeminence they could avoid imperial edicts directed at recovering the property of more ordinary monasteries. In pointing out this dialectic, Shahar describes Shaolin's motivation for cutting the stele of 728: "As Tonami Mamoru has suggested, it was probably this confiscation order [of 722]—which they so narrowly escaped—that convinced Shaolin monks of the necessity to engrave in stone their military exploits. The Shaolin Monastery Stele was erected to ensure that future rulers would be as mindful as Xuanzong had been of the monastery's contribution to the dynastic founding."[39]

In fact, besides affixing the emperor Xuanzong's handwriting at the top of Li Shimin's letter of 621, the Shaolin Monastery Stele includes a letter of 724 from the secretariat Zhangyue confirming that this was the current emperor's handwriting and that the 621 letter was legitimate, making it clear to all that the current emperor (Xuanzong) was endorsing what his distant predecessor Li Shimin had decreed. In effect, in the stele of 728, we have something like a smoking gun. The

37. Shahar, "Epigraphy, Buddhist Historiography, and Fighting Monks," 26.
38. See Wechsler, "The Founding of the T'ang Dynasty," 180.
39. Shahar, "Epigraphy, Buddhist Historiography, and Fighting Monks," 30.

single stone that holds these various documents from the seventh and eighth centuries basically says to the public and the throne: Look, here are the documents proving our legal ownership of this estate, here is our religious pedigree, here is a history of our close involvement with the throne, and here is the current emperor's handwriting at the top of a previous emperor's letter (his signature is included, too)—and all are vouched for by the secretariat, so don't doubt our claim to this land or our right to be the leading monastery of the nation.

Next to these distinctly political and economic concerns, there is another sphere of events that is equally important to keep in view in understanding the production of the Faru narrative. With the publication of Daoxuan's *Encyclopedia of Eminent Monks II,* in 645 and in a revised form in the 660s, there were several new, high-profile lineage claims in public. In particular, as mentioned above, there is clear evidence that after 645 someone rewrote the entry for Huike to make him appear to be the first Chinese master to receive an elite form of Buddhism from Bodhidharma. Key to interpreting this rewriting of Huike's biography is the way he has been turned into an especially "potent" master who transmits to other Chinese monks and who ultimately provides a lineage basis for master Fachong, who flourished in the mid-seventh century.

I explore this rewriting of Huike's biography below—relying on the scholarship of Jeffrey Broughton, Bernard Faure, Hu Shi, and John McRae—but for the moment, let me suggest that Daoxuan's *Encyclopedia* not only provided the Shaolin monks with raw material that was reworked into the Faru biography but also, in the case of Huike's biography, presented a highly visible example of manufacturing a narrative to canalize an elite form of Buddhism and bring it into the current moment. Thus, though owning the Cypress Valley Estate set the stage for Shaolin's seventh century and led indirectly to the writing of the Faru stele, the actual content of the narrative—and presumably the audacity to embark on such a writing project in the first place—derives from the growing body of published ancestral claims for a variety of Buddhist monks and, it would seem, Daoist monks as well.

FARU'S BIOGRAPHY: A CLOSE READING

In accord with the term for "biography" *(xingzhuang)* in the title of the stele, there are several things early in this account of Faru that are no different from a standard biography of a monk. Thus, the stele starts off recounting Faru's name, place of origin and so forth, and then turns to explain his induction into Buddhism and his contact with the perfect form of tradition that the stele is attempting to insert in his person.[40]

> The great master's dharma name was Faru; he was originally surnamed Wang, and was from Shangdang [modern Shanxi]. When he was young, he followed his maternal uncle to a post in Liyang where he served a teacher named Blue Robed Ming. He then became a monk at age nineteen, and earnestly sought the Mahāyāna *(dafa)*. [His master] Ming had concealed *(neiyin)* within him meditative wisdom *(chanzhi)*. When people saw [that this was the case] he declined [teaching it] and said [to Faru], "In Xingzhou [modern Hubei] there is the samādhi practiced by the Chan Master [Hong] Ren—you would do better to go to him and request [the teachings]." Faru respectfully accepted this advice, and then went to join that community.

In this sparse opening, Faru is given a name and place of origin, brought to Buddhism, and then, through the humbleness of a certain master Ming, sent off to learn a samādhi from Hongren. Thus, Faru's engagement with Hongren is made to appear as an unexpected turn of events—Faru was simply seeking the Mahāyāna, and his master sent him off to Xingzhou to find Hongren. This casual chain of events that leads Faru to Hongren appears more interesting when the narrative claims that Faru's reception of the Way from Hongren was based on prior karmic connections, making it seem that behind the superficial happenstance of this sequence of events there is a deep plot of sorts that various actors are acting out, albeit in innocence. In many of the later genealogies, we will see just this kind of innocent but predestined encounter, a combination that does the most to make the lineage grab look honest because it is simply reflecting a deeper plot line and legitimate because it is without desire.

It is also interesting how the above passage delicately handles Faru's first master's right to point the way to final authority. Master Ming is defined by having a kind of hidden internal wisdom whose source is never defined, or revealed, since he declined to teach. In effect, Ming is presented as a perfect signpost who owns a measure of wisdom that he doesn't transmit to anyone, yet stands tall enough to point the way to the real font of tradition. In fact, master Ming seems included in the story not for any formative impact he might have had on the young

---

40. In translating this text, I received very useful suggestions from Chen Jinhua and Brook Ziporyn. Brook, in particular, sat down with the text for an afternoon and solved (in his pajamas and without a dictionary) the more difficult passages.

Faru—something that is never said—but rather to function as a narra-tive tool that directs the hero on to his next stage—the encounter with perfect tradition.

The honesty and simpleness of Faru's encounter with tradition is developed in the next passage, where the narrative brings Faru to Hongren in a splashy moment of mystical transmission in which, based on those previous karmic connections, Hongren provides Faru with the totality of tradition, a moment that the latter part of the passage glori-fies with a range of quotes and allusions drawn from well-known sūtras and commentaries. Key here is that though this moment is loaded with textual allusions to explain its "reality," Faru has never been shown studying the sūtras or commentaries, and they are not depicted as part of the transmission of tradition that Hongren is bestowing on Faru. Instead, the language of the sūtras has become decorative; it now func-tions as a kind of wallpaper designed to convince the reader of tradi-tion's presence by providing a familiar backdrop to this supposedly historical happening. Following from the passage above:

> [Once in Xingzhou,] when Faru was done bowing and asking [for teach-ing], Hongren, the Master *(zushi)*,[41] didn't say anything, as there was a prior karmic connection *(xian ji)*. [Instead,] he just transmitted the Way *(shou qi dao)* to him. So with the secret meaning *(miyi)* of the Buddha opened, Faru *suddenly entered (dunru)* into the One Vehicle; and, of all causes and non-causes, both were finalized,[42] and he went to the pond of pure peace, and entered into the empty dwelling of nirvana. One could say that it was a case of not moving from the final limit of truth, and yet knowing all things.[43]

---

41. Yanagida *(Shoki Zenshū shisho no kenkyū,* 490) notes that this seems to be the earliest use of this term, *zushi* (lit., "ancestral master") in Chan-related material. He notes, too, that slightly earlier a parallel phrase is used by Daoxuan in his *Genealogical Record of Śākyamuni (Shijia shi pu): "with the ancestral Buddha as teacher (zufo wei shi)," T.50.84b. However, several centuries earlier one finds ancestral terms built from *zong* in works such as Mouzi's *Lihuo lun*, a text that, though difficult to date, likely was written before the fifth century. See Keenan's translation and discussion, *How Master Mou Removes Our Doubts*, esp. 64–65, where he explores Mouzi's use of the term *zongxu*, "ancestral link." A key passage in Mouzi's text comes when he defines the Buddha: "Buddha is the original ancestor of the Way, our ancestral link to spiritual understanding" (64). Keenan also notes the use of the term *zuzong*, "ancestral lineage/essence," in the early Buddhist apologetic text, *Zhengwu lun* (65).

42. Yanagida *(Shoki Zenshū shisho no kenkyū,* 490–91) links this line with a pas-sage from the *Mahāprajñāpāramitā Śāstra (Dazhidu lun),* T.25.742c.

43. According to Yanagida *(Shoki Zenshū shisho no kenkyū,* 491), the pond meta-phor is from *Dazhidu lun* (T.25.221c); the empty dwelling of nirvana is from the *Vimalakīrti* (T.14.549c); and the final line about not moving is from Sengzhao, *Buzhen konglun* (T.45.153a).

In this momentous encounter, the narrative demonstrates that tradition can be given, fully and absolutely, through some unexplained action on Hongren's part—a bestowal that has several implications for the future of tradition. For instance, Faru appears to have done nothing to receive tradition. The narrative's vague recourse to "prior karmic connection" does little to explain why this is happening or to clarify how one prepares to get in line to be the next master. Certainly, it is not the case that Faru practiced anything or prepared himself with meditation or such. Instead, the narrative makes clear that the power to give tradition was in the hands of Hongren, who, without words or deeds, simply bestowed the Way on him, and this effected all sorts of perfection in Faru, perfections cataloged with allusions to a range of Buddhist texts. More telling, the narrative makes clear that this is an esoteric form of Buddhism, the best form of Buddhism to be sure, but one defined as the "secret meaning of the Buddha." For the moment, then, the narrative has created the image of a perfect form of Buddhism that is secret and is only reproduced in this inexplicable encounter with the master Hongren.

Then, without explaining anything else about their relationship, and nothing more will be said, the narrative jumps to a quick discussion of how transmission worked in India in which we learn more about this secret mode of transmitting the essence of tradition. In this passage the author makes three things clear. First, there really is a highly secretive form of tradition that should be carefully guarded and kept away from unsuitable types. Second, this form of oral transmission, and the perfection it brings, is beyond what is found in the sūtras. And, third, and by implication, each master transmits to only one other master. Thus, we likely are being invited to go back and read Hongren's gift of the Way to Faru as Hongren's sole dispensation since the author explains this act by recounting a series of other gift-giving moments that also are singular and exclusive. Following directly from the above passage we read:

> In India, the essence (ben) was transmitted without written words
> (wu wenzi) and those who entered into this door (ru cimen) did so
> only through the transmission of mind/thought (wei yi xiangchuan).[44]
> Therefore, Huiyuan of Mount Lu wrote in his preface to the Meditation
> Sūtra, "Ānanda, who collected the oral teachings, was instructed [by

44. Yanagida (Shoki Zenshū shisho no kenkyū, 492) notes that the final phrase in this sentence is likely a reference to a line in the Laṇkāvatāra Sūtra, T.16.497b.

the Buddha] that if he met someone who was not [suitable], he should conceal the [teachings] in the spiritual court *(ling fu)*[45] [of the mind] whose secluded gate *(you guan)*[46] is so rarely opened that one hardly ever sees the palace."[47] Shortly after the Buddha died, Ānanda transmitted to Madhyāntika, Madhyāntika transmitted to Śāṇavāsa. These three responded to truth, and secretly tallied [their understanding] with the past [teaching]. Their achievements were beyond words, in that which the sūtras do not mention. They must have secretly modeled themselves on the original craftsman *(yuan jiang)*—there was not even a thread's width of difference. And they comprehended the measures and were good at transforming inwardly and outwardly without obstruction, and yet concealed their names and trusted it to their traces—[thereby rendering the whole project] unrecognized and unmanifest. Persons such as these cannot be categorized with names—it is clear that there was this other ancestral source *(zong)* [of truth].

Also, there was the southern Indian, the Tripiṭaka Dharma Master, Bodhidharma, who inherited this essence *(zong)*, and marched with it to this Eastern country. A biography *(zhuan)* says, "Magically transforming *(shenhua)* in hidden and mysterious *(youze)* ways, he entered into Wei and transmitted to Ke, Ke to Can, Can transmitted to Xin, Xin transmitted to Ren, Ren transmitted to Ru. Given that transmission cannot use words, if not for [finding] the right person, how could it be transmitted?

This section of the text first establishes an authorized Indian precedent for this esoteric form of tradition, supposedly established by the Buddha, and then jumps forward some thousand years to abruptly take up the story of how Bodhidharma brought this privatized form of tradition to China. Bodhidharma's given identity is decidedly simple: it consists simply of a locale, southern India, and a title, Tripiṭaka Dharma Master. And yet the narrative claims that he, too, inherited this secret essence of tradition and then brought it to China, though his own Indian master is never identified. Of course, what remains unadmitted is that the Indian lineage, as found in Huiyuan's text that is cited for proof of this esoteric form of tradition, had nothing to do with Bodhidharma or the rest of the story that will be divulged. In fact, Huiyuan's lineage was dedicated to shoring up the legacy of a certain

45. Yanagida (*Shoki Zenshū shisho no kenkyū*, 492–93) notes that Zhuangzi uses this binome in the fifth chapter, where *lingfu* is the house of the spirit. The term is also found in the *Meditation Sūtra* itself, T.15.301a.4.

46. Yanagida (*Shoki Zenshū shisho no kenkyū*, 492) has found this binome in Sengzhao's commentary on the *Vimalakīrti, Zhu Weimojing*, T.38.327b.

47. For a partial translation of Huiyuan's preface, see McRae, *The Northern School*, 81 ff.

Dharmatrāta. Thus, the author plugged that early Indian lineage drawn from Huiyan's preface into the figure of Bodhidharma, who then supposedly brought pure esoteric tradition to China and then transmitted it to the Chinese side of the lineage that led down to Hongren.

In this minimalist account of Bodhidharma, the author did not directly hook Bodhidharma to the prior list of Indian masters from the Buddha to Ānanda to Madhyāntika, and so on. Instead, Bodhidharma appears as a kind of free-floating connector that delivers the essence of tradition from India to China and is, somehow, able to cover that gap of one thousand years between the Buddha's supposed descendants and Huike. Bodhidharma's success in this role of inaugurating the Chinese side of the lineage—"to Ke, Ke to Can, Can to Xin," and so on, is vouched for by citing a "biography," which presumably refers to his biography in Daoxuan's *Encyclopedia*. However, this narrative of Bodhidharma and his lineage is not found in Bodhidharma's entry in Daoxuan's *Encyclopedia*. True, the entries for both Bodhidharma and Huike explain Bodhidharma's connection to Huike but in much less grandiose terms, and with mention of another inheritor, Daoyu—an inclusion that would have ruined the symmetry of the claim about a line of singular inheritance. Moreover, neither of these entries in Daoxuan connects Bodhidharma to that early Indian lineage from the Buddha to Ānanda, and so on, as the Faru biography does. Equally missing in Daoxuan's entries is an attempt to draw the lineage forward in China, in a singular man-to-man fashion, from Huike to Sengcan to Daoxin to Hongren, though Sengcan is mentioned in a rather random way in Huike's biography, along with several other students of Huike. (Below I clarify what is and is not in Daoxuan's entries and what the author of Faru's biography has done in adopting that material to his narrative.)

With this sketchiest of lineages in place, the author returns to the details of Faru's life. Here, we learn of Hongren's death and Faru's subsequent exit from East Mountain. This part of the narrative drifts underground as Faru's whereabouts in this period are kept vague and his eventual arrival at Shaolin is cloaked in secrecy. All this changes, though, in 686, when Faru supposedly hosts that massive dharma meeting in which he publicly performs as a buddha, in direct contrast to the secret life he had been leading after inheriting tradition from Hongren at some unspecified time in the past. This pattern of moving total tradition into a figure and then having him go underground until some later time will become a stock element in later genealogical writing.

After the above explanation of transmission, we learn that:

In 675, the master [Hongren] died. [Faru], having served him for sixteen years, then went to convert [people in] Huainan; then he went north to Zhongyue [on Mount Song] and finally settled at Shaolin Monastery. *He stayed three years without anyone recognizing him.* This was how he held on to his [spiritual] roots *(shouben)*, and kept intact his simplicity *(pu)*. He disdained the world and regarded glory as fleeting—such is the honest virtue and the spirit of a sage.[48] Externally, he hid his fame and talent, and internally he accorded with the mysterious merit *(xuangong)*—this is, basically, the way of keeping close to it, and such is the manner of lofty simplicity. In responding to questions, his words were simple, [but] they fully exhausted the essence and entered into the subtleties. His answers transcended the speculations of being, and escaped the confinement of emptiness. His engaged wisdom was courageous and succinct, and thereby he was able to construct the dharma city, and yet he was a friend who brought comfort—that was the wisdom of the master.

In the year 686, monks of the four directions congregated at Shaolin Monastery and requested him to reveal the Chan Dharma *(chanfa)*. Everyone said, "Beginning from the Wei [dynasty] up until the Tang [dynasty] there have been five generations of imperial representatives, who covered nearly two hundred years—[during these years] someone has always come forth to define the virtue of the age. All of them bestowed upon us, the descendants, the legacy of the peerless jewel *(wushang dabao)*. If again today you would shake the mysterious net *(xuan wang)* for your fortunate listeners, *(chao wenzhe),*[49] then your radiance would again correctly transform us."

When the master was done listening to their request, he declined, saying that "Even when words are silenced [lit., "nirvanized"], [your] thoughts won't die. But if I use wisdom, your worries won't be destroyed. How could I dare to accept your request, and deliver the Way of the former victors *(xian sheng zhi dao)*." He politely refused in this way three times. But after some time had passed, he agreed. "When we contemplate the intent of the Perfect Man, it is broad and vast, deep and far-reaching. Today, [I will teach] with just the Single Dharma which is capable of causing sages and commoners alike to enter into irreversible samādhi *(jueding)*. Those brave and intrepid listeners should carefully receive this teaching. When making fire, one must not leave off the task in the middle."

The whole assembly bowed and paid their respects, and obtained the original mind *(benxin)*. The master imprinted their minds secretly *(miyin)* with the Dharma of One Seal *(yi yin zhi fa),* and thereby the mundane world was no longer manifest, and instead it was the dharma

48. Yanagida (*Shoki Zenshū shisho no kenkyū,* 493) notes that binomes in this passage echo lines from Confucius's *Analects* and some from Wang Chong's *Lunheng* (27–97).

49. This line is alluding to the line in book 4 of the *Analects,* "If a man should hear of the Way in the morning. . . ."

realm. This dharma was manifested in the minds of those to be delivered like the moon's reflection [in water], and if the disciples energetically practice [his teaching], the Way is therein. Once his great transformation [of the congregation] had spread forth its deeds, it broadly covered all the different capacities of the crowd, and the degree of revealing and concealing always precisely matched [the crowd's capacity].

With this grand teaching moment achieved, the narrative quickly turns to Faru's demise, which capitalizes on a number of the issues "proven" in recounting the life of Faru, such as his noted ability to "deliver the Way of the former victors."

> After that, he repeatedly instructed his disciples to quickly ask about that which they doubted. Suddenly he manifested signs of illness, and the quick witted ones knew what the signs meant. On his last night he sat upright under a tree and pronounced his final words *(yixun)*, again clarifying the ultimate principles of the lineage *(zongji)*. He made seven days seem to be an eon and awakened them to the way [a buddha], with a finger-snap, shakes the world. The dharma neither comes nor goes. Thoughts of quickness or slowness were eliminated. Then at noon on the 27th day of the 7th month in the year of 689, he died in perfect quietude. He was fifty-two years old. He was buried on the plains of Shaoshi [the name of the wider area where Shaolin Monastery was located]. And, on the north side toward the high peak, all the close disciples erected a stupa and placed there a stone with an image of the Udayana portrait of the Buddha on it. Then they collected his biography and engraved it on [this] buddha-stele *(fobei)*. They set up this [document] in the temple courtyard, displayed in order for us to discipline ourselves, saying: "Our master had keen perception and his motion and stillness were unfathomable. He molded flat the ten thousand types of bondage and served as a bridge for the vast world. He ascended into the subtleties and thereby provided a staircase so that whoever applied themselves [accordingly] would certainly accomplish it. The merit of his legacy is limitless, equal in radiance to the sun and moon."

In this closing sequence, the majesty of Faru's buddha-perfection is made clear, and though there is no mention of him reproducing an heir, the final section of this passage presents him as an icon-to-be-replicated, and thus his example is said to function as a kind of staircase that, for those who would diligently follow his model, would lead to similarly grand results. Of course, inciting monks to replicate Faru's path, especially with reference to the analogy of the staircase, might appear rather odd here since the narrative has said nothing of Faru's practice, and, more worrisome, Faru's success came as a gift from Hongren in that sudden moment of transmission that broke any kind of causal movement along the path, or staircase.

FAMOUS FOR HUMILITY:
THE AGENDA OF THE FARU STELE

With the stele's narrative now in view, I suggest that though Faru is obviously the hero of the narrative, the fulfillment of the narrative is his death and permanent installment at Shaolin Monastery. And thus, the story is best characterized not as the life of Faru but the story of how total tradition came to Shaolin Monastery. Shaolin as the site of closure is underscored in the way Faru is buried next to the monastery, memorialized with a stupa and a portrait of the Buddha and glorified with this sensational biography. Note, too, that there is no mention of him transmitting total truth to any particular figure before his death. Truth, as a jewel-like entity, has been brought to Shaolin and installed there in an inert but still presumably potent form.

Read in this light, there are three places in Faru's narrative where we are asked to witness the crucial task of moving truth in and out of zones of ownership. Oddly enough, all three events occur without public knowledge. Like later Chan narratives, these silent or secretive moments are usually the place where the most important polemical work is accomplished. Or, more exactly, it is usually in these underground moments far from the public eye that the narratives work to fuse together previously unrelated textual sources. In the first case, Faru is said to receive total truth from Hongren in that sudden moment during their first meeting, but this transfer produces no noticeable effect in the narrative. There is no public surprise, no ritual of investiture, no State intervention, and no great teaching event like the one Faru will give once installed at Shaolin years later. Also, though the mystical aspects of this moment of inheritance are developed in the narrative with flowery language, we learn nothing of the time that Hongren and Faru spent together. Except for the line mentioning the sixteen years Faru served him, there are no details from Faru's life at Hongren's monastery, or Hongren's teaching. In short, the narrative works to explain this amazing connection between Hongren and Faru but doesn't give any details that might ground their connection in historical events or in the activities of other contemporaries. In fact, even the time of their fateful meeting isn't clarified, and there certainly aren't any witnesses mentioned.

The second moment of moving truth in and out of a particular zone of possession is Faru's exit from East Mountain, after Hongren's death. This, too, is odd. Why does Faru leave? In Daoxuan's biography of

Daoxin, the only detail we learn about Hongren is that he inherits Daoxin's stupa and appears to stay on-site at Huangmei.[50] This kind of fuzziness in the narrative's logic looks more suspicious when we learn that when Faru arrives at Shaolin he hid his identity for three years—the third example of the secret movement of truth. But why was this necessary? What demanded that the flow of truth again go underground in these various ways before it could reappear? The best answer seems to be that by making truth go underground, the author avoided the need to document these events, and then by setting up the supposedly public teaching event as the work of a Chinese buddha, he "proved" that buddhahood had arrived at Shaolin in just the way he claimed.

In effect, then, the spectacular teaching moment is designed as a rhyme scheme, with the assembled masses recognizing Faru's genealogy-of-truth in just the way that the author wishes the reader would. Similarly, the public (within the narrative) also vouches for the claim that the throne saw Faru this way, too, explicitly linking him to that chain of five previous imperially recognized masters. Then, with the lineage recognized publicly and governmentally for what it would like to be, the author has Faru perform as a buddha would, delivering the totality of tradition to the adoring audience, thereby confirming with actions the claims of the rest of the lineage narrative and the public's supposed assessment of Faru. In sum, with the lavish teaching event as a public "historical" event, the narrative has "visibly" ratified the secretive private history of Faru's truth-fathers that stretches back centuries to the Buddha. Thus, when Faru's magical gift *outward* turns the teaching site into the dharma sphere, we are simply seeing the effect of that magical gift *inward* in which Faru received total enlightenment from Hongren and, more distantly, the Buddha.

NARRATIVE AS PERFORMANCE: BOURDIEU'S TRIANGLE OF MAGICAL AUTHORITY

If we consider the Faru stele in light of Bourdieu's notions of legitimacy and authority, the text appears to be performing in a very standard manner.[51] The narrative, on a basic level, is designed to

50. For translation of this passage in Daoxuan's *Encyclopedia*, see McRae, *The Northern School*, 31–32.
51. I have used this Bourdieu-style analysis elsewhere; see my *Text as Father* and "Simplicity for the Sophisticated."

demonstrate religious authority by means of a three-part trajectory that bounces between a sanctified and sanctifying origin, a current delegate who represents that origin, and the public who are attracted to this representative based on his official capacity to deliver tradition.[52] Viewed in this manner, the Faru narrative clearly fulfills this three-part equation, with Faru as the current delegate who, with his private connections to pure Truth established through this newly concocted genealogy back to the Buddha—the santifying origin—is now legitimized to give tradition outward to be partially shared with an adoring public.

Also in line with Bourdieu's notion of how this process works, we can see that though this is an aggressive narrative that takes possession of perfect Buddhism, it is cloaked with a patina of innocence and simplicity. Hence, throughout the narrative we are given plenty of clues that Faru is innocent of ever wanting to own Truth. He didn't go to Hongren to inherit Truth; he was simply following the advice of his master to go to Hongren to study a form of meditation. Likewise, with Hongren, he asked for nothing; it was prior karmic connections that produced the transmission, and nothing in this life, such as greed or desire for fame, is admitted as a contributing factor. Equally demonstrative of his humble spirit, he remained Hongren's faithful attendant for sixteen years even after he had received tradition.

These items are telling in the narrative, but once Faru is about to be brought onstage in the role of a living buddha, his humble nature is again emphasized and in language marked by allusions to Confucius's *Analects*. For instance, by refusing to participate in the grand event three times, he is simply demonstrating again his self-effacing ways, ways that were thoroughly established in the preceding passages. This motif is one that will repeat frequently in Chan narratives, and I suggest that it is best read as an effect of attempting to cloak the aggressivity and audacity of the author-historian. The master, in other words, has to appear as the inverse of the historian: simple, uninterested in owning anything, or in moving the crowds, and certainly not drawn to nose around in other people's lineage narratives to try to find form and content to better claim ownership of tradition.

---

52. For Bourdieu's discussion of this triangular structure, see his *Language and Symbolic Power*, esp. the chapters "Authorized Language," 107–16; and "Rites of Institution," 117–26.

BACKFIELD IN MOTION: REWRITES IN DAOXUAN'S
ENCYCLOPEDIA OF EMINENT MONKS II

Reading Faru's narrative suspiciously seems all the more defendable when we look closely at the Chinese side of the lineage that was made up for Faru. One of the cotter pins in my argument about the fabrication of Faru's identity is the relationship between his lineage and a protolineage set up, for Fachong's benefit, in Huike's entry in Daoxuan's *Encyclopedia.* Hence, it is not simply that the Faru stele presents a lineage of masters that cannot be found in the *Encyclopedia*—in fact, it contradicts what is found there—but rather that the Huike biography in Daoxuan's text already shows clear reworking in a direction that the Faru biography extends. Hence, assuming that the Faru biography builds on the rewritten Huike biography—and there are good reasons to assume this—then its construction of the lineage of Bodhidharma –Huike–Sengcan–Daoxin–Hongren needs to be located in a sequence of rewriting history that prefigured the presentation of Faru more than any real historical event. Therefore, if it is the case that the Faru biography picked up pieces of Fachong's protolineage, then this means that the Faru lineage is not derivative simply on the level of content but also in terms of replaying the writing strategies that are evident in the "Fachong affair." Moreover, borrowing the rewritten part of Huike's biography and yet removing Fachong from the Huike lineage set the stage for a series of lineage "beheadings" that would mark genealogical writing in the decades to come.

To get a sense for the details, note that in Fachong's biography, which belongs to an added-on strata of the *Encyclopedia,* Fachong is set in a vague lineage of sorts as follows:[53]

Bodhidharma>Huike>Sengcan and others >Fachong.

Moreover, the *Laṅkāvatāra Sūtra* is identified as the transmitted object that holds the lineage together. Then, when the Fachong entry asks us to see the entry for Huike for more information, it is easy to see that Fachong's entry was designed in concert with Huike's now-jumbled biography, which clearly has been reworked to support Fachong's claim about a Bodhidharma lineage built around the *Laṅkāvatāra Sūtra.*

---

53. This mini-lineage is distilled from McRae's discussion, *The Northern School,* 24–26; for Faure's discussion of Fachong, see *The Will to Orthodoxy,* 145 ff; and *Le bouddhisme Ch'an.*

Thus, we have clear evidence that in the second half of the seventh century, the biographies of sixth-century Bodhidharma and Huike had become lightning rods for claims to status and legitimacy. Moreover, we see evidence of unseen authors attempting to pump up the authority of a certain Fachong, and to create a fetish to hold tradition in the form of the *Laṅkāvatāra Sūtra*—a popular sūtra that would on and off be put in this role as the conveyor of the totality of tradition. Obviously, since the agenda behind the Faru stele was the promotion of Shaolin Monastery as preeminent in the empire, they had no use for Fachong's claims that sought to pull tradition into himself or the parallel claim that tradition resides in the *Laṅkāvatāra Sūtra*. No surprise, then, that these elements are not present in Faru's biography, even though they figure so importantly in Daoxuan's material.

Reworking the Bodhidharma–Huike–Sengcan–Fachong segment of lineage to the benefit of Faru wasn't all that the Faru stele accomplished. It took this protolineage, sans Fachong and the *Laṅkāvatāra Sūtra,* and then joined it to another protolineage segment, also found in Daoxuan. This second segment is defined by a meager narrative detail that explains how Daoxin, at the point of death (in 651), picked Hongren to be in charge of his stupa at Mount Huangmei, an act that likely would be taken as a kind of transmission of legacy.[54] At first glance, joining these two protolineages seems to derive simply from the need to bring the Bodhidharma–Huike protolineage closer into the present of the writing moment so that Faru as the most recent incarnation of tradition can have up-to-date ancestors. This makes sense because clearly the Daoxin–Hongren link was just a couple decades in the past, but I suggest more was at play in this choice than simple chronological suitability.

By attaching the Bodhidharma–Huike protolineage to the Daoxin–Hongren connection and then, of course, pulling that essence out of Hongren and putting it in Faru, the author of the Faru biography found a way to own whatever cachet was imagined to exist at East Mountain in the figures of Daoxin and Hongren. That is, and here we see a trope that would be fundamental in later genealogical writing, in threading these two segments together, Daoxin and Hongren have been tethered to a lineage that now can be put to any chosen use. Thus, and with no regard for what any of these figures might actually have taught or prac-

---

54. T.50.606b.20. See McRae, *The Northern School,* 31–32, for a translation of Daoxuan's biography of Daoxin.

ticed, the Faru narrative relegates Daoxin and Hongren to place-holders who simply link Faru back to the Buddha and the font of tradition. For instance, that Daoxin taught the *Prajñāpāramitā Sūtras* and was good at magic is nowhere acknowledged in the Faru narrative, even though those are the details associated with his life in Daoxuan's biography of him. In Faru's biography, Daoxin simply needs to sit quietly behind Hongren, holding him in line with Sengcan and priming him with the heritage of the truth-fathers that will push its way on to Faru.

In sum, Faru's "family" of truth-fathers was put together with three disparate chunks of historical narrative, two from Daoxuan (the Bodhidharma–Huike and Daoxin–Hongren segments) and then the list of Indian masters from Huiyuan's preface, a text that can be found in several pre-Tang collections. Moreover, the author of the Faru biography has treated each segment in the same high-handed manner, with no regard for its prior function, focus, or context. In effect, and this is precisely why McRae's and Faure's approaches to this material won't work, there should be no expectation that there was transmission of *anything* from these prior masters, since they have only become masters in this newly concocted lineage when their literary remains, as found in Daoxuan's high-profile *Encyclopedia,* were later hooked together by adventurous genealogists. Similarly, by the end of the chapter, I will set out the argument that the content within the pipeline—items such as sudden enlightenment or sudden inclusion in the lineage—begins to appear in these narratives not because that is what was transacted between masters but because it facilitates this kind of identity theft and the aggressive overhaul of prior attempts to own tradition.

THE GRADUAL APPEARANCE OF SUDDENNESS

The daring with which the Shaolin authors rewrote prior Buddhist narratives and joined them willy-nilly in order to produce a convincing account of Shaolin's uniqueness suggests that we need to approach content in these narratives in a much more suspicious manner than Chan Studies has been accustomed to.[55] For instance, let's return to that moment when Faru meets Hongren and Hongren silently gives

---

55. Faure has argued, in *The Will to Orthodoxy* (8), against thinking that the content of Chan is a *function* of the polemics involved in producing genealogical claims to own tradition: "The need for a two-fold reading of Chan texts—historical-critical and hermeneutical approach—explains why this analysis of the Northern School and of the *Records* [Du Fei's *Chuan fabao ji*] proceeds along two major axes: the study of the

him the Way and the totality of tradition. Given the above evidence suggesting how the Faru narrative was sewn together from these previously separate protolineages, we have to consider the possibility that the suddenness of Faru's assumption of truth has everything to do with the suddenness of the author connecting those two disparate pieces of narrative taken from Daoxuan's *Encyclopedia*. That is, a deep reading would urge us to consider that Faru's sudden reception of total tradition from Hongren is a perfect distillation of the writing process—that "sudden" authorial gesture to hook together two pieces of literature that previously had nothing to do with one another and whose narrative connections could not be coherently explained otherwise. That is, suddenness between masters *in the narrative* is the effect of the way authors are, on the outside, handling various narratives that are being linked together to provide a continuous account of the history of truth.[56]

Grounds for reaching this kind of conclusion about the connection between suddenness and narrative construction are also found in the way that in Du Fei's genealogy, the next Bodhidharma genealogy that attempted to supersede Faru's (treated in the next chapter), Faru no longer is accorded a sudden enlightenment experience; instead it is now Shenxiu who is recognized by Hongren "in a glance" and who is presented as the real recipient of tradition. Clearly, sudden inclusion in the Bodhidharma lineage comes and goes rather suddenly, and this is because it is suddenness as the effect of literary fusion that makes the master who he is, not some human experience within the Real of history, as previous studies have assumed. Thus, it is no surprise that later

---

patriarchal tradition and its sectarian stakes on the one hand, and the ideology of the practice of Northern Chan on the other. *Here we must stress that there is no clear causal link between the one aspect and the other, even if there are apparently occasional correlations:* the analysis of sectarian infighting does not necessarily reflect the development of doctrine, and subitism [suddenness] is not, as has long been claimed, the sole prerogative of the Southern School." If I am interpreting this correctly, Faure's position here boils down to saying that there is real religion behind the sectarianism, and thus politics and practice can be separated. This is, it would seem, basically a faith-claim—and, at the very least, he has done little to explain how the content of any of these texts could be treated apart from the sectarianism that houses them. Obviously, I am arguing the opposite.

56. McRae, "Shenhui as Evangelist," 133, pursues a somewhat similar connection between sudden enlightenment and literary motifs, noting that this angle of his investigation grew out of a question that someone asked during a presentation at the University of California, Berkeley, on March 19, 2002. It is most likely not a coincidence that I had given a paper to this same group two days earlier in which I argued for just this connection between sudden enlightenment and the writing of the genealogies.

authors rely on suddenness to steal the Bodhidharma lineage throughout the rest of the eighth century, with the *Platform Sūtra* being a particularly clear case of how sudden enlightenment from Hongren would
get rewritten yet again to make a new master—this time, Huineng.
Hence, I suggest that, among other things, this suddenness that at first
looks like master-to-master contact actually is the effect of renarrating
previous narratives: it is the place where the chaotic, unconnected, and
heterogeneous elements of the past are fused into perfect teleological
succession—that place where tradition can appear as immaculately
self-caused and not the effect of the ongoing attempt to make it look
that way.

On another level, suddenness marks that dangerous power to give
and take identity which is arguably the workhorse of patriarchy.[57]
However, this strength of patriarchy is also its weakness, for just as
easily as ancestors can be created post facto, and even ex nihilo when
necessary, so, too, can they be stolen and whisked off to work in competing patriarchal lineage claims. In sum, suddenness, and especially
sudden identity, marks the prerogative of the genealogist, and his greatest fear.

THE LIFE OF LITERATURE

Faru's stele raises some important questions about recycling language.
For instance, it is hard to miss that, structurally, the stele works as a
vortex of textuality. Textual material, drawn from a variety of sources
named and unnamed, circles around two moments of sheer silence, the
two moments that, nonetheless, give the narrative its raison d'être. The
first moment of silence occurs when Hongren gives Faru the transmission of truth, termed "the Dao." At this juncture, nothing was said,
and what Hongren or Faru might have thought at that moment is left
unidentified. Instead, this section billows forth with sūtra and śāstra
quotes that have been culled from China's best-loved Buddhist texts
and set here to explain how wonderful the moment was. As briefly
mentioned above, the construction of the narrative makes it clear that
though nothing "onstage" is being said, the entirety of the Buddhist
textual tradition is implicitly present since quotes from key texts are
relied on to register this event. Thus, this old familiar Buddhist scrip-

---

57. I explore this dynamic in patriarchy in my *Text as Father,* chap. 1.

tural language has come alive in the figure of Faru, whose life now shimmers with the glamour of these classical quotes. And, by making this moment of transmission match what was said/written in older strata of beloved Buddhist scripture, Faru's life is now appearing as though he *lived* what everyone else was only reading about. Of course, this is not too different from narrating scenes from Jesus' life with passages from Isaiah or the Psalms, and in either case, the sage is made to "live literature" in a way that will have profound consequences for how tradition will be regathered and, equally important, how it will henceforth be written into the present. In short, though appearing casual at first, describing Faru's life in scriptural terms has front-loaded the essence of tradition from scriptural sources into his person in a powerful gesture that will become another crucial element in the literary ploys characteristic of Chan literature.

Faru's public teaching is the second moment when the narrative overflows with scriptural sources that mask a basic silence. One might expect that this teaching moment would be performed in language, but in fact Faru's "speech" is drowned out in a sea of sūtra quotes. Actually, after his three refusals to teach, which appear as real articulations in the narrative, he decides to teach, though we never hear what he said. Then, the narrative turns to explain what was *around* the discourse. Thus, we learn about a series of sanctifying elements supporting his discourse, from the cause of the teaching—"the intent of the Perfect Man"—which leads on to the means—"the Single Dharma which is capable of causing sages and commoners alike to enter irreversible samādhi"—to, finally, the effect: "The whole assembly bowed and paid their respects, and obtained the original mind *(benxin)*. The master imprinted their minds secrectly *(miyin)* with the Dharma of One Seal, and thereby the mundane world was no longer manifest, and instead it was the dharma realm." Obviously, these three descriptors are focused on his speech as a sublime object, coming from Faru the Perfect Man and going into the audience with total efficacy. Clearly, though, there is no content here in the formal sense of a record of discourse, and thus there is a match between Faru's silent reception of the dharma and his purported annunciation of it: in both cases what we learn about are its causes and effects, with no hint about its reality as an audible and thinkable Something.

Instead of assuming that this is simply the effect of what later Chan partisans would herald as Chan's truth-beyond-language, I think we would do better to consider that this silence or lack in the midst of the narrative about real tradition has several other factors structuring it. First, keeping the center of Faru's discourse empty of content, though its presence is narrated with quotes from sūtras and the Chinese classics, allows Faru to move beyond all literature by essentially standing on its shoulders. Thus, not only did the Shaolin monks want to avoid picking a text to be the final arbiter of tradition, and they had already deleted the emphasis on the *Laṅkāvatāra Sūtra* in the Huike–Fachong material from Daoxuan's *Encyclopedia,* they likely saw that in attempting to create the image of the final form of tradition, the sūtras could be used but only to provide the swoosh of the vortex around the silent and consummate center—the claim that Faru was a buddha.

Second, Chinese literature has a long tradition of juxtaposing literature and a nonliterate Real. Whether it is the "wordless teachings" *(wuyan jiao)* of the *Daode jing* offered in complex and witty poetry, or the *Zhuangzi*'s wily and hilarious conversations that speak of language beyond language found in the wind blowing through the world's holes, not to mention the wine-moon-nature poetry of pre-Tang and Tang eras, Chinese writers and readers presumably would have been quite predisposed to let content *be about content,* with final content remaining undefined and essentially silent.

Third, and most importantly, the Faru stele works as a piece of ideology only when its literary basis, and especially its complex and dubious use of prior texts, is annulled and overshadowed by the "history" that it is working to create—the history explaining how that fundamentally uncreated Truth of the Buddha somehow had been moving forward in time and finally ended up in Faru's person. Thus, not only does the Faru stele need a kind of suddenness to hook together recycled literary passages; it also can make good use of a profound literary silence to ground the noise of the literature that is creating the immensity and potency of this silence.

Fourth, and finally, this silence of the masters also works to keep tradition private and inscrutable. Imagine what would have happened if Faru had been made to articulate some specific content that would supposedly represent all the wisdom of tradition. Such a statement-of-content would automatically, like Jesus' normally covered genitalia, suddenly be vulnerable to a range of unwanted judgments that could not be countered by increasing or decreasing the size of the presentation. In sum, as I argue in the following chapters, the array of linguistic claims put forward to explain silent transmission—be it a mind-to-mind transmission, or a kind of samādhi, or being zapped into the "secret meaning of the Buddha"—can be read as elements involved in negotiating this tension between public textuality, including the Faru stele itself, and the silence that has to be in place to keep that claim to own tradition strictly private.

FARU THE MAN

Some readers may, at this point, be hoping for me to offer an opinion about Faru's historical reality. However, I believe that arguing for or against Faru's existence isn't that telling; presumably there were plenty of Tang Buddhist monks named Faru. Instead, what does seem worth focusing on is the way that the narrative shifts Faru's identity from being an ordinary man from Shangdang into a buddha replica. Given the above arguments, it seems clear that Faru, as he is presented in the stele, is who he is *only* because of his lineage: nothing else about him matters. It was never said that he was smart, well trained, or particularly articulate. Instead his "isness"—his content as a master and a quasi-buddha—stands or falls with his history as produced in the Faru biography, and thus he really has no content other than this personal history, which is also the history of perfect Buddhism in China. In other words, according to the logic at work in his biography, his personal content qua identity is a function of the past: he is a buddha-like figure precisely, and solely, because of a past that was made present in accord with the lineage mode of inheritance and its supposedly accurate representation in the narrative on the stele at Shaolin.

Thus, the problem isn't just that the Faru narrative seems wholly invented but rather that the Shaolin author has made Faru's identity totally dependent on history and on its truthful reportage in historical narrative, while at the same time treating history and its reportage with near-total disregard. Consequently, as fabricated history is turned into perfect tradition, in the figure of the living master and his track of predecessors, there is a gaping hole created at the center of both Faru and tradition, not simply because the history appears to have been knowingly fabricated, but because the narrative works from a logic in which Faru the man is overwritten—replaced, actually—with both this fabricated history and the axiom that this thin track of "living history" supersedes any other form of tradition and human being.

CHAPTER 4

The Future of an Illusion

Du Fei Hijacks Shaolin's Truth-Fathers

FARU'S UNWANTED LEGACY

In the decades after 690, the basic historical narrative that made up Faru's biography—the claim that perfect tradition had arrived, man-to-man, from the Indian Buddha to a set of Chinese masters via Bodhidharma—was adopted and redesigned by several authors. While historicizing these new histories explaining the local ownership of buddhahood is complicated for several reasons—a lack of dates for the composition of most of the texts, a clear tendency to invent events and masters, and, in some cases, later reediting that upsets the logic of the narratives—on a general level, it is not too hard to see what is going on: the Faru biography had successfully explained how the essence of tradition had been poured into Shaolin's Faru, and other leading Buddhists wanted both that essence and the genealogical container that supposedly held it. Thus, in some of the new versions of Bodhidharma's descendants, Faru is still mentioned but he is upstaged by a newly announced "brother," such as master Shenxiu (d. 706), who is said to have also inherited tradition from Hongren. In other cases, Faru is erased altogether, and the genealogy explains Shenxiu's singular inheritance from Hongren, even though this claim was presumably made under the general influence of the Faru biography. The following chapters explore three examples of this ongoing effort to reinvent the lineage of Bodhidharma—a process of rewriting the truth-fathers that I take to be the real "father" of Chan.

IN THE COMPANY OF TRUTH: FINDING
SHENXIU A MASTER (AND A DESCENDANT)

Of the various texts that rewrote the Faru genealogy, one of the earliest and most interesting is that by Du Fei titled the *Record of the Transmission of the Dharma-Jewel (Chuan fabao ji)*. This text is dense, well written, and a good bit more developed than the Faru stele. As the close reading below will make clear, Du Fei is an author to be reckoned with. Though owing much to Faru's biography, Du Fei's work is distinctive in several ways that reflect the fact that the *Record*, while also trying to lay claim to the totality of tradition, was not written for the benefit of a certain monastery. Instead, the *Record* seems designed, primarily, to manage the cachet of legitimacy that had been sunk into Shenxiu by Empress Wu when she invited him to court in 701 and bestowed on him the title National Teacher *(guoshi)*. Thus, Du Fei's text works to substantialize Shenxiu's unusually high level of court recognition into a jewel-like Thing so that it could be reproduced in a future line of descendants. That is, I believe the *Record*'s most basic agenda can be boiled down to the following statement: "What seemed to have been in the court's prerogative to give—the title National Teacher—is actually no more than the external recognition of a system of investiture that we Buddhists control and plan to wield in the future." In short, I believe the "coronation" of Shenxiu as something like the pope of Buddhism was the impetus for Du Fei to generate a back story that would allow him and others to canalize this instance of recognition into a living institution of sorts.[1]

Put this way, the structure of Du Fei's basic agenda was no different from Guanding's or Shaolin's, since each of these accounts is trying to turn contemporaneous and fully contingent political acts into religious realities that supposedly had deep histories reaching back to the Buddha. That is, and this takes a little getting used to, each of these narratives seeks to domesticate the action of the State by claiming that State recognition was, in fact, preordained by religious realities and was to be controlled, in the future, by religious actors and not the State. To effect this crucial shift in the background causality of national suc-

---

1. Adamek explores the coronation element in Chan genealogies in a different manner; see her *The Mystique of Transmission*, 156–57.

cess, each one of these genealogies works to situate the State-recognized master into a lineage in a manner that turns their individual identities into something like a company product that will outlive the tenure of any particular CEO.

The forward-looking nature of the *Record*'s "company agenda" is clear in the way that Du Fei linked Shenxiu's newly invented deep history to the claim that Shenxiu secretly transmitted that essence-of-tradition to another figure right before he died. Thus, the *Record* injects tradition into Shenxiu but then pushes that claim to own tradition forward into the present since Shenxiu's unidentified descendant stands as a promise that a representative of the family of truth-fathers is still alive. Consequently, Du Fei's narrative is spring-loaded, leaving the reader with the sense that he must discover Shenxiu's descendant in order to make the narrative come full circle and deliver the fullest form of its promise.[2] This shift toward current concerns would have dramatic effects: it opened the door for masters to begin performing "live" in their role as Chinese buddhas. But it is also telling that at this initial moment of invention, Du Fei only goes halfway since he keeps the living inheritor of tradition secret and thus only partially crowned as the real-time representative of tradition. In line with moving tradition into the zone of the living, Du Fei's text also marks the emergence of a legalistic theory for transmitting the tradition. Thus, whereas Faru did not transmit his inheritance in his biography, the *Record* is designed to manage the flow of this newly commodified version of tradition—"the dharma-jewel" *(fabao)*—and to manage it in perpetuity. No surprise, then, that there are in the *Record* specific ritual sequences mentioned for the future transmission of the dharma-jewel and similarly that the biographic material provided for the six masters focuses on the transmission moment, something that had been absent in the simple list of Faru's ancestors.

Besides moving the ownership of tradition into real time, there

2. Another text vaunting Shenxiu, an epitaph written for him by Zhang Yue (667–731), also works to create a similar kind of spring-loaded effect but does so more directly. Zhang Yue ends his eulogy for Shenxiu depicting his worried and awestruck disciples wondering who inherited *(fuzhu)* Shenxiu's legacy. For an edited version of this text with excellent notes, see Yanagida, *Shoki Zenshū shiso no kenkyū,* 497 ff. For discussion of this source and Zhang Yue, see Faure, *The Will to Orthodoxy,* 14–15, 34–36; see also McRae, *The Northern School,* 45–48. Zhang Yue was one of the more powerful ministers in the first three decades of the eighth century; for a synopsis of his life, see Faure, *The Will to Orthodoxy,* 192 n. 65.

is an equally crucial difference between Du Fei's *Record* and Faru's biography in terms of genre. As I argued in the preceding chapter, the account of Faru's life left the frame of the standard funerary biography and morphed into a history of Chinese Buddhism with Faru's life story opening up to reveal this subterranean lineage deriving from the Buddha. Du Fei turned Faru's neither-fish-nor-fowl biography inside out by externalizing that train of truth-fathers—Faru's supposed Chinese predecessors—and then giving each of these masters a biography basically parallel to Faru's. In broader terms, Du Fei invented the freestanding genealogy that functions as a history of real Buddhism, and which is independent of the funerary biography of any particular master, even though it was built, quite literally, out of the stuff of funerary biography.

As for the authorship of the *Record,* at least two Dunhuang manuscripts identify Du Fei as the author.[3] Unlike many attributions of authorship in Chan texts, this one seems likely. Du Fei does not claim a place in the lineage for himself and instead mentions briefly at the end of his work that he was asked to write the genealogy on behalf of a friend.[4] Who this friend might have been is hard to know. In a short time, however, two leading monks were recognized as Shenxiu's heirs—Yifu (661–736) and Puji (651–739)—and granted the imperial title National Teacher.[5] In light of these developments, Du Fei's text seems to have been successful in the sense that Shenxiu's lineage,

---

3. The Taisho version (T.85.1291) is based on Pelliot 2634 and only provides Du Fei's introduction up to Bodhidharma's biography. Pelliot 3858 is incomplete, and I have not consulted it. The other version, Pelliot 3559, is complete and is edited with copious notes by Yanagida in his *Shoki Zenshū shiso no kenkyū,* 559–93. I have consulted McRae's translation of the text in *The Northern School,* 255–69, and learned much from it, though I disagree with his rendering of several passages. Nonetheless, it is also the case that I could not have written this chapter without his impressive pioneering work on Du Fei's *Record.* Also, I want to thank Brook Ziporyn for correcting and improving my translations.

For other historical references to Du Fei, see McRae, *The Northern School,* 86–87. Similarly, for brief mention of master (Du) Fei see Faure, *The Will to Orthodoxy,* 35; Adamek, *The Mystique of Transmission,* 439 n. 109, points out that Rong Xinjiang has recently published articles on surviving manuscript fragments of the *Record;* see his "Dunhuang ben Chanzong dengshi canjuan shiyi" and "Youguan Dunhuangben *Lidai fabo ji* de xin ziliao."

4. McRae, *The Northern School,* 269.

5. For discussion of Puji, see McRae, *The Northern School,* 65–67; and Faure, *The Will to Orthodoxy,* 93–100. For discussion of Yifu, see McRae, *The Northern School,* 64–65; and Faure, *Le bouddhisme Ch'an,* 180 n. 2; and his *The Will to Orthodoxy,* 78 ff, 201 n. 1.

though apparently created posthumously, produced a new generation of inheritors. Thus, Du Fei's basic ploy to ancestrize the title National Teacher and muscle it into a reproductive lineage appears to have worked. Put in terms of a plumbing metaphor, Du Fei took Shenxiu's identity and hooked it to the pipeline of Faru's ancestors in order to create a conduit that was prized for delivering the essence of Buddhism, via Bodhidharma. Then, with Shenxiu as the final section of that conduit and Faru capped off to the side as a dead-end segment, the end of the pipe was threaded (the secret transmission) so that it could receive the next link of pipe, be it Puji and Yifu, or other figures that we haven't yet identified. Hence, on the shifting sands of political recognition, this pipeline was designed to undo other competitors' claims to own tradition, and to extend, posthumously, Shenxiu's State-recognized identity as the leader of Chinese Buddhism.

Ironically, for as clever as Du Fei's plumbing appears, it soon would suffer the same fate, since several decades later Shenhui (d. 758) claimed that his master Huineng and not Shenxiu had been the real spigot flowing from Hongren. In light of Shenhui's arguments (see chapter 6), it would seem that what Shenhui really learned from Du Fei's discourse was just this maneuver in Du Fei's text that capped Faru and created another spigot running from Hongren.

FISHING FOR BODHIDHARMA:
A CLOSE READING OF DU FEI'S *RECORD*

To build a close reading of the *Record*, I have divided the narrative into four sections, which are implied by the structure of the text: (1) an introduction that argues for the reality of a transcendent realm beyond words and texts, which nonetheless abides in the bodies of certain select men who transmit this truth-essence forward from one man to the next; (2) the introduction of Bodhidharma and his unique role in the transmission of tradition from India to China, a transmission that is recounted as a kind of rebirth for Chinese Buddhism since it brings an infusion of the truth where there had been only darkness and decadence; (3) the biographies of seven patriarchs from Bodhidharma down to Shenxiu; and (4) a closing, with more comments about the reality of truth-beyond-language and the state of affairs in the early eighth century. To keep my discussion brief, I focus on the introduction and Bodhidharma's biography and then make some general comments about the remaining biographies, with special attention given to the way Shenxiu is presented.

After listing his name and place of residence in the Northern capital, Du Fei begins his text with a homage, saying:[6]

> I bow down to the Good Spiritual Friends *(shanzhishi)* who are able to effect the protection of the fundamental mind *(benxin)* and who [function] just like a pearl that has the strength to suddenly clarify muddy water.[7] It was in this way [i.e. by way of good spiritual friends] that I was caused to prepare this record *(xiuji)* in order to illuminate this step-by-step transmission of dharma *(dichuanfa)*, in the hope that buddha-knowledge *(fo zhijian;* lit., "buddha knowing and seeing") would be extended as far into the future as possible.

In this fairly vague homage, Du Fei first signals a faith in the efficacy of Buddhist teachers identified as "good spiritual friends" and a special, "step-by-step transmission" that they share among themselves. He also establishes a confidence in his own possession of a "fundamental mind" that can be purified by these teachers. Thus, from the outset we have a basic tension between a very narrowly defined elite—the Good Spiritual Friends *(kalayānamitra)* who are in possession of buddha-knowledge—and the rest of humanity who have this "fundamental mind" but nonetheless need to rely on those within the chute of transmission to activate it. Du Fei also hints that it was these friends who led to the writing of this document, a fact that he announces much more clearly later in the text. I won't comment more on this opening passage until we have a fuller sense of what this text is going to present.

In the next line Du Fei starts mixing this pairing of private and public truth with a discussion of the truth realm that is completely beyond words. At first, this might seem peripheral to his overall agenda of creating a historical lineage, but, in fact, it is absolutely crucial that Du Fei posit this realm-of-truth-beyond-words, and more importantly, beyond tradition, so as to effectively set the lineage before the public as unique and incomparable in its privileged connection to the Buddha *and* to this realm-of-truth-beyond-words. Though similar logic had

---

6. My translation varies somewhat from McRae's; see his *The Northern School*, 255–69.

7. McRae's reading of the pearl analogy is different but plausible; however, he seems to have omitted the following sentence regarding the composition of the text. See *The Northern School*, 255.

been crucial in the Faru stele, Du Fei develops the trope more extensively here. He writes:

> What is realized by the dharmakāya buddha is my own true dharmakāya. It is separate *(li)* from the words and explanations of all the buddhas that appear in samsara *(huafo)*, and the texts that they transmit. Hence this door of thusness *(zhenrumen)* is transmitted by means of realizing the mind *(zhengxin)* in one's own awakening [or, "realizing the mind's self-awakening"].
>
> Thus it is said in a commentary, "All dharmas are originally separate *(li)* from the mark of words and explanations *(yanshuoxiang)*, separate from the mark of words and names, and separate from the mark of mental causes *(xinyuanxiang)*. They are ultimately equal, without change or difference—they can't be destroyed. [They are all] just this One Mind and therefore are called thusness *(zhenru)*."

This passage, laden with technical Buddhist vocabulary regarding buddha-bodies and thusness, is quite sophisticated in arranging a number of ideological tropes. The first line asserts that within Du Fei there is an internal truth-body that is identical to the truth-body of the Buddha, thereby signifying a kind of sameness between the final essence of the buddhas' being and the author's being, a claim that is presumably applicable to readers, thereby involving them intimately in this discussion. Thus, as the brashness of the opening line makes clear, the essence of Buddhism isn't to be thought of as distant or vague, since it is at the foundation of one's being. Making the reality of tradition an immanent presence is reinforced with the final line in the passage that collapses all being and truth into a single mind of thusness, which is presumably the same mind of the buddhas.[8]

The main point in this first paragraph, then, is to deny that buddhas move truth forward in time with their texts and teachings; instead we are to have confidence in a transmission of truth that somehow occurs without linguistic mediation since it is effected through enlightenment itself. Hence, Du Fei is purveying an image of a prelinguistic truth field that is communicable directly *in* truth such that the intrinsic enlightenment of the recipient is the basis

---

8. This kind of rhetoric of intimacy with the Buddha is found in a variety of Indian sūtras, but it also figures in the *Two Entrances and Four Practices* and in one of the letters appended to one version of the *Two Entrances and Four Practices;* see McRae, *The Northern School,* 103 and 106, respectively. Similarly, this promised fusion of sages and commoners had been mentioned in a line describing Faru's stupendous teaching session at the end of his biography (see previous chapter).

of receiving enlightenment with no intervention of nontruth, and certainly no intervention of language or anything else public since this transmission is to happen "in one's own awakening." What this implies is that Du Fei is rendering Buddhism, as it was previously known, largely superfluous, with all "the words and explanations of all the buddhas that appear in samsara" being downplayed as insufficient and perhaps even obstructing. In short, Du Fei is hollowing out other forms of Buddhism in order to posit another "form" of tradition that is altogether mystical in the sense of being beyond words, yet unique in holding the singular essence of the buddhas' truth.

There is of course a lot to consider in this claim. For instance, is language really being transcended, or is it executing itself to produce an image of not-itself that nonetheless can abide only in language? Thus, isn't it the case that Du Fei is using language to point beyond language in a way that is doubly dependent on language, first, since it is a claim that obviously exists within the medium of language, and, second, because language is the thing being negated to produce that prized otherness, that sphere beyond language? And why must Du Fei condemn the grand linguistic work of all the buddhas of the universe? Such a statement likely would have seemed blasphemous to Chinese readers, who took texts such as the *Lotus Sūtra* or the *Diamond Sūtra* to be reliable conduits back to the font of tradition and of transcendental value in their own right. Besides the first two problems that this is all taking place *in* language and *through* language, there is the third problem of legitimacy via language. Du Fei's first attempt to legitimize this surprising claim regarding truth-apart-from-language is to turn to Buddhist literature for proof, pointing to another text referred to simply as "a commentary." Hence, claims about the truth of truth-beyond-language require more language to firm themselves up, thereby opening up a kind of endless chain of language to deliver reliable language about the end of language.

Of course, there is the deeper irony that Du Fei's ostensible rejection of language nevertheless led him to initiate the entirely new Buddhist genre of the genealogy of truth-fathers, a genre that would develop unevenly over the following centuries but would, by the early Song, give birth to the standard "lamp histories" that are the basis of modern Chan and Zen. Consequently, Du Fei appears as a crucial inventor of a new way of writing and reading about Buddhist truth in which prior forms of Buddhist literature are disparaged (symbolically killed, actually) by historical figures imagined to be in perfect contact with truth due to their place in the genealogy of truth.

AWAKENING OF FAITH: LITERATURE TO PROVE THE REALM BEYOND LANGUAGE

The unnamed commentary that Du Fei quoted above is the famous *Awakening of Faith (Qixin lun).*[9] This text, written roughly one hundred fifty years before Du Fei's work, is equally interested in discoursing on a place beyond discourse and employs a variety of rhetorics to evoke this sphere beyond language. It also reduces all being to mind, one mind actually, in a total collapse of the universe into buddha-consciousness, which is accorded the name "thusness" and true being. Hence, in this passage Du Fei finds a bold statement of sameness-in-being that comes with the term *equality (pingdeng),* which, though used to describe dharmas, presumably also refers to all beings and the buddhas, who, like all dharmas, are really just this one mind that is beyond change and the threat of destruction.

Contrary to the ease with which Du Fei can move rhetoric on cosmic sameness from the *Awakening of Faith* into his own text, we should not overlook that the two texts represent diametrically opposed techniques for delivering tradition.[10] The *Awakening of Faith,* apparently written in sixth-century China, though pretending to be imported from India, is designed to function like a sūtra and not a lineage text. In fact, besides lacking a lineage, the *Awakening of Faith* concludes its discourse by offering itself as the object of veneration, the object that when tendered homage and transmitted to the next person produces infinite merit.[11] Thus, despite Du Fei's eagerness to rely on this work, the *Awakening of Faith* represents the very kind of sūtra-style cult-of-the-text that Du Fei is trying to overcome. Regardless of this basic antagonism on the level of form, the *Awakening of Faith* seems to have provided several positions that would become standard in later Chan writing.

9. McRae, *The Northern School,* 347 n.2, identifies the passage in *The Awakening of Faith,* T.32.576a; see Yoshito S. Hakeda, the *Awakening of Faith,* 32 ff, for the full context of this passage.

10. For discussion of the *Awakening of Faith*'s placement of itself vis-à-vis the totality of tradition, see my "A Plan for the Past."

11. See T.32.583a.23ff; and Hakeda, *The Awakening of Faith,* 103–4.

DOUBLING BACK: SAMENESS
AND DIFFERENCE ONE MORE TIME

Du Fei follows the quote on cosmic sameness with a longer passage from the *Awakening of Faith* that begins to hierarchize this field of sameness. In this passage we learn of bodhisattvas ascending the stages to total enlightenment; ironically, on their way to realizing total sameness, they create a great gap of difference between those who know this sameness and those who do not. Du Fei writes:

> It also says [in the *Awakening of Faith*], "For those [bodhisattvas] who have achieved bodhicitta *(faxin)* and then course from the level of pure mind *(jingxin)* up to the final [stage], what realm do they achieve? Well, that which is called 'thusness' is called a realm by the [mistaken] mind of rebirth *(zhuanshi)* when in fact there is no realm for this achiever. It is only that 'knowledge of thusness' is being called the dharmakāya."[12]

> Elsewhere a sūtra says, "The bodhisattvas, the great beings, reside alone in a quiet place, awaken themselves and perceive the limit—it doesn't come to them from someone else.[13] Separate from views and misconceptions *(wangxiang)* they ascend and ascend, making progress until they enter the stage of the Tathāgatha. This is what is called the self-enlightening sagely wisdom." Therefore without having obtained the nsurpassed vehicle *(wushangsheng)* and transmission *(chuan)* of the mind-ground *(xindi)*, how could one enter into the realm of truth *(zhenjingjie)*?

What probably first strikes the careful reader of these passages is a tension between realizing truth on one's own, as these bodhisattvas do, and a notion of transmission that is mentioned in the concluding sentence of the passage. In the second of these quotes, the one from the unnamed sūtra, we are invited to imagine bodhisattvas renouncing connections with others in order to achieve total truth on their own.

12. McRae, *The Northern School*, 255, reads this somewhat differently. Hakeda, *The Awakening of Faith*, 27, has yet another take on the passage.

13. This sūtra, it turns out, is the *Laṅkāvatāra Sūtra;* McRae identifies the passage as T.16.497b2. That Du Fei cites this sūtra is interesting because later in his discussion he works to downgrade its importance. Thus, that he chose to cite it in an unattributed manner may be more than happenstance. McRae, *The Northern School*, 256, translates the key line proclaiming the bodhisattva's self-reliance differently—"not depending on any method other [than the One Vehicle] . . ."—which I think is a bit of a stretch and doesn't reflect the self-other tension that seems key to the passage. Perhaps this is the meaning of the passage in the sūtra context, but here it would likely be read otherwise.

Not surprisingly, this vision of the bodhisattvas' success is given the name "self-enlightening sagely wisdom."

The tension between self-enlightenment and transmission becomes even more evident in the final line, where Du Fei turns to insist on exclusive transmission of tradition. This move to privatize enlightenment is clarified in the next line when Du Fei cites the lineage from Huiyuan's preface to the *Meditation Sūtra,* as the Faru stele had, thereby putting this tension between self-enlightenment and a private lineage in clearer relief. He writes:

> The former worthy of Mount Lu, [Hui] Yuan wrote in his preface to the *Meditation Sūtra,* "The Buddha gave it *(fu)* to Ānanda, Ānanda gave it to Madhyāntika, and Madhyāntika gave it to Śāṇavāsa."[14] Thus, [the Buddha] understood perfectly that if henceforth [this transmission] was not to be lost, it must depend on being maintained in the appropriate people.[15] How could those clinging to causes and effects, and investigating the meaning of words and sentences, ever enter into this [truth]?

The first obvious conclusion to draw from this ongoing juxtaposition of self-enlightenment and the genealogical inheritance of tradition is that Du Fei wanted, for some reason, the self-enlightenment of the solitary bodhisattvas, as portrayed in the sūtra quotations, to sit next to a short discussion of a very narrow lineage holding pure tradition. Without addressing this uneasy cohabitation, by citing this short lineage from Huiyuan's preface, Du Fei gives the reader the sense that truth not only follows a conduit but also is held by only one person at a time. Also, the quotations suggests that one shouldn't expect a sharing outward from this lineage that moves from the Buddha to Ānanda to Madhyāntika, and so on, presumably because it moves forward singularly, man-to-man. Furthermore, Du Fei clarifies that this lineage has what others want but can't get due to their various attachments to ineffectual techniques, which are cited as (1) "clinging to causes and effects"; and (2) a kind of scholasticism focused on language.

14. For Huiyuan's preface to the *Meditation Sūtra,* see T.15.301a–b; or T.55.65c–66a; for discussion of Huiyan's text, see McRae, *The Northern School,* 80–82; see also Morrison, "Ancestors, Authority, and History," 19–22.

15. This passage evokes the line from the *Analects* (19.22) about the Way of King Wen and King Wu not yet being lost (lit.: fallen to the ground). Thus, Du Fei is presenting the Indian Buddha as one who understands the transmission of tradition in Confucian terms. This is ironic, in a way, but is of a piece with Du Fei's larger project of convincing Chinese readers of the legitimacy of the imported Buddhist lineage.

BODHIDHARMA'S ARRIVAL

Du Fei follows the above passages with another section on self-caused enlightenment, but, following in this zigzag manner, he then moves on to the explanation of Bodhidharma's lineage:[16]

> Among those who traveled from India and came to this land there was Bodhidharma. Because there was at that time in China a supremely benevolent one [Shenghui zhe: pun on Huike's name], he transmitted *(chuan)* it to him, silently indicating the truth realm. This [transmission of truth to China] was like a weak and moribund person suddenly returning to health. Or again, it was like a great torch being illuminated in a dark room. There are no words that could describe it. But, just as there were some with uniquely lofty dispositions, there were others who just played with what they had studied, and didn't seek supreme wisdom [from Bodhidharma]. Those who were completely changed in receiving [the teachings] were extremely few. It was only Huike of the Eastern Wei, who sought it *(zhi)* with his life; the great master transmitted it *(zhi)* to him and then left.

This passage initiates one of the main themes of the text. Du Fei is beginning to explain the radically superior transmission of total truth from India to China, via Bodhidharma. And, as the metaphors of darkness and sickness make clear, along with the potshots at scholarly decadence, Du Fei's discussion of this perfect form of transmission is energized with a range of insults for other forms of tradition.

Before we analyze what is said in this crucial passage, let's note that by this time in his text, Du Fei has bounced between sections on self-enlightenment and sections on transmission twice. The repetition of this juxtaposition suggests that it isn't accidental or simply an effect of inattentive writing. Quite the contrary, since this juxtaposition seems designed to produce a certain desire in the reader—a desire that was first stoked by the openness of self-enlightenment—but was then postponed or even disavowed as entirely impossible for the reader by the lineage system of moving enlightenment and tradition forward. That is to say, the promise that truth can be won by all, as though it were just a question of effort, is promoted only to be undercut by the assertion that in fact truth is exclusively owned by men in a very elite family who do not share it out except to the next unique master. Clearly, of

---

16. McRae's translation differs significantly here; see *The Northern School,* 256.

the two positions, the latter position that encases truth in the lineage is the one that will dominate, but the prior promise of self-enlightenment seems to rest at the beginning of this privatizing discourse both as an enticement and as an alibi. Moreover, this zigzagging was prepared for by Du Fei's opening lines about the ubiquitous truth-body and the step-by-step transmission system that, though private, would lead all into awareness of buddha-wisdom.

In the above paragraph that introduces Bodhidharma, Du Fei develops a number of other agendas. First, and most aggressively, Chinese Buddhism is being thoroughly undermined. Whatever other Buddhists have been doing in China, they have been far from finding truth and, according to Du Fei, have been lazy, self-satisfied, and unreceptive. Against this background of failure and decadence, Du Fei claims that Bodhidharma had only one full convert, Huike, to whom he transmits "it" *(zhi)*. However, "it" isn't clarified at all here. In fact, Du Fei seems reluctant to say that "it" is enlightenment or buddhahood, or something equally complete. He certainly had plenty of chances to define it or at least label it, though up to now he preferred simply to call it "it" and let the resonances of total truth and super-linguistic realization, established in his introduction, glimmer around this vague attribution of the thing transmitted.

Second, in explaining Bodhidharma's triumphant arrival, Du Fei makes it clear that this singular transmission to Huike was all that mattered, since after Bodhidharma transmits to Huike, he leaves. There isn't any mention here of Bodhidharma caring for the masses or searching out other disciples, something that Daoxuan had explained in his account of Bodhidharma in his *Encyclopedia*. In Du Fei's writing, one recipient is enough, and, in fact, Bodhidharma's abrupt departure suggests that transmission is inherently singular, and, thus, as soon as it was accomplished, Bodhidharma has no reason to stay in China. In fact, this narrowing of Bodhidharma's students to one had already been accomplished; Faru's biography had excluded Bodhidharma's other special student, Daoyu, who in Daoxuan's biography of Bodhidharma had been given status equal to Huike.

Standing back from Du Fei's introduction a couple of things are now clearer. It seems fair to say that the passages cited from the sūtra about self-enlightenment are quite contrary to what Du Fei is saying about Chinese Buddhists, who, supposedly, aren't making any progress, just playing with what they have learned. Arguably, then, according to Du Fei, these self-enlightening bodhisattvas are somewhere else besides

China, and it is only in that *other* sphere that they are making progress toward truth. In short, Du Fei is giving us a decadent China in juxtaposition to another, far superior realm that seems to be none other than India. This conclusion makes sense for a number of reasons. First, the very fact that the account of these self-enlightened bodhisattvas comes in a sūtra means that the reader would be expected to think that it was the Buddha talking about his disciples. Second, though Du Fei doesn't admit it as a problem, he will need to justify Bodhidharma's ownership of enlightenment. Later, when he gives Bodhidharma's biography in detail, there is no mention of Bodhidharma's teacher or Bodhidharma's place in an Indian lineage or his enlightenment moment. Thus, it seems that Du Fei needs to imply that in India there are lots of these self-enlightened bodhisattva types, and Bodhidharma was one of them.

Really, though, Du Fei's rhetoric works to avoid having to get that technical. In place of spelling all this out, he has created an alternative sphere of Buddhists who are the opposite of Chinese Buddhists and who send one of their own to China to stretch that one thin line of truth into an otherwise dark and sickly country. All this adds up to a nostalgia for the perfect Buddhism of India, that wholly other place where Buddhists really practice and where bodhisattvas really achieve enlightenment on their own.

DU FEI'S ANTHROPOLOGY OF THE OTHER

Making these damning generalizations about China in order to proclaim a single redeeming lineage means that Du Fei has to pretend to have knowledge of his contemporaries' spiritual status. Naturally, then, he has to pose as one who really knows, universally, what is and is not known in China. Thus, for the Bodhidharma truth-lineage to be put forward as the unique conduit of total truth, it had to be conjoined with a kind of anthropology of the Other. Just this kind of vision-of-the-Other will manifest itself over and over in Chan rhetoric, since the speaker of total truth is *also* in charge of the global denunciation of all the Others, a denunciation that requires all sorts of impossible knowledges. In the case of Du Fei's introduction, he has quite cleverly established two radically different fields of Buddhist practice: first there is this place of excellent pure practice where bodhisattvas make progress on their own, and then there is this diseased place of laziness where no one makes any progress. With these polar opposites defined, Du Fei has a singular spark cross just this divide. This divide, besides being geographic, represents the divide between those in and outside the lineage in China, since the wholesome valor of that other land of practice will be given to Huike as Bodhidharma supposedly succeeds at being a moving receptacle who condensed all of Indian Buddhism and its unquestionable enlightenment and brought it to otherwise faux-Buddhist China.

What this all implies is that for a Chinese reader to love Bodhidharma, and his Chinese lineage that Du Fei is constructing, he needs to engage in some measure of self-hatred. It is no surprise, then, that throughout the rest of the *Record,* Du Fei keeps reminding his readers that without finding a good teacher they will be completely lost. In essence, then, this vision of nostalgized India not only establishes Bodhidharma's legitimacy; it functions to produce a gap or loss that binds Chinese readers all the more to the lineage since Chinese consumers of the text learn that they have no right to insist on the legitimacy of their Buddhist traditions, nor should they have confidence in their efforts to achieve Buddhist goals on their own.

SHENXIU'S INHERITANCE

Having sketched this split-frame scenario, Du Fei moves into an explanation of the lineage that Bodhidharma established. Following the above passage that recounts how Bodhidharma transmitted to Huike and left China, Du Fei writes:[17]

> Huike transmitted *(chuan)* to Sengcan, Sengcan transmitted to Daoxin, Daoxin transmitted to Hongren, Hongren transmitted to Faru, Faru *passed it (jihu)* to The Great Perceiver (Datong, Shenxiu). From Bodhidharma on down, teacher and disciple *(shizi)* [in turn] opened the Way. All were skilled in using upāya to obtain verification of the mind *(guzhen yuxin);* and they responded [only] to what was asked and didn't offer complicated explanations.

While this short passage efficiently moves Bodhidharma's pure origins into the present, it also reveals a rather interesting problem that T. Griffith Foulk pointed out to me many years ago.[18] Clearly, Du Fei wants to put Shenxiu in this track running back to Bodhidharma, but the suturing isn't smooth because Du Fei doesn't say that Shenxiu got

---

17. See McRae, *The Northern School,* 257, for a slightly different rendering.
18. Pers. com., 1992, University of Michigan.

perfect tradition directly but rather that it was "passed" to him by Faru and not formally transmitted. Similarly, Du Fei doesn't tell us that Hongren gave transmission to both Shenxiu and Faru. In short, Du Fei is keeping things decidedly ill-defined. The parameters of this problem will become clearer when we consider Shenxiu's biography as Du Fei develops it below, but for now let's note the irony of this indirectness and vagueness right where there is supposed to be absolute directness in a perfect kind of extralinguistic transmission of total truth. Similarly, we shouldn't overlook the contradiction of Du Fei insisting that all the truth-ancestors "didn't offer complicated explanations" when, in fact, creating just this image of simple truth-telling masters is taking a lot of complicated maneuvering.

BAD VERSIONS OF BODHIDHARMA

With the basic lineage recounted and Shenxiu's place at least tenuously established at the end of it, Du Fei's next gesture is to refute another text's attempt to present Bodhidharma. He writes:[19]

> Nowadays in oral and/or written form, there is a discourse called "Bodhi-dharma's Treatise" *(Damo lun)*. This must be the work of some students who, on their own initiative, took it to be a true discourse, wrote it down and treasured it, but it is full of errors *(duo miu)*. Transcendent enlighten-ment *(chaowu)*, which is received in the succession *(xiangcheng)* [of the lineage], is obtained in mind. Thus how could there be any sound, not to mention language and written words, which would be interposed between them [i.e., the masters]?

Du Fei's denunciation of "Bodhidharma's Treatise" warrants reflection. Why is Du Fei attacking the supposed attempt to record Bodhidharma's teaching? Aside from accusing these student-stenographers of being immature, he hasn't really explained the inherent impossibility of the situation. Whatever his motivations might have been vis-à-vis "Bodhidharma's Treatise," at the very least we can see that with this vehement charge Du Fei is moving the discussion of Bodhidharma away from content—that is, away from any supposed teaching—and confining discussions to the history of Bodhidharma, that is, his role in delivering total tradition from India. In short, Du Fei focuses on the function of Bodhidharma as the connector to India and has no use for

---

19. See McRae, *The Northern School*, 257, for an alternative reading.

any content that had been previously associated with him, content that could disrupt the image of total tradition that Du Fei needs to both put in and pull out of Bodhidharma in order to establish Shenxiu as a Chinese buddha.

Key to reading this passage is the fact that Du Fei is directly invalidating his main source—Daoxuan's *Encyclopedia*—since Daoxuan's entry for Bodhidharma had endorsed the claim that Bodhidharma taught the *Two Entrances and Four Practices,* which is presumably what is being called "Bodhidharma's Treatise" in the above passage. (A later statement by Du Fei makes this connection clearer.) Moreover, Daoxuan had approvingly quoted from the *Two Entrances and Four Practices* in his entry for Bodhidharma, so this seems to be an especially glaring moment when Du Fei undermined his sources to strip Bodhidharma of any specific teaching and to disenfranchise all those who had been following his public, textual teaching.[20] Seeing how Du Fei so fully upended Daoxuan's account of Bodhidharma is crucial since Du Fei will do something similar to Huike.

ABOUT THIS BOOK

In the wake of denouncing the attempt to identify any content in Bodhidharma's teaching, Du Fei offers an analogy for understanding the relationship between texts and truth that leaves little doubt regarding how he wants to position truth in the eyes of the public:[21]

> For those who can't see to the ultimate, it is convenient to point to small things in order to elucidate large things. This is like the case of mundane [i.e., non-Buddhist] teachings on the smelting of true cinnabar in order to [consume it and] ascend to heaven in broad daylight—you have to find a celestial being *(xian ren)* to physically [lit., "by body and hand"] give you transmission of the smelting [process] for true cinnabar to be obtained. If you rely on the emerald-like words in the jade-like books you will, in the end, be lost. This is just a worldly example of such an exigency [of relying on a teacher], so what need is there to mention the case of the unsurpassed essence of truth *(wushang zhenzong)*—how could it be wrapped up in words and explanations? Thus this Way is subtle and secret; rare it is to obtain this door.
>
> Though dharma doesn't rely on men, and meaning doesn't rely on language, still how could I watch the demise of these true good spiritual

---

20. For Daoxuan's entry for Bodhidharma, see T.50.551b.27 ff.
21. See McRae, *The Northern School,* 257, for his rendering of the passage.

friends? Today these outstanding men are not invoked, and it is not easy
to name them. Thus, to dispel the ignorance of those in future times, and
to allow them to admire [these matters], I have today prepared a short
account from Bodhidharma onward, [explaining] how the dharma was
handed down in successive transmissions *(xiangcheng chuanfa)* in the
text that follows, which is called the "Record of the Transmission of
the Dharma-Jewel" in one folio.

This passage presents a classic example of the rhetoric that became
essential to Chan literature. Starting at the top, there is the conde-
scending trope that positions the reader as short-sighted and in need
of a technique for vision, a technique that will be given but with the
understanding that it will be incomplete and temporary. Like Du Fei's
comments about the state of Chinese Buddhism before Bodhidharma
arrived, here the reader learns that Du Fei has to dumb down the message and speak metaphorically, only partially indicating the "large
things" by referring to the small. This unavoidable gap between (little)
presentation and (big) referent then is developed in the metaphor about
trying to get alchemical success out of a recipe book in the absence of
a celestial being who presumably has already effected the alchemical
success himself.

Clearly, Du Fei's point is that just as a Daoist recipe book for
alchemical transformations is useless without an accomplished teacher
on hand, so, too, is a Buddhist text on enlightenment. The implication
is that Du Fei is including his own text in this category of public texts
and is insisting, as he will later more explicitly, that his own writing is
useless unless one finds the private lineage that owns the "unsurpassed
essence of truth." Put metaphorically, the reader is being handed one
line of a couplet whose content is none other than directions for finding
the other line that rhymes with it, with the second line being essential
not simply for completing the rhyme but also for giving the first line the
right to speak about the second line. Thus, what is being transmitted
in this text about transmission is clearly not enlightenment but this
desire to complete the couplet—to find the lineage that rhymes with
this lineage text. In short, the reader enters into the lineage fantasy,
not by becoming a member, but by being the conduit-of-recognition
that receives the literary account of the lineage and then links it to
living representatives who supposedly belong to that lineage and own
the pure content of tradition.

Having given an official raison d'être for the text, Du Fei briefly
mentions his technique for writing it. He announces that he is simply

combining the "traces" of what was personally seen and heard, or what was recorded in books. Thus, his account lays claim to a kind of historical certainty based on the retrieval of first-person perceptions and trustworthy archives. This, of course, is one of the soft spots in Du Fei's discourse: he is admitting that he is relying on language and narrative, and in some cases narratives admittedly quite distant from him, to produce a narrative about an essence that pretends to be beyond narrative.

After establishing the sources of his account, Du Fei softens his exclusionary focus on these few masters by saying that in any era there are enlightened ones, and he adds that he regrets not mentioning such figures here. This comment seems odd here since it goes against the position he took in the introduction, where he denounced Chinese Buddhism as decadent and misguided, and it will run counter to what he will say below in his account of jealous monks and pedantic scholars who supposedly regularly attacked Bodhidharma and his lineage members. It would seem that this gesture of respect for those excluded masters sits right here because he is in the midst of talking about his archival sources, and clearly these sources present many more masters than the six that Du Fei pulls out. Thus, when discussing his historical sources, he wants to appear gentle and not destroy the literary font of his narrative, but when it comes to the general politics of Chinese Buddhism, he allows himself to be harsh and partisan. Of course, once we can compare Du Fei's "history" with what must have been his sources, we will see that he has done much more than simply piece together textual narratives and first-person accounts, and thus it could be argued that he has committed more than a little symbolic violence on the living and the dead.

With this basic introduction in place, Du Fei lists the lineage members and the monasteries where they lived. This list serves, in part, to provide the reader with an outline of the biographies to follow, but it also sits in the text as a more vivid presentation of the lineage as one essential body that can be "seen" at once. Presumably Du Fei added this redundant listing—he had just listed the series of transmissions in prose format—simply to give a condensed version of the lineage that otherwise might be diluted by the series of biographies that follows, as well as to focus attention on their respective places of residence.[22]

22. As McRae and others have noted, it is interesting to see that in this earliest of lineage texts, no numbers are offered to clarify placement in the lineage; see his *The Northern School*, 88.

THE BODHIDHARMA REMIX

Before giving a close reading of Du Fei's presentation of Bodhidharma,
I should remind the reader that Du Fei's biography of Bodhidharma
comes in the wake of at least three prior textual statements about the
life of Bodhidharma.[23] However, Du Fei's is the most developed of these
early accounts and clearly has embellished contents found in the earlier
accounts. Following the above discussion, Du Fei writes:[24]

> Bodhidharma was the third son in a Brahman family in southern India.
> He was gifted spiritually *(jishen)* and completely enlightened *(chaowu),*
> and he transmitted *(chuan)* the great dharma-jewel with enlightenment
> and sagely wisdom; and, for the sake of gods and men *(rentian),* he widely
> opened the knowledge and insight of the Buddha.[25] [Then], for the sake
> of those of us in the country of China, he navigated the oceans, and came
> to Mount Song. At the time, he was hardly recognized. It was only Daoyu
> and Huike, with the potential to understand derived from previous lives,
> who vigorously sought it, serving the teacher for six years, intent on
> obtaining thorough enlightenment *(tongwu).*
> At that time, Bodhidharma said to Huike, "Would you be able to
> give your life for the dharma?" Huike cut off his arm to prove his sincer-
> ity *(chengken). (Another account says that it was cut off by bandits,
> but that was an erroneous account circulated for a brief time.)* From
> then on [transmission] was secretly effected *(kaifa)* with upāya [skillful
> means]. *(This upāya for effecting [transmission] is something that only
> masters and their disciples (shizi) secretly employ, thus there is no way
> to represent it in language.)* Then Bodhidharma suddenly *(dun)* caused
> his [Huike's] mind to directly enter *(zhiru)* into the dharma realm *(fajie).*

In the first half of this cryptic passage we only learn about the spectacular qualities and achievements of Bodhidharma. There are no details
given about his entry into the sangha, his teachers, his teaching, the
texts he preferred, the practices he advocated, or what he felt about his
entourage. Instead the account focuses on his successes. He transmitted
the dharma-jewel with enlightenment and sagely wisdom, presumably
for the chosen elite, though this isn't made explicit, and gave the masses
a vision of buddha-knowledge, thereby fulfilling the two tasks that Du

---

23. See chapter 3 for more discussion of these sources.
24. See McRae, *The Northern School,* 258–59, for an alternate translation.
25. McRae (*The Northern School,* 258) reads this to say that Bodhidharma received
transmission, but the grammar and context suggest the opposite: he is supposedly transmitting the dharma-jewel but, in line with Du Fei's prior comments, this kind of open
transmission to the public is only happening in India, before he arrives in China.

Fei will assign to each of the following truth-masters that he is in the process of creating.

Once in China, everything changes, however. Bodhidharma's capacity for successfully reproducing and exteriorizing the dharma is completely squelched. Whereas in India his success appeared unrestricted in both the public sphere of teaching and the private sphere of transmission, in China he meets with resistance and nonrecognition. This image of rejection, in fact, serves a number of polemical purposes. First, it allows Du Fei to funnel Bodhidharma into an exclusionary lineage, since by making Huike Bodhidharma's only "real" student, Du Fei can cut off any other attempt to create a lineage back to Bodhidharma. However, there is an obvious problem here: Du Fei notes that Bodhidharma gave transmission to Huike *and* Daoyu, even though Du Fei will clarify in other sections of his text that only Huike is the real inheritor. This problem seems to reflect the conflict between the need to singularize the flow of transmission and the fact that in Bodhidharma's entry in Daoxuan's *Encyclopedia,* Daoyu appears as a full recipient of Bodhidharma's teaching and an equal to Huike. In the above passage, Du Fei allows Daoyu to be an earnest seeker of Bodhidharma's truth, but in the next paragraph he focuses solely on Bodhidharma's relationship with Huike, thereby effectively removing Daoyu without explaining what happened to him.

Actually, creating this uniqueness in Bodhidharma's transmission performs a more important function. By saying that Bodhidharma gave his transmission only to Huike, due to the blindness of everyone else, Du Fei has created an alibi for himself along the lines of, "Don't accuse me of favoring the privatization of enlightenment in the early eighth century, since, after all, when it was publicly given some two hundred years ago, China universally rejected it. Thus enlightenment's eighth-century privateness is a function of China's past ignorance, not my own current partisanship." Moreover, in this alibi, a thoroughly privatized enlightenment is poised to be given back to those Chinese Buddhists who, in light of Du Fei's charges, exist with a kind of original sin against Bodhidharma. The Chinese, save for Huike and his companion Daoyu, rejected Bodhidharma, and more, as we will read, persecuted him and even killed him.

Thus, the reader is given a sense that not only is there a treasure to behold here—a chance to glimpse a jewel that earlier Buddhists ignored—but it is doubly worth revering Bodhidharma, given the injustices that were visited on such a kind and innocent figure during his stay in China. Implicit, too, is the attempt to draw the reader into righting the wrongs of history (as constructed by Du Fei, of course) by respecting that history-of-wrongs—Du Fei's narrative, that is. Thus, one can rise above one's ignorant predecessors to give due respect to such an august character by respecting Du Fei's account, since to believe Du Fei's reconstruction is to side with "truth" against injustice and ineptitude. Along with this offer to right the evils of history, one is being given an explicit example of failure-to-recognize truth, making any resistance to Du Fei's text appear as an echo of this prior resistance. In short, there is the subtle suggestion that whatever resistance there is to Du Fei's text, it is just a replay of a long series of Chinese failures to recognize Bodhidharma and his truth.

TRUTH: JUST AN ARM'S LENGTH AWAY

In Du Fei's construction of the transmission moment between Bodhidharma and Huike, it is crucial to see that, as with Faru's moment with Hongren, Huike isn't said to actually learn something new, or awaken to some Buddhist truth. Instead, Bodhidharma "suddenly *(dun)* caused his [Huike's] mind to directly enter *(zhiru)* into the dharma realm *(fajie)*." Moreover, the overall structure of the vignette suggests that this happens after Huike has shown his sincerity by serving Bodhidharma for six years and, of course, by cutting off his arm. Thus, there is a clear quid pro quo logic organizing this crucial juncture when real Buddhism enters China and takes up residence in a Chinese body. By creating the story of Huike's arm offering, Du Fei is obviously implying that the gift of total truth can only be given to one who has risen above notions of selfish ownership, for that is what Bodhidharma's question implies: you must be willing to die for this in order to inherit it. As in most mythologies with this sort of suicide trope, all that needs to happen at this impossible juncture is for a facsimile of the willingness to die to be demonstrated. This is exactly what Huike does; he offers his arm in a gift that solidifies the parameters of their exchange by proving his boundless sincerity, his ardor, and his selflessness.

The gift structure of this moment has a number of interesting implications. First, according to Du Fei's logic, the dharma comes to China through the unique conjunction of Bodhidharma's wisdom with Huike's filial willingness to sacrifice himself. As these two elements meet, truth now is installed in China, with Huike's bodily offering and his total submission anchoring that reception. Moreover, the terminology here is telling. By using the Confucian-tinged adjective *chengken* to label Huike's sincerity, Du Fei is painting Huike as something like the only good son in China. He is the only one who knew, in a Confucianesque manner, how to treat the father, and consequently got the father's patrimony. Second, the structure of this gift-giving ought to encourage us to see that Chan isn't the further sinification of Chinese Buddhism simply in terms of doctrines, but also in terms of how it has formulated the "life" of tradition. Thus, regardless of content, in terms of form, Du Fei has installed Buddhist truth in China via a Chinese model of a father-son exchange wherein the son offers up his body, sincerity, and his service, as the father coldly passes on his essence and then disappears. That is, just when Du Fei is explaining the full entrance of Buddhism into China, he relies on Confucian forms and terms to frame this moment and make it appear legitimate and attractive. Or put negatively, Du Fei has said nothing about Huike's Buddhist qualities that made this event occur; rather, for Du Fei, it was Huike's fully Chinese, that is, Confucian, qualities that got foreign Buddhism into a Chinese body.

HOW HUIKE TWICE LOST HIS ARM TO BUDDHIST HISTORIANS

The Confucian aspects of this transmission moment appear more clearly when we consider Du Fei's comment that according to another account, bandits amputated Huike's arm. In fact, this account of the bandit attack is in the reworked section of Huike's entry in Daoxuan's *Encyclopedia*, which is presumably Du Fei's primary source for the Bodhidharma-Huike relationship. Also, no other prior source has been found to corroborate Huike's arm offering as Du Fei has presented it, nor does he cite one. Thus, assuming that Du Fei went to Daoxuan's *Encyclopedia* for source material, and this seems undeniable, he would have found in the second part of Huike's biography a strange passage that explains that not only was Tanlin's (ca. 506–74) arm cut off by bandits but Huike's was as well. It seems that Tanlin was known as "one-armed Lin" in other sources prior to Daoxuan, so we are probably right to assume that Tanlin actually lost his arm to bandits.[26]

---

26. For more details on Tanlin and his activities in the sixth and seventh centuries, see Broughton, *The Bodhidharma Anthology*, 143 n. 24. Broughton (144 n. 26) supplies pre-Daoxuan sources for Tanlin's moniker "Armless Tan"; for instance, see T.37.22a.19, where Jizang refers to him as *wubi Lin*, "no-arm Lin."

However, in the case of Huike, whereas the first part of his biography doesn't have this remarkable detail, the second section presents him as one-armed Tanlin's doppelgänger. In a brief sketch we learn that Tanlin complained about his arm loss, but Huike accepted the pain stoically. Thus, in this interpolated section of Huike's biography, which was dedicated to lionizing Huike and identifying him as Fachong's dharma-ancestor, Huike's overall master status was upgraded with this story of his magical ability to accept enormous pain. Of course, the irony is that the material for this story emphasizing his uniqueness was generated by transposing details from Tanlin's life on to Huike and then having Huike play the hero while Tanlin was reduced to serving as a whimpering foil.[27]

To really get at what Du Fei has done with these prior narratives about Bodhidharma and Huike, we also need to note that in Daoxuan's account of their interaction, there is a transmission of sorts, but it isn't sudden, and it lacks the violent arm offering. Thus, Daoxuan writes, "Huike came to cherish him [Bodhidharma] as a treasure, realizing that Bodhidharma embodied the path. In a single glance Bodhidharma was pleased with him, and Huike came to serve Bodhidharma as his master."[28] Though the rest of this passage contains comments about Huike's further mastery of Bodhidharma's teaching, there is no mention of an arm offering, or Bodhidharma's stern question, "Would you be able to give your life for the dharma?"

Thus, in Daoxuan's entry, Huike plays out his full relationship with Bodhidharma without offering his arm or facing such a challenging sudden moment. Similarly, in Daoxuan's entries for Bodhidharma and Huike, transmission wasn't specified as a particular event, save perhaps for that knowing glance from Bodhidharma, but at any rate it wasn't

---

27. Adamek (*The Mystique of Transmission*, 146–52) deals with the expansion of the Huike stories. However, her reading of the stories seems hampered by never clarifying what they were intended to do (their seduction value and polemical purposes) and never explaining how authors read each other and then deformed the stories as they saw fit. Instead of building a discussion from these elemental issues, Adamek, following Faure, jumps to read these stories as articulating and dramatizing philosophic paradigms of no-thought. Of course, some readers might find this "philosophical" style of interpretation more to their liking (and certainly this has been the overall tendency in the field), but, as I have been arguing, this style of reading misses how and why these stories were so regularly rewritten. Also, as a point of fact, and it certainly isn't a big problem: the account of Bodhidharma giving Huike his name "Able" *(ke)* first appears in Duge Pei's *Treatise Defining the True and False*, not in the *Baolin zhuan*, as Adamek claims (147); see chap. 6 below for references and more discussion.

28. Translation from Broughton, *The Bodhidharma Anthology*, 57–58; see T. 50.552a.3.

dressed up as a sudden entry into truth. Thus, we have to ask, How did these bland narrative segments get turned into this much more dramatic episode? My guess is that Du Fei not only recombined elements already present in Daoxuan's entry—reworking Huike's arm loss into an arm donation, for instance—but he also combined these elements with material from Faru's stele, especially in terms of the suddenness of the Hongren–Faru transmission. It was presumably in this way that he took the Hongren–Faru transmission scene from Faru's biography and transposed it onto Bodhidharma and Huike in order to renarrate that encounter in a way contrary to Daoxuan's presentation but in line with Faru's sudden encounter with Hongren, as found in the Faru biography.

Reading Du Fei's narrative as the effect of transposing a variety of earlier mini-narratives makes good sense when we consider that this Bodhidharma-Huike scene was already doubled in the second section of Huike's biography in Daoxuan's *Encyclopedia*. Hence, against the simplicity of the first layer's account of Huike's relationship to Bodhidharma—just quoted above—the second layer of Huike's biography in Daoxuan explains that Bodhidharma gave Huike a specific kind of transmission, and it came in the form of handing over the *Laṅkāvatāra Sūtra*, set up in this section of Huike's biography as the fetish-of-tradition. In Daoxuan's *Encyclopedia*, Bodhidharma supposedly said to Huike, "When I examine the land of China, it is clear that there is only this sūtra. If you rely on it to practice, you will be able to cross over the world [to nirvana]."[29] This version of their encounter is obviously designed to highlight the *Laṅkāvatāra Sūtra* as the essence of tradition—a trope that was the basic point of rewriting Huike's biography so that he would serve as Fachong's distant ancestor from whom he received the essence of tradition in the form of the *Laṅkāvatāra Sūtra*.

What comes next in this section of Huike's biography is that passage describing how Huike lost his arm to bandits, along with a bizarre meal scene that contrasts Tanlin's failure to handle the pain to Huike's unshaking stoicism. Thus, in Daoxuan's *Encyclopedia*, Huike's arm loss isn't hooked to the transmission of tradition at all but seems designed solely to make Huike look more like an unthinkably tough master. Following the meal scene with Tanlin, we learn that Huike often taught the *Laṅkāvatāra Sūtra*, but he complained that in four

---

29. Translation from Broughton, *The Bodhidharma Anthology*, 62, with addition of the bracketed phrase; T.50.552b.20ff.

generations, study of it would "degenerate into mere doctrinal terminology." After this prediction, the narrative jarringly launches into a proto-lineage with mini-biographies for Huike's supposed students—masters Na and Huiman—set within the claim that pure Buddhism is moved forward by transmitting the *Laṅkāvatāra Sūtra*. Clearly, then, in the rewritten section of Huike's biography, there is a series of awkward narrative elements that contradict the first section of Huike's biography and seem clearly designed to accomplish three things: (1) to fetishize tradition into the *Laṅkāvatāra Sūtra*; (2) to explain how Huike came to properly "own" this text, with the promise from Bodhidharma that it would deliver Buddhist success like no other text; and (3) to build a quasi-lineage of masters of the *Laṅkāvatāra Sūtra* who supposedly descended from Huike.

With such extensive rewriting evident in Daoxuan's *Encyclopedia* entry for Huike, it seems likely that Du Fei wrote his own account of the Bodhidharma–Huike relationship by piecing together elements from someone else's messy attempt to build a transmission story for Huike. Besides seeing this rather startling rewrite in Daoxuan's *Encyclopedia*, Du Fei would have most assuredly also known how this material had been rewritten in Faru's biography (more on this point below). Thus, I believe Du Fei rewrote Huike's biography, and the whole Bodhidharma story, knowing full well that he was the third author to take up the task of recombining these elements to make a convincing story about how the essence of Buddhism came to China.

The way Du Fei reconstructed Huike's arm loss is actually quite ingenious. With a subtle sleight of pen, Huike's arm no longer is lost in a moment of casual violence as it is in the second layer of Huike's biography in Daoxuan's *Encyclopedia,* and instead it is now cut off as the grand offering that allows Huike to fulfill his side of the exchange with the life-demanding Bodhidharma. Of course, in generating this mini-narrative, Du Fei is recycling an arm that had, actually, never been lost; this fact, however, did not prohibit it from being offered as the gift that won China access to perfect Buddhism.

Creating Huike's fleshy offering does two other things as well. First, Huike's dedication to Bodhidharma's dharma gets ample proof in the cutting of Huike's flesh. Daoxuan's account noted that Huike, after the bandit attack, simply took care of the wound and went about his business, but in Du Fei's hands, Huike *performs* this auto-mutilation and does so heroically. In a later passage Du Fei notes that there was "no change in his expression," and thus clearly the auto-amputation becomes a mark of Huike's fortitude in the face of the brutally demanding father and unthinkable pain. In all this, there can be no doubt that Huike appears as one who has fully won the title, "master." Second, invisible enlightenment that supposedly passed from mind to mind gains some reality with the stunningly visible gift of the amputated arm. "Seeing" this arm in the narrative, the reader naturally assumes that Huike must have gotten something equally weighty in return.

Since Huike's gift became a central node of Chan mythology and Chan art, it is worth considering, more closely, the logic of this founding myth.[30] Like so many gifts in religion, the gift "upward" is useless to the recipient. What is Bodhidharma going to do with an amputated limb, anyway?[31] Thus, the arm gift functions on another level where the gift given isn't received; it simply needs to be given. Thus, it is the degree to which Huike will suffer loss of himself—his happiness, his wholeness—that causes Bodhidharma to restore another kind of happiness and wholeness to him. This point warrants reflection because Du Fei has already established a rhetoric of "fundamental mind" in his preface, and thus Huike is the one who gives of himself to get himself back from the master, a dialectic that I think is key for Chan rhetoric in general.

In addition to demonstrating the structure of this kind of gift exchange, Huike's founding gesture works as a kind of forbidding challenge. If it took Huike this much of an offering to get truth, many readers are going to think maybe it would be better just to admire truth from a distance. On this level, Du Fei's story reads much like a popular Confucian story regarding what an especially filial son would do for his parents. Thus, in line with a splendidly filial son like Wang Xiang who lay on the ice to melt a hole so that he could retrieve fish for his

---

30. If I am right about Du Fei reworking Huike's biography, then we ought to pause to appreciate the ironic imbalance between the ease of altering a given historical account and the effect that this alteration has had on generations of readers. After Du Fei's creative reworking of a phrase or two from Daoxuan's account, the rest of China (then Japan, Korea, and Vietnam and now the whole world) had to labor under the image of Huike's awe-inspiring sacrifice.

31. The uselessness of the "flesh from below" that moves backward in time from youth to seniority is to be contrasted with later accounts of this exchange that have Bodhidharma explain which of his students will receive essential parts of his body—his skin, flesh, bones, and so on—with Huike getting his bones, thereby turning the origin of Chan in China into a kind of human sacrifice—but now a sacrifice of the master, Bodhidharma, instead of the disciple, Huike. For an example of this later trope, see *Jing de chuandeng lu*, T.51.219c1 ff.

mother in winter, Huike's story is an extravagant homily on the devotion expected toward the parental figure, who holds truth and access to one's fullest identity.

SUDDEN MASTER-MAKING

Besides seeing what Du Fei has done with Huike's arm, we need to recognize how he has inserted suddenness into this scene, a suddenness that had not been in Daoxuan's version. In the above passage, Du Fei writes, "Bodhidharma *suddenly (dun)* caused his [Huike's] mind to directly enter into the dharma realm." What might this suddenness mean? Clearly, Bodhidharma is the one who has the capacity to effect such drastic shifts in the Other. And the suddenness of Huike's entrance into total truth seems to rhyme with the suddenness of his self-mutilation; both are abrupt actions that cross lines to establish new frontiers: a piece of Huike goes from his side to Bodhidharma's, and the dharma-jewel of Bodhidharma goes in the opposite direction into Huike. Thus, Bodhidharma refathered Huike in a mighty moment that ends Huike's old identity and installs him in the lineage of truth-fathers who, apparently, abide in the "dharma realm."[32]

This suddenness warrants reflection on another level, too. Writing at a time when Chinese Buddhists were continually unsure of how to interpret Indian Buddhism, Du Fei has created a remarkable hermeneutical scheme that can be put this way: total truth came from India and was directly and suddenly lodged in Huike. Consequently, suddenness serves as an end to interpretation, as well as the basis of a very defendable polemical position. Du Fei isn't claiming that Huike actually learned some new content, content that then could be challenged by other Buddhists as secondary or incomplete, given their own construction of Buddhist truths. Suddenness in Du Fei's hands means

---

32. In thinking about the violence of the sudden boundary-crossing that is being effected in this narrative, we shouldn't forget the story of how Guṇabhadra supposedly learned Chinese perfectly, after he dreamed that a man dressed in white and carrying a sword and a head appeared to him and cut off Guṇabhadra's head and replaced it with the one he had brought, thereby allowing him to speak Chinese fluently upon waking. For a translation of this story from the first *Gaoseng zhuan*, see Robert Shih, *Biographies des moines éminents (Kao Seng Tchouan) de Houei-Kiao. Part I,* 151. Obviously, in this story, the swapping of heads is used to signify Guṇabhadra's new Chinese-speaking identity and thereby supplies the ground for a more intimate translation/transmission of Indian Buddhism into China.

that there is no room for debate. Huike's mind was *put suddenly and directly into truth*—end of discussion. Arguably, the model at work here is much more akin to a coronation or formal investiture in a public office than to a meditative experience.

Given the importance that Du Fei is hanging on this kind of master-disciple moment of suddenness, it is no surprise that he reminds us that this exchange is secret and beyond words. Thus, that crucial link between master and disciple remains something that can be known only as an abstract fact, never in terms of real content known to pass from the patriarch to his descendant. Thus, this secret upāya can only be known negatively. The reader now knows that he can't know about that private exchange between the two links in the chain. Thus, as usual in these texts, Du Fei is publicizing an open secret for the clear purpose of making that link desirable in the eyes of those who will not be privy to the content of the secret, content that they are, nonetheless, being asked to believe in.

THE *LAṄKĀVATĀRA SŪTRA:* NOTHING BUT A HAND-ME-DOWN

With this part of the transmission between India and China in place, Du Fei turns to the problematic role of the *Laṅkāvatāra Sūtra,* a topic that he will treat in an ambivalent manner. The problem was that this Indian text figures in Daoxuan's account of Bodhidharma and Huike in a complex way, because in Bodhidharma's biography there is no mention of the text, but in the rewritten section of Huike's biography, as we have just seen, there are awkward lines explaining that Bodhidharma transmitted the *Laṅkāvatāra Sūtra* to Huike as the Thing that made transmission real. Thus, if Du Fei was intent on lodging tradition in a Chinese body, as he most assuredly was, he had before him the task of first taking it out of the *Laṅkāvatāra Sūtra.* Following the above passage, Du Fei works to harmonize his preferred man-to-man transmission with the contradictory claim in the second part of Huike's biography that transmission of the *Laṅkāvatāra Sūtra* is the standard. He writes:[33]

> Four or five years later [after the transmission], looking for textual confirmation *(wenzhao),* he [Bodhidharma] took the *Laṅkāvatāra Sūtra* and

---

33. See McRae, *The Northern School,* 259, for a slightly different reading.

gave it to Huike saying, "I see that in the land of China, this text alone
is suitable for converting students *(huadaozhe)*."[34] For students who
did not yet understand [truth], he personally transmitted it *(shouchuan)*
many times saying, "Take this as the future cause [of enlightenment]."
*(According to another extant biography [zhuan] there is mention of
wall-contemplation and the four practices, but they were just provisional
[techniques] for conversion, used once upon a time. There may be traces
of this teaching in circulation and someone may have collected them, but
they are not his final position [zhilun].)*

In this passage, and it seems obvious once you look at it closely, Du
Fei is deftly working against alternative accounts of Bodhidharma's
transmission, acknowledging them but only as secondary techniques
designed to accommodate beginners. Thus, in addition to claiming
that Bodhidharma transmitted the *Laṅkāvatāra Sūtra* to Huike as
a supplement useful for instructing future students, the mention of
"wall-contemplation" and the "four practices" makes it fairly certain
that we were right in assuming above that when Du Fei denounced a
Bodhidharma text that he referred to as "Bodhidharma's Treatise," he
was referring to the *Two Entrances and Four Practices (Erru sixing
lun)*, which includes "wall-contemplation" and the "four practices."
Hence, in this passage Du Fei takes on the two texts that other works
had claimed were associated with Bodhidharma—the *Laṅkāvatāra
Sūtra* and the *Two Entrances and Four Practices*—and disparages them
as second-rate techniques, even as he gives them a place at the table.

The first part of the passage downplays the importance of the transmission of the *Laṅkāvatāra Sūtra*, relegating it to a secondary teaching for those who did not understand truth, thereby undermining its
singular importance in Huike's and Fachong's biographies in Daoxuan.
Moreover, in terms of narrative construction, by saying that this textual
transmission event between Bodhidharma and Huike occurred four or
five years after the more dramatic transmission involving Huike's arm
sacrifice, Du Fei seems to be separating the two transmissions, with the
first being the one that matters. Moreover, Du Fei has cleverly identified
textuality, and the *Laṅkāvatāra Sūtra* in particular, as a stigmatized,
secondary measure that Bodhidharma employed in a dumbed-down
version of tradition in order to match Chinese limitations. The derisive
attitude toward the text is made clearer in the line about giving it to

34. This line seems close to the one in the reworked section of Huike's biography in
Daoxuan's *Encyclopedia;* see T. 50.552b.20.

students "who did not yet understand," a point made even clearer when Du Fei adds that this kind of transmission was a cause for their future enlightenment, signaling again that the transmission of the text was not a final transmission at all, as the one to Huike supposedly was.

The above passages also draw an opposition between the way Bodhidharma adapted his teaching for the lesser recipients but demanded a total sacrifice of Huike. Thus, in the exchange of enlightenment for the arm, though Du Fei labeled it a secret upāya, Bodhidharma's sudden installation of Huike into the dharma realm doesn't appear as an expedient means in the sense of being a watered-down version of the truth. On the other hand, according to Du Fei, all the other lesser students got expedient means in the sense of these partial and yet more palatable dispensations of truth. Thus, on one level, Du Fei is arguing, in line with the logic of the *Lotus Sūtra,* that to make the message palatable to the student is a mark of the message's secondary, and even decadent, nature.

This position is particularly interesting given that one could see Du Fei's whole project as one of adapting Indian truth to a Chinese situation and therefore decidedly decadent according to the logic Du Fei just constructed. That is, in the passage on Huike's arm offering, he has constructed a theory for transmitting truth that appears more Indian in *content* but only by housing that supposedly pure Indian content in a Chinese-looking *form,* with a Confucianesque "direct" exchange between master and disciple making the transmission look legitimate. In other words, for Chinese readers, this construction of transmission will appear more legitimate not because its content matches its assumed foreign source but because its form of delivery matches Chinese notions of a legitimate source and its rightful trans-mission to the recipient—a Confucian-style paternal transmission, that is.

In the second part of the above passage, Du Fei casts doubt on the other textual account that he was apparently familiar with. This other text with wall-contemplation and the four practices is undercut as "provisional" *(quan),* which simply means secondary teachings given in consideration of the audience's limitations and not representative of the teacher's final view. Having hollowed out these competing claims to authenticity via textuality, content, and practice, Du Fei fills the void with nothing other than the image of an India-to-China lineage, and the promise that buddhahood is in fact passed on through that conduit. Du Fei's content, then, is an explanation of pure content's arrival in historical time, an explanation that does not in any way describe that content but clarifies who owns it and why.

THE MASTER'S DEATH: A DAOIST TRIUMPH

The few lines that Du Fei gives us on Bodhidharma's death are fascinating for invoking a kind of Buddhist sectarian violence, and for adapting a scenario that had been closely associated with Tang-era stories describing Laozi's death. Following directly from above:[35]

> After this, Bodhidharma's students grew daily and at this juncture well-known monks became deeply jealous and, after biding their time, found an occasion to put poison in his food. . . . The great master knew of this and ate it, but the poison was unable to harm him. After this, one saw many occasions when he ate poison. He told Huike, "I came due to the dharma, and now I have transmitted it to you, there is no point in me staying here, I am going to leave." Gathering his followers *(menren)* he again explained the ultimate meaning of his teaching *(zongji)*, and again ate poison, in order to manifest the transformation [of death]. *(Henceforth, all transmissions occur at the point of death, when the master repeats an explanation of the true essence/lineage (zhenzong). [This case] is to be taken as a model for future reenactments.)* At this time, it was said that he was 150 years old. That day the emissary of the Eastern Wei, Song Yun, was returning from the West at Conglin and met the great teacher as he was returning to the West. He was told, "Today the master *(jun)* of your country died." Song Yun asked, "On whom will the master's disciples rely?" Bodhidharma answered, "Forty years from now there will be a Chinese man of the Way who will continue the transmission." When Bodhidharma's disciples heard this news, they opened his grave and saw that it was empty.

A number of polemical objectives are established in closing out Bodhidharma's biography in this manner. First, we have an interesting tension between private and public success. In the discussion of Bodhidharma's relationship to Huike and Daoyu, there were no other persons in China who knew of Bodhidharma's worth, but now suddenly after that transmission, there are masses of people recognizing Bodhidharma's immense value. So what changed? What narrative logic might be satisfied by situating this public recognition after the account of the successful private transmission? All we are told is that "After this, Bodhidharma's students grew daily and at this juncture

---

35. See McRae, *The Northern School,* 259–60, for an alternate translation.

well-known monks became deeply jealous." In lieu of any details about the causality between these two events—secret transmission and public recognition—I think we have to say that what changed was that Du Fei, once he had narratively installed enlightenment in a single descendant, then wanted to show the reader how that event was valued by the public. Hence, all those earlier comments about China's lazy unresponsive tendencies are now exchanged for accounts of energetic enthusiasm for Bodhidharma. In doing this, Du Fei is showing how the private core of transmission is supposedly manifesting its value for the public, a public now shown demonstrating devotion but, according to Du Fei's earlier comments, surely only receiving secondary teachings.

Moreover, Du Fei uses this shift to public success to explain Bodhidharma's death, which he presents, at least on one level, as a magical transformation and not a death at all. However, Bodhidharma's magical power to ingest the poison without suffering harm does not absolve the unnamed jealous monks who are shown trying to murder him. Thus, on a more basic level, the jealous monks are still presumably guilty of at least trying to kill him. This narrative ploy has, I think, more than a little to do with the politics of Du Fei's writing moment. Du Fei in this gesture is depicting the criminal extremes that the opposition to Bodhidharma could take, and is again creating a kind of original sin for China. But this time it comes with a distinction in class: the students came in droves, but the well-known monks were uncontrollably jealous. Thus, Bodhidharma is positioned as a kind of counterculture hero: his Buddhist perfection supposedly wins the hearts of the innocent masses and reveals the villainous nature of the established teachers.

Actually, reading this passage more closely, it seems that Du Fei is registering Bodhidharma's public success in a way that strings together several elements in a mutually confirming sequence. Du Fei sketches a circle of meaning in which (1) masses of people were devoted to Bodhidharma, and (2) this made the other, former recipients of Buddhist devotion jealous, and (3) they sought to kill him, and then (4) he died or at least disappeared. In this causal progression, his death becomes proof of each prior moment in the circle. His death, or rather his absence, is caused by the greed of the monkly competition, and this greed is caused by the success that Bodhidharma had with the masses, and this was due, one is to believe, to their finally recognizing his value and the transmission that he supposedly held.

On another plane, this passage makes Bodhidharma's arrival in

China even more intensely teleological. As Du Fei has Bodhidharma exclaim, "I came due to the dharma." This alone is his mission, and once it is installed in Huike, there was nothing left to do but leave; again, Bodhidharma appears without any other desires. Bodhidharma's transmission of truth to China is satisfied by its injection into Huike, and thus the teaching of the masses, however it was portrayed a few lines earlier, is completely secondary to this single gift of truth to Huike. Bodhidharma then is one whose identity is as singular as his function: he is a conduit of truth leading from India to China, and nothing else is found in his persona. He is essentially hollow save for the truth that he pours into Huike, along with the will required for that transmission to be effected.

What shall we say about Bodhidharma's death, with its magic and its rescripting of a familiar Daoist narrative? First, let's be clear that Du Fei's account seems completely innovative here, since Daoxuan, save for mentioning Bodhidharma's reputed age of one hundred fifty years (drawn presumably from a similar comment made in the sixth-century *Record of the Buddhist Monasteries of Luoyang*), has nothing to say about the poison, Bodhidharma's appearance on the frontier on the same day as his death, or the empty coffin. Actually, there is a parallel threat of murder in Daoxuan's *Encyclopedia,* but it is directed at Huike, and thus it might be that Du Fei is mixing and matching biographic material from multiple sources to achieve maximum effect.[36] Daoxuan's account of Bodhidharma's death is completely different from the one that Du Fei offers. In the first part of Huike's biography, a much more prosaic death for Bodhidharma is narrated: "Bodhidharma died at Lo River Beach. Huike concealed the body [or buried the body without the proper ceremonies] on a bank of the river, but Bodhidharma had enjoyed a fine reputation in the past, and so a proclamation was transmitted through the imperial domain."[37] Apparently, then, even Daoxuan's version of Bodhidharma's death already seems problematic since the narrative seems designed to explain why Bodhidharma's remains aren't locatable, and this despite the claim that he was well known and even given imperial recognition of some sort.

But what, exactly, is Du Fei trying to do in offering this new version of Bodhidharma's demise to the reader, and in what context should

---

36. For translation of the Huike material, see Broughton, *The Bodhidharma Anthology,* 58–59.
37. Ibid., 58.

it be interpreted? Anyone familiar with Tang-period religion would immediately recognize a cluster of Daoist tropes, ranging from the empty coffin to the "exit interview" with a government official at a border on his death day.[38] Moreover, this death sequence fits what is called the *shijie* model of the master manifesting death and yet recovering his body, leaving no trace. So let's conclude that Bodhidharma is being typecasted according to some very generic forms: he is another master who dies and yet continues to live elsewhere, taking his body with him.

BORROWED PLENTITUDE:
THE VALUE OF THE OTHER'S VALUE

To understand Du Fei's construction of Bodhidharma's identity, we have to see that the newness of Du Fei's position was found in recombining older elements that he culled from a variety of disparate sources.[39] Thus, Bodhidharma is made to look like an awe-inspiring master by giving his biography details that rhyme with the details of other masters, Buddhist and Daoist, a rhyme scheme that presumably would have been recognized by Du Fei's audience. However, though his audience would have presumably recognized the familiarity of Bodhidharma's biographic details, they might not have noticed that they had been *asked to recognize* that familiarity—the familiarity would, instead, appear as a natural effect of Bodhidharma actually being the same as other stereotypical masters. Orchestrating just that moment of recognition in which the act of recognition itself is not recognized as the effect of authorial artifice has to be ranked as one of Du Fei's major accomplishments. And it is just this process of recycling prior elements that warrants careful attention, not only to get past naive readings of Chan as antinomian and revolutionary, but also to begin to see how a dense set of literary precedents were so central to the emergence of the Chan tradition. Or put otherwise, it took a mountain of Chinese literature—from various eras and various traditions—to make the awesomely simple Bodhidharma and his perfectly filial descendant, Huike.

---

38. Faure mentions that Bodhidharma's death matches this Daoist model; see his "Bodhidharma as Textual and Religious Paradigm," 193–94. More recently, John Jorgensen also argues that Bodhidharma's death is being dressed in Daoist garb; see his *Inventing Hui-neng, the Sixth Patriarch,* 250.

39. For a thoughtful discussion of various aspects of syncretism in Chinese Buddhism, see Robert H. Sharf, *Coming to Terms with Chinese Buddhism.*

Seeing the syncreticism in Bodhidharma's regularly revised "biography" risks ruining two major attractions in Chan: (1) the fantasy that Chan is new and in some way pristine, and certainly not the product of cultural mastication that owes much to several diverse sectors of Chinese and Buddhist culture that had been developing for centuries; and (2) the heartening claim that Chan somehow is a movement that breaks away from prior literary forms. To think about Du Fei's text as a contrived pastiche of all sorts of prior elements is suddenly to vanquish the idea that there is something beyond language and culture here. If we really take into account Du Fei's deft manipulation of various literary precedents—Buddhist biographies, imported sūtras such as the *Laṅkāvatāra Sūtra,* Faru's stele, commentaries of uncertain provenance such as the *Awakening of Faith,* Daoist hagiographies, Daoist notions of truth and the value of inversion logics (to be seen shortly), and Confucian models of sonship and reproductive patriarchy—then the promise to deliver that one pure realm of truth beyond language and literature that Du Fei set out at the beginning of his discourse seems decidedly compromised if not laughable. In short, we haven't gotten very good at noticing that the idea of truth beyond language and beyond all cultural formatting is itself a culturally formatted item that has value only when it rests inside that cultural system of meaning.

Reading Du Fei's Bodhidharma as the product of what we ought to call "partisan-tinged syncretism," let's consider Bodhidharma's mode of dying more closely. The *shijie* model goes back to Daoist sources and is also associated with the alchemical traditions that Du Fei alluded to in the analogy for the esotericism of Buddhist wisdom. But we needn't assume that Du Fei was pulling this format for Bodhidharma's death directly from Daoist sources, since one sees evidence of Buddhist biographers casting famous Chinese Buddhists in this mold at least two centuries earlier.[40] Thus, we ought to posit a rather long history of Buddhist authors adopting Daoist formulas to prove the eminence of their masters. Of course, the influence went both ways. For a long time we have been aware of the Buddhist details that were brought into Daoist biographies. Laozi's growing biography, in particular, was given a variety of elements that seem adapted from Chinese accounts of the Buddha. For instance, Laozi is born from his mother's armpit (the

---

40. For pre-Tang Buddhist uses of the *shijie* model, see Robert Ford Campany, *Strange Writing,* 329.

Buddha supposedly came from his mother's side), he came out talking
(as did the Buddha), and so on. In short, a fair appraisal of hagio-
graphic writing in the Tang would conclude that Daoist and Buddhist
elements have been passed back and forth several times, probably with
the result that their Buddhistness or Daoistness was no longer evident
to most readers.

   This isn't to say that there was some happy sharing of desirable
biographic elements drawn from Buddhist and Daoist sources. Quite
the contrary. Throughout the seventh and early eighth century there
was a good deal of bitterness between the Daoists and the Buddhists.
One vantage point for seeing this struggle is the angry debates over
the Daoist text called the *Sūtra on Converting the Barbarians (Huahu
jing)*.[41] This text has a long and involved history, having grown
enormously over the centuries, but its central argument was that the
Buddha is actually a misrecognized form of Laozi.[42] In brief, Laozi's
exit from China, via a western outpost, is taken as the beginning of
an account of how he then went to India to "convert the barbarians."
Thus, the *Huahu jing* invites the reader to appreciate that the arrival
of Buddhism in China is simply a perverted form of Laozi's teaching
coming back "home" after having passed through the demented misunderstanding of the barbarian Indians. In short, imported Buddhism
is just bad Daoism that had been purposefully dumbed down for the
barbarians but then reintroduced to China by those barbarians who
didn't know the Chinese origins of their own teachings. Put another
way, the Daoists were claiming to be the progenitors of Buddhism, and
casting the Buddhists as unwitting sons who didn't know who their
real father was.

   To add to the various ironies here, it would seem that the *Huahu*
theory relies on the Buddhist notion of upāya, as found in the *Lotus
Sūtra*. That is, by claiming that Laozi's original message was transformed into second-rate teachings in the form of Buddhism—due to
the limitations of the barbarians—is to tar and feather the Buddhists
as unwitting, second-rate Daoists, unaware of the deeper "history" of
their tradition, a very *Lotus Sūtra*-like strategy, after all. In short, all
sorts of elements, including both form and content, are getting passed

---

   41. For discussion of seventh-century debates over this text, see Barrett's *Taoism
under the T'ang*, 31–32; see also Weinstein, *Buddhism under the T'ang*, 37.
   42. For materials on the earlier form of the *Huahu* "debate," see Zürcher, *The
Buddhist Invasion of China*, chap. 6.

back and forth in this battle to define who is really legitimate in claiming truth and the Dao. With a sense of these dynamics, let's return to Du Fei's account of the other six masters to develop a fuller interpretation of Du Fei's attempt to fetishize tradition.

THE CHINESE MASTERS: TRANSMISSION IS EVERYTHING

In the interest of keeping this reading of the *Record* reasonably short, I will summarize the biographies of the six masters who follow Bodhidharma: Huike, Sengcan, Daoxin, Hongren, Faru, and Shenxiu. In line with the above discussion, two thematics work well in establishing the form and content of these biographies. The first is simply a focus on Du Fei's presentation of transmission — how the moment of transmission is presented within the biographies and what rules or expectations are associated with it. The second theme is the issue of simplicity, which comes to the fore in several of the biographies.

As for transmission in these biographies, on each occasion Du Fei locates it at the end of the master's life. For instance, Du Fei tells us in the case of Huike:[43]

> At the time of his death, [Huike] said to his disciple Sengcan, "The dharma that I have received in transmission, I now entrust *(fu)* to you. You must use it, extensively, to save others." [Huike] also personally *(shouchuan)* transmitted the *Laṅkāvatāra Sūtra* to people, saying, "This sūtra will become only a title in four generations. How lamentable."

In this scene, Du Fei does little more than establish a link between these two men and push the dharma forward to the next generation. Huike seems to know that he is about to die and hands over the dharma with the vague instruction that Sengcan is to use the dharma to save others. This seems to be the most economical version of transmission in Du Fei's text; it mentions no funeral details, no other members in attendance, no postmortem magic, and no public recognition.

Especially noteworthy in this paucity of detail is that Sengcan, whose life is not well documented in any pre-eighth-century source, is said to have "served Huike and had the capacity to awaken to the perfect and sudden [teachings], and then entered into the [master's] room,

---

43. See McRae, *The Northern School*, 261, for a slightly different translation.

[to receive transmission]."[44] This vague comment is particularly telling as Du Fei is simply explaining that Sengcan's enlightenment was part of a filial relation with the master, without specifying any details of teachings or practices. It turns out that Daoxuan's *Encyclopedia* had nothing to offer on the details of Sengcan's life, other than mentioning him at the top of a list of Huike's students in the odd biography of Fachong.[45] Thus, Du Fei had little to go on for constructing a life and certainly didn't have materials for creating a rich story like Huike's arm gift.

The way Du Fei has Huike treat the *Laṅkāvatāra Sūtra* in this exchange is in keeping with the transmission moment that he worked up for Bodhidharma and Huike. In both cases, Du Fei brings the *Laṅkāvatāra Sūtra* onstage and acknowledges it but in the next moment undermines it and prepares for its future obsolescence. In this case, Du Fei has Huike transmitting the *Laṅkāvatāra Sūtra* but only to nameless recipients and with no lineage effects mentioned; it is only after the singular dharma "received in transmission" had been passed on to Sengcan that the vague transmission of the *Laṅkāvatāra Sūtra* is mentioned, introduced with an "also." The limits of this secondary form of transmission are confirmed when Du Fei has Huike predict that in four generations this text will become no more than a name. In sum, by including mention of the *Laṅkāvatāra Sūtra* as a kind of minor double of real transmission while also preparing for its demise, Du Fei appears to be working hard at reducing the power of the *Laṅkāvatāra Sūtra* that was so much a part of the reworked version of Huike's biography in Daoxuan's *Encyclopedia,* from whence he drew his material.[46] Clearly, as Du Fei took biographic information from Daoxuan's *Encyclopedia* and inserted it into the skeleton form of the lineage, as defined in the Faru stele, he carefully selected and rearranged material to create the image of a lineage of truth-fathers

44. McRae, *The Northern School,* translates Sengcan's entrance into the master's room as a metaphor—Sengcan "developed into [one of Huike's] most trusted students" (261)—presumably to reflect the way the *Analects* presents successful moral cultivation as gradual movement into the master's private dwelling space; see, for instance, 11.2, 11.15, 11.20, and 19.23.

45. See McRae, *The Northern School,* 25–26.

46. In fact, predicting the demise of the *Laṅkāvatāra Sūtra* is found in the reworked version of the Huike biography, but this prediction isn't set next to an account of a perfect moment of transmission to Sengcan: "Each time Huike discoursed on dharma he would end by saying '[Interpretations] of this sūtra, after four generations, will degenerate into mere doctrinal terminology. How sad." (trans. in Broughton, *The Bodhidharma Anthology,* 62).

who had the content of total tradition but in a form not identified with any particular content and certainly not with the *Laṅkāvatāra Sūtra*.

In comparison to the Bodhidharma–Huike transmission, with its suicide motif and spectacular amputation, Du Fei's account of the Huike–Sengcan transmission seems easy and uninvolved. What could account for such a shift in the drama of transmission? Presumably, on one level, the problem is simply that Du Fei didn't have any material from Daoxuan to work into the narrative. Consequently, although Du Fei employs the vague terminology of perfect and sudden [teachings] to explain Sengcan's reception of the dharma, these terms appear quite free of the hype that would surround sudden enlightenment in the decades to come. In fact, Du Fei's comments on the nature of Sengcan's enlightenment seem much closer to boilerplate, included to assure the reader of the validity of the connection between the two men but not developed into a site of desire. Apparently, Du Fei just needed to insert a brief biography for Sengcan to flesh out the conduit of truth from Huike to Daoxin.[47]

This perspective on the narrative function of Sengcan's biography is strengthened when we read how Sengcan transmits to Daoxin, a moment that Du Fei also treats in a minimalist manner:[48]

> Because he had completed his teaching *(hua)*, he wished to speak to Daoxin and said, "From the patriarch Bodhidharma *(Damozu)* on, the dharma has been transmitted up to me. Now I want to go south, and [thus] leave it with you to extend and protect."

Here, nothing about Sengcan's teaching is mentioned, and instead we get vague statements from the master about the lineage's past and future. In fact, it seems that in concocting this scene, Du Fei is just making sure that the reader "sees" the gift of dharma being passed down the chain of masters.

Three other elements are noteworthy in this short transmission scene between Sengcan and Daoxin. First, the *Laṅkāvatāra Sūtra* has disappeared altogether. At the end of the Huike–Sengcan transmission moment, Du Fei had brought it onstage to demote it, but here in the Sengcan–Daoxin moment, freed of the need to work against elements in Daoxuan's *Encyclopedia*, he leaves the *Laṅkāvatāra Sūtra* out of the

---

47. In the mid-eighth century a new biography for Sengcan was concocted and cut in stone. See Chen Jinhua's forthcoming study of Sengcan.

48. See McRae, *The Northern School*, 261, for a similar rendering.

picture completely. Consequently, it seems appropriate to conclude that what is driving the depiction of content in Du Fei's account of the genealogy is twofold: (1) the need to work for or against haphazard precedents found in the material borrowed from Daoxuan's *Encyclopedia*—as in rejecting the *Laṅkāvatāra Sūtra* or reworking Huike's arm loss; and (2) the narrative constraints defined by having to convince the reader of the reliability of this conduit back to the Buddha; that is, Sengcan needs to get sudden and complete enlightenment, too, even if this seems like a vapid moment in the narrative.

Second, in the above Sengcan–Daoxin transmission, Bodhidharma is called a patriarch, a *zu*. This term is notably rare in this text, though it soon would be used extensively in Chan texts to describe past masters. It would seem that Du Fei hadn't felt fully at ease calling these masters "patriarchs," though here, in a line where Sengcan needs to restate the coherence of the lineage, this is the language that Du Fei relied on to underscore a sense of continuity. Third, Du Fei describes Sengcan going south after the transmission, and this seems to be part of a general trend to send masters south when they are finished with teaching and/or life.

In contrast to these two bland transmission moments involving the obscure Sengcan, other transmission scenes are much more theatrical in Du Fei's *Record*. For instance, in narrating Daoxin's transmission to Hongren, Du Fei includes the information that students competed with one another to be the chosen heir to the lineage, that there was a mausoleum-building project under way, and that Daoxin's death was accompanied by magical earthquakes and mists. In all this, Daoxin's death appears as a mysterious moment that no longer is a death per se, and which Du Fei labels a "transformation" *(huabi),* a term with strong connections to the magical death of the Buddha. Du Fei writes:[49]

> In the eighth month of the second year of the Yong Hui era (651), Daoxin ordered his disciples to build a crypt *(kan)* on the side of the mountain. His disciples knew he was about to die [lit., "transform and finish," *huabi*], and thus started to debate and dispute over who would be the rare dharma heir *(xifasi).* They asked Daoxin to whom he would transmit *(chuanfu)* and he sighed for a while, and then said, "Hongren is slightly more capable." Then with an exhortation about belonging [to the lineage], he again explained the ultimate principle [to Hongren]. Learning that his crypt was finished, he peacefully died, sitting upright. At this time there were great earthquakes and mist rose up all around.

49. See McRae, *The Northern School,* 262–63, for an alternate translation.

This account tells us a good bit more about how Du Fei wanted his readers to understand transmission. The need for transmission here is apparently caused by Daoxin's impending death, with the distinct implication that transmission works not as a kind of enlightenment but as a kind of investiture and, of course, as a narrative device designed to move truth from the past into the present. Clearly, Du Fei depicts the students' understanding that Daoxin's death represented an occasion to inherit his position because they know that his death will open up something like the Chair of Enlightenment, which presumably wasn't available as long as Daoxin was alive.

Having gotten used to Du Fei's reworking of Daoxuan's material, we shouldn't be surprised to note that in Daoxuan's biography of Daoxin, there is no rush at the end of Daoxin's life, and the students simply ask if a transmission has been effected, a question that in the context of Daoxuan's *Encyclopedia* would not have implied that the transmission of total truth was expected of this moment. In the *Encyclopedia* entry, Daoxin replies that he has given many transmissions throughout his life, and nothing more is said, though Hongren is put in charge of building the stupa and later leads the students to visit it.[50] This means that while Daoxuan had left Daoxin's transmissions numerous and ill-defined, with Hongren implicitly identified as a leader since he was put in charge of the stupa, in Du Fei's hands Daoxin's death is dramatized as a public scene wherein Hongren is explicitly identified as the sole heir among a field of contenders. Comparing these two accounts, it would seem that Du Fei redesigned Daoxuan's account to make it conform to Du Fei's notion of a singular truth-lineage with one master per generation, even though Daoxuan's account said the exact opposite.[51]

Daoxin's death scene, as created by Du Fei, also includes a variety of magical elements worth keeping in mind, something that many modern Chan and Zen enthusiasts play down. Daoxin, like Sengcan, clearly has a mystical foreknowledge of his death, a death that he seems to control, not just by dying seated, but also by timing it so that it comes only after the crypt was complete. Again, Du Fei's language is telling. He chooses

---

50. See McRae, *The Northern School*, 32.

51. Jorgensen has argued that it is only with Shenhui's writing that we get the one-master-per-generation rule, but it is clear that it is already at work here in Du Fei, though Du Fei will have to break this rule in order to insert Shenxiu into the Faru lineage. That Shenhui pointed out this bulge in the lineage simply means that he saw both the rule and its exception. For Jorgensen's discussion, see his "The 'Imperial Lineage' of Chan Buddhism."

terms like *transformation (huabi and zuohua)* not simply to be polite but also to suggest that Daoxin's death is merely an apparent death, not an actual disappearance and decomposition. The transcendent nature of Daoxin's death is clearer when Du Fei adds the details about the earthquakes and mists, which resonate with the Buddha's death and perhaps with generic Chinese images of the sage-dragon.

Though in Du Fei's narrative only Shenxiu will be accorded similarly grand postmortem honors, the descriptions of the deaths of the next two masters, Hongren and Faru, are parallel in linking death, transmission, and a kind of mastery over death, demonstrated with a mystical foreknowledge of death, an unhurried completion of tasks, and a seated death moment. In setting up his narrative of transmission in this manner, Du Fei is again indicating that there should be only one master per generation. Death, in other words, is the moment of reproduction when the jewel is installed in another body, thereby transforming that new body into a buddha-like being.[52]

Between these accounts of death and transmission, Du Fei gives some details about what these masters did, where they went, how they taught, and so on. Despite the thickening of biographic details as Du Fei works his way toward his writing present, it is hard to discover a common teaching in the accounts of the masters, a common teaching that would match the fixity of Du Fei's jewel metaphor for the dharma that is supposedly transmitted. This lack of specific teaching content among the various masters is bothersome only if we assume that early Chan was in fact a teaching and not a *theory* regarding the right to teach, which of course is a very different matter.

As for the details given about the masters' teachings, despite Bodhidharma's and Huike's choice of the *Laṅkāvatāra Sūtra* as a supplement to transmission and as a text for beginners, Du Fei explains that Daoxin taught the recitation of the *Perfection of Wisdom Sūtras* (and here Du Fei is paraphrasing what was in Daoxuan's account), Sengcan develops himself with meditation and wisdom left in an unspecified

52. The details of the triumph over death probably ought to be read in a register that covers at least three realms of reference: (1) these masters are transcendent figures that aren't subject to laws of life and death as other mortals are; and here Buddhist and Daoist models of this kind of transcendence are combined, such that replications of the Buddha's death are conjoined with the alchemical and *shijie* details already given for Bodhidharma's death; (2) these masters are powerful and fertile in a postmortem manner that warrants the special treatment they are accorded; and (3) death marks an occasion for fusing together public and private realities as the lineage extends itself privately, but the body of the deceased serves as a ritual site for everyone else.

form, and Hongren does not read sūtras, whereas Shenxiu read extensively in Buddhist and non-Buddhist literature. Furthermore, outside of the equally vague comments of "activating the fundamental mind," or teaching the "abstruse principle," and so on, we learn nothing about what was supposedly in the transmission. Thus, it is enough for Du Fei to announce the presence of truth and to explain its flawless, legalistic movement forward. In lieu of homogeneous contents that might represent Chan teachings or something recognizable in the lineage's claim to truth, we get the narration of several other themes that shed some light on what Du Fei wanted his readers to think about these masters and the truth that they possessed.

The first theme is magic and is relatively straightforward. In addition to the magical occurrences that might be mentioned at a master's death, many of the masters are accredited with magical powers. For instance, Sengcan is said to tame wild beasts, and Daoxin creates illusionary giants to scare away bandits and makes dry wells flow again. These magical events seem included not only because, for instance, they were mentioned in Daoxuan's account of Daoxin but also because the magic motif worked nicely with the overall project of displaying these men as superhuman. Thus Du Fei added magical elements to Sengcan's life when there was no precedent for that detail. Given the prominence of the magic theme, it is worth considering the possibility that the gift of enlightenment, for instance the way Bodhidharma made Huike's mind enter into pure truth, is part and parcel with these other kinds of magical displays.

SIMPLY PERFECT:
THE FULLNESS OF LACK IN THE MASTERS

The second major theme in the biographies is simplicity. Throughout the seven biographies that constitute the middle section of the *Record*, Du Fei employs tropes of simplicity that can be divided into four categories: simplicity in desires, teachings, practices, and culture. The first and most prevalent simplicity is the way these masters are depicted as living only for the dharma. Contrary to later developments, in Du Fei's writing the masters show no interest in the arts, or in other diversions that are not centered on furthering the lineage through establishing an heir and proselytizing the populace. Moreover, the masters never appear in need of validation from the Other and thus are simple in the sense of being beyond intersubjectivity, beyond competition, and beyond the complications of contemporaneous Buddhism. Thus, they are often depicted off by themselves, or just with their own master, receiving truth apart from any previously established institutional framework. Similarly, these masters are set up as the complete antithesis of Du Fei the historian, since Du Fei's stated goal was to make the lineage known to others, and known in a way to create desire and admiration.

The second simplicity is found in Du Fei's construction of the masters' teaching. Two of the masters—Huike and Hongren—are said to teach in a direct and uncomplicated way that Du Fei likens to an echo. Of course, this suggests again that the master has no desire and is like a bell to be rung or a drum to be sounded. But his echolike reaction also marks how his lack of desire is perfectly in accord with the students' desire, since the master's lack of desire means that he can fulfill the students' desires perfectly and instantaneously. Hence, it is no surprise that Du Fei tells of the multitudes that come to study with these masters once this kind of relationship has been established. Arguably, this echolike quality of the master functions as a kind of solicitude to the reader, who is invited to think of the masters as automatically dispensing the dharma discourse most useful to the student. This seems sensible, but an equally viable interpretation would be that Du Fei is positioning these masters to appear like Chinese deities that one contacts within a call-and-response structure, technically called *ganying*.

The simplicity of the masters' teaching takes on other dimensions when Du Fei briefly mentions, in lieu of any details from Daoxuan, how Daoxin instructed his students in practice: "Make effort and be diligent in your sitting; sitting is the root. You should be able to sit for years [lit., "three or five years"], with but one mouthful of rice to satisfy your hunger and illnesses—just close the door and sit, don't read sūtras, don't talk to anyone. If you are able to go on like this, in time it will be effective, like the way a monkey [eventually] gets at the meat of a chestnut."[53] Here the simplicity of the master seems transferred on to the student, who is instructed to take up a kind of seated meditation and brutal austerities. Given that Du Fei does not develop the meditation motif anywhere else, we have little to go on to make sense of this comment other than to assume that Du Fei wants the

53. Yanagida, *Shoki Zenshū shiso no kenkyū*, 566; for McRae's slightly different rendering, see *The Northern School*, 262. Again proving the fluidity of these texts, this passage was later attributed to Shenxiu; see Faure, *The Will to Orthodoxy*, 212 n. 1.

reader to see how demanding Daoxin's teachings were. However, with truth and enlightenment depicted in Du Fei's narrative as items given by the master, effort on the student's part remains rather problematic. At the very least, we can say that in this quotation on meditation from Daoxin, the emphasis is on things beyond language. Daoxin's instructions include meditation, but clearly this meditation has its value partly due to being separate from reading sūtras and from talking to anyone.

Also, the machismo in Daoxin's comments is not out of context with other things Du Fei wants to suggest about these masters. For instance, in one anecdote from Faru's life, we learn that Faru was so simple *(wu suo xiuqu)* that he was just like an empty boat on a river, which, if you knocked against it, would not get angry, presumably since there was no one there to have a conflict with. Faru's impassive nature had already been emphasized when Du Fei recounted how he fell in the river and was completely unfazed when fished out sometime later, as though death was of no concern to him.[54] It would seem, then, that Du Fei wants to show the reader how the masters are always at ease and never moved by desire or fear, and this impassiveness is completely in line with simplicity, for simplicity also speaks of desirelessness and unshakable calm.

HONGREN

Hongren's simplicity is particularly telling and leads on to the final kind of simplicity—the simplicity of culture, with the important sub-

---

54. For these two passages, see McRae, *The Northern School*, 264. The motif of the monk as an empty boat was known in pre-Tang texts; see Zürcher, *The Buddhist Conquest of China*, 261. Also, for a parallel story about a monk surviving a boating accident unfazed, see the biography of the meditation master Daoying in the *Ming bao ji* in Gjerston, *Miraculous Retribution*, 164–65; T.51.789b.15. This entry for Daoying (a monk who died in the first half of the seventh century) is replete with themes that later would be taken up for depicting the rustic, carefree Chan master who could answer everyone's questions. Supposedly, Daoying, though a monk, ate and drank what he wanted, wore layman's clothes, tended cattle, and kept his hair long. Similarly, he was an abrupt teacher who gave his questioners mind-bending answers. And, most importantly, "He did not concern himself with acting dignified, but when it came to obscure meanings in the sūtras and the monastic regulations, there were none that he could not explain upon first hearing them" (Gjerston, *Miraculous Retribution*, 164). In short, Daoying looks like an early version of the perfect Chan master who, though appearing common, rude, uncouth, and in touch with nature, is naturally endowed with the essence of tradition that he can spontaneously produce, just like Hongren and Huineng would in later literature.

categories of (1) being beyond the literary tradition; and (2) inverting hierarchy—tropes that will dominate in later Chan writing.[55] Thus, Du Fei's biography of Hongren explains that he does not read sūtras and instead associates with the servants. Moreover, he does manual labor all day and meditates all night. In this biographic space where Du Fei had no details to draw on from Daoxuan's *Encyclopedia*, or from Faru's stele, he chose to paint Hongren as a master of simplicity who rejected societal hierarchies and the literary side of the Buddhist tradition. Du Fei develops Hongren's disinterest in hierarchy with the detail that as a younger man Hongren was often ridiculed and yet never responded. And, yet, Hongren's minimalist style of Buddhism supposedly had an immense effect on the world of culture that Hongren supposedly forsook, since Du Fei notes, "Because of his reputation, after he received the transmission, the number of noblemen who gathered around him doubled everyday." Similarly, "After a little more than ten years, eight or nine of every ten ordained and lay aspirants in the country had studied with him."[56] In this passage, Hongren's upside-down approach to Buddhism and society are shown to produce amazingly broad effects precisely in the two realms that he supposedly renounced—Buddhism and society. In fact, Du Fei is claiming that Hongren became China's de facto National Master because eighty or ninety percent of the clergy and laity supposedly studied with him.

With this "illustriously low" profile so clearly informing Du Fei's version of Hongren, it is hard not to read Hongren's biography as an indictment of famous, well-educated, and certainly well-connected monks. Hongren has the truth and has no use for secondary markers of status or pleasure, and this of course fits nicely with his echo style of teaching, which was notably spontaneous and beyond "general pronouncements." In short, not only is Hongren depicted as beyond class considerations, in and outside the monastic institution, he is also in fact implicitly free of Buddhism. He doesn't need Buddhist texts, Buddhist rituals, or Buddhist hierarchies. He has got it all, wherever he is, and meditation is the only Buddhist activity that he engages in.

I will say much more about this "simple" image of the master in my discussion of Huineng in chapter 6. For now, let's admit that Hongren's

---

55. I agree with McRae when he argues that Hongren's biography in the *Record* was in part the template for Huineng's biography, which would emerge several decades later. For his discussion, see *Seeing through Zen,* 68 ff.

56. Translations from McRae, *The Nothern School,* 263.

simplicity appears to function in some rather complicated ways. For instance, it produces a very potent kind of innocence, since the master's simplicity removes him from the realm of religious or political competition—a very useful profile given the competitive polemic that Du Fei is pushing. Hongren's simplicity also serves as a mark of authenticity: he is a master whose identity is at one with truth, and thus he has absolutely no interest in anything else, and certainly no interest in polemics. Conversely, the simplicity of his at-oneness-with-the-law stands as a mark for his being-solely-for-the-Other, just as the echo metaphor suggests.

More bothersome for the credulous reader, Hongren's disregard for reading puts the reader in a double bind, since he is reading about the perfection of one who doesn't read, and certainly doesn't read about past masters. Thus, if the reader comes to long for Hongren and his simplicity beyond literature and the Buddhist establishment, then he has de facto disparaged his own literary abilities and his respect for the Buddhist institution. In short, Du Fei has arranged for a reader seduction that involves a measure of self-condemnation. Hongren's simplicity sets the master up as an impossibly perfect figure who cannot be contained or countenanced by any figure—high or low—in the hierarchy, and especially cannot be domesticated by the desirous reader. In fact, he is literally that reader's opposite in form and content since Hongren neither reads nor desires the Other. Obviously, because Hongren is located at *both* the top and the bottom of the social hierarchy, he becomes even more "menacing" *and* desirable as an absolute master, since he is one who is beyond the ken of the Other precisely due to his rejection of the Other's notion of the symbolic order.[57]

FARU

Faru fits well in this lineage of prodigiously simple masters that Du Fei is creating. Faru, as we have seen, is described as simple in several ways, yet he also is portrayed as a very successful teacher. To understand Du Fei's construction of Faru's biography, which bears little likeness to the one presented at Shaolin, we have to remember that, earlier in his

57. Of course, given what we saw with Xinxing's aggrandizement in the Sect of the Three Levels, a sect that was still being proscribed at the time of Du Fei's writing, we would do well to assume that Du Fei was aware of that precedent in which Xinxing was depicted as the ultimate Buddhist leader who stepped beyond the lines of the clergy, engaged in manual labor, and nonetheless was presented as the epitome of tradition.

narrative, Du Fei had accorded Faru a place in the lineage, even as he claimed that Faru did not reproduce, thereby leaving Shenxiu as the sole inheritor of Hongren's transmission. Thus, like his treatment of the *Laṅkāvatāra Sūtra,* Faru will be accorded some prestige but ultimately will be written out of the lineage.

As for the details, Du Fei describes Faru as the son of an official, well read in Buddhist literature, and a diligent student of master Hongren. However, in a telling lacuna, Du Fei doesn't recount the transmission moment between Hongren and Faru, as he had for all the other masters. Instead, though he had mentioned in Hongren's biography that Hongren had transmitted the dharma to Faru, Du Fei now pushes this moment from view, saying that Faru, "having secretly received the seal of dharma transmission *(jier michuan fayin),* traveled about practicing the Way."[58] In this phrasing, the dharma is given, but only secretively, and Du Fei oddly chose not to identify Hongren as the gift giver or to depict that crucial moment of contact with Hongren—a dramatic moment that was surely available to him from the Faru stele. Given what we have seen Du Fei do at other critical junctures in rewriting prior material, I think we have to conclude that this is part 1 of detaching Faru from a source of legitimacy that Du Fei wants for his own ends.

Faru then has a brilliant career teaching, and he attracts students and court invitations. Du Fei even allows that "in accord with the patriarch model of masters and disciples, he activated the great upāya and caused the minds [of his students] to directly enter into [truth] without complicated [explanations],"[59] a line that echoes the description of the teaching event in the Faru stele. However, Du Fei does not label this great upāya as a transmission per se, even though many of the elements are there. And, of course, these generic master-student relations produced no named descendants. Thus, it seems that Du Fei is trying to say that Faru did what all the other masters did, but somehow nothing specific was achieved. Consequently, everything is decidedly incomplete, especially in comparison to the transmission moments that Du Fei presented in the other biographies.

The sense that something is lacking in Faru's ownership of truth becomes more acute in his death scene, which in some ways is like the other masters' death scenes but again is missing just that element of a

---

58. See McRae, *The Northern School,* 264, for a slightly different reading.
59. Ibid.

specific transmission. Like all the other precedents in Du Fei's account, Faru announces his death and ends his life peacefully in a seated position. The problem is that instead of picking a successor and transmitting the "dharma-jewel" to him, Du Fei tells us that Faru's final advice to his students is to go study with Shenxiu. He says, "From now on, you must go study under Chan Master Shenxiu at Yuquan Monastery in Jingzhou."[60] Thus, Faru leaves no direct descendants and, even more oddly, ends his life with a final message that sends his students off to another master who, we are led to believe, will take over where he left off. This sequence of events appears to be part 2 of Du Fei's hollowing out of Faru. The lineage form is all perfectly present, but there is an absence of transmission, an absence that can only be recovered by following Faru's instructions, which point away from himself and to the "real" patriarch. In short, Faru is endowed with a limited legitimacy that is good only for passing on a trustworthy assessment about where legitimacy is.[61] And in this sense, Faru's transmission at death isn't a transmission of content to a new student-inheritor; it is, functionally, a transmission of master status that is getting moved from his person over to Shenxiu.

Given the complexities and irregularities surrounding Faru's reception of dharma and this curious twist at the end of his life, I think we have to say that Du Fei is carefully hollowing out Faru, keeping him as a placeholder but stealing his reproductive capacities in order that Shenxiu can take over as the new holder of tradition. This maneuver is doubly effective as it first cancels any claim that a student of Faru's might try to make and then installs Shenxiu as Hongren's real successor based on the authority of Faru's final teaching. This complicated splicing becomes clearer when we consider Shenxiu's biography.

SHENXIU

Shenxiu's biography is the longest in the *Record,* and Du Fei provides abundant details on his pre-Buddhist life, his training, his travels, and, most importantly, his relations with court. The first thing that strikes the reader in this biography is that Du Fei is eager to present Shenxiu

---

60. See McRae, *The Northern School,* 264–65, for a parallel rendering.
61. This position makes Faru function a lot like master Ming in Faru's biography who, as discussed in the previous chapter, supposedly has wisdom but only acts to direct Faru to Hongren's wisdom. In chapter 6, we will see Shenhui use a parallel trope.

as a know-it-all. With a description of his precocious childhood, followed by an account of his wide reading in the non-Buddhist classics,
followed by a listing of all the masters he studied with and all the
doctrines he mastered, we get the sense that Shenxiu is simply the most
remarkable teacher in China. Despite this well-wrought and flattering account, Du Fei has trouble explaining the transmission between
Hongren and Shenxiu.

Instead of public death scenes in which the transmission is fully
scripted, as given for the other masters in the lineage, Du Fei claims
that Shenxiu studied with Hongren, "who recognized his worth immediately *(yijian zhongzhi)*" and then, after guiding him for some years,
"led him into the truth realm *(daoru zhenjing)*."[62] Clearly, there is no
mention of a specific transmission moment, and their relationship is
not fulfilled with the standard death-day transmission. In fact, Du Fei
had already said in Hongren's biography that Hongren transmitted
to Faru before his death in accordance with the rules of transmission
that he established back in his account of Bodhidharma. So, Shenxiu's
relationship with Hongren is set off to the side of the straightforward
advancement of the dharma from Hongren to Faru. Or, rather, Shenxiu
has this glancing contact, literally, with master Hongren, who nonetheless gives transmission later to another master who, when he dies,
directs his students to go to Shenxiu.

The awkwardness of this doubling is clearer when Du Fei recounts
what happened next. Du Fei quotes Shenxiu as saying on the occasion
of Hongren's death, a death for which he is notably absent, "There was
a prior entrustment *(xianyou fuzhu)*."[63] The meaning of this statement
is clarified by the next line when we learn that Shenxiu "didn't transmit
the dharma *(chuanfa)*, for the next ten-some years, until after Faru
died." The logic here seems to be that with Hongren's death, Shenxiu
would have been expected to take over the role of the master, and yet
he postpones assuming the mantle of the master because that role had
already been bequeathed to Faru. This sequence makes it clear that Du
Fei wants to uphold his logic of one master per generation, or at least
one *active* master, even though he needs to have two transmissions in
place in order to splice Shenxiu into the Bodhidharma lineage, as it had
been written at Shaolin Monastery.

---

62. See McRae, *The Northern School*, 265, for a different reading.
63. See ibid., 265, for a slightly different rendering of this line and the one that follows it.

Odder still is the fact that Shenxiu's comment, "There was a prior entrustment," is given in the narrative without reference to place or internal audience and seems, evidently, to be aimed at the reader. That is, Du Fei is trying to set things right with the reader, whose expectations vis-à-vis transmission he has organized in specific ways, and thus he is having Shenxiu explain to no one in particular in the narrative why he came into this inheritance in such a complicated manner. In sum, Du Fei has created a very tangled story with an overlap of masters, a transmission from Hongren long before he died (thus breaking the transmission rules that Du Fei had invoked earlier in his narrative), and, stranger still, a transmission going into someone (Faru) who does not give it to the next master in line. And finally he has to have his chosen master, Shenxiu, vouch for this bulge in the transmission with a quick sotto voce comment endorsing the oddness of the situation, just as one might add his or her initials next to a corrected error on a bank check. Standing back from the details, it seems evident that Du Fei has simultaneously stolen Faru's lineage, "capped" him, and turned him into Shenxiu's promoter, all in order that Shenxiu could appear to be in singular possession of truth and transmission.

With this replumbing of the Faru lineage explained and defended, Du Fei goes on to narrate Shenxiu's successes, the first of which is that Shenxiu is nationally popular, with "students not thinking ten thousand miles too far to come to take refuge at his dharma platform *(fatan).*"[64] In this claim Du Fei wants us to see that Buddhism has coalesced in Shenxiu, who is now located at the center of the Buddhist world, the singular place where one ought to take refuge, the place where those on the distant periphery, even if ten thousand miles away, ought to come calling and cross over Shenxiu's "dharma platform" to become legitimately Buddhist.[65] Announcing Shenxiu's ownership of the gateway into authentic Buddhism is of special interest, since it

64. See McRae, *The Northern School,* 265–66, for a parallel translation.
65. This claim about Shenxiu's "dharma platform" *(fatan)* probably needs to be read in the context of contemporaneous efforts to rearticulate the practice of taking refuge, along with reconfiguring the actual platform used in the ritual. For a useful account of Chinese efforts to reestablish platform traditions of various sorts, see John McRae, "Daoxuan's Vision of Jetavana." Of particular interest in this essay is McRae's assessment of the possibility that the Buddhist platforms of the mid-Tang in part owed their design to patterns and precedents established in Daoist platforms and the imperial *feng* and *shan* rites (84, 89, 96 n. 16). For equally useful comments on the expansion of various kinds of "ordinations" for the public, see Adamek, *The Mystique of Transmission,* chap. 3.

echoes Faru's grand teaching moment in the stele at Shaolin, and it will reappear with a vengeance in the *Platform Sūtra,* a text dedicated to taking Shenxiu's legitimacy away from his self-proclaimed descendants even as it constructs this kind of privately owned platform that is offered to the public as the place for gaining, or rather, *regaining,* their Buddhist legitimacy.

Du Fei's account of Shenxiu's success includes another element that is equally important for understanding the polemics of this text. Du Fei explains that Shenxiu was invited to court by Empress Wu and was received in a lavish manner—an event that actually seems to have happened, even if the details likely have been embellished. Most notably, Du Fei explains that *she* bows to him, and along with the other court ladies takes refuge with him, having previously purified themselves.[66] In fact, supposedly everyone at court took refuge with him and regarded him as their parent *(youru fumu),* and Du Fei adds that the emperor Xiaohe (Zhongzong) became involved, repeatedly demanding teachings of Shenxiu and preventing him from returning to his home monastery in Yuquan.[67] In this depiction, Du Fei seems to be working to establishing a precedent whereby the court pays homage to the leader of the Buddhist community, a striking inversion of power relations as they had been established in the preceding centuries. However, the situation is a little more complicated, because Du Fei seems to be claiming, discreetly, that the imperial lineage—Empress Wu and her two sons, Zhongzong and Ruizong, who would assume the throne after her death in 705—submitted to a Buddhist master and by default his lineage. Moreover, they did so in the context of taking him to be a parentlike figure. In short, this is a radical assertion in which Du Fei claims that the throne, finally! submits to a religious leader established as something like a paternal Buddhist pope. That Du Fei then adds that these two emperors cared for Shenxiu's remains after his death implies that not only is Shenxiu the National Teacher, but he is in effect, also becoming a National Ancestor.

---

66. The claim that Empress Wu bowed to Shenxiu has to be read in the context of the vociferous debates that had circled around the issue of clergy refusing to bow to their parents and the throne. For an overview of the problem, see Weinstein, *Buddhism under the T'ang,* 32–34. This is doubly interesting since I believe McRae is right to suspect that Shenxiu, under the name Weixiu, might have been the leader in the 662 effort to block the recently issued imperial proclamation requiring monks to bow to the emperor. For his discussion, see *The Northern School,* 48–50.

67. McRae, *The Northern School,* 266.

After the details of the transmissions that led to Shenxiu's inheritance, along with this account of his public success in his final years,
Du Fei rather abruptly closes out his text by going back to the rhetoric
of truth-beyond-language with which he had opened his discourse, but
this time it is much clearer what he has in mind. First, he reaffirms
that there is a realm beyond words, and to this end he supplies brief
quotations from the Buddha, Confucius, the *Zhuangzi,* and the *Book
of Changes.* This panoply of disparate authorities reflects the heterogeneous nature of Du Fei's sense of tradition, as well as his expectation
that the reader will also be familiar with all these sources and respect
them. Of course, he is back to citing words to prove the claim about
the truth-beyond-words, but, more importantly, this gesture now is
linked to his studied effort to install this realm-beyond-words into the
lineage.

   In this final section he underscores the privilege of the lineage by
saying that those who read Buddhist texts without finding masters "get
further and further away from the truth."[68] Thus, just as with his earlier
alchemical example, he is establishing the two-tier system of Buddhists,
sages and ordinary types, with the ordinary types now bereft of the
chance for advancement through their own work in reading or practice, a position that would seem to parallel rather closely Xinxing's
claims, as seen in chapter 2. Du Fei continues in this vein by heap-
ing criticism on those Buddhist scholars who invested their energies in
extended exegesis vis-à-vis the translated Indian texts. He lampoons
their notion of truth and the public favors they won for themselves.
These supposedly arrogant and deluded Buddhist teachers are juxta-
posed to Bodhidharma in the next section, where Du Fei emphasizes
that Bodhidharma was the one who had truth-beyond-words. In all this
criticism of those addicted to the literary tradition, and as yet unwilling
to submit to this image of the transmission of tradition that Du Fei is
propagating, we shouldn't miss that Du Fei's undermining of the literary tradition is accomplished by means of the literary tradition. And,
equally important, Du Fei's strategy involves creating the new genre of
the genealogy in which we learn of Chinese buddhas whose perfection
undergirds these radical claims to authority and renders the old literary
forms of tradition defunct.

   Put another way, Du Fei has created a new theory of tradition that

68. Ibid., 267.

both empties and completes the past system of signification in that it claims that the prior system of signification actually does not reach its referents—the Dao, truth, buddhahood, authenticity, and so on—and that only those chosen few who have received transmission from the truth-fathers reach those prized referents, and own them, dispensing them as they see fit. And to put this development in some kind of comparative context, it seems fair, on the fly, to argue that the Gospels work in a similar fashion since they, too, work around an overhaul of a previous system of reference and devotion in which, for example, it becomes sensible to claim that, as John has Jesus say to his disciples, "I am the way, and the truth, and the life. No one comes to the Father except through me. If you know me, you will know my Father also" (14:6). And a little later, "Whoever has seen me has seen the Father. How can you say, 'Show us the Father?' Do you not believe that I am in the Father and the Father is in me?" (14:10–11). The key point of interpretation in Chan and the Gospels is to see that the past symbolic order is overcome and finalized by introducing this hitherto unknown patriarchal conduit that comes from the Father (or the Buddha) and leads everyone back to the Father, as long as they believe the narrative that explains how this esoteric father–son lineage owns tradition and the rights to its distribution.

CONCLUSIONS: A HISTORY OF PROBLEMS WITH THE LAW

There are four conclusions that I would like to draw from the above discussions. First, it seems clear that Du Fei's *Record* comes after Faru's biography at Shaolin Monastery, works from it, and reproduces many of its elements and assumptions in a calculating manner. Concluding that Du Fei knew Faru's stele is not, of course, a new opinion. Yanagida, McRae, and others have thought the same. However, in previous discussions, noting this dependence did not lead to further reflection on how we ought to interpret Du Fei's writing vis-à-vis the Faru stele. By avoiding consideration of Du Fei's "anxiety of influence"—something particularly interesting in a discourse fixated on connecting the past to the present—we miss the chance to understand this new style of writing, with its objective of claiming national preeminence. Moreover, without analyzing this literary link, we cannot appreciate that it was at this point in history that Faru's biography qua history-of-Buddhism essentially reproduced itself with Du Fei's text as a kind of unwanted bastard son. Surely the monks at Shaolin were less than delighted to see a version of their story floating around at court with a new buddhified master at the business end of their lineage and their master Faru written off as an oddly unreproductive uncle of sorts. In sum, we need to see Du Fei's text as proof of that key moment when the newly invented genealogy of truth moving from the Buddha to Bodhidharma to Tang China metastasized itself as a kind of literary meme that escaped from the perimeter of Shaolin and would henceforth float freely in the textual world of Chinese Buddhism, where it would be so often reappropriated in a cycle of new efforts to own tradition.

The second conclusion is already implicit in the first: a close reading of Du Fei's text reveals how much liberty he took with his sources. Hence, Du Fei, though clearly erudite and in control of his writing, appears altogether untrustworthy as a narrator of history. For instance, in looking at how he turned Huike's supposed arm loss into the foundational gift that brought perfect Buddhism to China, or the way that he simultaneously included and undermined the *Laṅkāvatāra Sūtra,* or the way that he bounced between images of self-enlightenment and dependence on the master at the beginning of his text, it seems undeniable that he has made shrewd choices that reflect his hopes for influencing the future and not simply reflecting the past. Of course, to this short list of literary "inventions" it seems crucial to add the sin of omission when he chose not to admit his reliance on the Faru stele. In thinking of Du Fei's penchant for writing "public relations history," we ought to see that that metastasizing jump from Shaolin's stele to Du Fei's text was accomplished through Du Fei's calculated manipulation of not just his sources but his readers, too, for in cloaking the origins of his theory of origins, he was withholding just the kind of information that would have made his task of seducing them a whole lot harder. That is, the past was written into existence not just for the present but for denying the actual past, along with the specific way that the contrived past had been written into existence.

Too, we should remember that Du Fei very likely set out on these literary adventures knowing full well that he was mimicking what the author(s) at Shaolin had done because he would have known that the historical record, most notably Daoxuan's *Encyclopedia,* did not support Shaolin's claims. Surely, Du Fei knew what was and was not in Daoxuan's entries for the masters lined up in Faru's lineage, and thus we ought to surmise that he saw Shaolin's fraudulent "historicizing" for what it was and then decided to produce more of the same when invited to do so by his "friend(s)." In short, Du Fei's text represents a crucial node on that track of aggressively reading and rewriting the history of truth, which, throughout the eighth century, was to produce the genres and literary tropes that would be recognized as Chan Buddhism.

Third, and this is probably obvious by now, given Du Fei's overall untrustworthiness and his basic agenda of setting up Shenxiu as the connecting link for the next generation of masters, there is no reason to imagine that Shenxiu ever met Hongren. As we saw, Du Fei's account of Shenxiu's reputed contact with Hongren is altogether vague, unbelievable, and positively against the rules of transmission that Du Fei had set up for all the other moments of transmission. This means that the forward movement of the writing of genealogies does not reflect some history of real contact between these masters. Outside of Du Fei's literary act of stealing Faru's ancestors, along with the narrative inventions that held them in place, there is no "religious" tradition of Chan pushing its way forward in time. Consequently, we have no grounds to speak either of a "Chan movement" taking form or of Shenxiu's supposed disciples inheriting what he inherited. Shenxiu had no inheritance to give because he hadn't received any. And, more to the point, there never was anything to inherit since all these claims to inheritance are simply taking place in fuzzy and unreliable narratives borrowed from other fuzzy and unreliable narratives. In short, there is quite a scandal here at the origin of the theory of origins of truth.

Fourth, Du Fei's text has gone a long way toward creating an expectation for truth beyond sūtras, beyond literature, and beyond language. And this, in effect, translates into the claim to know and own the real form of tradition behind any form that tradition actually had taken in the past and present. With masters now supposedly directly linked to the ultimate source of tradition, future authors and spokespersons were at liberty to recast tradition as they wished. Of course, there would be some restraints in what the public would accept as legitimate statements about Buddhist content, but the door had been opened for the Chinese to remake Buddhism with a new kind of freedom based on the image of having supposedly received it all *already* via Bodhidharma.

With this admittedly dense discussion behind us, we are ready to turn to another major rewriting of the Bodhidharma lineage—Jingjue's *History of the Teachers and Disciples of the Laṅkāvatāra Sūtra*—to see how Shenxiu would be given a brother, Xuanze, who was spliced onto

Du Fei's lineage just as Du Fei spliced Shenxiu onto Faru's. Moreover, in this new Bodhidharma lineage we will see Jingjue develop a number of gestures and strategies that are already apparent in the Faru stele and Du Fei's work, making clear that he represents another node in the genealogy of genealogists—that series of writers who sought to benefit from the inventions of their "forefathers" as they went about the business of inventing forefathers.

CHAPTER 5

My Life as a Buddha

Jingjue's Version of the Truth-Fathers

OVERVIEW: FIRST-PERSON ACCOUNTS OF THE TRUTH-FATHERS

Early in the preface to his *History of the Masters and Disciples of the Laṅkāvatāra Sūtra (Lengqie shizi ji)*, Jingjue (683–750?) explains his relationship to his master, Xuanze. Jingjue claims Xuanze was a perfect buddha-like monk who received transmission from Hongren, and who was recognized at court as an "imperial teacher" *(dishi)*. Jingjue writes:[1]

> Among those to whom the Great Teacher Hongren had given predictions [of enlightenment], there was one from Anzhou—this was my great teacher [Xuanze]. In appearance he was like an ordinary monk, but in his realization he shared the stage of the buddhas. He was the imperial teacher *(dishi)*, a national treasure *(guobao)* to whom people throughout the land gave their allegiance. Since I had karmic connections with him from past lives, I personally received his instructions: only then did I come to know that the inner heart is fully endowed with True Thusness.

With the virtually unheard of Xuanze baldly presented as a buddha-like figure, Jingjue enters into a retelling of the history of the truth-

---

1. Translation from J. C. Cleary, *Zen Dawn*, 19–20, with minor changes; T.85.1283a.9. Later in the text, Jingjue speaks of Xuanze as a National Teacher *(guoshi)* (72; T.85.1290a.22). Yanagida's useful critical edition of this text is in *Shoki no zenshi, I*; Faure provides a French translation with excellent references in his *Le bouddhisme Ch'an*, 87–182.

fathers that mimicks Du Fei's *Record* but reworks it in several ways. For instance, though Jingjue lists Bodhidharma's descendants down to Shenxiu in a manner parallel to Du Fei, he changes the end of the lineage to recount how he came to inherit tradition from Xuanze, who, as the above passage makes clear, looked like an ordinary monk but was in fact equal in status to the buddhas. Hence, in Jingjue's gene-alogy Shenxiu now has a lineage "brother" named Xuanze because Jingjue claims—completely against Du Fei's *Record*—that Xuanze and Shenxiu shared equally in Hongren's patrimony of truth. Of course, doubling Hongren's "progeny" is *exactly* what Du Fei had done in his *Record* when he awkwardly gave Faru a lineage brother, Shenxiu, so that both Shenxiu and Faru could inherit Hongren's patrimony. Thus, though we don't know exactly when Jingjue wrote this work, it seems logical to assume that Jingjue's *History* came after Du Fei's *Record* and participated in that curious process of recycling and appropriat-ing other people's ancestors, or more exactly, other people's ancestral claims.[2] Moreover, in Jingjue's *History,* we have good evidence that the Bodhidharma lineage form was reinvented yet again not just by Jingjue stealing previously published lineages but also by *stealing their techniques for stealing ancestors.* That is, I will be arguing that Jingjue did to Du Fei's *Record* what he saw Du Fei do to the Faru biogra-phy, which, itself, had done something similar to the protolineage for Fachong in Daoxuan's *Encyclopedia.*

That Jingjue's *History* derives from Du Fei's *Record* seems clear from several facts. First, there are the parallels in design: Jingjue builds from the basic Bodhidharma-to-Hongren sequence that Du Fei had pulled out of the Faru stele. And, like Du Fei, after an orienting intro-duction, Jingjue hooks together accounts of the masters in a trainlike fashion. Besides these structural similarities, Jingjue's *History* seems to postdate Du Fei's because there is a certain taken-for-grantedness about Chinese truth-fathers in it—a confidence that assumes that a number of arguments presented in Du Fei's text can now be considered established. Thus, Jingjue does not devote much time to explaining transmission, either in the abstract or in specific historical instances. While the transmission moment was Du Fei's principal concern in link-ing the various biographies into a contiguous conduit, Jingjue treats

2. T. H. Barrett argues that the text had to be written before 716 because it refers to Ruizong, who died in 716, as *taishang huang* (retired emperor), implying that he was still alive when the text was written. See his "The Date of the Leng-chia shih-tzu chi."

these events with single phrases such as, "It was Master Y who took it up after Master X." Similarly, Jingjue does not cite sources to explain the Indian side of the genealogy—that list of inheriters that ran from the Buddha to Ānanda to Madhyāntika, and so on, that had figured in both the Faru stele and in Du Fei's *Record*. In brief, a host of battles that Du Fei felt he had to win in order to write his *Record* aren't pressing issues for Jingjue, and thus he launches into his genealogy with a kind of ease that isn't like Du Fei's more combative and legalistic text. Of course, too, if Du Fei's text had come after Jingjue's, then Du Fei would have taken pains to write Xuanze out of the lineage in just the way that he wrote Faru out of the lineage, but that didn't happen because, as I will attempt to prove, Jingjue had not yet created Xuanze as one of Hongren's inheritors.

Despite the many parallels between Du Fei's and Jingjue's genealogies, Jingjue's *History* shows major innovations, innovations that, in general, reflect a burgeoning audacity in rewriting the past in order to claim buddha-status in the present. These innovations have not been explored carefully, and McRae, for instance, argues that the two texts are essentially brother and sister works happily belonging to the Northern School and reflecting the growing early Chan community.[3] Moreover, since McRae doesn't see the antagonism between the *History* and the *Record,* he misses how the *History* represents a key reproductive moment in the cycle of ancestor thefts in which Du Fei's *Record* "fathers" Jingjue's *History* precisely because it was from the *Record* that Jingjue got his fathers. To get started understanding this antagonistic and reproductive relationship between these texts, I will outline Jingjue's three innovations and then develop a close reading of the more interesting aspects of his *History*.

As for the first innovation, though Jingjue builds from the genealogy of ancestors that Du Fei had lined up for Shenxiu, he reworked both the initial and final ancestor slot. Thus, Jingjue gave Bodhidharma a specific predecessor in the form of the Indian translator Guṇabhadra,

---

3. For McRae's sense of continuity in the early Chan School and its supposed movement from the provinces to the capital, see *The Northern School,* 30, where he concludes, "In other words, we can trace the growth of Chan from Daoxin to Shenxiu and beyond in an unbroken line." For McRae's more recent comments, which are basically the same, see *Seeing through Zen,* 18, 36 ff. Faure presents the *Record* and the *History* as "the two 'histories' of the Dongshan School [the East Mountain School]"; see *The Will to Orthodoxy,* 2. Later in that same work (162–64), Faure argues that we can't be sure which work came first and that we should assume that Jingjue didn't know the *Record.* The details, considered below, suggest otherwise.

who it seems came to China in the first half of the fifth century.[4] As discussed in the previous chapter, Du Fei had left Bodhidharma without a direct ancestor, Indian or otherwise, and had just mentioned that he was the third son of a Brahman family from south India. Identifying Guṇabhadra as Bodhidharma's predecessor is wholly implausible since no prior account mentions that they had met; in fact, even accepting Bodhidharma as a real sixth-century century personage means that there would have been no way for these two to have met, separated as they were by about one hundred years. However, Guṇabhadra was known for a popular translation of the *Laṅkāvatāra Sūtra,* and thus by planting him at the beginning of the lineage, Jingjue appears intent on underscoring the importance of this text for his notion of the essence of tradition.[5]

Jingjue's juggling of historical figures is clear, too, in the way that he has apparently transposed Bodhidharma's biography, as found in Du Fei's *Record,* onto Guṇabhadra. Thus, in Jingjue's *History,* there is no mention that Bodhidharma suffered from the jealous attacks of contemporary monks or that he had a thoroughly negative opinion of Chinese Buddhists, elements that were key in Du Fei's depiction of Bodhidharma's life in China. Instead, in Jingjue's *History,* both these themes are central in his account of Guṇabhadra, with Guṇabhadra discoursing at length on the evils of jealousy and the absolute lack of authentic Buddhism in China.[6] Hence, with a kind of literary slumping, part of Bodhidharma's biography, as Du Fei had created it, seems to have slid backward and landed on Jingjue's version of Guṇabhadra, who now has to play the front man for that crucial first moment when real Indian Buddhism landed in China. Clearly, Jingjue appears quite at ease manhandling the supposedly august figures in his patriline, a tendency that was apparent in the previous genealogies but here is starker.

The most plausible explanation for how Jingjue came to name Guṇabhadra as Bodhidharma's predecessor begins by assuming

---

4. For translation of this early biography of Guṇabhadra, see Shih, *Biographies des moines éminent,* 148–55; see also T.50.340a. His biography is also in Sengyou's *Chu sanzang ji ji,* T.55.105b.17–106b.21.

5. See Faure, *The Will to Orthodoxy,* 141, for his assessment of the politics at work in Jingjue's choice to put Guṇabhadra as Bodhidharma's predecessor.

6. Guṇabhadra's life in China, as presented by Huijiao in his *Biographies of Eminent Monks,* is altogether different from Jingjue's account and is mostly dedicated to explaining Guṇabhadra's translation activities, his relations with court, and a particularly ill-advised association with a prince who plotted a coup and failed; for details, see Shih, *Biographies des moines éminents,* 148–56.

that when Jingjue read Daoxuan's *Encyclopedia*—and he cites the *Encyclopedia* by name—he saw that in the biographies for Huike and Fachong, the *Laṅkāvatāra Sūtra* had been singled out as the fetish of tradition.[7] In fact, Fachong's biography mentioned Guṇabhadra as the translator of this text, and in the context of a protolineage in which Bodhidharma later transmitted the *Laṅkāvatāra Sūtra* to Huike and others. Thus, it would have been easy for Jingjue to stretch the story and create a direct connection between Guṇabhadra and Bodhidharma, based on their supposed commitment to the *Laṅkāvatāra Sūtra* as the essence of tradition.[8] Hence, whereas Du Fei worked on muffling the emphasis on the *Laṅkāvatāra Sūtra,* as found in the protolineage of Huike to Fachong in Daoxuan's *Encyclopedia*, Jingjue chose to accentuate it. In effect, Jingjue has responded to Faru's stele and Du Fei's *Record* by saying, "I see that you are building lineages by reworking that protolineage of Huike in Daoxuan's *Encyclopedia*. Thanks for the idea. I think I'll do likewise, but I'm going to do it more in line with what was already started in that entry." Thus, Jingjue's *History* represents one of those moments when, as text D, it appears to be written with a knowledge of what texts B and C did to text A, but then it reappropriated text A in a way that reflects B and C's treatment of A but also works up angles to push against B and C.

On the other end of the lineage Jingjue was equally creative, though again his inventions ought to be read as distinct imitations of preceding genealogical fabrications. Whereas in Du Fei's *Record* Hongren transmitted, awkwardly it must be admitted, to both Faru and Shenxiu, Jingjue gives Hongren ten disciples but focuses on three as the only full-fledged inheritors—Shenxiu, Xuanze, and Lao An (n.d.). In Jingjue's *History,* Lao An remains ill-defined and probably is just a diversionary figure for cloaking Jingjue's more pressing task of creating a new master, Xuanze, who will be Jingjue's spigot for tapping into Du Fei's

---

7. For this important passage in Fachong's biography, see McRae, *The Northern School*, 24–25: "[The Laṅkāvatāra] Sūtra was originally translated by Tripiṭaka Master Guṇabhadra of the Song and transcribed by Dharma Master Huiguan. Therefore, its text matches well with the truth and its practices correlate with reality. It emphasizes only the contemplation of wisdom, not just [beautiful] words. Later, Dhyana Master [Bodhi]dharma transmitted it to [both] north and south [China. Bodhidharma's] teaching *(zong)* was that of 'forgetting words, forgetting thoughts, the true contemplation of non-attainment.'" See also Faure, *The Will to Orthodoxy*, 146, for an alternative translation. For Jingjue's citation of Daoxuan's *Encyclopedia*, see T.85.1284c.25; and Cleary, *Zen Dawn*, 32.

8. For translation of this passage, see McRae, *The Northern School*, 24–25; and Broughton, *The Bodhidharma Anthology*, 65.

ancestors. Jingjue's exclusive focus on Shenxiu and Xuanze is visible in the crucial death scene when Hongren supposedly speaks to the relative merits of the ten inheriting masters and concludes by praising Shenxiu and Xuanze as the chosen duo: "To Xuanze he said: 'You yourself must properly maintain and cherish your combined practice. After I die you and Shenxiu must make the sun of enlightenment radiate anew and the lamp of mind shine again."[9] Clearly, at this climatic moment when Xuanze is defined by the truth-father Hongren as Shenxiu's equal, Jingjue saw no reason to mention Lao An, since Lao An has no value for Jingjue other than shrouding his basic task of doubling Shenxiu in order to get back to Shenxiu's purported ancestor, Hongren.[10]

One of most interesting elements in Jingjue's effort to double Shenxiu is that it seems that he created Xuanze virtually from thin air. If this is true, then, whereas Du Fei's basic agenda was to canalize, posthumously, the symbolic capital that Shenxiu had really won at court, Jingjue's basic strategy was to create a phantom double for Shenxiu and argue, essentially, "If you liked Shenxiu, you're going to love Xuanze." Or put metaphorically, as Du Fei sought to pull the hose of the Faru lineage up to the nozzle of Shenxiu's life, Jingue built on that accomplished linkage and simply doubled it off to the side with a new nozzle in the form of his invented master Xuanze.

The second main invention in Jingjue's *History* is that he wrote himself into the lineage. Thus, whereas Du Fei stayed off to the side as he wrote Shenxiu into the Bodhidharma lineage after Shenxiu's death—probably for the sake of Puji and/or Yifu—Jingjue wrote for himself. In line with this kind of self-promotion, Jingjue as a living truth-father writes in something like the first person—another striking novelty—and gives a brief description of his movement into the sphere of enlightenment. Though his quasi-first-person account appears constructed from literary clichés and though he refers to himself in the

9. Cleary, *Zen Dawn*, 69; T.85.1289c.16.

10. In his preface, Jingjue admits that he studied with Shenxiu when Shenxiu was at the capital but that Shenxiu never gave him transmission. Shortly thereafter, Shenxiu died. Just after narrating this loss, Jingjue turns to explain the life and success of Xuanze, giving the distinct impression that Xuanze functions as a kind of supplemental truth-father for Jingjue, giving Jingjue tradition and authority in place of Shenxiu, who apparently didn't fulfill this function and then died. Of course, because I believe Du Fei and others (most notably, Zhang Yue) constructed Shenxiu's identity as a lineage member after Shenxiu's death, Jingjue's narrative ought to be read as a kind of post facto desire for transmission from Shenxiu, born of reading Du Fei's text. A French translation of the preface (absent in the manuscript that Cleary was working from) can be found in Faure, *Le bouddhisme Ch'an*, 87 ff.

third person, it still represents a further closing of the gap between the genealogical narrative of tradition and the act of claiming tradition in real time, in a living body, and in the writing moment. Thus, and this is worth some reflection: the local buddha in the form of Jingjue was now also the historian of local buddhas, which means that the ownership of tradition is now based on the dual ownership of transcendental truth (from India) and the historical truth of how that Indian truth got into Chinese men.[11]

Despite this claim to immediacy with the lineage of truth-fathers, Jingjue's relationship to tradition, history, and truth appears quite vexed. All this will get worse if it turns out that I am right to suspect that Jingjue's master, Xuanze, never existed, or if he did, he did not play the crucial buddha role that Jingjue has foisted on him. Such a glaring zero at the base of Jingjue's relationship to tradition will be particularly damning, since Jingjue, like Du Fei, also argued that without transmission one doesn't have access to tradition. Thus, once writers like Du Fei and Jingjue began to assert the rule that tradition only comes in a lineage and once these lineages are shown to be *knowingly* fabricated, we have to face the problem that the content of tradition at this point has turned into *this particular style of claiming ownership of tradition.* That is, Buddhism, in Jingjue's hands, is most fundamentally the explanation of how Jingjue has come to own the essence of Buddhism. Consequently, despite the superficial obsession with the past, this cycle of rewriting tradition is accomplished with little regard for historical accuracy or respect for tradition as it used to be.

Jingjue's third innovation involves giving content to the teachings of the truth-fathers—an effort that also appears as troubled as his attempts at historical verisimilitude. Whereas Du Fei, like the Faru stele, had left truth qua tradition basically vague and ineffable, Jingjue announces that tradition flows with the *Laṅkāvatāra Sūtra,* as the title of his genealogy promises. However, he doesn't keep to this position at all and instead fills out the interior of each master's boxcar-like biography with two basic kinds of language: (1) semi-live accounts of the masters supposedly reciting their favorite sūtra quotes, quotes that rarely come from the *Laṅkāvatāra Sūtra;* and (2) pithy enigmatic questions and zany comments, given in more venacular phrasing. In brief, not only is Jingjue bringing "history" to life by claiming to be a living

---

11. The same arrangement informs the *Platform Sūtra.*

inheritor of the lineage; he is turning the biographic sketches of the masters into a place where the reader can watch masters perform tradition and articulate tradition's truths in their "own voices," even if their "spoken" rhetoric is a borrowed sūtra-ese, spiced up with some bizarre, jivey language, such as "Can you enter a jar?"[12]

In sum, by depicting passages of the Indian sūtras spilling out of the Chinese masters, Jingjue has accomplished a very basic goal: "real Buddhism" — or at least what the Chinese took to be real Buddhism — now comes out of the mouths and bodies of Chinese masters who supposedly lived in recent history. And, by putting these sūtra quotes into their bodies, albeit bodies that exist only in his text, Jingjue has effected the most basic insemination of "real Buddhism" into China since now the discourse of the Indian Buddha is mingled with the "biology" of Chinese men in a way that subtly suggests that these men didn't just read tradition and then ape it, but that tradition comes out of them in a natural way, proving that tradition is truly inside them — a claim that Jingjue made for his master Xuanze from the first lines of his text. Actually, Jingjue underscored this claim by mentioning that five-colored relics popped out of Xuanze's eyes one day when he was meditating, a detail surely designed to imply that the essence of tradition was present in a perfect form within Xuanze's physical body.[13]

In this effort to portray Chinese men as buddhas, I ought to mention that Jingjue's limits as a writer are rather noticable; it turns out that the oral content that he tries to "extract" from the masters is totally chaotic, with the sūtra quotes articulated without any reference to time, place, or their intended audience. Thus, intent as he was to manufacture the new "orality of tradition" to prove the extraliterary nature of these figures, Jingjue shows little skill in staging their performances or making his literary accounts of their orality look live. More troubling for those who would insist on reading this text as reliable reportage is the fact that the content that Jingjue so haphazardly pours into each master looks much like the content of his preface, where he wrote in his own voice and where he establishes clear perferences for certain sūtras

12. Poceski has done important work on the role of sūtra snippets in later Chan writing; see "*Mazu yulu* and the Creation of the Chan Records of Sayings." However, he seems to have overlooked how important it was to get this "buddha-talk" to appear to come out of Chinese bodies.

13. For a French translation of this passage, see Faure, *Le bouddhism Ch'an*, 90; T.85.1283a.3.

and certain themes, preferences that will repeat in the biographies of the masters. In fact, even the jivey comments that the masters supposedly uttered are repetitive and cliché, with those given to Guṇabhadra being the norm:[14]

> "Can you enter a jar? Can you enter a pillar? Can you enter fire? Can you go through a mountain? Do you enter bodily or do you enter mentally?" He also said: "In a room there is a jar. Is the jar also outside the room or not? Is there water in the jar? Is the jar in the water? Are there jars in all the waters in the world? What is this water?"

As one reads parallel lines for Bodhidharma, Hongren, and Shenxiu, it is hard to avoid the sense that Jingjue's efforts to bring these masters to life was rather uninspired, and worse, that Jingjue was altogether unimaginative as a ventriloquist since his masters speak with a kind of univocality that matches Jingjue's own "voice" in his preface.

To gain confidence in this assessment of Jingjue's manipulations, one need only ask: How does Jingue know what the masters said at all? He never once cites a source for these long-dead masters' orality, nor does he try to explain how their teaching might have gotten passed down to him. In sum, he writes with the abandon of a rather naive omniscient narrator who pretends he can breezily repeat the oral articulation of three hundred years' worth of tradition without explaining how this orality was recorded or set in his narrative, or why his account of their teachings contradicts much of what was written in other texts about these men.

BUILD IT, THEY'LL COME

To close out this overview of Jingjue's *History*, I need to mention an odd thing about Jingjue's *History*: as we have it, it ends with an ill-formed mini-chapter that lists Shenxiu's four supposed descendants: Puji, Jingxian, Yifu, and Huifu.[15] The problems that come along with

---

14. Cleary, *Zen Dawn*, 31; T.85.1284c.13.

15. Puji and Yifu, as Shenxiu's supposed descendants, were mentioned in previous chapters. At some point Jingjue (660–723) was ancestrized as one of Shenxiu's inheritors; for a brief discussion, see McRae, *The Northern School*, 63–64. Huifu is harder to identify; see McRae, *The Northern School*, 293 n. H, for several theories. For more discussion of Jingxian, see also Faure, *The Will to Orthodoxy*, 207 n. 33, where he explains that the surviving stele for Jingxian, written in 735 or 737, has him buried at Mount Song (presumably Shaolin Monastery), survived by numerous disciples, and granted imperial calligraphy for his stupa stele.

this mini-chapter are manifold. First, though all the other truth-fathers receive biographies, or at least partial biographies, no details are given about these four, and they are oddly treated as a group, something that doesn't happen in the other chapters of the *History*. Moreover, earlier in his narrative, in Shenxiu's biography, Jingjue says absolutely nothing about Shenxiu transmitting to anyone. Thus, given that Jingjue had not prepared to include these four descendants in Shenxiu's family history, it seems likely that they were tacked on later by envious "editors" who sought to burrow into Jingjue's lineage text by attaching this new set of supposed descendants.[16]

Thus, as Jingjue redid Du Fei's pipeline and put himself on the end as a working spigot in a manner that *did not* conclusively cap Shenxiu, his *History* appears to have been given a different ending in which the want-to-be-descendants-of-Shenxiu simply attached themselves, or rather their masters, to Shenxiu. That is, since Jingjue never denigrates Shenxiu in his effort to make Xuanze his double, and since Shenxiu's biography held the final position in the *History*, it was not too difficult to attach a quick transmission narrative regarding Shenxiu's four supposed disciples and sidestep the Xuanze-Jingjue segment. The structural problem here is that this addition of the four disciples of Shenxiu, who are not connected to Xuanze or Jingjue, breaks the logic of Jingjue's narrative in which the whole lineage is known to Jingjue and, in effect, arrives in his mind, his body, and then his prose. Thus, that the *History* now ends with four masters who have no connection with Jingjue, or his master, Xuanze, ruins the voice of the *History*, which had, in the preface, been speaking of what it saw, knew, and felt. Clearly, if this whole history is coming out of Jingjue's "mouth," one simply cannot put new characters on the end of the history, as though Shenxiu was in charge of the forward movement of the lineage, instead of the author, Jingjue.

In another sense, the work that Jingjue put into generating a history of this esoteric tradition independent of literature, and directing it into his own body, has been rerouted so that this history smoothly slides past Jingjue's body and actually attaches to the bodies of others. That is, his *History* was essentially a long account of Jingjue's own identity, and yet this edifice of language that sought to give him a buddha-identity apart from language was, with a couple brush strokes, turned into the

---

16. Faure also suspects this is what happened to the end of Jingjue's text; see *Le bouddhisme Ch'an*, 179 n. 1; and *The Will to Orthodoxy*, 207 n. 33.

edifice for someone else's claim to perfect identity. Keeping this final chapter's politics in view helps explain the text's success, since the eight manuscripts of Jingjue's *History* found at Dunhuang most likely do not represent Jingjue's success but rather the success of the four tacked-on masters and their descendants.

A THICKER HISTORY OF HISTORIES

To really be convinced of this cycle of appropriating the Other's identity-giving ancestors, it is worth mentioning, in advance of a close reading of Jingjue's *History,* that a couple of decades after Jingjue's writing, a certain Shenhui (d. 758) claimed Hongren's legacy in a manner basically no different from Du Fei and Jingjue. Given this cycle of rewriting the past—and it would continue for several more centuries—it seems imperative that we build a model to explain how lineage texts produced more lineage texts. To date, Chan Studies has offered little to imagine what kind of motor was driving all this writing, and except for Bernard Faure's notion of the "double" in the writing of hagiographies, the topic has not been given much attention.[17] Faure's interest in looking for doubles is, in my opinion, a promising track: it lends itself well to understanding the construction of identity via mimicry and the absorption of the Other's mana into one's own body, or the body of one's master. However, in Faure's writing, this process remains passive and essentially innocent. What I think fits the evidence much better is a model based on envy and jealousy, coupled with the growing force-of-genre in which the success of one lineage claim requires other prominent figures to work up lineages in order to remain part of the competitive discourse. Imagining these forces as part of the engine responsible for genealogical invention matches the evidence better, but it does offer a further insult to the living tradition, which was, in some measure, already scandalized by the Dunhuang Chan texts that revealed the complicated and corrupt genesis of Chinese enlightenment.

Actually, there is another layer of trouble to confront here. It seems beyond a doubt that these genealogies were written by those figures who distrusted and/or devalued the genealogical texts *they* were reading. Thus, Faure's gentle paradigm of doubles has to be exchanged for something much more involved with bad faith because participants could join

17. For Faure's interesting discussion of Bodhidharma and Seng Zhou as doubles, see his "Bodhidharma as Textual and Religious Paradigm."

the game only by recognizing its rules and its fundamentally fraudulent nature. For instance, I think by the end of this chapter it will be quite clear that Jingjue could only have written his *History* by reading Du Fei *against the grain,* that is, not as history but as seductive narrative, and in that ironic reading of Du Fei, Jingjue took from him the techniques for extending the literary practice of fathering one's truth-fathers, even as this repetition of the game would require him to know its fraudulent nature. In short, the mechanisms by which the Bodhidharma lineage was reproduced leaves little doubt that the authors of the lineage did not believe the lineage texts that they were reading *or the ones they were writing.* To close one's eyes to these problems of bad faith and duplicity is to cloak the Chinese tradition of writing genealogy in an aura of honesty and simplicity that I think it never recognized in itself.

Since obviously quite a lot rides on whether or not we acknowledge this level of invention and bad faith in the composition of these texts, below I will use Jingjue's presentation of his master, Xuanze, as a kind of courtroom case by means of which we can rethink the basic expectations with which we read these lineage histories. Of course, that I have to do this after McRae and Faure assumed Xuanze's existence—as Jingjue's master and a national teacher, and so on—is a little out of order. Once we saw the unreliable nature of these narratives, the burden of proof should have been on the historian who would claim that any of this was reliable information. Reading with the assumption of veracity should have died long ago and been replaced by its opposite: if someone writing a lineage text is asserting something to be historical, one ought to suspect the opposite, given the nature of the genre.[18]

JINGJUE, THE ARRIVISTE

The basic facts of Jingjue's *History,* such as its date of composition, its intended circulation, and its intended readership, are difficult to establish.[19] However, we can begin to historicize the text by setting out what solid evidence we do have. First, there were seven Chinese manuscripts

18. Though he has recently promoted the easy-to-remember rule, "Lineage assertions are as wrong as they are strong," at the beginning of *Seeing through Zen,* xix, McRae has not clarified what level of suspicion is appropriate in reading these lineage claims.

19. In moving into a more detailed discussion of Jingjue's *History,* I want to first applaud Faure's study of the text that he published in 1989 under the title, *Le bouddhisme Ch'an en mal d'histoire.*

of the text found at Dunhuang, as well as one Tibetan translation. Only three manuscripts of Du Fei's *Records* were found at Dunhuang, and thus the apparent willingness of copyists to reproduce Jingjue's *History,* and translate it into Tibetan, will become important for considering the logic of the final mini-chapter that, as argued above, most likely represents yet another attempt to hijack the lineage.

One way to begin to get a sense for Jingjue's place in the world of early-eighth-century polemics, is to clarify his literary sources. I note five sources, besides the plethora of Mahāyāna sūtras, that he draws on; three are labeled, and two can be divined from content. First, there is the ever-present *Encyclopedia* by Daoxuan, along with Bodhidharma's biography as supplied in the preface to the *Two Entrances and Four Practices,* both of which are mentioned by name. In his use of Daoxuan's *Encyclopedia* entry for Bodhidharma, Jingjue is basically no more devious than Du Fei. Like Du Fei, he expands and deforms the given details of Bodhidharma's relationship to Huike and Daoyu in order to present them as a node in the transmission sequence up to Shenxiu and Xuanze, something obviously quite absent in Daoxuan. In the actual content of Bodhidharma's teaching, Jingjue is more faithful than Du Fei to Daoxuan since he repeats the text attributed to Bodhidharma, the *Two Entrances and Four Practices.*

However, Jingjue has a much more complicated relationship with Daoxuan's *Encyclopedia* in another place. In his presentation of Huike, Jingjue offers an odd reconstruction of Huike's reception of transmission from Bodhidharma in which Huike is imagined standing in snow all night, a scene that will become an important iconic element in the Chan tradition. Jingjue has Huike say, "When I first generated the mind intent on enlightenment, I cut off one arm and stood in the snow from twilight until midnight, not noticing the snow pile up past my knees, because I was seeking the Supreme Path."[20] The problem is that Jingjue seems to have lifted this detail about withstanding a snowstorm from the mini-biography of Huiman, a narrative that was tacked on to the end of Huike's rewritten biography in Daoxuan's *Encyclopedia.*[21] In that passage it is Huiman, not Huike, who stands in the snow all night, and the event is recounted in the third person, with no connection to Bodhidharma. Thus, just as Du Fei remade the

---

20. Cleary, *Zen Dawn,* 41–42; T.85.1286a.14.
21. T.50.552c.13. For a translation of Huike's biography in Daoxuan's *Encyclopedia,* see Broughton, *The Bodhidharma Anthology,* 62–63.

account of Huike's random arm loss into the most important sacrifice in the history of Chinese Buddhism, Jingjue took another story of heroism about another monk, Huiman, and pasted it on to Huike. That Jingjue has Huike announce this event in the first person when the snow story of Huiman is told in the third person makes it is hard to believe that Jingjue's adoption of this story was due to a simple clerical error in which he mistakenly wrote the details from Huiman's story into Huike's life, for he altered its voice to amplify the impact of the narrative and to make the event parallel the machismo of the arm offering. Clearly, then, Jingjue, like Du Fei, made use of Daoxuan and distorted him in the interest of his own lineage-building agenda. And both their efforts appear parallel to Guanding's attempt to re-create Zhiyi's life by recycling details from the lives of other monks as presented in the encyclopedia of his era, Huijiao's *Encyclopedia of Eminent Monks* (see chapter 2).

Jingjue's third admitted literary source is a curious text, supposedly by Xuanze and with a title much like Jingjue's text—the *Legacy of the Men and Dharma of the Laṅkāvatāra Sūtra (Lengqie renfa zhi)*. Since I doubt the historicity of Xuanze, naturally I am suspicious of this text. Below, I detail the reasons for this suspicion, but for now let's just note that despite the expansive coverage that the title of Xuanze's text promises, Jingjue ignores his supposed master's work in developing the "biographies" of the early masters and only cites the text to narrate the lives of the final two figures in the lineage—Hongren and Shenxiu—precisely the two that Jingjue needed to rework in order to insert himself in the lineage that Du Fei had created for Shenxiu.

Then there are two literary sources that we can only suspect. The first is the *Encyclopedia of Eminent Monks* by Huijiao, which was Daoxuan's template and was completed in the early sixth century. Presumably, Jingjue relied on this older encyclopedia for a sketchy biographic framework for Guṇabhadra that he employed and yet rewrote in improbable ways.[22] For instance, he claimed that Guṇabhadra was particularly attached to the *Laṅkāvatāra Sūtra* and that he spoke in these jazzy riffs that look like idiomatic Chinese and are not what an esteemed Indian monk might say.[23] Thus, there is a clear sense that the

---

22. See Faure, *Le bouddhisme Ch'an,* 100 n. 4, for a discussion of what Jingjue might have taken from Huijiao's *Encyclopedia of Eminent Monks.*
23. Faure also comments on the oddness of making an Indian monk speak slang Chinese; see *Le bouddhisme Ch'an,* 111 n. 47.

masters in Jingjue's text belong to a floating world where they, and any details associated with them, can be mixed and matched as needed.

The second of these unnamed texts on which Jingjue relies is the most problematic—Du Fei's *Record*. Generally scholars have seen Jingjue's text as following in the wake of Du Fei's *Record* but haven't clarified how this "coming second" actually occurred. McRae asserts that Jingjue did not know Du Fei, but the only reason he gives is that Jingjue doesn't cite Du Fei, a position that holds only if we assume that Jingjue was an honest, source-citing historian simply interested in informing his audience of certain historial realities.[24] In general, Jingjue has been seen as a supporter of Shenxiu's school, since much of Jingjue's text follows Du Fei's buddhification of Shenxiu. However, while I agree that Jingjue's work follows Du Fei's, since it is essentially intent on appropriating Shenxiu's buddhahood, I do not accept the assumption that Jingjue was a Shenxiu supporter, or just another writer in the supposed Northern School.

In fact, this tension between Jingjue's and Du Fei's construction and use of Shenxiu is precisely why the relationship between the *History* and the *Record* is an issue. If Jingjue was writing *for* Shenxiu and Shenxiu's descendants in line with Du Fei's manuevers, why didn't he just cite Du Fei? On the other hand, if Jingjue didn't know Du Fei's work, how did he know about this particular formulation of the Bodhidharma-to-Shenxiu lineage that appears in Du Fei's *Record*? Admittedly he might have known of these claims from other sources,[25] but without having read Du Fei's *Record,* how did he know about specific deformations that Du Fei had wrought in Daoxuan's accounts? For instance, Jingjue includes that Huike cut off his arm for the dharma, a detail that does not appear in any contemporaneous work other than Du Fei's *Record*. Of course, too, going back to rework Daoxuan's account of that snowstorm in Huike's biography is a gesture that Jingjue presumably learned from seeing what Du Fei had done with Huike's arm. Last, if in a more general sense Jingjue did to Du Fei what Du Fei did to Faru's stele, where else but from Du Fei would he have learned this trick? This final point is, in my mind, the clincher, and I develop it below. It is this

24. For McRae's opinion, see *The Northern School,* 89. Faure also believes that Jingjue didn't know Du Fei's *Record;* see *The Will to Orthodoxy,* 162.

25. Zhang Yue's stele for Shenxiu puts Shenxiu in the Bodhidharma lineage, as Hongren's sole inheritor, but it is not clear whether it came before or after Du Fei's *Record.* For an edited version of this stele, see Yanagida, *Shoki Zenshū shiso no kenkyū,* 497 ff.

very copycat kind of "grandfather stealing" that makes Jingjue's text look like the son of Du Fei's *Record,* even as it works to push Du Fei's "father-text" out of the way. And, should it be thought that we need to reverse the order of influence, with Du Fei copying from Jingjue, I think we have to say that the structure of trying to attach Xuanze to Shenxiu makes it clear that Du Fei's buddhification of Shenxiu came first and that Jingjue's work presupposes it as a "target lineage."

ANXIETY OF INFLUENCE:
JINGJUE'S UNADMITTED RELIANCE ON DU FEI

In light of the above discussion, assuming Jingjue's familiarity with Du Fei looks quite defendable, but there are other reasons as well. First, and only circumstantially, Du Fei's text was most likely written at the capital and contained many claims about imperial actions taken vis-à-vis Shenxiu, and thus it would be unlikely that Jingjue, as both a former empress's brother and a well-regarded monk, would be ignorant of what was happening as Du Fei turned Shenxiu into an imperially recognized buddha. News like that would have traveled fast, especially at the elite level. Jingjue's connections with court are also confirmed by the fact that a preface to his *Commentary on the "Heart Sūtra"* was written by Li Zhifei, one of the more powerful ministers during the 720s and also the author of one of Shenxiu's epitaphs.[26]

Second, in assessing Jingjue's literary influences, we ought to pay attention to Jingjue's treatment of Faru. Faru is listed in Jingjue's *History* as being one of the ten who received Hongren's transmission, but Faru's status is specifically minimized when Jingjue has Hongren say that Faru and several others will be "fit to be people's teachers, but will only be local figures."[27] Assuming that Jingjue knew Du Fei's text, he would have received a rather rosy picture of Faru, since in Du Fei's hands Faru was a full-fledged master, like the others in the lineage, albeit without an heir. Similarly, if Jingjue knew of Faru from Shaolin Monastery, he would have had the same image from the Faru stele but in even more glowing terms, since in that narrative Faru wasn't

---

26. For an edited version of this preface, and the text, see Yanagida, *Shoki Zenshū shiso no kenkyū,* 594 ff. For a discussion of Jingjue's life, see Faure, *The Will to Orthodoxy,* 130–44.

27. Cleary, *Zen Dawn,* 69; T.85.1289c.13. McRae accepts Yanagida's opinion that Faru was deliberately slighted by later authors but doesn't develop a theory to explain why this happened; for his comments, see *The Northern School,* 43 ff.

overshadowed by Shenxiu. So how did it happen that Jingjue knew of a Hongren-Faru connection and yet seems eager to dismiss Faru as an unimportant bush-league teacher against the accounts of the earlier sources?

The most likely explanation for demoting Faru involves understanding what I take to be the basic motor driving the rewriting of the Bodhidharma lineage. Jingjue saw what Du Fei did to Faru and then did exactly the same thing to Shenxiu: he built up a "brother" figure to the last figure in the target lineage, his shadowy master Xuanze, and then used that double to siphon off the splendor of Shenxiu. But in dragging the patriarchal inheritance away from a prior source (Hongren), he had absolutely no use for Faru. In fact, Faru's presence as a full disciple of Hongren would have signaled to readers familiar with Du Fei's *Record* that Jingjue was repeating Du Fei's gesture of moving the lineage inheritance "laterally" to a new, previously unrelated recipient. I think that in order to hide this track of doubles, Jingjue knocked Faru down in stature so that Shenxiu no longer looks like Faru's double, as he so clearly does in Du Fei's text; thus, with Shenxiu's independent eminence clarified in Jingjue's version of Hongren's transmission, one would never suspect that Jingjue's depiction was the third phase in a cycle (after Shaolin Monastery and Du Fei) of rewriting Hongren's disciples.

Jingjue did two other things to obscure his borrowings of form, content, and literary technique from Du Fei's text. First, he peopled his narrative with extraneous figures like Lao An and the others mentioned in the list of ten inheritors who seem to serve no function other than to divert attention from his basic effort to get at the marrow of Du Fei's lineage. Thus, Jingjue introduces Lao An as another fully qualified inheritor at the beginning of Shenxiu's biography, but he is never again mentioned, nor is he included in Hongren's speech that glorifies only Shenxiu and Xuanze. Thus, Lao An is a kind of deflection, turning the reader's suspicious eyes away from the basic invention of Shenxiu's "brother," Jingjue's supposed master, Xuanze.

Second, Jingjue presented this whole Hongren scene, along with Shenxiu's biography, as long citations from a text by Xuanze.[28] Since Jingjue brings his supposed master's text onstage only for the tricky joint between Hongren and Shenxiu, it is worth thinking that in work-

---

28. McRae assumes that this text by Xuanze existed; see *The Northern School*, 9. Faure concurs; see *The Will to Orthodoxy*, 158–59, 166–67.

ing to double up Shenxiu, Jingjue also saw that he could benefit by doubling himself as an author, and thus he gave his imagined master, Xuanze, the literary task of handling these delicate moments in the narrative. In short, by ghostwriting this section of the genealogy under the nom de plume of his purported master, it appears that Jingjue hoped to gain authority for his narrative, and to further cloak the idiosyncratic and self-centered agenda that seems to have motivated his construction of this history of Chinese buddhas, which, of course, is really a history of himself.

Presumably, Jingjue also thought that readers would find these two crucial biographic clips—for Hongren and Shenxiu—more convincing if they appeared in his text as a narrative already written elsewhere, and by a buddha at that, and thus exempt from the scrutiny that otherwise might be visited on a narrative written by the one who was also currently claiming to own tradition. If this is what happened, then not only did Jingjue father his father in order to be his son by creating the narrative in the preface about Xuanze-the-buddha, but he also presented himself as a reliable historian by creating for himself a "historian-ancestor" in the figure of his master who supposedly gave him truth and the text with which to prove it to the world—the *Legacy of the Men and Dharma of the Laṅkāvatāra Sūtra*. In sum, there are good reasons to believe that while Jingjue made the other masters speak according to his needs, he made Xuanze write, and write in such a fashion to hide Jingjue's writing and the overall work of the text.

THE MASTER-PUPPET DIALECTIC

To get a better sense of Jingjue's writing, let's look more carefully at Jingjue's construction of the masters' speech. Though he reports the masters' words, these conversations are not integrated into the development of the plot—as they often are in Du Fei's *Record*—and instead are quickly forgotten in the deluge of long sūtra quotes that are usually strung together with no markers of time, place, or the persons on hand receiving the discourse. For instance, in presenting Bodhidharma's arrival in China, Jingjue avoids any depiction of the moment of transmission to Huike and instead first explains that the "teaching" that Bodhidharma gave was the *Two Entrances and Four Teachings*, which Jingjue then gives in a condensed form. But then, with no clear account of what is happening in the narrative, Jingjue next reproduces a nearly full version of the *Two Entrances and Four Teachings*. Apparently, Jingjue was interested in giving Bodhidharma a speaking voice, but he hesitated about what to put into his mouth and in the end decided to provide nothing more than a summary of a text attributed to Bodhidharma, followed by the text itself. To close out this messy compilation, Jingjue explains that the text was what the Chan Master [Bodhi] Dharma "personally taught" (qinshuo).[29] One doesn't have to work too hard to see that Jingjue is trying to create a speaking figure for a text by pouring that text back into the mouth of its supposed author.

In other cases there isn't even this much of an attempt to produce the appearance of speaking masters. Instead, sūtra quotes are just lined up as the masters' orality, and no effort is made to make them come alive in a particular setting or discourse moment. Thus, though Jingjue tried to produce the image of the *actual* teaching of the masters, content that Du Fei largely eschewed, his presentation of these sūtra-quoting masters is unsatisfying as it seems fabricated, insubstantial, and totally textual. In fact, one gets the odd sense reading the string of quotations supposedly coming out of the masters' mouths that Jingjue has simply done a cut-and-paste job, collecting his own favorite sūtra quotes and putting them, in their awkward literary form, into the mouths of these masters, just as he did with Bodhidharma's *Two Entrances and Four Practices* at the supposed moment of transmission to Huike and Daoyu.

Thus, in his presentation of direct dialogue, Jingjue falls short of just the elements he is after: "orality," "directness," and "authenticity." In sum, against his poetic writing in the preface to the *History,* these masters are stick figures, arranged to mechanically mouth the words of the Buddha while filling out the needed passage of time so that Jingjue could appear to be hooked, in history, back to Bodhidharma and the Buddha in India.

"IT'S ALIVE"

Besides his use of fairly random sūtra quotes to fill out the "teachings" of the masters, Jingjue's other style of writing for the masters—or, at least Guṇabhadra, Bodhidharma, Hongren, and Shenxiu—is based on a set of aggressive non sequiturs, such as "Can you enter a jar?" as seen above. McRae has identified these phrases as an early form of the pithy dialogues that would make up later *gong'an* (koan) material. That is,

---

29. T.85.1285b.15; Cleary, *Zen Dawn,* 37.

these non sequiturs supposedly represent nascent moments of "master-disciple encounter" in which the master relies on "shock therapy" to lead the student into enlightenment.[30] And, yet, whereas McRae argues that these supposedly off-the-cuff comments represent spontaneity and orality, I think the evidence suggests that these riffs are another of Jingjue's literary efforts to give the *impression* of orality and have nothing to do with the emergence of a new teaching style, or the beginning of a new shock therapy form of Buddhism. Instead, like so many things about Jingjue's work, these snappy lines are inseparable from his efforts to publicly claim ownership of tradition and to make that effort look innocent, coherent, and, of course, separate and superior to the older literary forms of tradition.

To get a sense for how Jingjue's literary agenda is being advanced by including these jivey passages, the first thing to notice is that they appear to be the opposite of the sūtra quotes since they are colloquial, usually directed toward non-Buddhist topics, and presented in much shorter chunks. Also, these jivey passages are usually set at the end of the biographic entry and not integrated into the body of the masters' supposed teaching. Thus, Jingjue first "quoted" the masters reciting a range of Indian sūtras with little or no commentary, and certainly nothing cheeky or snide implied, but then closes out his account of their teachings with these aggressive colloquialisms that either have nothing to do with India and the sūtras or seem designed to prove a kind of transcendence over language and the authority of the sūtra genre. For instance, Shenxiu supposedly said, "The *Nirvana Sūtra* says there is a bodhisattva with a boundless body who comes from the east. Since the bodhisattva's body is boundless, why then does he come from the east? Why not from the west, the south, or the north?"[31] Clearly, this question is designed to overcome the finality and sanctity of the *Nirvana Sūtra,* and, by implication, sūtras in general. However, it also gives the reader the impression that Shenxiu was just the kind of towering master who could ask such insulting questions of an Indian sūtra, questions that, presumably, would have been read as upending the foundations of the old tradition. Thus, this awkward shift to local "orality" that Jingjue is presenting seems put here to offset the masters' reliance on the sūtra and to cast the masters as figures larger than tradition, as it had

---

30. For McRae's assessment, see his "The Antecedents of Encounter Dialogue in Chinese Ch'an Buddhism," esp. 56–58.
31. Cleary, *Zen Dawn,* 76, with a small change; T.85.1290c.10.

been defined by the imported sūtras. Hence, I suspect that it was precisely Jingjue's dependence on the sūtra language that made this kind of locally inflected anti-sūtra language appear as a helpful additive to the discourse he was brewing. Or in other terms, for these local buddhas to really look like the Buddha, they had to jive a bit and diss tradition in order to look as big as the founder of tradition, the Buddha.

In effect, then, Buddha language from the sūtras was put *into* the masters to prove their august identity, but now a different kind of language had to be extracted from them to prove their independence from that distant Indian source even as that independence will also prove their sameness with the Buddha. And it had to happen in that order—sūtras first, jive second. In short, this is that crucial moment in which sameness and difference vis-à-vis tradition collapse into one reality: the new Chinese buddhas are the same as their Indian precedents, but they aren't simply beholden to that tradition as this snappy, aggressive language presumably proves.

Thus, against the McRae's assumption that Jingjue's text reflects the emergence of religious techniques for instructing students, I believe that Jingjue's literary obligation to find and prove sameness with tradition appears as the mother of invention here, with the jive of the master presented because of the complicated pressures of writing for an audience whose expectations of authority and tradition had to be both evoked *and* overcome in the way that I sketched above. This explanation is consistent with other aspects of Jingjue's agenda, but it is also useful for understanding the mercurial and iconoclastic trends that one sees in later accounts of masters' orality. Thus, here at a kind of ground zero for rewriting tradition, we can see that anti-literature literature [*sic*] was designed to prove that these masters could give and take with the best of them and, of course, that their relationship to tradition was not based on literature.

And here Faure's comments on the origin of this style of discourse are especially interesting and useful. He argues that this style of "speech" has much in common with a range of Buddhist and non-Buddhist literary precedents.[32] I would agree with this aspect of his analysis and would emphasize the way that images of orality were passed down through tracks of literature. Ironically, then, even as Jingjue looked for ways to produce for his readers the image of live discourse in his

---

32. For his comments, see *Le bouddhisme Ch'an*, 111 n. 47.

string of masters, he relied once again on literary forms that he thought would make the readers recognize the vitality and reality of these figures. Judging from the lasting enthusiasm for this portrayal of the rough-and-tumble master, his gamble paid off.

A REAL PIECE OF WORK

My various charges of bad faith in Jingjue's uses of historical sources culminate in the question of whether or not he created his master, Xuanze. Though Daoxuan mentions the name Xuanze as one of the monks in attendance at an ordination ceremony in 667, this does little to support Jingjue's claim that Xuanze was a buddha, a National Master, and his own master, or the equally crucial claim that Xuanze was the author of the text that explained how Xuanze was Hongren's descendant.[33] That is, like Faru, we might be able to find the name in the historical record, but this does not support the basic claims that are being made about these supposedly towering figures in Tang Buddhism. Doubts about Xuanze's historicity come from two categories of evidence: (1) straightforward inconsistencies in Jingjue's presentation of Xuanze in this text and in his other works; and (2) structural problems in Jingjue's assembly of the history of the masters. As I mentioned above, I will present my argument that Jingjue invented his master in the form of a courtroom case to give the reader a fuller sense of the choices that we have for reading and interpreting Jingjue's text.

As for the first type of evidence, Jingjue mentions Xuanze in several places in the *History*. He first invokes his master in the preface, mentioning several tidbits about Xuanze's life that climax in his arrival at court soon after Shenxiu's death in 706. Then, in the biography of Hongren, Jingjue cites the text supposedly written by Xuanze, the *Legacy of the Men and Dharma of the Laṅkāvatāra Sūtra,* which recounts how Xuanze was chosen to lead in the construction of Hongren's stupa and accorded a status equal to Shenxiu.[34] Xuanze's

33. For mention of Xuanze on Daoxuan's list, see McRae, "Daoxuan's Vision of Jetavana," 78; and *The Northern School,* 59–60.

34. T.85.1289c.16 ff; Cleary, *Zen Dawn,* 67–69; Faure, *Le bouddhisme Ch'an,* 163 ff. McRae, as mentioned above, takes the existence of Xuanze's text as a historical fact, yet also allows that this passage is dedicated to building up Xuanze by aligning him with Shenxiu as a parallel inheritor of Hongren's prestige: "Xuanze's references to Shenxiu and himself are a bald attempt to appropriate some of the recently deceased monk's glory" (*The Northern School,* 38).

relationship to Hongren is sealed with the mention of how Hongren's portrait was painted on a wall *(bihuaxiang)* at Xuanze's monastery in Anzhou.[35] The final time Jingjue mentions Xuanze, he is listed in the group of Hongren's top-tier descendants: Shenxiu, Xuanze, and Lao An.[36] Though all three masters are listed at the top of this chapter as Hongren's favored descendants, the chapter only gives a biography of Shenxiu. Thus, although Xuanze explains how he himself received the highest honors from Hongren, in his supposed text the *Legacy of the Men and Dharma of the Laṅkāvatāra Sūtra,* which Jingjue quotes from throughout this section, somehow neither Xuanze nor Jingjue was willing to write Xuanze's biography.[37] What is equally troubling in Jingjue's presentation of Xuanze is that, save for a preface by Li Zhifei to another text by Jingjue—his *Commentary on the "Heart Sūtra"*—and Wang Wei's stele for Jingjue, there is absolutely no other text, stele, or memorial that mentions Xuanze.[38] Xuanze, then, is an oddly obscure figure, and despite Jingjue's insistence on his fame at court and national renown, his existence is visible only in the texts connected to the person who hoped to inherit his patrimony.[39]

Most modern readers would already be skeptical of this arrangement, especially in the hands of a "historian" as unreliable as Jingjue has shown himself to be in other sections of the text, but let's review some other kinds of evidence that cast more doubt on the existence of Xuanze as a National Teacher and Jingjue's master. First, besides not being mentioned in any non-Jingjue-related text, Du Fei doesn't mention him, which turns out to be a useful piece of evidence. Obviously, Du Fei's account of Hongren's transmission doesn't match Jingjue's, so presumably one or both of them are fabricating their version of the events. And, given that Du Fei works to cap Faru, it is quite odd that he doesn't mention Xuanze, since if Xuanze was really at court in the

---

35. T.85.1289c.22; Cleary, *Zen Dawn,* 69; Faure, *Le bouddhisme Ch'an,* 167.

36. T.85.1290a.19ff; Cleary, *Zen Dawn,* 72; Faure, *Le bouddhisme Ch'an,* 171.

37. One might think that Xuanze's biography was already given in the preface to the *History* where Jingjue does give Xuanze's name, place of origin, and the account of his arrival at the capital. However, this is all tucked into Jingjue's account of his own life, which, right before this section, explains his relationship to Shenxiu. Since Shenxiu was then accorded a full biography despite being covered in the preface, we can still count the absence of Xuanze's biography as noteworthy.

38. For Wang Wei's stele for Jingjue, see Yanagida, *Shoki Zenshū shiso no kenkyū,* 517 ff; see 518, for mention of Xuanze. For Li Zhifei's preface, see Yanagida, *Shoki Zenshū shiso no kenkyū,* 596–97.

39. Faure sums up prior opinions about the dubious aspects of the presentation of Xuanze; see *Le bouddhisme Ch'an,* 91 n. 18 and n. 19.

capacity of one of Hongren's elite inheritors, as Jingjue claims, then Du Fei presumably would have needed to shut him down so as to keep the dharma flowing singularly from Shenxiu to his secret descendant(s). Again, nothing like this is mentioned in Du Fei, even though he is writing just at the time when this would have been an issue—in the wake of Shenxiu's funeral, when Jingjue claims Xuanze was at court. In short, Xuanze would have represented a massive threat to Du Fei's work; yet Du Fei has nothing to say about this figure who Jingjue claims was an "imperial teacher" and the tutor of two emperors. Arguably, just on this evidence, Xuanze did not exist as Jingjue is insisting. Moreover, despite this supposed high-profile life, there are no court records mentioning him, and there is no surviving stele cut for him or stupa erected, such as was done for other National Teachers such as Puji and Yifu. Clearly there is much to doubt here even in terms of negative evidence.

Next, and rather damaging given his general emphasis on Hongren's death and remains, Jingjue gives us no details about Xuanze's death and burial. His death is not mentioned, nor is a date or locale given for the burial, and there is certainly nothing like a sumptuous court funeral that is described for Shenxiu. Again, if Xuanze was the figure who Jingjue said he was, this all should have happened, and it would have been to Jingjue's advantage to recount it in his text. Given these absences, one has to ask the detective's question, "Where's the body?" with the justified suspicion that there is no body because Jingjue never had Xuanze for his master. Not only is Xuanze ultimately missing a body but Jingjue doesn't give him any specific teaching or doctrine: neither in the *History* nor in Jingjue's later writing are Xuanze's teachings ever mentioned. And, in the *History*, Xuanze, unlike the other masters, never gets the normal biographic entry with all the sūtra quotes to flesh out his image as a legitimate representative of the Buddhist tradition. In short, in Jingjue's structuring of the *History*, Xuanze appears as a master with neither a body nor a set of teachings, and yet he provides the hugely beneficial service of delivering a conduit—physical and textual—back to Hongren and the already established lineage that was being promulgated at court by Du Fei and the want-to-be-descendants of Shenxiu.

Now, for the second kind of evidence—structural problems in the *History*. Jingjue's *History*, like Du Fei's *Record*, recounts a singular line of inheritance up to Hongren, when suddenly there are two main inheritors onstage, Shenxiu and Xuanze (against Du Fei's Faru and Shenxiu). Besides this doubling, the problem with the *History* is that it doesn't end properly, even if one removes the final mini-chapter about Puji and the other three inheritors, since the final figure onstage is Shenxiu and not Xuanze or Jingjue himself. Du Fei had handled this doubling better by making Faru's biography spill into Shenxiu's, with Faru made to say at his death, "Go study with Shenxiu." Du Fei then gave Shenxiu a full biography that, with an account of his state funeral, rounds out the lineage with a satisfying account of the final hero who, in his last days, supposedly gave a secret transmission. In short, Du Fei's text ends where it should, with the final lineage holder dying, having passed on his patrimony to the living descendant. Jingjue, on the other hand, finishes his narrative with Shenxiu fully onstage and still loaded to give his patrimony to a chosen descendant who can't be Jingjue since Jingjue mentioned in the introduction that he failed to be Shenxiu's heir.[40] Thus, in terms of the plumbing metaphor, Jingjue ends the story of the pipeline celebrating a capped figure to whom he is unrelated and who plays no role in the future of the lineage that he is generating. Apparently what has happened is that Jingjue needed the image of Shenxiu to reproduce Xuanze as his double but then couldn't figure out how to get him out of the way, and thus Shenxiu remains as a vestige limb.

This awkwardness in Jingjue's text is matched by other odd things in the structure of the *History,* such as Jingjue's use of this text by Xuanze, the *Legacy of the Men and Dharma of the Laṅkāvatāra Sūtra,* a text that is not mentioned in any other source. If this text really existed, and especially given its name implying the same attempt to put the *Laṅkāvatāra Sūtra* back into the Bodhidharma lineage, why didn't Jingjue rely on it for entries for the other masters besides Hongren and Shenxiu? Surely he could have used some help for the Guṇabhadra entry, which likely struck readers as implausible. Instead, as mentioned above, Jingjue relies on Xuanze's shadowy text solely for that "zone of suspicion" where Du Fei's account had to be opened up and doubled so as to allow Jingjue's claim to inheritance look legitimate.

The real oddness of such a text by Xuanze comes through in a final problem: Why would Xuanze bother to write Shenxiu's biography, as he is made to do in Jingjue's citation of Xuanze's *Legacy*? He was supposedly Shenxiu's equal and occupied the same rung on the genealogical ladder, and thus he would have had no specific motivation to enshrine

---

40. See Faure, *Le bouddhisme Ch'an,* 88–90.

Shenxiu in this version of the Bodhidharma lineage, especially because the logic of the situation, as Jingjue has scripted it, is that Shenxiu does not reproduce an heir, but Xuanze does, so the flow of tradition ought to move from Hongren to Xuanze to Jingjue since Shenxiu is basically a dead end in this account.

In light of all these oddities surrounding Xuanze, not to mention Jingjue's proven unreliability as a narrator, it seems reasonable to conclude that Jingjue invented Xuanze and his text, the *Legacy,* to solve one basic problem—providing Jingjue with a truth-father, as grand and legitimate as Shenxiu, who would connect him to Hongren. With this doubling as the goal, Jingjue generated Xuanze, who fills that gap physically and textually since his body and his writing provide just the connecting tissue that Jingjue needed—to fill in the space between Hongren and Jingjue. And Jingjue uses him and his text for nothing else. Thus, in Jingjue's narrative, Xuanze's main contribution to Jingjue's text and identity isn't a moment of truth-transmission or a specific teaching—neither of which is mentioned—but rather a text in which Xuanze "writes" Shenxiu's biography and then stands equally tall next to Shenxiu, basking in the reflection of his "dharma brother." Consequently, Xuanze's real fertility as a reproductive truth-father isn't in any content but in the ability to deliver the *narrative of content* to the one who wants to be his son. Thus, Jingjue the want-to-be-buddha, generated his truth-father not as a teacher but as a "historian," with the faux-transmission of this history of the truth-fathers being the real thing that makes the next generation of truth-fathers.

THE MASTERS OF THE SŪTRA QUOTES: THE GEOGRAPHY OF INNOCENCE AND AUTHENTICITY

Now that we have a sense of Jingjue's zeal for reworking tradition and authority, it is worth discussing briefly two themes that run through the sūtra quotes that he has chosen to assign to the masters in his *History* and which he, too, cites in his preface. First, many of the masters both quote and discuss sūtra passages that evoke a kind of monism, usually in the form of the One Mind that encompasses everything, a trope central to the *Laṅkāvatāra Sūtra.* Part of this emphasis on oneness in Jingjue's sūtra citations is the insistence that sentient beings and the buddhas are essentially the same. Thus, in his preface, Jingjue articulates this as a fact, in his own voice, and then has Guṇabhadra utter the same thing slightly later in the text.[41] This theme then reappears when Jingjue has Bodhidharma rehearse the text that is attributed him, the *Two Entrances and Four Practices;* Huike, then, says something similar, too.[42] Sengcan is made to "preach" on the topic of the sameness of buddhas and sentient beings, and similar passages can be found in Daoxin's more extensive set of sūtra quotes.

Though this hierarchy-defying sameness might seem like a normal topic for Jingjue to insert here, it underscores that fundamental tension which exists between these motifs of sameness and the exclusivity of the Bodhidharma lineage—an exclusivity that apparently allows only one representative per generation, at least until Hongren, when a certain plurality takes over. At any rate, Jingjue insisted on a monism, and a collapse of hierarchy and difference, and yet worked to re-create an esoteric genealogical form of Tradition-beyond-tradition that was designed specifically to appear different from, and better than, all other forms of Buddhism. In effect, though ostensibly contradictory, these two claims end up being paired in a complementary manner that I think becomes standard fare in Chan discourse: knowing the supposed deep sameness of the Real is what makes you different, and access to this kind of deep knowledge beyond tradition is supposedly what the lineage of exclusivity delivers.

Put this way, the play of sameness and difference in this rhetoric has important public relations effects, especially in view of locating tradition in such a narrow and forbidding chute of truth-fathers. Apparently, as part of a strategy to soften this exclusivity, Jingjue appears as yet another genealogist who offers the reader a heady rhetoric equating the reader with the Buddha and yet sets this rhetoric within the frame of a "history" that is devoted to explaining why the reader is now to find himself excluded from enlightenment and in a strictly dependent relationship with the lineage members (and their texts). Thus, Jingjue starts off his preface affirming, as Du Fei did, that the secret of Buddhism isn't transmitted publicly and that real Buddhism is esoteric and far from literature, words, and even the two vehicles, Hīnayāna and Mahāyāna.[43] This drive to underscore the privateness of enlightenment reappears

---

41. Cleary, *Zen Dawn,* 20–21, 29; T.85.1283a.21 ff, 85.1284b.8.

42. Cleary, *Zen Dawn,* 34, 41; T.85.1285a.14, T.85.1286a.13. Actually, parallel passages can be found in the second section of Huike's biography in Daoxuan; see Broughton, *The Bodhidharma Anthology,* 61.

43. For a translation of the opening of the text, see Faure, *Le bouddhisme Ch'an,* 87–88.

several times in the discourses that Jingjue gives to his masters. For instance, he has Guṇabhadra explain, "In our land [India] we have the Correct Teaching, but it is secret and not openly transmitted. Those who have an affinity with it and whose faculties are fully prepared meet good and wise men on the road who bestow it on them. If not for encounters with good and wise teachers, there would be no transmission from 'father' to 'son.' "[44] The recounting of this secret patriarchal truth, however, is set next to a thorough condemnation of Chinese Buddhism, just as Du Fei had made Bodhidharma dismiss all forms of Chinese Buddhism. Guṇabhadra supposedly said, "Since coming to this country, I have not even seen people who cultivate the Path, much less anyone who has pacified mind. I often see people who go along creating karma, who have not merged with the Path. Some are concerned with fame and reputation; some act for the sake of profit and support. They operate with the mentality of self and other; they act with the attitude of jealousy."[45] As Jingjue inserts these criticisms of Chinese Buddhists into Guṇabhadra's discourse, he has handily picked up a stick with which to beat the competition, who, just like the supposed contemporaries of Guṇabhadra, will be guilty of practicing bad Buddhism if they can't point to their lineage inheritance won in a secret "father to son" transmission that Guṇabhadra supposedly held as the sine qua non of tradition.

Equally important to notice here is that, as in Du Fei's *Record*, and of course in Xinxing's teaching, there is an implicit rejection of reading sūtras on one's own. Just as Du Fei argued that reading about Buddhism apart from a real lineage master was like reading alchemy books without an accomplished Daoist saint on hand, and just as Xinxing argued that reading the sūtras and interpreting them was the cause of slandering the buddhas, Jingjue has the masters say, in effect, "We can read the sūtras, but you'd better not, or at least not without us on hand." The structure of Jingjue's text essentially has the masters say, "The sūtras, that's us."

Actually, with the sūtras swept up as the special purview of the masters, something else is happening. As long as a reader "falls into" the text and believes that he is getting live comments from the masters, he won't notice that these masters have been positioned to articulate and encourage a fundamental genre shift: don't read imported sūtras

44. Cleary, *Zen Dawn*, 26; T. 85.1284a.9; Faure, *Le bouddhisme Ch'an*, 103.
45. Cleary, *Zen Dawn*, 27; T.85.1284a.19; Faure, *Le bouddhisme Ch'an*, 105.

on Buddhism; read about the Chinese masters who not only "speak" in the same voice as the sūtras but also somehow know what is what in these texts and are able to distill the essence of tradition for the public. In fact, as in the case of Daoxin's biography in the *History*, these teachings are specifically labeled for beginners.[46] Thus, in his rendering of the masters in these biographies, Jingjue has performed an astounding alchemical transformation of Chinese authority: these masters stand before the reader with a mass of sūtras at their backs, and yet only a few select quotations from various sūtras come popping from their mouths, and as they combine these short quotations and offer commentary on them, the totality of tradition is now mediated through their "physical presence," and consequently tradition seamlessly moves not just from India to China but from sūtra literature to Chinese orality and then back into Jingjue's literary presentation of all this to the public.

TOTALLY CONTENT WITH FORM

In this literary alchemy that so quietly succeeds in reforming and relocating tradition, there is a fundamental shift in content as well. Above, I argued several times that content was disappearing as the genealogies invariably were more interested in developing the form that was to convincingly hold content than in working up discussions of content itself. In this vein of thinking about how form and content work together, I believe that we can speak of Jingjue, and Chan in general, working to create three kinds of legitimacy that fit together to mediate a triangle defined by genealogy, tradition, and the public. First, there is the legitimacy of the historian in which Jingjue as narrator expects the reader to trust him to immaculately deliver a historical narrative true to the Real of history. Here the narrative of the lineage is offered as historically accurate, with the promise that it, as narrative, was born of the Real of history and not from Jingjue's machinations, not from a growing competitive literary field, and certainly not fundamentally beholden to a long Chinese tradition of reading, writing, and reconfiguration.

Second, in the narrative of the lineage, there is the captivating promise-of-legitimacy based on the assumption that tradition moves immaculately in and out of the masters' bodies with no heresy, dilution,

---

46. See, for instance, Cleary, *Zen Dawn*, 61, 63; T.85.1288c.12, T.85.1289a.9.

or partiality. Each of the masters *is* tradition and a spokesperson as reliable as the Buddha—end of discussion. In effect, this form of legitimacy annuls all anxiety about the forward motion of tradition in time, since the deep sameness of total tradition is imagined to bump along perfectly, master by master, with nothing lost, reduced, or distorted by time, history, interpretation, illness, insanity, human desire, or cultural differences.

The third form of legitimacy is the one that offers up the most food for thought. Jingjue, and again Chan in general, has the masters insist on the preestablished legitimacy of the reader in the form of innate buddhahood, or by belonging to an inclusive truth-body or "One mind," or because of a fundamental sameness between buddhas and sentient beings. This final form of promised legitimacy actually has within it a set of expectations that simplify into three elements. First, it tempts the reader with a deep invisible totality that joins the public, en masse, to the lineage and the text articulating master public relations. With legitimacy announced on either side of the line dividing masters from the public, this form of ubiquitous legitimacy presumably incites desire in the reader, who reasons: "Aha, I myself am already legitimate, and the lineage-of-legitimate-masters is the means by which I am going to get at my own legitimacy." Conversely, to deny the lineage's legitimacy is to lose a chance to lay claim to one's own legitimacy that, though supposedly always already present, would be lost if it couldn't be vouched for by the Chinese buddhas in the lineage.

Second, this ubiquitous and yet invisible legitimacy effects a fusion of truth and being such that truth is not only no longer linguistic, but it is socked into the stuff of the Real in such a manner that it *can't* have content anymore. That is, legitimacy is now pitched not just as one's relationship to one's Real Self but also as one's relationship to the whole of reality. Thus, whereas nongenealogical forms of tradition are occupied with explaining how they are legitimately traditional via the transmission of language, texts, practices, understandings, and so on, Jingjue has produced an always already perfect form of tradition that is dispersed universally in the warp and woof of reality. Thus with Tradition = Truth = Reality, tradition as it had been known in all its multiforms is rendered superfluous in view of the masters who are both the true and the Real and know that this equation is true for all beings as well.

Third, with invisible but ontic legitimacy deployed in both this public and private manner—and designed to join the two—the door is open to promote and promise any form of actual Buddhist practice, whether silent meditation, nothing at all, or, ironically, sūtra reading, provided that it is done in reliance on a master and within the understanding of this ubiquitous form of tradition qua reality. In all cases, as long as the master–masses dialectic is in place, undergirded by the lineage legitimacy and the preestablished ontic legitimacy on either side of the master–masses divide, then the day-to-day forms of Buddhism are relatively unimportant. Or rather, with the absolute master established as the guarantor of real Buddhism, and any particular "common" practitioner already endowed with both the Real and real Buddhism, the only game in town is to keep in view that line which delineates masters from the "common" practitioner so that masters can keep telling everyone, believably, that this or that is deeply traditional.

Standing back from this arrangement, we ought to notice that the masters' exhortation to collapse the inauthentic "self" into the buddha-nature essentially mimics China's agony vis-à-vis India. Thus, the success of a Huike or a Hongren in incorporating the totality of tradition meant that all Chinese could do the same, and in fact were in some measure required to see that this was also their most basic obligation and destiny. In short, a kind of cultural alienation that existed between China and the source of Buddhism in India was resolved by fully converting a track of Chinese men into figures supposedly identical to the longed-for Indian templates and then transposing the gap of China and India on to the gap between masters and the masses, a gap that, too, was transposed on to the interior of each individual, who now had to resolve the abyss between his mundane self and his buddha-nature.

HONGREN AND THE IMAGE OF NATURAL SIMPLICITY

Before leaving Jingjue's *History,* it is worth considering how Jingjue employed Daoist motifs in creating his string of masters. This angle not only reveals the level of literary ingenuity in Jingjue's text, something that hardly need be proven again for the *History,* but also gives a clearer sense of how Tang authors formulated a kind of innocence for their masters, an innocence that not only borrowed from Daoist templates for the masters' profiles but also worked to cloak the entire genealogical writing enterprise in the gauze of disinterest and ease.

Though nature motifs and various images of innocence come and go in Jingjue's text, his treatment of Hongren reveals the most about how pre-Buddhist literary values were gradually worked into the

Bodhidharma lineage claims.[47] As detailed in the preceding chapter, in Du Fei's *Record,* Hongren's rejection of formalized Buddhism and cultural distinctions was presented as the background for his monumental success in just the zones that he was shown rejecting—society and the Buddhist hierarchy. In short, Du Fei's Hongren was a cultural hero qua buddha who went down in the symbolic order in order to land on top. Thus, arguably Du Fei has given us a profile of Hongren in which Hongren's simplicity is a mark of his transcendence of Buddhism itself, for in Hongren, Buddhism has ceased being a religion with a past, a textual presence, an institutional reality, and a political and economic life and instead has returned to its "natural" state of simply being Truth known by a buddha. With this transcendental naturalism purifying Hongren, his truth becomes all the more desirable and truthful since it is supposedly free of any inflection due to culture, literature, or politics.

Jingjue, it would seem, correctly identified the promise and function of the simplicity motifs that Du Fei put into Hongren and enhanced them with Daoist terms and a fairly explicit allusion to the *Zhuangzi,* as we will see below. Thus, as Jingjue appropriated Du Fei's lineage, he also parsed the nature and simplicity motifs for what they were, and then developed them in order to increase the allure of his pitch and to cloak his thievery in a more innocent-looking wrapper. In sum, Jingjue saw the mileage Du Fei was getting out of the simplicity-beyond-culture thematics and adopted them to make a more enticing cultural product. Of course, in moving Daoist motifs from one text to another, a literary conduit was emerging for trafficking in the image of a perfect counterculture, an image that besides being attractive to Chinese literati was also a camouflage for that very literature that delivered it and the restless spirit of competiton that created it.

In the following passage it is clear that Jingjue positions Hongren to claim ownership of truth and tradition by insisting that he was essentially buddhified by nature, in the depths of the mountains, far from culture, literature, and the Buddhist elite at court. Thus, Daoist motifs in Chan genealogies hide the literary cycle of manufacturing masters since

---

47. For McRae's reflections on Hongren as a template for the creation of Huineng, see *The Northern School,* 36. Though he argues that literary creativity was at the basis of the construction of Huineng, McRae doesn't explore the possibility that Hongren, too, was a literary product. The biographic sketch that McRae gives for Hongren is unwisely based on compiling "information" from four different sources without regard for their particular agendas; see *The Northern School,* 35 ff.

the reader becomes convinced that it was truth itself, acting in some Dao-like simplicity, that created the masters and stands behind them and not their literati "historians." Consequently, in Jingjue's reworking of Du Fei's biography for Hongren, Hongren claims that he is like the heavy timber of the deep forest far from the city. Jingjue writes:[48]

> Someone asked, "To study the Way, why is it that you don't go to cities and towns, and instead live in the mountains?" Hongren answered, "The timbers for a great hall come from the remote valleys *(yougu)*, not from inhabited areas. Because they are far from humans, they have not been chopped down or damaged by their axes. One by one they grow into giant things: only then are they fit to serve as ridgebeams. Thus we know how to rest the spirit in remote values, to stay far away from the hubbub and dust, to nourish our true nature in the mountains *(yangxing shanzhong)*, and forswear conventional affairs always. When there is nothing before the eyes, mind is, of itself, peaceful. From this the tree of the Way blooms and the fruits of the Chan forest come forth."
>
> The Great Master Hongren sat alone in purity. He produced no written record. He explained mystic truth orally and imparted it to people in silence.

This passage makes clear that Jingjue wants to promote Hongren as a remarkable treelike figure grown far from the city and far from language and given all the Daoist vocabulary of nourishing the spirit in the remote valleys, far from traditional forms of Buddhism. In fact, with only nature in view as the cause of Hongren's buddhahood, one might even be tempted to say that in his zeal to make Buddhism a totally natural Truth, Jingjue has stripped it of any content, Buddhist or otherwise. However, when Hongren is made to say that it is only under these circumstances that such timber is "fit to serve as ridgebeams," it is clear that Hongren's perfection in nature has some perfectly viable cultural functions, since the best of nature is brought in to literally bear up culture. And, given that this motif of the tall trees in out-of-the-way places is probably alluding to the discussion of big trees in the *Zhuangzi*, we have a good example of Jingjue apparently reading Du Fei's construction of Hongren, seeing the implicit Daoist motifs, and adding to them with more explicit Daoist language and allusions.[49]

---

48. Cleary, *Zen Dawn*, 66–67, with minor changes; T.85.1289b.14.

49. Faure notes in his translation of this passage that the timber motif is from the *Zhuangzi*. For this and his reflections on the Daoist imagery, see *Le bouddhisme Ch'an*, 162; later on other allusions are made to the *Zhuangzi* (e.g., 164). For an English translation of the tree passages in the *Zhuangzi*, see Burton Watson, trans., *Chuang Tzu: Basic Writings*, 59–61.

Seeing Jingjue's rewriting of Du Fei's Hongren, we have to conclude that this is not simply the gentle and unconscious process of "naturalizing" Chinese Buddhism by slowly adding in the ingredients of China's supposed love for nature. In fact, two things stand in the way of such a simple interpretation. First, Hongren's naturalism seems to be snowballing in an emerging genre of genealogical competition where naturalism is part of that very competition—certainly Jingjue has gone further than Du Fei, and Shenhui will go even further, though he will spill all this naturalism into his own master, Huineng, who he wants to be identified as Hongren's sole descendant. Second, within this spiral of faux-naturalism, the manner of developing the master's natural appeal is to attach even more literature to him; in this case, Jingjue's lines are apparently partially drawn from the *Zhuangzi*. The naturalism of the big trees is evidently being designed to support claims of cultural ascendency at court as the line about making "suitable ridgebeams" makes clear. Thus, in the hands of Chan authors, Daoist motifs might proliferate, but they also might get turned upside down, since now Zhuangzian ideals are being dragged from the idyllic distant fields and woods, where people knew "their mothers but not their fathers," into the enclaves of patriarchy and political power.[50]

Reading these Daoist motifs as having been carefully chosen to further the work of making more perfect-looking Buddhist masters while also keeping the historians-of-the-masters looking honest, innocent, and beyond court concerns, is more believable when we remember that Jingjue has several of his masters in the *History* explicitly evoke Daoist texts and teachings in order to denigrate them. Hence, for instance, Daoxin is made to disparage Zhuangzi's teachings and then Laozi's at the end of his biography.[51] Thus, in line with Jingjue's use of the sūtras, he is quite happy drawing on the established allure of Daoist texts and discourses, but he certainly doesn't want to show that borrowing as a kind of indebtedness or a reason to lodge Chan in a matrix of equally interesting and viable non-Buddhist ways to look at reality and human being. Instead, doggedly engaged in the game of one-upmanship, Jingjue even picks up discourses on noncompetition in order to gather more ammunition in his zeal to present his lineage of absolute masters.

---

50. For this phrase extolling primitive utopia, see the Robber Zhi chapter of the *Zhuangzi*, trans. Burton Watson, in his *The Complete Works of Chuang Tzu*, 327.
     51. See Cleary, *Zen Dawn*, 65; T.85.1289b.2.

SMALL CONCLUSIONS: MASTER PIECES

In this chapter, as in the others, I believe I have shown that the old model of half-believing Jingjue's *History* isn't going to work. As long as we keep looking for what Faure calls the "vertical" component of religiousity, or what McRae wants to laud as the real and authentic teaching techniques that were emerging at this time between masters and disciples, this text and the other early Bodhidharma genealogies will remain largely incomprehensible. Clearly, the evidence doesn't fit that paradigm that seeks kernels of honesty and evidence of straightforward religion, and we ought to face that fact head-on. Those generous and unsuspicious models will fall even shorter when we try to understand these texts as belonging to a reproductive sequence that, like advertisements or sit-coms such as *Happy Days,* needs to be read sequentially in order to understand its trends, its intertextual pressures, and, most telling, the way that genealogists seemed to have been carefully and ironically reading other genealogies.

Given this state of affairs, I believe we have essentially four approaches to choose from. We can keep reading half-believing, and just avoid the difficult elements, patching together a narrative-of-sincerity as needed, even while admitting the fabrication of *some* things—an approach that I am obviously trying to discredit. Second, we can avoid these early Chan texts and read only the later ones in which this messy lineage warfare is swept under the rug and we aren't brought up short by so many contradictions and glaring "inventions." And, yet, when Chan goes to Japan in the twelfth century, it is clear from the work of Carl Bielefeldt and others, many of these same dynamics of eighth-century China play out again. Thus, the ostrich model probably won't work very well either. Third, we can dismiss Chan and Zen as more religious bunk designed to win power, fame, property, pleasure, and so on, while keeping the masses moderately opiated with some heady rhetoric about salvation and innate buddhahood.

The fourth and final choice, the one that I am advocating, is to read these texts not to find out about truth, enlightenment, and human perfection but to see how these items were created, dispensed, and enjoyed. On this track, we have the basic liberal arts agenda squarely in view—trying to figure out what other people did and why, all in the hope that such a venture will tell us something somewhat more universal about being human. This means reading Chan literature to see that it was very particular, very local, and very time-bound processes that created the supposed universals of Chan, and it is just these processes that are the most interesting and most revealing of human nature. In arguing for this kind of treatment of the faux-universals of Chan, I am advocating that we read these texts hoping to learn more about human nature but only in a once-removed sense of learning how and why Chan authors created *particular* visions of human nature. And here the most important liberal arts element is catching sight of how humans make that stunning shift from the particular to the universal, that is, that alchemical moment when readers believe that it isn't some guy "talking" on a piece of paper, in a certain well-concocted narrative, but rather it is a *buddha* discoursing, flawlessly, on total truth.

Perhaps such a distanced approach that concerns itself with these dramatic shifts in the human assessment of humans will sound tepid, privileged, and a suitable target for the standard rebuttal that there are no atheists in foxholes (or cancer wards). On the other hand, it may be that in watching others create doctrines of innate perfection *for others to desire,* we have the best chance to understand similar longings within ourselves. Thus, it may turn out that reading in this distanced way will give us a rather workable and satisfying way to get at some of the more perennial "spiritual" questions, questions that swirl around identity, its supposed basis in the Real, and its relationship to the Law—issues that are inevitably set within the porous, shifting, self-opaque human subject that encompasses these elements and yet rarely comes to terms with them.

In the next chapter I work through one more iteration of the Bodhidharma lineage and have more occasion to pursue these questions regarding Chan Studies' place in the liberal arts and Religious Studies.

CHAPTER 6

Shenhui's "Stop Thief" Bid to Be the Seventh Son

OVERVIEW

After Jingjue's *History,* the next major attempt to rewrite Bodhidharma's supposed legacy came when Shenhui (d. 758)[1] argued that the current "descendants of Bodhidharma" were all fraudulent and that he was the sole inheritor of Bodhidharma's dharma.[2] At the base of Shenhui's strategy was yet another replumbing of the Hongren section of the lineage pipe: Shenhui claimed that it was his master, Huineng (n.d.), who had really received transmission from Hongren—not Shenxiu as Du Fei insisted, or Xuanze as Jingjue had argued. While this gesture of inserting oneself in the Bodhidharma lineage by creating a father who supposedly was Hongren's real inheritor hardly appears original, there are a number of innovative elements in the four texts associated

---

1. Like everything with Shenhui, even his year of death has been disputed and confused. I think it is safest to follow the date of 758 given in the stele recently discovered at Longmen in 1983. For an English translation of this important stele, see Jan Fontein, "The Epitaphs of Two Chan Patriarchs," esp. 102. I should add that Fontein's credulous assumption that the stele for Sengcan (the other stele treated in his essay) was actually written by Daoxin in 592 is most unlikely. For what I expect to be a much more careful assessment of Sengcan's posthumous "life," see Chen Jinhua's forthcoming study on Sengcan.

2. For reasons of space I have had to omit discussion of the steles written for Puji and Yifu. For Faure's treatment of Puji, see *The Will to Orthodoxy,* esp. 93–100; for his discussion of Yifu, see 78–82. For McRae's treatment of these two masters and their descendants, see *The Northern School,* 64–71.

with Shenhui that reveal much about developments in mid-eighth-century genealogical writing and the effort to make Chinese buddhas. Prominent among these innovations are techniques for bringing the ownership of enlightenment more visibly into the present. For instance, several of the Shenhui texts develop strategies for depicting Shenhui performing as a living buddha, both in his pronouncements and in nascent rituals that feature him as an officiating buddha. In addition, there is a new vitriol in Shenhui's attacks, or at least in one of the four works associated with him. In this text (considered below), Shenhui was not only more aggressive vis-à-vis prior claimants, but he also named the tricks of the trade—explicitly charging his predecessors with lineage fabrication, ancestor theft, and bad faith. Given these detailed charges, the Shenhui material, though as partisan as that of the previous genealogists, reveals the contours of mid-eighth-century lineage combat in a particularly clear manner.

Also with Shenhui came the nomenclature of the Northern and Southern Schools of Chan, a polemical invention that has bedeviled Chan Studies for decades.[3] The problem has basically been that we have been slow to recognize that there never was a Northern School of Chan and that the categories are no more than Shenhui's calculated refiguration of the field, with his predecessors now tarred as "Northern" Chan, while Shenhui and his master, Huineng, are the sole representatives of good, legitimate, Southern Chan. In fact, the figures who Shenhui labels "Northern"—Shenxiu, Puji, et al.—actually spoke of themselves as Southern but only in the limited sense that they claimed to have inherited tradition from Bodhidharma, who supposedly came from southern India, as described in the works by Du Fei and Jingjue and, even earlier, in Daoxuan's *Encyclopedia*. Shenhui, in his effort to oust the prior claimants, simply called them all "Northern," preserving the title "Southern" for himself and his invented master, Huineng. In short, by switching the meaning of "Southern" from Indian origins to contemporaneous Chinese masters, he was able to appropriate the legitimacy of the term *Southern* and dismiss all other lineage claims. Thus, with this division of good and bad Chan, Shenhui did to all prior Bodhidharma genealogies exactly what the Bodhidharma genealogies did to Chinese Buddhism: he established a new conduit of tradition and voided the claims of everyone outside of that conduit.

3. McRae makes a similar point; see his "Shenhui as Evangelist," 125.

We could explain Shenhui's take-no-prisoners approach to lineage combat simply as the result of his personality, but it is also worth considering that by the time he was writing, an increasing facticity had gathered around those claiming to be Shenxiu's dharma-descendants, and this would have made Shenhui's new "historical" claims all the harder to push into public view. The surviving evidence from the mid-eighth century suggests that the court, and several prominent writers, thought that the singular truth that Bodhidharma had supposedly brought from India was in Shenxiu's descendants, most notably Puji but also Yifu and others mentioned in that tacked-on chapter in Jingjue's *History*, as well as in new sources explaining Puji's descendants. Thus, whereas Du Fei only had to struggle against the Faru biography at Shaolin Monastery, Shenhui's task was much more daunting: how to unseat a claim to legitimacy that had all the marks of being permanently entrenched since it was recognized by a sector of the public, stamped with the imperial imprimatur, legitimized by the passage of several decades, and apparently rendered visible in public art at Shaolin Monastery and perhaps other sites where Puji's version of the seven patriarchs was erected.[4] True, Jingjue's rewriting of the lineage had already contested Du Fei's account, but it wasn't aimed at unseating Shenxiu's patriarchal place and merely sought to siphon off a portion of its patrimony by creating a brother for Shenxiu—Xuanze—who was positioned as an equally deserving inheritor of Hongren's legacy.

FOUR NEW WAYS TO BE A BUDDHA

While Shenhui's overall agenda fits the pattern of stealing ancestors, he employed four new techniques that I want to outline in advance

4. For brief mention of Puji setting up ancestor halls at Mount Song, see the vitriolic section of Shenhui's *Treatise Defining the True and False (Ding shifei lun)*, in Hu Shi, *Shenhui heshang yiji*, 289. It also seems that Emperor Zhongzong had a thirteen-story stupa set up for Shenxiu at Songyuesi, which would again have concretized the claims of Shenxiu's descendants. This is asserted in Li Yong's (678–747) "Stele of Songyuesi" (*Quan Tang wen*, 263); for this detail, see Faure, *The Will to Orthodoxy*, 188 n. 27. I believe Faure is right to explore, in this useful note, the hypothesis that locating Shenxiu's cult at Shaolin Monastery was a multilayered project supported by Puji. In fact, there is a glaring problem here: the Shaolin Monastery Stele (728) makes no mention of Shenxiu or Puji and gives Faru an heir—Huichao. Thus, there are grounds for thinking that the "installation" of Puji at Shaolin Monastery happened later than one might think, and through complex processes of negotiation. One hypothesis worth pursuing is that Yixing (683–727), as student of Puji, close confidant of Emperor Xuanzong, and friend of Shaolin Monastery, is the linchpin. For Yixing's role in the writing of the Shaolin Monastery Stele, see Tonami, *The Shaolin Monastery Stele*, 36.

of a close reading of the Shenhui texts. First, and not in the historical order of events, he directly accused Puji and others of just the kind of ancestor theft that he, too, was seeking to accomplish. No previous writer had included direct reference to the tricks of the trade, but Shenhui explicitly condemned a number of strategies found in the earlier Bodhidharma lineages. Of course, it seems that these strategies had been implicitly recognized by other lineage authors, since they copied them, but they didn't bring these gestures to the surface as part of the hostile takeovers. Thus, ironically, Shenhui attempted to insert himself into the lineage by publicly pointing out, and with some significant evidence, that Puji had done just the same thing at an earlier moment in the eighth century. In short, Shenhui tried to undo Puji et al. by copying their ancestor-stealing techniques *and* condemning them for practicing just these techniques, all in order that his own mimicry of this gesture would take hold—hence this chapter's title.

Second, Shenhui claimed that transmission of truth in China was only effected by passing down Bodhidharma's robe. Though there is some mention of the Buddha's robe being transmitted to Kāśyapa in Indian narratives found in Chinese sources, the nearest precedent for Shenhui's claim was probably Li Zhifei's rather undeveloped comment in his preface to Jingjue's *Commentary to the "Heart Sūtra,"* where he mentioned that Xuanze had given Jingjue "the robe that he had worn, his bowl, staff, and such."[5] In that context, this detail seems to serve no other function than to give form and visibility to Jingjue's connection to Xuanze. Nowhere else is the transmission of personal effects mentioned in Li Zhifei's preface, or in Jingjue's writing, and thus it seems to be a detail included here to shore up what was probably the weakest part of Jingjue's case—the absence of anything physical related to Xuanze's existence. Also, Li Zhifei's comment only connects Xuanze and Jingjue since the passage doesn't say that this was Bodhidharma's robe or that the robe stood for the essence of the whole lineage.[6] In writing the requirement of the robe and bowl into the rules of transmission, Shenhui seems to have found a powerful tool to chip away at Puji's

5. For an edited version of this text, see Yanagida, *Shoki Zenshū shiso no kenkyū,* 594–614. (This line is found on p. 597.) For more on the Chinese discussion of the Buddha's robe in India, see Shinohara, "The Kaṣāya Robe of the Past Buddha Kāśyapa in the Miraculous Instruction Given to the Vinaya Master Daoxuan (596–667)"; see also Adamek, *The Mystique of Transmission,* esp. 128–35 and chap. 5.

6. For a general discussion of Buddhist robes and bowls in Tang China, see John Kieschnick, *The Impact of Buddhism on Chinese Material Culture,* 83–112.

legitimacy. Actually, Shenhui would go further by condemning Puji not simply for lacking the robe but also for trying to steal it from its rightful owner, Huineng, thereby revealing three layers of Puji's supposed lack of integrity: (1) Puji doesn't have the robe and therefore can't be legitimate according to these new transmission rules; (2) by trying to steal the robe, Puji proves that he wanted it and thereby acknowledges both his lack and the fundamental importance of this talisman; and (3) Puji has shown himself to be a common thief and not a perfect buddha at all.

Third, Shenhui, or whoever wrote these accounts, created new literary genres for publicizing this revised version of Bodhidharma's lineage, genres that by definition increasingly treated Shenhui as a buddha-like figure whose language rivaled the Buddha's. One of these new formats was based on gathering up the supposedly "live" dialogues of the master and turning them into independent texts. In such a text, Shenhui is shown engaging in dialogue with supposedly historical spokespersons, in real Chinese places, sometimes even with the decor mentioned. Despite the emphasis on things Chinese, it turns out that in these conversations Shenhui is often quoting sūtras or giving commentary on them; in fact, Shenhui's words are, in some cases, indistinguishable from the Buddha's, as found in familiar Mahāyāna sūtras. The blending of Shenhui's "voice" with the "voice" of the Buddha is so complete that in some cases it is not clear who actually is talking; and even when a quotation is marked, it is still difficult to tell where the Buddha's "voice" ends and Shenhui's begins. Thus, as in Jingjue's *History,* the masters are still speaking sūtra-ese, but in Shenhui's writing, the dialogue model set around the Chinese master absorbs and overcomes the genre of the Indian sūtra in a more thorough manner.[7]

---

7. Adamek is likewise concerned with how sūtra language is repositioned in Chan masters' discourse but, at least in the case of Wuzhu in the *Lidai fabao ji,* seems overly hasty in treating the sūtra snippets as markers of "'Southern School' orthodoxy" and ignores the shifts in literary presentation and "housing" that these borrowings announce. In short, she doesn't explore the way that these texts were designed to get the supposed words of the Buddha to come out of the body/mind of a Chinese master, unencumbered by Indian origins and cut free of the cult-of-the-text that supports this Indian language in its sūtra context. For an example of her treatment of sūtra-ese in the Chan master's discourse, see *The Mystique of Transmission,* 59. I should add that, despite the subtlety of her arguments, Adamek appears to miss the way that negation, no-mind, "formless transmission," and patriarchal claims to exclusive ownership of truth, and so on, all go hand in hand; figuring out this package that contains the negation of content *and* the privatization of truth and tradition would have strengthened her discussions, which, though well researched and elegantly presented, seem content simply to appreciate the cohabitation of nondualism (in the form of no-mind, formless precepts, etc.) with genealogical claims.

Fourth and last, but certainly not the least of the four innovations in the Shenhui material, is the intensely interesting image of Shenhui's phantom father—Huineng. This newly created patriarch was to serve as Shenhui's place of entry into the lineage, just as Xuanze had for Jingjue. However, whereas Xuanze garnered no attention in the later rewriting of the lineage, interest in the figure of Huineng would grow throughout the Tang. Ironically, then, in Shenhui's effort to create the most desirable truth-father *for himself,* he gave birth to a father who, in time, would become the father of virtually all later Chan and Zen claimants. Equally interesting, Huineng represents a radical shift in the image of buddhahood in China for some fascinating reasons that I touch on below.

A NEWBORN FATHER: HUINENG

As many scholars have noted, up until Shenhui's writing, Huineng appears just once in the literary record. In his biography of Hongren in the *History,* Jingjue had Hongren identify Huineng as a minor figure:[8]

> In my life I have taught numberless people. Many good ones have perished. I only give approval to ten as the ones who can transmit my path in the future. With Shenxiu I have discussed the *Laṇkāvatāra Sūtra,* and he has penetrated its mystic truth: he is sure to bring much benefit. . . . Faru of Luzhou, *Huineng of Shaozhou,* and the Korean monk Zhide of Yangzhou are all fit to be people's teachers, but will only be local figures.

This list of ten masters seems quite suspect—as is everything about Jingjue's construction of this transmission moment—since several of the ten masters aren't identifiable, and, more important, the number ten seems designed to match the Ten Great Virtuous Ones *(shi dade)* that Shaolin Monastery supposedly had set up as a kind of national committee of elite masters.[9] Also, it will turn out that giving a master ten disciples shows up in several later texts, including the *Platform Sūtra* and the *Lidai fabao ji,* suggesting that a coterie of ten disciples was seen as a stock trope before and after its usage here by Jingjue

8. Translation from Cleary, *Zen Dawn,* 68–69; for Faure's translation, see *Le bouddhisme Ch'an,* 165–66; T.85.1289c.9.

9. For mention of Shaolin's ten-monk system, see the Shaolin Monastery Stele, trans. in Tonami's *The Shaolin Monastery Stele,* 37.

and thus we should expect that several of these masters are essentially placeholders to fill out the needed set of ten.[10]

Huineng was most visibly born, it would seem, when Shenhui invited the famous poet-functionaire Wang Wei (701–61) to write a long and elegant epitaph for Huineng.[11] Though the epitaph is poetic and well wrought, the life story that Wang Wei's stele created for Huineng looks most improbable, and for two very distinctive reasons. First, there is a total lack of historical details: no dates at all for Huineng or his actions—not even a place of birth or death.[12] Second, the details that are given about Huineng's life are generated by quoting lines from the Chinese classics and Buddhist sūtras. Thus, apart from recycled snippets from China's favorite texts, there is a noticeable absence of real "events" in Huineng's life; in short, he appears to be a paper tiger of sorts. To reveal the density of this kind of literary Frankensteinism in Wang Wei's stele, I have marked the references for some of the more interesting allusions in the following translation, which represents the first third of Wang Wei's text.[13]

> The Chan Master was surnamed Lu, and was from such and such [sic] region and province. Names are empty and vain, [and anyway] he was not born of an aristocratic family. As the dharma has no center or periphery (fa wuzhongbian), he did not dwell only in China (buju huaxia zhi di). Good habits were manifest [even] in the way he played games as a child, and his sharp intellect was displayed in his youthful mind. He was not selfish, and was a companion to the stench of farming and silk production (chouwei yu gensang zhi lu—Zuozhuan), and simply taking whatever came along, he followed the rank way of his barbarian land (shanxing yu manmei zhi xiang—Zhuangzi/Analects).[14] When he had a couple years

---

10. For this passage in the Platform Sūtra, see Yampolsky, trans., 170.

11. Wang Wei also wrote an epitaph for Jingjue, which suggests that he was essentially a pen for hire since the two lineage claims are contradictory. For the stele written for Jingjue, see Yanagida, Shoki Zenshū shiso no kenkyū, 517–34.

12. A similar vagueness—and the use of "such and such" to fill out absent details—is found in Wang Wei's stele for Jingjue. For a partial translation, see Faure, The Will to Orthodoxy, 135.

13. I have relied extensively on Yanagida's identification of these references; for his edited version of this stele and footnotes, see Shoki Zenshū shiso no kenkyū, 539–57. I frankly don't have the encyclopedic knowledge of Chinese literature needed to identify these lines. This in itself is interesting—who but someone equal to Wang Wei would have been able to recognize more than a glimmer of the vastness of his reference scheme? Because the allusions are so numerous, I have only pointed out a few; those readers interested in every binome should consult Yanagida's amazingly detailed work. Also, I would like to thank Brook Ziporyn and Chen Jinhua for solving some of the more difficult translation problems in the stele.

14. Yanagida (Shoki Zenshū shiso no kenkyū, 545) notes the use of the binome shanxing ("rank way") in chapter 24 of the Zhuangzi; for an English translation, see

of age, he served the great master [Hong-]Ren of Huangmei with all his
strength *(yuan jie qi li—Analects)*.[15] [At Huangmei,] he was installed in
the [work] of the well and the mortar *(History of the South, Nanshi)*,[16]
and it was there that he gouged out his mind *(kuxin—Zhuangzi)*[17]and
attained enlightenment in the wild grass *(tibai—Zhuangzi)*.

Every time the master [Hongren] ascended the seat, students filled the
hall, and among them one could find the capacities of the three vehicles,
as they listened together to the one-sound-dharma. The Chan master
[Huineng] was silent in receiving the teachings and didn't introduce
anything [new or private] *(zeng bu qi yu—Analects)*. And then with
careful private investigation *(tuixing—Analects)*, he far transcended them
all [the other students] to reach no-self, realizing that the self's putative
had been no more than deluded thoughts, like a thirsty deer thinking of
water *(Laṅkāvatāra Sūtra)* or hoping to trace the tracks of birds in the
sky *(Vimalakīrti)*.The perfumed rice *(Vimalakīrti)* not digested, and dirty
clothes still worn, but everyone could tell he had ascended the hall and
entered the room *(Analects)* to fathom the ocean and survey the heavens.
It was said that he had obtained the Yellow Emperor's pearl *(huangdi
zhi zhu—Zhuangzi)*,[18] and that he merited the seal of the dharma-king
(Lotus Sūtra). The Great Master [Hongren] knew of his achievements *(zhi
huo de—Shiji)* and [knew] that due to his modesty, he was not trumpeting
them. Heaven, how could it speak *(tian he yan zai—Analects)*? Sage-
liness and Benevolence, who would dare claim them *(sheng yu ren qi
gan—Analects)*?[19] You and me [reader and Wang Wei] are not as good

---

Watson, trans., *Complete Works of Chuang Tzu*, 276. The other binome, "barbarian
land" *(manmei)* is found in the *Analects* (15.6); for an English translation, see D. C. Lau,
Confucius: The Analects, 132.

15. This line alludes to the passage in the *Analects* 1.7: "who exerts himself to the
utmost in the service of his parents" *(nengjie qi li)*. See Lau, *Confucius: The Analects*,
60.

16. It is likely that this random reference to Huineng's involvement with food and
food production later gave rise to accounts of how he worked in the monastery's threshing
room *(dui fang)*, as explained in the *Platform Sūtra* (trans. Yampolsky), 128, 131, 132.

17. Yanagida interprets this phrase based on the binome *kuxin* "gouge out your
mind" (or, "to pluck out your mind") to mean that he was enlightened in his everyday
activities; for this passage in the *Zhuangzi*, see p. 127 in Watson's *Chuang Tzu*: "The
Way covers and bears up the ten thousand things—vast, vast is its greatness. The gentle-
man *(junzi)* must pluck out his mind! To act through inaction *(wuwei)* is called Heaven.
To speak through inaction is called Virtue." The binome "wild grass" is in the *Zhuangzi*
in a riff about finding the Dao in everything, even in lowly things like wild grass, "tile
and shards," and "piss and shit"; see Watson, 241, where he translates "wild grass" as
"panic grass." I think this passage may have been influential in establishing scatological
elements in later Chan discourse.

18. Watson, trans., *Chuang Tzu*, 128–29: "The Yellow Emperor went wandering
north of the Red Water, ascended the slopes of K'un-lun, and gazed south. When he got
home, he discovered he had lost his mysterious pearl *(xuanzhu)*."

19. "The Master said, 'How dare I claim to be a sage or a benevolent man? Perhaps
it might be said that I learn without flagging and teach without growing weary.' " See
Lau, *Confucius: The Analects*, 90.

as he *(Analects)*. As Hongren was about to die, he secrectly transmitted the patriarchal robe and bowl, and said to him [Huineng], "All creatures hate those who are uniquely worthy. And people hate those who are better than themselves *(Hanshu)*. After I am dead, you should go."

Despite relying so heavily on this bevy of Buddhist and non-Buddhist source materials to create Huineng's life, it is clear that Wang Wei's basic agenda is to make Huineng look like a bumpkin buddha. Thus, against the kingly image of the Indian Buddha, Huineng is rural, unlearned, plebian, and directly involved with odiferous food production. The net effect is that Huineng appears as the magically apt, if somewhat stinky, redneck who is naturally endowed with all that it takes to be a buddha, independent of the cultural and institutional techniques normally relied on to generate buddhas and Buddhist authority. Hence, like the shifts in the artistic rendering of the Buddha's face and body throughout Asia, this was a key moment when the profile of human perfection was radically altered and the Indian Buddha now appeared as a Zhuangzian sage. Henceforth, this shift toward radical naturalism, already evident in the budding biography of Hongren, as seen in the narratives by Du Fei and Jingjue, would be a favored leitmotif in Chan.

In taking stock of Wang Wei's bumpkin buddha, we should not miss that Huineng's unlettered down-homeness is obviously a literary image generated by one of the most educated writers of the era who wrote this figure into existence by stitching together a staggeringly diverse set of quotations from Chinese literature, Buddhist and non-Buddhist. This means that there is a funny mismatch between form and content here: Huineng is presented as an all-natural, backwoods buddha, but this image is evoked with quotations from a wide range of sophisticated books, lightly alluded to, in an elegant eulogy. Similarly, there is a tension between observer and spectacle. Wang Wei's dense writing is accessible only to those literati for whom the figure of super-simple Huineng stands as a kind of polar opposite, and thus to get the literary references about Huineng's down-home innocence is already to find oneself on the wrong side of the fence.

By locating pure Buddhism in this rural and completely unadorned figure, far from court and high culture, Wang Wei has given Shenhui a heavy stick to beat the establishment with since Shenhui has positioned himself to inherit perfection from one who apparently never sought confirmation of his perfect status from the public or from the Buddhist hierarchy. Thus, though appearing contentedly unwashed and completely uninvolved with institutional status, Wang Wei's Huineng is

turned into a site for collecting a spectrum of Chinese values and organizing them so that they can be "harvested" by his son, Shenhui, for
some rather institutional purposes. Or, rather, this image of Huineng
seems designed as a kind of triple threat: Huineng has the perfect truth
of a buddha, but it is held with an earthy old-style Daoist simplicity
that cleanses him of any sectarianism or self-aggrandizing polemics,
while this amalgam of innocent perfection is ready to be harvested
according to Confucian models of inheritance and probity.

The question of Chineseness in Huineng's identity also warrants
attention. Early on in the epitaph, Wang Wei, after clarifying that
Huineng was not an aristocrat, writes, "The dharma has no center or
periphery *(fa wuzhongbian),* and he did not dwell in China *(bu ju hua
xia zhi di).*" With this line Wang Wei positioned Huineng as a kind of
crossover figure who is beyond the cultural and racial divides that seem
to have so interested eighth-century writers. Huineng was presumably
Chinese in a certain sense—Wang Wei said he was surnamed Lu—and
yet Huineng is also residing outside of China, and thus, as a liminal
figure, is not restricted by the divide between Chinese and non-Chinese
and, like the nature of dharma mentioned in this line, appears beyond
notions of center or periphery. I suggest that with this comment, Wang
Wei is trying to mediate the India-China divide, which would have to
be overcome if Huineng was going to be a site of both Buddhist and
Chinese perfection.

Huineng's ambiguous, extraterritorial Chineseness works in tandem
with another of Wang Wei's tropes. Though Wang Wei has Huineng
receive formal transmission from Hongren at Hongren's death, in
the narrative details leading up to this moment, Wang Wei has taken
pains to show that Huineng *already* had within himself the totality of
Buddhism and clearly needed nothing in the way of a final transmission
from Hongren, from India, or from the Chinese Buddhist establishment. He was, so we are told, enlightened on his own, in "the wild
grass," and certainly was not zapped into enlightenment as Faru and
other masters supposedly were. In fact, in the lines preceding the transmission, Wang Wei makes clear that Huineng had already been recognized as enlightened by the people, and thus the transmission from
Hongren appears anticlimactic.

Equally clear, Huineng appears constructed as a father who was
never really a son vis-à-vis his formal truth-father, Hongren, and this
serves two purposes. First, Huineng's biography is proving that Chinese
ground is as good as Indian ground; innate buddhahood isn't restricted

to racial origins, a theme that will be associated with Huineng in other texts written slightly later.[20] As one who has become what he always was, he is proving the most crucial point for asserting China's independence from India: buddhahood can be Chinese, and it can be manifested apart from imported Buddhism. Second, when this self-reliant Chinese buddha transmits perfection to Shenhui we know that this version of Buddhist perfection has its origins not only in the foreign Indian father but also in the "soul" of China—as evoked by all the Confucian and Daoist references that give Huineng his identity—a position that will have subtle effects for generating desire for Huineng and Chan in general.[21] In other words, perfection in the figure of Huineng just got a little more perfect as it moved closer to home.

Moreover, by creating a figure from thin air, Wang Wei and Shenhui drew an invisible but invincible line around a site that could house all the literary values that mattered—the Chinese literati tradition with its spectrum of Confucian and Daoist tendencies, the Indian Buddhist traditions with its sūtras and images of perfection, and so on. In that immaculate creation of the perfectly empty (and full) father, all these values found a home away from the matrixes that traditionally housed them: books, academies, governmental libraries, real historical figures, Buddhism, India, and so on. Once Wang Wei wrote Huineng into existence in this manner, the die was cast for centuries of enjoying, in literature, the image of the perfect Chan master beyond literature.

In short, Huineng as a historical figure was immaculately produced simply by gathering up literary references and putting them into the

---

20. In the *Platform Sūtra* this is just the theme that Huineng is made to play up in his first encounter with Hongren; see Yampolsky, trans., 127–28. In what is referred to as "Huineng's Unofficial Biography," this, too, is his main discussion point with Hongren; for a translation, see Jorgensen, *Inventing Hui-neng*, 681–82. Unfortunately, despite the massive amount of research for this book, Jorgensen seems not to have found a stable theoretical paradigm for reading and interpreting Chan literature. For a particularly unsatisfying discussion of fabrication in the writing of Huineng's biography, see 10 ff, where he tries to fold literary deceptions into the upāya-based practice of Buddhism such that one consents to be liberated by the lies of the master, with this being no more than a reflection of Chan enlightenment and Mādhyamika thought (13). This confusion is heightened when Jorgensen's narrative about the development of tradition makes clear that he, like McRae and Faure, is treating Chan literature as largely reliable for establishing historical facts.

21. It might be worth exploring how this situation parallels Germany's difficult relationship with Greece, especially in light of Germany's nineteenth-century Greek mania that was followed by Heidegger's darker attempt to reclaim Greek wisdom and anchor it in German soil with his beloved notion of rootedness *(Bodenständigkeit)*. For discussion of this tension, see Charles Bambach, *Heidegger's Roots*.

image of a body. Thus, Wang Wei's fathering of Huineng involved creating a perimeter, notably sealed off from any natal lineage, and injecting that circumscribed space with the literary values that the literati generally cared about. In this displacement, the literary chunks don't exactly change their meaning, but their context now is defined as living through a real body and not through mere words and the encumbering physicality of texts. Similarly, in receiving this literary content as his interior and as the basis for his life, Huineng is purified of being ordinary and particular, since now his person is the quilting point for the cachet associated with these various literary allusions of "universal" acclaim. Thus, there is an interesting dialectic at work here: literature, after chosen pieces of it have been recombined and injected into the body of the rustic, shines back to the literati as an image of itself housed in a zone most distant from itself, thereby purifying itself of itself, even as it has manufactured a new literary form qua container for focusing desire on itself.

Of course, something else has happened. With this immaculate relocation of literature in a man's body, Wang Wei easily moves that perfection forward into Shenhui's body, and with the most partisan of intentions, one suspects. Thus, the dialectic of recombining Chinese literary values with its opposite—Huineng's smelly body—comes hand in hand with the most private kind of self-aggrandizement: Shenhui is now the sole inheritor of this repackaged image of tradition that holds Confucian, Daoist, and Buddhist values in a new synthetic totality. Put otherwise, the whole maneuver focuses desire for tradition onto the figure of a singular man, a gesture that is exciting for the immediacy and intensity it promises, even though this gesture is also the one that will keep those desires from doing anything other than appreciating those elements from afar, since, according to the logic of inheritance, only Shenhui will come to fully own them.[22] Of course, the irony of the situation only deepens when Wang Wei codes even this moment of transmission from Huineng to Shenhui as replay of literature: Wang Wei writes that Shenhui inherits Huineng's perfection just as suddenly as the Naga princess does in the *Lotus Sūtra*.[23]

In sum, Wang Wei's account of the Huineng-to-Shenhui transmission

22. Careful readers likely will see here a workable template for reinterpreting the figure of Jesus in the New Testament. I plan to take up this comparison in a forthcoming book, *Fetishizing Tradition: Desire and Reinvention in Buddhist and Christian Narratives*.

23. This scene occurs in chapter 12 of the *Lotus Sūtra;* see Watson, trans., 185–89.

transforms literary values into human perfection and establishes this amalgam in a historical framework that, once it looks historical, erases Wang Wei's role in just this creation and thereby allows for new levels of desire for these forms of perfection that are captivating precisely for the series of purification that they incarnate: literature purified of itself, humanity purified of itself, the writing of history purified of itself, and, perhaps most important, polemics purified of itself. With this sense of Wang Wei and Shenhui's involved literary and symbolic strategies in creating Huineng—strategies that replayed many of the previous strategies for stealing ancestors, along with coming up with new tricks as well—let's begin sorting through the other Shenhui-related material by first considering Shenhui's situation on the field of religious politics.

SHENHUI THE BARKER: THE POLITICAL ECONOMY OF ORDINATION CERTIFICATES

To give some context for Shenhui's bid to be Bodhidharma's descendant, we need to remember that the scant historical evidence for Shenhui suggests a tumultuous career that culminated in his on-again, off-again success at the capitals where he was known, apparently, for holding large public dharma meetings where he sold ordination certificates—a most interesting conjunction of activities worth theorizing on several fronts.[24] Treating the surviving evidence judiciously, it seems that Shenhui arrived at court in 745, five or six years after Puji died, and was widely recognized as a powerful public speaker well able to hold the attention of large crowds. Of course, this talent was a useful skill for any monk who wished to draw attention to himself and gain cultural capital, but it was also crucial for situating Shenhui as a conduit between the throne and the people. With Puji and Yifu dead, Buddhist power at the capital seems to have entered into a period without a clear leader. Though other monks went on to claim inheritance from these masters, no singular figure stands out at court after Puji, except for Shenhui, for the rest of the eighth century.[25]

24. Evidence for this comes from the *Lidai fabao ji*. For discussion of Shenhui's life, see McRae, "Shenhui as Evangelist"; see also his "Shen-hui's Vocation on the Ordination Platform and Our Visualization of Medieval Ch'an Buddhism." For another discussion, see Jorgensen, *Inventing Hui-neng*, 62–68; see also Yampolsky, *The Platform Sūtra*, 23–42.

25. For discussion of the various claimants to the Puji and Yifu lineages, see Faure, *The Will to Orthodoxy*, 91–100; and McRae, *The Northern School*, 69–71.

Soon after Shenhui arrived in the capital, the empire was racked by nearly a decade of civil war—the An Lushan Rebellion—during which the capital had to be evacuated and the country fell into considerable chaos. A major concern of the government was raising enough funds to field its armies while maintaining control over the areas that it had not ceded to the rebels. Apparently to bolster the imperial coffers, the court decided to sell Buddhist ordination certificates, which the government had long been in control of. These documents basically defined who was officially recognized as a Buddhist monk, and since the status of monk carried with it exemption from tax and corvée labor, winning court recognition of one's monkhood had significant economic consequences. Given these privileges that accompanied monkhood, it is no surprise that for centuries the Chinese government tried to limit the disbursement of these documents for fear that otherwise a significant portion of the male population would find a shelter from taxes and government service. Throughout the centuries, however, it was normal for the court to offer, usually as part of an amnesty or a sign of imperial goodwill, a crop of certificates, say, on the scale of one thousand or more in excess of the yearly rate.

During the An Lushan Rebellion, however, the throne decided that its economic situation was so dire that it needed to immediately raise money any way it could, and to that end, it was decided that ordination certificates could be sold to the public.[26] Though it isn't clear how widespread this practice became, it does seem that the government was essentially mortgaging its future since each certificate represented a future loss of revenue for the State. At any rate, it appears that the government enlisted Shenhui to sell these certificates, presumably at the large public meetings, a setting that suggests that they weren't just sold but likely auctioned off to the highest bidders and hence the government's interest in enlisting the services of a barker-style Buddhist leader like Shenhui. Given this situation, the State would probably have been little bothered to see Shenhui make new and exorbitant claims about his identity, provided that it finessed the sale of the certificates at high prices. That is, given the State's urgent needs, it would have cost the State little in terms of symbolic capital to grant Shenhui, informally or formally, the right to claim whatever identity or heritage he chose, even if it ran counter to identities that the State had conferred on

---

26. For more information on ordination certificates, see Faure, *The Will to Orthodoxy*, 89–90.

figures such as Shenxiu (posthumously) and then, more recently, Puji and Yifu. In short, Shenhui's ascendance seems linked to another hot spot in Chinese dynastic history when the State was in a particularly vulnerable situation and the parameters for negotiating Buddhist-State relations were relaxed and perhaps even in disarray.

Put in other terms, the State was in charge of manufacturing the commodity of basic Buddhist legitimacy in the form of the ordination certificate, while Shenhui was enfranchised as its salesperson but in a way that only worked insofar as he would appear as a legitimate purveyor of these key Buddhist rights. Thus, whereas Guanding set up the memory of Zhiyi to be an ongoing Big Other to the throne, as did the monks of Shaolin with Faru, here the State seems little interested in seeing Shenhui as a "deep" representative of tradition whose endorsement of the State will carry weight with the masses, but rather the State is interested in having Shenhui play that Big Other role for the masses in order to secure steady revenue for the State. Hence, below, when we consider two of Shenhui's texts that are oriented toward organizing public meetings, it is worth wondering if part of what instigated the movement from simple genealogical claims made at court to announcing such claims at publicly orchestrated events had to do with the State's need to sell formal rights to Buddhist identity during this extraordinary midcentury crisis.

THE SHENHUI MANUSCRIPTS

There are four texts that are grouped around the figure of Shenhui.[27] Two texts are set up as dialogues between Shenhui and various interlocutors—one in private, one in public—the third is something like a public ritual text organized around Shenhui converting an audience with his *Platform Sermon (Tanyu),* and the fourth is a short poetic piece on "no thought" *(wunian)* and the robe of transmission, known as the *Record Clarifying the Essence (Xianzongji).* For reasons of space, I will treat only the first three.[28]

In reading these texts, one quickly senses that they reflect rather diverse styles and contents. For example, within the numerous conversations in the longer dialogue text that is called *Questions and*

27. Yampolsky charts these four texts on pp. 24–25 of his *The Platform Sūtra.*
28. Robert Zeuschner translated the *Record Clarifying the Essence;* see his "The *Hsien Tsung Chi* (An Early Ch'an [Zen] Buddhist Text)."

Answers on Various [Topics] Confirming the Doctrine (Wenda za zhengyi, title based on S. 6557), there is no mention of Huineng, the lineage of Bodhidharma, the evils of Puji, the robe, or the value of the *Diamond Sūtra.* Instead, the main topics are sudden enlightenment, the internal perfection of every sentient being—their buddha-nature, that is—and the need to find a buddha, bodhisattva, or Good Spiritual Adviser to gain access to that internal perfection. On the other hand, the other dialogue text, *The Treatise on Defining the True and False for the Southern School of Bhodhidharma (Putidamo nanzong ding shifei lun),* has a rather involved preface and then a short account of a public debate between Shenhui and Dharma Master Chongyuan (n.d.), which has very little content and ends with Shenhui claiming victory when Chongyuan slanders the *Lotus Sūtra.* The second part of this text, which seems largely unrelated to this first part, bristles with attacks on Puji and then extensively explains the logic and function of the robe of transmission but then trails off into tedious discussions of the *Diamond Sūtra* that seem contrary to the thrust and tenor of the attacks on Puji, and certainly are not in line with the tempo and content of the first part of the text or the other dialogue text, *Questions and Answers.*

To draw out the major differences between these texts, one could build a typology of structural and thematic differences—for example, noting the presence or absence of first-person voicing, the narrator's choice to emphasize dates and supposedly historical events in the narrative, the intrusion of an omniscient narrator, the presence or absence of an audience onstage, the inclusion of emotional reactions in the encounters, the importance of a lineage history, and so on. When the four texts are read searching for some consistency in these elemental themes, one quickly concludes that the texts don't represent the work of one author, or if they do, he changed his position and his discourse style radically. Actually, we don't need to work that hard to try to shoehorn these texts into the oeuvre of a single author since the two dialogue texts, the *Questions and Answers* and the *Treatise Defining the True and False,* come with prefaces announcing that they were compiled by disciples of Shenhui—Liucheng and Dugu Pei, respectively. Thus, we have to admit that these texts are not by Shenhui and likely are not the direct reporting of his teachings either. In fact, the supposedly live dialogues turn out to be complicated by a number of factors that warrant careful attention and that preclude assuming, as modern researchers regularly have, that these texts directly represent Shenhui's speech or thought.

There are two surviving epigraphs having to do with Shenhui—one by Wang Wei that is undated (discussed above) and another cut in 765, seven years after Shenhui's death. Wang Wei's epigraph tells us next to nothing about Shenhui's life other than the most important claim that he was Huineng's only disciple who received total enlightenment. Still, assuming that Wang Wei actually wrote it, and this seems likely, this puts Shenhui's time of activity in the mid-eighth century. The second epigraph, by Huikong, likewise claims that Shenhui was the seventh patriarch—"the seventh leaf," that is—having received transmission from Huineng and having been recognized as a National Master *(guoshi)*.[29] This stele asserts that Shenhui had been invited to the capital by Songding, vice president of the Ministry of War, in order to teach publicly and to "set up stelae and images." Then there is a brief description of his teachings: "Explaining the true vehicle of Prajñāpāramitā; directly pointing to reveal the [buddha-]nature; discussing the Tathāgata dharma seal—all this was only to understand the buddha-mind." This very brief mention of Shenhui's preferred teaching topics does match some of what is in the texts associated with him, but there is obviously nothing here to clarify his public teaching style.

Oddly enough, this epigraph is cut on a rock that clearly bore another epigraph before Shenhui's. Of the seven characters that are still legible from the effaced epigraph—according to the modern Chinese author, Wen Yucheng, who reported the discovery—one of them is the character *zu,* "patriarch," suggesting that the prior epigraph might have been involved in a similar kind of patriarchal claim.[30] Despite the likelihood that Shenhui's only surviving funerary epigraph was written over another one—an interesting fact since Shenhui accuses Puji of erasing stelae—we still can be fairly sure that Shenhui died on the date given, 758, and that he had claimed a place for himself in the Bodhidharma lineage, now designed to flow from Hongren to Huineng to himself. We also can't be wrong in noting that this stele is roughly cut, brief, and lacking literary quality. In short, these few elements around the stele provide but the most basic contours of Shenhui's life and point to his very marginal success even if the audacity of his efforts was to leave a lasting impression on Chan writing.

29. For this epitaph, see Wen Yucheng, "Ji xin chu tu de Heze dashi Shenhui taming"; for an English translation, see Fontein, "The Epitaphs of Two Chan Patriarchs," 102.

30. The seven characters are ground *(di),* patriarch *(zu),* and Śākyamuni *(Shi,* twice) and Monastery of Ten Thousand Treasures *(Wanzhen Si);* for this information, see Wen, "Ji xin chu tu de Heze dashi Shenhui taming," 78.

SHENHUI'S *QUESTIONS AND ANSWERS*
AND THE RECONSTITUTION OF THE SŪTRA GENRE

For its overall simplicity, I have chosen to first address the *Questions and Answers,* since starting here will work well to explore a number of important themes in the Shenhui material. In particular, throughout these forty-eight dialogues of varying length, Shenhui is presented as one who, with never a hesitation, answers key questions about the essence of Buddhism, defines the routes to enlightenment, gives permission for certain practices, explains the shortcomings of other masters, and, maybe most important, explains sūtra quotations. In short, Shenhui is serving as a buddha-like figure who has the final word on all the topics that lead to truth and salvation, and moreover, he is set up as the undeniable authority on other forms of authority, be it local masters or the sūtras.

The structure of *Questions and Answers* is quite straightforward.[31] It begins with a very short preface by Liucheng wherein he proclaims the "orthodox" transmission of Indian Buddhist truth via Bodhidharma into China through the succession of patriarchs. He then plainly identifies Shenhui, "the Master of Nanyang Monastery," as the seventh inheritor of the dharma, adding that he should be seen as the center of the community of all Buddhists. He adds further that everyone loved him like a father or mother and that when anyone asked him a question, he responded simply, like a great master.

Following the preface is a series of forty-eight conversations of various lengths that aren't strung together with a narrative or organized around any discernible principle. Liucheng, as the supposed redactor of these conversations, doesn't return to explain exactly how he came to know the content of the discussions or by what procedures he rendered these conversations into their written form.[32] None of the conversations

31. The three surviving manuscripts for this text vary considerably on the ordering of the conversations. Paul Demiéville has collated the different ordering of the texts; see "Deux documents de Touen-houang sur le Dhyana chinois," 9. I have followed P3047 as this is the one Hu Shi edited and that Gernet translated into French in his *Entretiens du Maître de Dhyāna Chen-houei du Ho-tsö.* For the preface of the text, see Demiéville, "Deux documents," 9–10.

32. One conversation does have two lines that sum up the conversation as occurring today, a comment that might represent an effort to make it seem that Liucheng was on hand for these conversations and then wrote them down later in the day. See conversation 5, in Gernet, *Entretiens,* 12; Hu Shi, *Shenhui heshang yiji,* 101. On the other hand, Liucheng mentions in the preface that he interviewed many people in preparing his text; see Demiéville, "Deux documents," 10.

is given a setting, decor, or even a date or place. Nor do any of these conversations have an introduction that would set the stage or indicate through representative details other orders of meaning implicit in the account of the conversation. Thus, here Shenhui as a personage has no specific attributes and functions much more like a cipher constituted solely from the language that emerges from his speaking position.

What these conversations in *Questions and Answers* have in abundance is sūtra quotes. Actually, a large part of what Shenhui is made to say is based on passages taken from a fairly small set of Māhāyana sūtras. Without doing a character count, I think it is fair to say that roughly half of the dialogues derive from quotations drawn from Māhāyana sūtras such as the *Lotus Sūtra*, the *Nirvana Sūtra,* and the *Vimalakīrti.* Sometimes these quotations run on for five or ten sentences, and one gets the distinct impression that the text is far from representing a conversation and instead is providing an essayist with a convenient and very traditional model for developing a set of doctrinal positions, even as that model is now shifting slightly to prove Shenhui's ability to define tradition on demand. Moreover, there seem to be repeating patterns in some of the questioners' phrasing, suggesting that the various Others that are brought onstage to interrogate Shenhui might be designed by the author to play the straight man so that Shenhui can respond with his favorite sūtra quotes. Below, I explore these problems surrounding the stylized Other in these dialogues, but a preliminary hypothesis is that these dialogues aren't dialogues at all but rather represent a fairly minimalist mimicry of the Māhāyana sūtra genre in which a discourse on truth is set up between the Buddha and a docile interlocutor who asks all the right leading questions and reliably moves the discourse in just the desired direction.

FAUX-ORALITY IN THE *QUESTIONS AND ANSWERS*

Putting borrowed sūtra-ese into Shenhui's mouth presents another problem. The Indian sūtras themselves were intended to deliver orality and inspire confidence in the reader that, after all, they weren't literary compositions but instead the Buddha's orality—the most basic form of authority in Buddhist discourse. Thus, we have something like a doubling of faux-orality with Shenhui's literary orality only looking oral because of its resemblance to the earlier form of literary orality found in the sūtras. But unlike the Indian sūtras that often had rather plush discourse scenes sketched, Liucheng as redactor has done little to mock up a convincing presentation of Shenhui's orality. What is notably missing is anything that would mark the current dialogue as in tune with its moment of delivery and not drawn from some other distant source, such as the imported sūtras.

Though lacking annunciations of real-time events, another kind of historicity is apparent in the dialogues. Several times, Shenhui is questioned about the teachings of other Chinese masters, and each time, Shenhui smoothly points out their errors and seals the conversation with a sūtra quote. Though this doesn't break with the preponderance of the sūtra-ese, it still represents an attempt to bring sūtra quotes, and the pure authority of the Buddha that they contain, to bear on contemporary Chinese matters via the figure of a living person—Shenhui. In these performances, Shenhui is shown effortlessly responding to current dharma matters by delivering the perfect sūtra quote that resolves the problem. Thus, in terms of performance, Shenhui is set up as the great distiller and redactor of tradition—one whose knowledge first goes backward to the origin of tradition in India and then forward to contemporaneous China, just as a lineage claim would, obviating in every way any argument over interpretation. Tradition in the *Questions and Answers,* then, is totally in Shenhui's hands.

Also, whereas Bodhidharma or Hongren might be narratively defined as perfectly enlightened in Du Fei's *Record* or Jingjue's *History,* these vignettes of Shenhui holding "court" both proves his status and shifts ownership of truth from a narrative claim to a performance, a shift that, though still in literature, aligns authority closer to a living Chinese body since it is not narrative-based as lineage claims are. However, at this early juncture in formulating literary models for "dharma combat," all decisions are rendered at a distance from the other masters. Hence, in the cases in which a ruling on a contemporary master is sought, the questioner first gives an account of some other master's conduct or teaching, and then Shenhui responds with a decisive judgment, though this judgment never is taken back to the "offending" master for his rejoinder. Thus, the intervening interlocutor, positioned much like the reader, is still the place of resolution, since Shenhui's pronouncements never reach the field of dispute to which they were *supposed* to apply.

Another point to note about the interplay of sūtra quotes and Shenhui's "orality" is that nowhere in these forty-eight dialogues does Shenhui attack sūtra legitimacy. He never even argues for the reality of truth behind the sūtra tradition as Du Fei, Jingjue, and the monks of

Shaolin had. Instead the authority lodged in the sūtras has been front-loaded into his own person. Given that there is no mention of lineages in these discussions, Shenhui would be completely lost if he denounced the sūtras as lacking the core of truth in the Buddhist tradition. He absolutely needs this literary conduit, or he has no other route back to his avowed source of legitimacy.

In fact, not only does Shenhui blend his own person with the Buddha and Vimalakīrti by comfortably juxtaposing their dialogues with his, but there are also several dialogues that work at having Shenhui inhabit sūtra space. In these discussions, the current discussion moves from the present into the past space of the sūtras, where the Chinese questioner's qualms are cleverly blended with the questioner in a sūtra and then the Buddha's answer is made to satisfy both questions, with Shenhui sealing the explanation with his own phrases. Consequently, there is a subtle kind of mapping at work in which the Chinese questioner poses a problem, sometimes verbatim from one of Shenhui's choice sūtras, and Shenhui responds by drawing them explicitly into that sūtra where Shenhui and the Buddha go to work answering the question. The effect is a tight fusion between the Buddha and Shenhui, as well as between the sūtra and this collection of dialogues.

With Shenhui presented as a flawless, ever-ready sūtra commentator, we have an image of a Chan master quite at odds with what many modern readers might have expected. Shenhui as the supposed great champion of sudden enlightenment and "no-thought," shows himself to be rather involved in one of the oldest Chinese preoccupations—sūtra exegesis—but with two important differences. First, as we have seen above, Shenhui performs live, and thus instead of writing out his exegesis, he speaks it, or rather, performs it, since in the context of a question-and-answer dialogue his responses appear spontaneous and unprepared. In fact, if his interlocutors are taken as real Others arriving from the world-beyond-literature, then this situation is not only much more alive; it demonstrates Shenhui's unfailing confidence in real social intercourse, a zone that is always fraught with unexpected dangers, dangers that are totally absent within the controlled process of writing "armchair" sūtra commentary. Second, and by implication, besides dispensing with the cumbersome outline apparatus of the sūtra commentary, these dialogues bridge the gap between the language of the sūtras and Shenhui's own voice. This shift into a "spoken" and therefore living register, though still completely rooted in the language of the sūtras, brings Shenhui up to the level of a buddha, since the

Buddha's words and logics pass through Shenhui "naturally," without the filtering of an academic apparatus.[33]

THE CONTENT OF THE MATTER

Despite the word *various (za)* in the title *Questions and Answers on Various [Topics] Confirming the Doctrine,* there is a very narrow range of topics addressed in the conversations.[34] In fact, there are five main topics that, it turns out, are rather involved with one another and work to form a gestalt of sorts.

1. The inherent purity of all sentient beings, described as their buddha-nature *(foxing)*, which renders them, in an ultimate way, identical to the buddhas;

2. The indispensable role of sudden enlightenment, usually explained with the example in the *Lotus Sūtra* of the Naga princess's offering of the jewel to the Buddha, though two examples of sudden advancement in bureaucracy are also mentioned;

3. No-thought as a singular item in the achievement of enlightenment—that which all the buddhas and bodhisattvas used;

4. The claim that all non-buddhas need to find a teacher to effect this recovery of their internal purity, since no other technique will work; and

5. A certain tendency to discuss opposites as correlative; that is, there is long because there is short—though the domain of application for this kind of logic is very limited.

While apparently disparate, these five topics can be read as constituting one paradigm, though this paradigm has three sides. First, Shenhui is shown arguing that all beings are inherently perfect in a way that matches the *Nirvana Sūtra*'s position and several other of his favored

---

33. To clarify the audacity of this kind of writing, one could imagine an early church father such as Tertullian or Origen moving away from exegetical discussions of various passages in the Gospels to redeploy Jesus quotations in their own texts without clearly marking the passages. The intimacy suggested by fusing voices like this certainly would have appeared blasphemous within the early Christian church, especially if this fusion of voices was presented in a literary format that suggested that it was performed in public.

34. Gernet supplies a useful summary of the topics covered in the forty-eight discussions; see his *Entretiens*, 1–3.

Māhāyana sūtras. This topic is clearly the mainstay of the conversations. Then, with this ontology in view, Shenhui argues for sudden contact and reappropriation of this "lost" purity—hence the pitch for sudden enlightenment. This serves, it would seem, to incite desire in the reading audiences since the ultimate good is clearly on hand in an immediate form, and its recovery is a forgone conclusion since it has been established as an always-already ontic reality. Third, though enlightenment is inherently at the base of one's own nature, Shenhui says at least eight times that the only way one is going to get at one's internal reality is through the assistance of a master who is identified as a buddha, a bodhisattva, or a Good Spiritual Friend *(shanzhishi;* Skt. *kalyānamitra).* Here, of course, the wide open field of universal buddhahood is narrowed down to specific figures who, inexplicably, are set up as the gatekeepers to these goods. Similarly, nothing in particular is going to help regain this lost purity: meditation and other normal practices are worthless and will even obstruct one's bid for self-reclamation. Thus, implicit here is the claim that though total truth is completely public and ubiquitous, access to that truth can only be gained by finding a qualified master, a decided shift in emphasis from prior forms of Chinese and Indian Buddhism. (The discourses on opposites and spontaneity seem to be more demonstrative of Shenhui's prowess and play less of a role in the ideological package.)

In taking stock of this three-sided gestalt, we shouldn't miss that it reconstructs the relationship between truth and authority, as portrayed in the Māhāyana sūtras, in two major ways. First, the need to read sūtras and believe them has been overwritten with the need to place one's faith in a real historical person; this was stated numerous times, but the overall structure of the text makes this clear as well. In effect, this text is offering itself as a kind of key for "reading" Buddhism, and Liucheng says as much in the preface. Second, installing faith in Shenhui's perfect identity is the function of a certain kind of reading that is elicited by dialogues that demonstrate Shenhui's perfect identity in lieu of directly claiming it. Shenhui never calls himself a buddha in these discussions; instead he *performs* as a buddha, in real time, in China, mimicking all the forms that the sūtras provided to define the Buddha's actions and annunciations. This then seems to be a major advance in the writing of Chan rhetoric: Shaolin's or Du Fei's dry history of the patriarchs' deeds is a far cry from this intimacy with the living, breathing, truth-speaking master that one at least partially senses when reading the *Questions and Answers.*

Unfortunately, making sense of how the text organizes belief and desire around itself has been overlooked in modern readings. However, once we pay attention to the modes for constructing Shenhui's perfect identity, we can appreciate how this "live" literature works and why it was so successful from the Tang period down to the present. In sum, viewing these "live" performances as refined status claims will put us in a good place to understand how this literature grew directly out of the sūtra precedent and how it would overtake that precedent and lay the groundwork for several new Chan genres.

SHENHUI'S MANY VOICES: AN INTRODUCTION
TO THE *TREATISE DEFINING THE TRUE AND FALSE*

In another collection of Shenhui conversations we see a completely different image, not only of Shenhui, but also of the mode in which his buddha-status could be presented. Whereas the *Questions and Answers* linked a series of thematically related discussions together, the *Treatise Defining the True and False,* compiled by Dugu Pei, works up one single conversation into a richly choreographed event that concludes with Shenhui's triumphant public victory over a certain Dharma Master Chongyuan, who had been introduced as the leading master of the nation. In short, Dugu Pei's text represents a very different strategy for using dharma debates to advance polemical claims.

Unfortunately, the *Treatise* presents a number of manuscript complications since a complete manuscript of it was not found at Dunhuang; instead, it has been put together from two partial Dunhuang manuscripts, P3047 and P2045, which don't, in fact, join perfectly.[35] P3047 gives a full preface for the *Treatise* and then the account of one encounter between Shenhui and Chongyuan at Great Cloud Monastery in Huatai, in modern Henan. When the encounter ends, Shenhui is declared the victor, and the omniscient narrator picks up the narrative to claim that Shenhui had "on just that day distinguished the heretical from the orthodox, and defined the true and false."[36] This passage replays lines that had been used in the preface to introduce the encounter, giving the

35. There is a third manuscript of the text from Dunhuang, P3488, but it isn't useful for reconstructing the *Treatise* because it contains only the final third of the work, which is already found in P2045. P2045 is a multitext manuscript that also contains another text related to Shenhui, *The Platform Sermon,* which I consider at the end of this chapter.
36. Hu Shi, *Shenhui,* 267; Gernet, *Entretiens,* 90.

sense that the agenda established in the text's title and in the preface had been fulfilled at the end of this single triumphant encounter.

Moreover, just after these lines the narrative informs us that there were more than forty other great dharma masters (they are referred to as Great Virtuous Ones, *Dade*) on-site who confirmed the validity of the discussion and sealed the exchange as authentic. This group gesture generated in the narrative has even more finality to it since Dugu Pei uses the term *confirmed, zhengyi,* to explain the action of this impromptu committee of forty masters. So, clearly we have several markers of closure at this juncture, and yet with matters apparently resolved to the narrative's satisfaction, the conversation restarts in a different key, with Chongyuan asking about Shenhui's spiritual achievements and whether or not he is a buddha. However, we never learn where this line of questioning is headed because the manuscript breaks off just after these two opening questions. And yet, with just this evidence in view, we have several reasons to suspect that this resumption of the debate represents an attempt to piggyback more material into the original form that Dugu Pei had established.

Coincidentally, the second manuscript, P2045, begins to be legible roughly around this question of Shenhui's buddha-status. Thus, though P2045 lacks the preface and the account of the encounter between Shenhui and Chongyuan at Great Cloud Monastery, it shares with P3047 these two lines about whether Shenhui is a buddha. Based on these shared lines and the fact that P2045 uses the title *Treatise Defining the True and False* for itself later in the manuscript,[37] Hu Shi argued that these two chunks of narrative from manuscripts P3047 and P2045 ought to be joined to form one text. This seems logical, but with minor caveats. First, we shouldn't overlook the fact that the long conversations in P2045 that grow out of reopening the debate develop a whole series of positions that seem quite at odds with the style, form, and content of the first cycle of debate as found in P3047. Furthermore, as Jacques Gernet, the French translator of this text, has pointed out, P2045 has material just before the two lines it shares with P3047 that doesn't exactly match P3047.[38] Thus, my opinion is that while it is correct to fuse the manuscripts, we still have to see that the resulting ensemble set under the title *Treatise* represents several layers of writ-

37. See Hu Shi, *Shenhui,* 314, for this passage.
38. See Gernet, "Complétement aux *Entretiens du Maître de Dhyāna Chen-houei,*" 459 n. 4.

ing with one fold visible just before those questions about Shenhui's buddha-status, giving the impression that an original preface and a single encounter made up the earliest strata of the text, which was then supplemented in both manuscripts.

Actually, there are several other problems with hooking together these two manuscripts to produce a single text. For instance, not only does P2045 drift away from the "live" debate setting into long commentarial prose on the *Diamond Sūtra,* it flirts with giving itself a new title as well—"The Treatise on the Sudden Enlightenment of the Unsurpassed Vehicle" *(Dunwu zuishangcheng lun).*[39] Moreover, within P2045 there are at least two sections that are different enough in style and content to be separated from one another, as well as from the initial debate found in P3047. Given the layers of writing apparent in these supposed dialogues, I will first work through the preface and the first encounter that are found only in P3047 and then compare it to Liucheng's *Questions and Answers* to point out how different these two images of Shenhui are. Then I will explore the form and content of the later sections of the *Treatise* as found in P2045 where Shenhui's comments are largely dedicated to smearing Puji's reputation, comments that are mixed with a kind of hysteria and violence not found in either P3047 or Liucheng's *Questions and Answers.* In fact, of all the Shenhui material, this is the only place where we find such extreme language.

Also, given these different strata of content in the *Treatise,* we ought to resist assigning a single date to the ensemble.[40] In particular, it is altogether possible that these later sections so full of venom were added on to the first part of the *Treatise* that, though decidedly aggressive in its own right, had been written in a calmer and more hopeful time. In previous studies, it has been assumed that the text (as reconstructed from P3047 and P2045) represents one seamless event, and thus we have been asked to believe that Shenhui made these attacks on Puji and the Shenxiu "school" in 732 or so, based on the dates that Dugu Pei gives in the preface of P3047 for the dharma debate at Great Cloud Monastery. However, if I am right that these later sections attacking Puji and Shenxiu were added to the initial strata presenting the debate, then we need to consider that several pieces of this text might have been

---

39. Hu Shi, *Shenhui,* 310.
40. McRae, while he takes the text to reflect a real debate in 732, notes that he believes the text has been edited several times; see his "Shenhui as Evangelist," 125 n. 1.

written a good bit later than the early part of the 730s as claimed by Dugu Pei in the preface.

In sorting through these possibilities, the key date of 739 has to be kept in mind. This is the year that Puji died, and it seems likely that it was around this time that Shenhui would have made his more far-fetched claims in the effort to dislodge Puji's legitimacy. As we will see, in the most hostile section of P2045, Chongyuan is made to ask Shenhui why he waited so long to make these attacks on Puji since it has been more than several decades since Puji has been teaching (as the seventh patriarch).[41] This query obviously seeks to resolve what the author perceived as a potential point of resistance to his discourse, that is, Why all this *now?* In short, this query about the lateness of advancing these particularly nasty attacks on Puji and company suggests an admission that Shenhui's tactics shifted radically at some point in the middle of the eighth century.

THE *TREATISE DEFINING THE TRUE AND FALSE*

The preface to the *Treatise* begins with the otherwise unknown writer, Dugu Pei, announcing that he wrote the text after sitting at the foot of the mat of his master Shenhui as Shenhui debated the Dharma Master Chongyuan: "It was after these discussions that I composed this *Treatise.*" However, the simplicity of this writing is undermined when the following perplexing sentence announces that the writing process was rather drawn out.[42]

> In the years 731, 732, and 733, this text *(lunben)* remained unfinalized *(bing buding)* because the writing wasn't complete since the words [of the discussion] and the text didn't match *(yanlun butong)*. Now I take the 734 version *(ben)* to be definitive. Also, since then, there is [another text] in circulation entitled the *Biographies of the Teachers and Disciples in the Bloodline (Shizi xuemai zhuan)*.

This comment, sketchy as it is, seems to portray a drawn-out process of writing and rewriting, and leaves completely in doubt the actual date of the encounter that supposedly led to the text.[43] One would think that it should have happened in 731 or just before, but in fact,

41. Hu Shi, *Shenhui*, 290.

42. For a French translation, see Gernet, *Entretiens*, 81; for an edited version, see Hu Shi, *Shenhui*, 260.

43. Equally problematic is the manner in which Dugu Pei established an accord between his text and what was actually spoken. What or who served as the guarantor of the "words" as Dugu Pei drew up the text that was supposed to preserve the words?

several lines later, when Dugu Pei actually gives a date for the encounter, he claims it occurred in 735, a distinct impossibility given the
claim that the text was written and rewritten in 731, 732, 733, and
734. So what's going on? Hu Shi decided to backdate 735 by two
years and to change the date of the writing as well, so as to get a logical order of events.[44] McRae and Gernet, on the other hand, seem to
take the three writing years as the years of a series of debates and/or
lectures.[45] Frankly, in light of the contradictory evidence, I think we
should just conclude that the text has quite a problem assigning dates
to both the actual event and the later writing process. Below, when
we sort through the narrative's account of the "debate," we will have
even more reason to doubt its historicity and thus the question of its
date becomes more a question of determining when this narrative was
constructed and put into public space and less an investigation into a
supposed encounter.[46]

Following Dugu Pei's enigmatic statement about the writing process, he begins a fairly standard refuge poem that at first matches, in a
general way, the one that Du Fei gave at the beginning of the *Record*.
However, the second half of the preface shifts into more lineage-related
claims:[47]

> I take refuge in the dharma of the Three Jewels,
> And, in the Dharma Nature that is the Tathāgata Storehouse *(zhenru
> zang)*;
> And, in the Truth Body and the Effect Body [of the buddhas]—
> Those who save our world with their great compassion.
> With the understanding of the essence establishing the [next] under-
> standing of the essence *(li zongtong),*[48]
> Like the moon in the empty sky,
> May only the dharma of the sudden teachings be transmitted,
> Which is supramundane and destroys the heterodox teachings/sects
> *(zong).*

44. Hu Shi, *Shenhui*, 261.

45. McRae's comment—which I suspect he would no longer support—can be found
in his "Shen-hui and the Teaching of Sudden Enlightenment in Early Ch'an Buddhism,"
234; for Gernet's comment, see *Entretiens*, 43 n. 1.

46. Jorgensen, though he believes the debate was a historical event, suspects that the
text has been falsified; for his position, see *Inventing Hui-neng*, 64.

47. See Gernet, *Entretiens*, 81, for a French translation.

48. Gernet has edited this line so that it matches one from the *Platform Sūtra*, but I
think the line reads fine the way it is. Presumably, the image of the moon in the empty
sky is a mark of the singular "understanding of the essence," which nonetheless can be
counted on to reappear.

Having set up his notion of truth as singular—with the vague notion of transmission and the image of the moon in the sky—Dugu Pei makes clear that the "sudden teachings" that he is setting out to convey are to be launched into a rather contentious atmosphere with the hope of destroying "heterodox teachings/sects."

After this preface, the text gets under way with a question that Dugu Pei poses to himself: "For what reasons was this Treatise written?" I have translated this question in the past tense, "written," but the question could also be rendered, "For what reasons are you writing this Treatise?" In either case, the question clearly is a narrative device and not a question posed from outside the discourse's own space. Moreover, it reveals that Dugu Pei is writing with a clear Other in mind and is, from the outset, establishing his text for this reading Other by first addressing what he assumes to be the reader's primary concern, that is, Why are you writing to me? However, relying on a faux-dialogue format for the introduction to a text that is itself supposedly a dialogue between Shenhui and Chongyuan soon becomes complicated because Dugu Pei is going to use Shenhui's discourse, as he has constructed it, to answer this invented query, thereby using content from the "historical" event to solidify *the writing of that "historical" event.*

To finesse this reflexive history, Dugu Pei first establishes the site and date of the event and then turns the narrative voice over to Shenhui, once he has set Shenhui on the Lion's Throne in the middle of Huatai's Great Cloud Monastery in 735. From this throne of truth, Shenhui, as quoted indirectly by Dugu Pei, explains the history of the transmission of truth from Bodhidharma to Huineng, and by implication, to himself. Oddly, though, once Shenhui has finished this monologue, Dugu Pei addresses the reader, saying, "That's why I wrote this treatise." Thus, Dugu Pei has provided Shenhui with a long offstage whisper in which Shenhui gives the patriarchal history back to Bodhidharma but with absolutely no effect noted in that "historical" sphere at Great Cloud Monastery, and yet this monologue serves to answer the question that Dugu Pei had posed between himself and his reader.

In building this layered sequence, Dugu Pei's treatise is a long way from Liucheng's unconnected and undirected dialogues as seen in the *Questions and Answers*. Dugu Pei presents a dialogue that is one uniform event (however multilayered), directed toward very specific polemical goals, and quite self-conscious of what is at stake. Equally important, Dugu Pei has created Shenhui as a more visible actor, an actor who speaks of his own identity and who forces that identity on to others, supposedly in public, and from the most prestigious place in the monastery, the Lion Throne, the site from which the head of the monastery normally gives teachings in a manner that replicated the Buddha, who preaches from a Lion Throne in various Mahāyana sūtras.

OFFSTAGE LINE: THE SHORT
VERSION OF THE BODHIDHARMA LINEAGE

To understand how this dharma combat is to proceed, let's first look at the lineage claim that Dugu Pei puts in Shenhui's mouth in that opening, offstage whisper. This mini-history of the lineage is heavy on new stories for Bodhidharma and Huike and altogether uninterested in the rest of the ancestors leading up to Shenhui. Thus, it would seem that whereas Du Fei had to work hard to make this lineage look believable and whereas Jingjue felt obliged to fill out each master's life with sūtra quotes, this version of the lineage bolsters the two head figures with new stories and then jumps forward to Shenhui, ignoring the four other holders of the lineage, including Shenhui's supposed master, Huineng. In the new material for Bodhidharma, Shenhui recounts a supposed encounter between Bodhidharma and Emperor Wu in which Bodhidharma responds to the emperor's question about the amount of merit he has won from his pious deeds, such as building monasteries, making Buddhist statues, and copying sūtras—activities that would have been taken to be very typical ways to make merit. Bodhidharma declares that he has made no merit at all, and the emperor, angered, banishes him.[49] In this brief exchange, Bodhidharma identifies a fundamental lack in these standard practices and, given that Shenhui had mentioned that Bodhidharma had the "dhyāna of the Tathāgata," it would seem that we are to assume that Bodhidharma had the right to make this kind of determination because he presumably was the one directly owning tradition. However, by having the emperor banish Bodhidharma for his critique of mainstream Buddhism, the vignette also sets up a template for thinking that perfection, though fully present, might not be recognized by the throne—an important concern given Shenhui's overall agenda of undoing the throne's recognition of Shenxiu and his two supposed descendants, Yifu and Puji. Actually, when we look closely at the conflict between Shenhui and Chongyuan,

---

49. Gernet, *Entretiens*, 82–83; Hu Shi, *Shenhui*, 261; McRae, "Shenhui as Evangelist," 137.

there are reasons for thinking that the Bodhidharma – Emperor Wu conflict is arranged to resonate with Dugu Pei's own narrative: Bodhidharma and Shenhui both lack national recognition and yet claim to have a deeper legitimacy supposedly from the Buddha. At the very least, the "no merit" story sits here as an example of Real tradition rightfully denouncing derivative or ordinary versions of tradition, and doing so "in the face" of the one who was assumed to be Buddhism's Big Other—the throne—thereby reestablishing, at least in the narrative, perfect Buddhism's right to stand independent of imperial recognition—a right that Shenhui is distinctly in need of.[50]

The next major invention in the lineage history is Bodhidharma's encounter with Huike.[51] Though Dugu Pei follows Du Fei's account of Huike's arm offering, he links that event more closely to the snow-storm drama that he presumably picked up from Jingjue's *History*. In integrating these narrative details, Dugu Pei seals the encounter with a name change for Huike. We are told that Huike received his name, literally, "Wisdom Able," from Bodhidharma because of his ability to preserve and win wisdom through the hardship of offering his arm and standing all night in the waist-deep snow. In short, Dugu Pei is trying to make the event look more real by having the now widely known name *Huike* function as a marker of the historic event when Huike received transmission from Bodhidharma.

Right after explaining Huike's name, Dugu Pei has Shenhui give a key line: "Bodhidharma then opened up buddha wisdom-seeing *(kai fozhijian)* [in Huike], by means of a secret tallying *(miqi)*, and then transmitted to him the robe as a guarantor of the dharma *(faxin)*."[52] With the robe passing from Bodhidharma to Huike at the moment that buddha-identity was magically transmitted, Shenhui briskly closes out the rest of the patriarchal history up to the present. In fact, one sentence covers the transmission of the robe up through the other four Chinese patriarchs. Clearly, these later masters aren't of any

---

50. Adamek finds in this story proof of Shenhui's attempt to move the public away from pious giving and toward his focus on "the goal of 'seeing the nature' "; see *The Mystique of Transmission*, 144–45. I don't find this interpretation convincing because it takes the story out of its place in a narrative that appears designed to prove that Bodhidharma and his lineage, and in particular Shenhui, have tradition and no one else does, even if they are emperors practicing the most standard forms of Buddhism. Her early comments that we should see in this story "echoes of Bodhidharma's 'actual' milieu, in which merit-making began to be shadowed by the possibility of karmic retribution for spiritual greed" (98) seem far-fetched.

51. Gernet, *Entretiens*, 83–85; Hu Shi, *Shenhui*, 262.

52. Gernet, *Entretiens*, 84; Hu Shi, *Shenhui*, 263.

particular interest to Shenhui other than to provide a conduit that will run from the Buddha to Bodhidharma to Huineng and then to himself. Shenhui then says, "Six generations transmitted it [the robe] without any interruption," implying two things: first, that Shenhui has an intimate relationship to that history which, as mentioned in the interaction between Bodhidharma and Huike, was secret; and second, that this history has something to do with what is to follow in the narrative.

Actually, this brief lineage history that Shenhui just recounted is fused to the following events in a more telling manner. Dugu Pei reappears as narrator at this point and writes:[53]

> I also saw Shenhui on the Lion Throne say, "No one understands the unique teachings of the Southern School of Bodhidharma *(Putidamo nanzong yimen)*. If there was someone who understood it, I wouldn't speak of it. That I am speaking today is just to clarify the true and false for all those who practice the Way—it is for those who practice the Way that I am defining the essence of this lineage *(zong)*."

Here, Dugu Pei's firsthand testimony—"I also saw Shenhui on the Lion Throne say . . ."—leaves little doubt why he had Shenhui recount the Bodhidharma lineage in the preceding passage: Shenhui is supposedly the only one who understands the "Southern School of Bodhidharma," just as he is the only person who has the right to define the true and false for all Buddhists, and the "essence of this lineage," and these three powers are, apparently, due to Shenhui having received the transmission.

This passage is important, too, because it is the pivot where Dugu Pei fuses Shenhui's "historicizing" voice—pitched for the reader—with Shenhui's "live" voice, which will henceforth be directed toward the audience at Great Cloud Monastery. In effect, Dugu Pei first prepared *the reader* for Shenhui's performance by having Shenhui recount the Bodhidharma lineage in the long offstage whisper and then turned to narrate Shenhui's supposed performance in public. That no one at Great Cloud Monastery is aware of Shenhui's supposed place in the Bodhidharma lineage puts the reader in the rather privileged position of knowing more than the onstage audience, who will have to learn this history the hard way. Of course, it would seem that this entire public

53. Gernet, *Entretiens*, 85–86; Hu Shi, *Shenhui*, 263–64; McRae, "Shenhui as Evangelist," 140–41.

performance is produced for the reader as well, but to maximize the impact of the reading experience, this part of the text is cast as an event fully Other to the text.

In fact, like Faru's supposed teaching session for monks from all over the nation—as found in the Faru biography—the very publicness of this event at Great Cloud Monastery appears designed to neutralize the private claims being made for Shenhui. This is even clearer when at the end of the encounter Dugu Pei mentions the numerous dharma masters onstage who verify the conversation and uphold Shenhui as the victor. That is, Dugu Pei is seeking to drive his account of Shenhui's private family into the rock of a totally public event in which a host of reliable figures confirmed the event's integrity. Dugu Pei's ploy, then, is to argue that legitimate public recognition of Shenhui's private claim *already* happened, thereby cloaking his demands on the reader who might not notice that he is, in fact, reading a text that is asking him to rewrite history by believing this new version of the past. Consequently, by demonstrating to the reader that this kingmaking moment already happened, and legitimately so, given the august forty "dharma masters" on hand, Dugu Pei can seduce the reader into participating in the real act of kingmaking—assenting to Dugu Pei's narrative—precisely because he thinks it has already happened.

TRUTH AND ETIQUETTE

Up to this moment in Dugu Pei's narrative there has been no one else visible onstage besides Shenhui. However, now that all the historical and narrative issues have been carefully set up, Dugu Pei introduces Dharma Master Chongyuan. To get another set of reasons for doubting the historicity of the debate at Great Cloud Monastery, we would do well to first ask, Who was this Dharma Master Chongyuan with whom Shenhui supposedly debated? He is described as the most famous monk of the time, known in the two capitals, and of such stunning stature that Dugu Pei compared him to the Indian master Āryadeva, the disciple of Nāgārjuna. But, as far as I know, besides the Shenhui-related material, there is no other text or epigraphic evidence that mentions him.[54] And, given that we have evidence that Puji and others were accorded unique

---

54. A certain Dharma Master Yuan appears in the *Questions and Answers,* but it is unclear if this is the same person. See Gernet, *Entretiens,* 43.

national honors by the court during these years, it is hard to imagine who this supposedly grand figure might have been. Thus, until triangulating evidence appears, it is probably best to treat Chongyuan as a huge straw man—the imaginary owner of national recognition who, once he disgraces himself, yielded that identity to Shenhui. Ironically, then, in a narrative sense, it is from the nonexistent Chongyuan and not the other two nonexistents—Huineng or Bodhidharma—that Shenhui will get transmission, and, of course, on a deeper level, it is from the throne that this national master identity is being wrested, albeit in narrative.

The text's construction of Chongyuan as a temporary container for fame and public legitimacy is visible in another telling way. Never is it said that Chongyuan had any particularly nefarious doctrine that needed to be refuted, or that he had dubious habits. In short, there is nothing wrong with Chongyuan, and that is just the point. All that is good and traditional about Chongyuan, as inserted there by Dugu Pei's narrative, will just as easily be removed by the narrative and put in the body of Shenhui.

Equally dubious in the construction of this historical event is the institutional framing of the encounter. Why would Chongyuan allow Shenhui to organize such a dangerous-sounding meeting—to decide the true and the false—at his monastery? Obviously, the very premise of the discussion is an insult to Chongyuan and implies that tradition, under his tutelage, is adrift and in need of restoration. Similarly, though modern scholars treat this event as something like an invitational debate, the *Treatise* presents a much different kind of combat. Chongyuan's first words question the proceedings and are, in fact, a reproach to Shenhui: Chongyuan wants to know why somebody got out the decorative screens for the hall, as if there were important guests coming. Chongyuan seems not to have been on the planning committee when Shenhui was invited and not at all a party to the choices leading up to this event. Weirder still, it will soon be clear that establishing the legitimacy of the event turns out to be the only topic debated. Thus, actually, there is a beautiful rhyme here between the inside and the outside of the narrative since Dugu Pei's fundamental relationship to the reader is predicated on winning the reader's trust for his history of this supposedly real debate, and, within the text, the debate is itself structured around winning the legitimacy to have the debate in the first place.

SPECIAL SONSHIP AND DIRECT
ACCESS TO THE TRADITIONAL TEXTS

In the encounter between Shenhui and Chongyuan that follows, neither candidate develops a position with specific content. Instead, there is a kind of competition that is directed, not toward elucidating points for the Other or for the public as promised, but toward unseating Chongyuan and humiliating him. Hence, when we look closely at how the narrative develops, it seems that the structure of the encounter allows Shenhui to simultaneously annul and appropriate Chongyuan's status and legitimacy in a way that parallels how the *Lotus Sūtra* and the *Diamond Sūtra* supplant traditional Buddhism while also relying on traditional Buddhist figures to secure and ratify their coups. It is no surprise, then, that these sūtras are the ones cited since, most likely, they are providing both the form and the content of the engagement.

For this narrative to work, the violent victory over Chongyuan must be read *not* as a contingent bid to win recognition and status. Instead, Chongyuan's symbolic death must appear as the simple result of bringing pure, "old," independent truth—delivered from the Buddha to Shenhui via the Bodhidharma lineage—in contact with the current and decidedly second-rate form that it had taken in the figure of Chongyuan. In their meeting, Chongyuan's defeat must look like the natural effect of encountering Shenhui's perfect Buddhism that has this "deep" patriarchal heritage behind it. The overcoming of imperfect tradition, then, should appear to the reader as the natural and even undesired consequence of the "return" of Real tradition, which, supposedly, has no interest in overcoming the prior site of authority and only wants to define the true and false. As I argued in the preceding chapters, establishing desire for the master as a perfect figure works only when he is shown completely free of the desire to be recognized as such.

In terms of reading for this plot, by having Shenhui's first words onstage be an account of his connection to the Bodhidharma lineage of truth, Dugu Pei has given the reader a fundamental frame for interpreting why Shenhui trounces Chongyuan. The violence of the narrative is softened because it appears that Chongyuan's humiliation is simply the effect of letting truth out of the bag on to an unsuspecting figure who had always been a stranger to truth. Thus, in Dugu Pei's text, the reader is set up in the position of knowing much more than the figures onstage about the deeper forms of legitimacy directing the flow of events. Watching Shenhui upend the most renowned Buddhist monk in China comes as no surprise: the reader already knows why—it is because Shenhui is in the Bodhidharma lineage and Chongyuan isn't. Or better, it is because Shenhui is a buddha and Chongyuan isn't. Given that gross difference in identity, the reader is presumably not fazed by the outcome and simply feels satisfied that the foreknowledge that he had been given in the preface played out as expected in the account of the public debate.

In all this, the historicity of the onetime event at Great Cloud Monastery proves the historicity of the deeper chain of events—the lineage's movement forward in time from India to China and ultimately into the figure of Shenhui. This overlap of historical claims works just as it does in the Gospel narratives. For instance in the Gospel of Mark, after the narrator's voice, John the Baptist, the "voice from heaven," and a large number of demons and patients have testified to Jesus' divine sonship, we-the-reading-audience know why Jesus' supposedly historical conversations with established authority—the synagogue priests, Pharisees, and scribes—went the way they did. In both Dugu Pei's *Treatise* and the Gospels, the historicity of the particular "public" encounters are presented to the reader as proof of the "deeper" historical claims about perfect sonship that had hitherto been unknown and unregistered by public authorities. Thus, in both cases we ought to recognize that the narrative manages to create enough of a sense for the Real of visible history outside of the text that it can then harvest in order to prove its other, invisible historical claims, such as Jesus' God-given divinity or Shenhui's buddhahood.

Within this dharma combat that Dugu Pei has asked his reader to witness, it turns out that sūtra quotes predominate. Moreover, Chongyuan's defeat is registered once he is shown slandering the *Lotus Sūtra,* a crime that apparently Dugu Pei expected his readers to recognize as an unpardonable sin. Moreover, the sūtras provide the phrases for most of the onstage orality, and thus in a sense the sūtras serve as progenitors for the encounter, for without them there would be nothing to say. Clearly, then, Dugu Pei is moving language from one genre to another, from the sūtra genre to this new genre of "live history." However, there is a basic tension in relying on the sūtras in a text dedicated to explaining the flow of truth and tradition through the narrow chute of the Bodhidharma lineage. That is, for this supposedly historical event to look legitimate, it must look like Shenhui has truth from another source—the Bodhidharma lineage—for him to be in charge of sūtra language, and yet it is also true that all this sūtra language, rearranged as "dharma combat," is presented to sanctify just those lineage claims. Consequently, lineage and sūtra articulation are set up to stand arm-in-arm, even though they are fundamentally opposed to one another since Dugu Pei claimed from the outset—as did Jingjue, Du Fei, and the Shaolin monks—that tradition moved in the lineage and did not need the sūtras. In sum, just as the gospel writers relied on selections from Isaiah, the Psalms, Leviticus, and so on, to prove Jesus' relationship to his truth-father, even as this relationship will fundamentally undermine all such previous literature, so, too, the Māhāyana sūtras are relied on to certify and sanctify Shenhui's relationship to his truth-father, even as that relationship likewise undercuts the value of the sūtras.

COMBAT REPORT:
CHONGYUAN'S SUDDEN UNENLIGHTENMENT

After Shenhui has recounted his lineage history from the Lion's Throne, in that long offstage whisper, Chongyuan appears onstage and upbraids him in a manner that proves he has profoundly misrecognized Shenhui. Thus, from the first moment, Dugu Pei's narrative functions to negotiate two versions of truth, one sanctified by the narrative that claims to know of a special father-son connection between Shenhui and ultimate authority and the other that does not have this knowl-edge (Chongyuan's position) and that is about to be voided. Apparently seeing the hall decorated as if to receive important guests, Chongyuan takes Shenhui by the arm and addresses him with a trick question from the *Diamond Sūtra*:[55]

> The Dharma Master Chongyuan took the Monk's [Shenhui's] arm and scolded him asking, "Chan Master, do you call this ornamenting *(zhuang-yan)*?" "Yes," replied the Monk [Shenhui]. [Chongyuan said,] "As the Tathāgata said, 'ornamenting is not ornamenting.'"

In giving Chongyuan this leading question, Dugu Pei has him initially assume the role of the Buddha in the encounter since this question about ornaments is the Buddha's line in the *Diamond Sūtra*.[56] Thus, Dugu Pei

---

55. Gernet, *Entretiens*, 87; Hu Shi, *Shenhui*, 265.
56. See T.8.749c.18; for discussion of this passage, see my *Text as Father*, 187 ff. It is interesting to note that Dugu Pei has cleverly taken a conversation regarding the orna-menting of Pure Lands, as found in the *Diamond Sūtra* where it means something more like creating Pure Lands, and applied it to the ornamentation of the monastic hall.

starts Chongyuan off in the role that the rest of the narrative had given him as well: Chongyuan is the leading master in China. Shenhui, on the other hand, starts off with underdog status: he has to defend the choice to decorate the hall, as well as handle Chongyuan's more philosophic question about the ontic irreality of ornamentation, a question that if he fails to answer will ruin his bid for that social status marked by the ornamentation. Actually, this tension between an empty ontology and the hope to win publicly recognized leadership underlies the entire Chan gambit—how to assert the ultimate equality of all beings and yet claim to be the privileged owner of tradition, a conundrum that we have seen Du Fei and Jingjue wrestle with too.

After the above initial encounter, Shenhui evades the *Diamond Sūtra* question by responding with a quote from the *Vimalakīrti*. Shenhui replies, "It is also said in the sūtras that one doesn't pass beyond the composite *(bujin youwei)*, and one doesn't abide in the uncomposite *(buzhu wuwei)*." Chongyuan replies, "But what is the meaning of 'one doesn't pass beyond the composite, and one doesn't abide in the uncomposite'?"[57] In this exchange, the shift in power has already been announced. Whereas, Shenhui evaded Chongyuan's sūtra trap and countered it with another sūtra quote, Chongyuan is shown falling into the narrative of the *Vimalakīrti*. As Chongyuan asks for an explanation of the passage, the narrative has advanced three "facts." First, it has just demonstrated Chongyuan's incompetence vis-à-vis a widely revered text, the *Vimalakīrti;* presumably, any dharma master should not have to ask these basic questions about composite and uncomposite reality. Second, in getting drawn into the *Vimalakīrti*'s narrative, Chongyuan is shown unable to dodge Shenhui's parry and unable, too, to move the conversation into another authority structure where he could dominate. Thus, the exchange reveals that Chongyuan can't dance between sūtras, which marks him again as someone who has yet to master tradition. Third, and maybe most interesting from a narrative point of view, given that Shenhui quotes the rest of the passage to him, Chongyuan's question allows Shenhui to establish himself in the role of the Buddha and Chongyuan in the subservient role of the bodhisattva since the next line from Shenhui is actually taken from the Buddha's response to a bodhisattva in the *Vimalakīrti*.[58] Consequently, as Chongyuan's question shows his own lack of mastery, it opens the

---

57. Gernet, *Entretiens*, 88; Hu Shi, *Shenhui*, 265.
58. See Watson, trans., *The Vimalakīrti Sūtra*, 126; T.14.554b.3.

door for Shenhui's speaking identity to be fused with the Buddha's. In brief, Chongyuan started out speaking like a buddha, but now he is getting lectured by one.

The redistribution of power and authority in this short conversation is immediately underscored when the narrator adds, "The Dharma Master Chongyuan didn't have anything to say at that moment, and waited a long time until he said the following. The Dharma Master said, 'Lust and anger are the Way; it is not in ornamentation.' "[59] This is a rough paraphrase from the *Vimalakīrti*,[60] but it doesn't succeed in trapping Shenhui, who answers with the realistic comment, "If that is the case, then common people *(suren)* should currently obtain the Way." Shenhui's retort again throws Chongyuan off balance, and he has to ask, "Why do you say that common people should obtain the Way?" Shenhui proves his point, saying, "You say that desire and anger are the path, and since the common people are just those who follow desire and anger, how could they not obtain the Way?"[61]

With this clarification, Shenhui has shown the absurdity of Chongyuan's claim that desire and anger are the Way. Of course, in the process Chongyuan's failure as a dharma master has been demonstrated again. The line about desire and anger *is* basically put forward by Vimalakīrti in the *Vimalakīrti*, but in Chongyuan's mouth it doesn't work. Thus, Dugu Pei is proving that Chongyuan can't play his role in expressing and defending well-known Buddhist positions. Furthermore, in voiding Chongyuan's citation of this famous antinomianism from the *Vimalakīrti*, Dugu Pei is showing that Shenhui's words, not Chongyuan's, "cap" sūtra lines. That is, Shenhui can take tradition and *speak for it*—as when he quoted the *Vimalakīrti* to good effect in the exchange preceding this one—or *against it*, as he does here when he refutes Vimalakīrti's line about desire and anger. Chongyuan, on the other hand, suffers tradition in both directions; he can neither quote tradition and sustain it nor overcome tradition by refuting Shenhui's quoting of tradition. Then, of course, there is yet a third level: Chongyuan can't overcome Shenhui's overcoming of the *Vimalakīrti* line, which leaves Shenhui's ingenuity untouched.

Before considering the next shift in the conversation, whose outcome seems altogether preordained, we ought to note that even at this

59. Gernet, *Entretiens*, 88; Hu Shi, *Shenhui*, 266.
60. See Watson, trans., *The Vimalakīrti Sūtra*, 41–43.
61. Gernet, *Entretiens*, 89; Hu Shi, *Shenhui*, 266.

point in the encounter, it is clear that the event itself is formulated around similar kinds of dharma combat found in the *Vimalakīrti* where Vimalakīrti as an outsider to the Buddhist establishment verbally abuses the members of the Buddhist hierarchy, pointing out both their errors and their lack of legitimacy to hold their respective titles.[62] This again shows the power of the literary tradition to shape later literary "events." Thus, it is not too surprising that Dugu Pei would have been drawn to this scenario in the *Vimalakīrti* for demonstrating Shenhui's prowess because, in effect, Shenhui is ousting traditional figures of authority and overcoming visible tradition with something supposedly more traditional—pure timeless Buddhist wisdom—just as Vimalakīrti is shown doing in the *Vimalakīrti*.

After his failure with the Vimalakīrti line, Chongyuan drops the topic of fusing desire to the Way in order to return to the Yes/No kind of question that he advanced at the outset with the question about ornamentation from the *Diamond Sūtra*. Now he says, "Does the Chan Master [Shenhui] understand?" When Shenhui says that he does, Chongyuan tries to force a *Diamond Sūtra*–esque negation on him, asserting, "Understanding is not-understanding." To this Shenhui gives a quote from the *Lotus Sūtra* that makes Chongyuan's negation look unfounded. Shenhui says:[63]

> "The *Lotus Sūtra* says, 'Incalculable eons, without measure or limit, have passed since I became a buddha.' So according [to your comment], he didn't become a buddha and he didn't traverse the limitless eons."
> [Chongyuan] responds, "This is devil's talk *(Moshuo).*"

While it is not immediately clear what Chongyuan is cursing—the *Lotus Sūtra* quote or Shenhui's application of it, and, of course, it doesn't really matter—this is the place in the text where Chongyuan's authority is fully exploded. Shenhui turns to the audience and explains Chongyuan's comment as an absolute insult to tradition:

> "Listen everyone, laity and clergy. From the two capitals to the end of the seas, everyone transmits *(xiangchuan)* the opinion that Chongyuan understands the meaning [of tradition] and is intelligent, and that he can explain the sūtras and commentaries of the Mahāyāna without error. And yet today he calls the *Lotus Sūtra* the devil's word *(Moshuo).* [If this is the case,] what is the Buddha's word?"

---

62. For more discussion of the *Vimalakīrti*, see my *Text as Father*, chap. 6.
63. Gernet, *Entretiens*, 89; Hu Shi, *Shenhui*, 266.

> The Dharma Master [Chongyuan] knew at this moment that he had gone too far. He stood lost, facing the crowd. After a long time, [it seemed] that he wanted to say something. The Monk [Shenhui] said, "When you have been pinned to the ground, what's the point of getting up again?"[64]

This most crushing defeat, generated by having Chongyuan slander the *Lotus Sūtra* as "devil's talk," essentially ends the dialogue, though there will be another short exchange that softens Shenhui's aggression, even as it seals his victory with legitimacy and public recognition.

Standing back from this exchange between Chongyuan and Shenhui, it is clear that the real topic of the conversation isn't the truth and falsity of Buddhist claims but truth and falsity in the identity of the two combatants. There are not two "philosophic" positions represented here. Instead, there is a kind of combat that appears as the mutual attempt to rid the other of the right to speak, a kind of verbal jousting in which the value of a jab is solely determined by the damage it can do to the Other. Shenhui wins at this battle in the first three rounds—the ornamentation debate, the question of desire and the Way, and understanding as not-understanding—and this is marked in the narrative by Chongyuan's increasing inability to speak. His pauses become longer, and he can't hold a topic. These small failures then climax in his utter implosion when he claims that a line from the *Lotus Sūtra* is the talk of the devil, Mara.

The climax of this combat warrants a little more reflection. It was at this most precipitous point in the dialogue that Shenhui turns to the audience and repeats what Chongyuan has said, after reminding them of Chongyuan's national and international reputation. Apparently Dugu Pei is counting on his reading audience to know how heinous it is to slander the *Lotus Sūtra,* and thus Chongyuan's embarrassment seems to confirm the finality of his lapse even more fully. What has happened, then, is the formal and sudden unenlightenment of Chongyuan. Chongyuan, who though supposedly recognized as the most famous speaker for the Mahāyana sūtras and commentaries, shows himself in the end not only unable to explain Mahāyana texts but also willing to confuse the most basic facts about the Mahāyana—claiming that the *Lotus Sūtra* isn't the Buddha's word and instead is the word of the devil, Mara. In short, Chongyuan's

---

64. Gernet, *Entretiens,* 89; Hu Shi, *Shenhui,* 266–67. I didn't understand the wrestling motif in this final passage until I read McRae's translation; see his "Shenhui as Evangelist," 125.

statement is being taken as a kind of apostasy since he suddenly loses all his rights to speak for tradition in an act that is the inverse of the sudden investiture of truth and legitimacy regularly explained in the lineage texts. Thus, Shenhui's implicit claim to be the seventh patriarch here is manifest not by any particularly new dharma position or some new special Chan content but by a narrative sequence that radically, suddenly, and unequivocally divests old authority of its legitimacy and then just as radically, suddenly, and unequivocally relocates authority elsewhere — in Shenhui's person — and directly asks the audience to recognize and verify this shift.

A DIVIDE IN THE *TREATISE* AND A SHIFT IN POLEMICS

For those who assume that Shenhui's position is about sudden enlightenment and the robe, along with his wild accusations of Puji's violent deeds, the form and content of the first section of the *Treatise* will appear unexpected. Clearly, in Dugu Pei's hands, Shenhui got along fine without relying on arguments regarding sudden enlightenment, the robe, and so on. Equally important, if this public event was held in the 730s and was to be a correction of heterodoxy, we have to ask, Where is Shenhui's principal enemy, Puji? Where is the debate over the real Southern School of Chan? And, why is Shenhui shown demolishing Chongyuan, the supposed leader of Chinese Buddhism, instead of Puji, especially when it is not clear that Chongyuan even existed?

If Chongyuan's identity as a nationally recognized master remains unproved outside the Shenhui texts, I believe that we ought to accept the following. Chongyuan is not only a straw man enabling Shenhui's literary bid for power, but he is also a stand-in for Puji, and thus there is an extended analogy running through this event that Dugu Pei has constructed: just as Chongyuan falls, so should Puji. Both masters are currently the supposed leaders of Chinese Buddhism, and both lack the transmission from Huineng, so both should go by the wayside. Presumably, attacking Puji in this indirect manner seemed particularly prudent when Puji still had too much power and court recognition to make a direct assault feasible. In effect, just as Liucheng had written accounts of Shenhui judging the actions of current masters, but only at a distance with the dubious masters' actions recounted to him by a proxy, here, too, Dugu Pei seems to be showing Shenhui working on a current master but only at a distance, and only via a proxy; it is Chongyuan who goes down, not Puji. Still, if this text was written in the 730s, it would have been read as an implicit attack on Puji simply because Chongyuan is set up as the current leader of Chinese Buddhism. If Shenhui is shown replacing Chongyuan and winning the day by means of an argument about the singular inheritance of the Bodhidharma lineage, Puji clearly is at risk, first, because of his formal similarity to Chongyuan, but, more importantly because he also lacks what Chongyuan lacked—the inheritance from Bodhidharma that Shenhui has laid claim to and that is shown as the sole item guaranteeing legitimacy. Given the subtlety of this indirect attack on Puji, the later sections vilifying Puji, as found in P2045, have to be seen as supplements written under very different circumstances, presumably when Shenhui thought it was suitable to launch this kind of direct ad hominem attack—most likely after Puji was dead, in 739.

THE *TREATISE* IN COMPARISON
TO THE *QUESTIONS AND ANSWERS*

Since it seems appropriate to treat the above account of that singular encounter at Great Cloud Monastery as one full text, let me round out the above analyses of the two dialogue texts, the *Questions and Answers* and the *Treatise*, by concluding that vis-à-vis the earlier lineage texts by Du Fei and Jingjue, these two texts seem inventive in a new direction. Instead of the staid historical account of Du Fei with the loose boxcar format that Jingjue then picked up, there is much more life and engagement here. Except for those odd jivey lines from several masters in Jingjue's *History*, the earlier genealogies do not deploy this kind of dialogue genre to demonstrate living Buddhist legitimacy. Really, no one had dared to apply the format of the sūtra discourse in the presentation of a Chinese buddha, and thus these two Shenhui texts show a blend of audacity and cleverness for proving local buddhahood.

Despite the literary borrowings used to construct this image of Shenhui as a buddha, the *Questions and Answers* and the *Treatise* are largely free of the specific contents of the earlier lineage texts and, more important, aren't playing the game of stealing ancestors in the same manner that both Du Fei and Jingjue had. Thus Liucheng's collected conversations in the *Questions and Answers* completely lacks lineage arguments, save for the brief preface that explains the Bodhidharma lineage and that Shenhui was the seventh patriarch. And, in the preface, though the idea of turning someone into a buddha with a lineage back to Bodhidharma was presumably picked up from the current milieu, nothing in particular from the form or content of Du Fei's or Jingjue's writing seems to have structured the text.

Similarly, Dugu Pei's text is clever in an unprecedented way: his narrative of the dharma combat intertwined public and private histories, mixed his own voice with Shenhui's and the Buddha's, and wound sūtra discourse into supposedly contemporaneous, historical events. While Dugu Pei's account of the Bodhidharma lineage was more expanded than Liucheng's, this expansion occurs *only* around Bodhidharma and Huike. Thus, in Dugu Pei's preface to the *Treatise* there are new stories about Bodhidharma and Huike, but the other patriarchs, from Huike to Huineng and Shenhui, are covered in one sentence, and there is absolutely no mention of conflict over the inheritance from Hongren. Given these facts, that the rest of the *Treatise* as found in P2045 shows itself to be extensively involved in the section of the lineage after Hongren seems telling. In effect, explicit lineage warfare is missing in the two sets of conversation collections discussed above, since Shenhui is shown vanquishing his interlocutors and proving his status without directly claiming it and without directly attacking the powers that be and their lineage claims.

SHENHUI THE BUDDHA, IN THE LATER SECTIONS OF THE *TREATISE*

In leaving P3047 to read how this initial debate scene likely was expanded in P2045, the first thing to admit is that the length of P2045 prohibits giving this text a line-by-line reading as I did for P3047. Thus, after a brief introduction to this section, I will consider five topics that represent the bulk of the text: (1) Shenhui's buddhahood, (2) the logic of the robe-of-transmission, (3) the history of the Bodhidharma lineage, (4) the evils of Puji, and (5) the power of the *Diamond Sūtra*.

In the final lines of P3047, which themselves seem to have been added on to Dugu Pei's original text, Chongyuan, apropos of nothing, asks Shenhui what bodhisattva level he might be on. Shenhui answers that he has fulfilled them all, and so Chongyuan asks him to perform a miracle, since obviously he is claiming to be a buddha.[65] P3047 breaks off at this point, but switching over to P2045, one can see that same line of questioning developing: in response to Chongyuan's demand for visual proof

65. Gernet, *Entretiens*, 91; Hu Shi, *Shenhui*, 270; McRae, "Shenhui as Evangelist," 141.

of his buddhahood, Shenhui backpedals a little and responds by citing a situation in the *Nirvana Sūtra* where a carpenter's son named Cunda learns, from the Buddha, that at least in some certain ways Cunda isn't different from the Buddha.[66] Though the passage in P2045 is badly smudged in the Dunhuang manuscript, it is clear that Shenhui's retort includes a line in which the Buddha says, "Cunda's mind is the same as the Tathāgata's mind *(Cunda xin tong rulai xin)*." A rough equivalent of this line is found in the *Nirvana Sūtra*, where the Buddha compared Cunda to his own biological son, Rahula: "Excellent Cunda, though you have received [from birth] a human body, your mind is like a buddha's mind *(xin ru foxin)*. And, today Cunda, you are a true son of the Buddha, just like Rahula, not at all different."[67] Despite the bad state of P2045 here, there is no doubt that Shenhui is arguing that his sameness with the Buddha is, like Cunda's, based on the sameness of mind and not body, a distinction that will allow him to speak as a buddha but avoid having to perform miracles as a full-fledged buddha would.

BASICALLY A BUDDHA, BUT . . .

This brief exchange about Shenhui's sameness with the Buddha is a crucial moment in the history of Chan rhetoric. Shenhui is claiming a shared identity with the Indian Buddha, and yet this sameness only comes by establishing a new, diminished version of buddhahood. It is only Shenhui's mind that is the same as the Buddha's since his body is still "ordinary" *(fanfu)*. This distinction in modes of buddhahood is clearly readable in one of the lines that Shenhui cites where the Buddha defines Cunda's identity. P2045 reads, "your body, though ordinary *(fanfu)*, your mind . . ."[68] Given how tattered P2045 is at this point we are lucky to have a version of this exchange quoted in the *Lidai fabao ji*, written several decades later, where it is confirmed that this passage is about establishing a new, diminished form of buddhahood.[69]

---

66. See Hu Shi, *Shenhui*, 276; McRae, "Shenhui as Evangelist," 141.

67. T.12.372b.26 (Hu Shi notes this borrowing; see his *Shenhui*, 276). The *Nirvana Sūtra* in other places also constructs the trope of "true son of the Buddha" via sameness with Rahula; see, for instance, T.12.380c.3 ff.

68. Hu Shi, *Shenhui*, 276. In quoting from the *Nirvana Sūtra*, Dugu Pei seems to have changed "human" *(renshen)* to "ordinary" *(fanfu)*.

69. See T.51.185b.22. Adamek deals with Shenhui's place in the *Lidai fabao ji* and hints at how McRae is going to treat this passage in his forthcoming work on Shenhui; see her *The Mystique of Transmission*, 171–79; see also her translation of this passage, 339–42.

In effect, the full spectrum of buddhahood as it had been explained and developed in India is getting knocked down to a simple mental sameness that allows Shenhui to join himself to the Indian Buddha with a claim to sameness that doesn't involve the vast magical powers associated with the Indian Buddha, not to mention a glorious body.

The question of sameness with the Buddha takes a different tack in the next exchange between Shenhui and Chongyuan.[70] Here, Shenhui seeks to find sameness with the Buddha by claiming that he *sees* his internal buddha-nature, a topic that is also treated extensively in the *Nirvana Sūtra*.[71] In this brief exchange Shenhui explains that seeing his buddha-nature qualifies him in two ways. First, because he sees his buddha-nature he is therefore equal to Cunda—whose sameness with the Buddha's mind had just been established with the quotation from the *Nirvana Sūtra*. And, second, seeing his buddha-nature gives him the right to lecture on the *Nirvana Sūtra*, whereas Chongyuan, who apparently is not claiming to have seen his buddha-nature, is divested of his right to explain that sūtra or any other. Thus, in Shenhui's hands, this quotation from the *Nirvana Sūtra* serves as a pivot for first establishing his own sameness with the Indian Buddha, despite physical differences, and then creating a litmus test for laying hold to that sameness. In effect, one's ability to actually see this ultimate human sameness is taken as the basis for determining leadership roles, which, of course, are about the radical difference between master and disciple. These two points are then focused on Chongyuan and used to prove to him why he doesn't have the authority to lecture on the *Nirvana Sūtra*. In sum, as in their first encounter that worked around the *Vimalakīrti*, the logic put forward in the *Nirvana Sūtra* has been repackaged into Shenhui's body and then used as a weapon against his interlocutor, Chongyuan.

NOTHING TO KNOW

Slightly later in P2045, Shenhui and Chongyuan are debating the Perfection of Wisdom *(Prajñāpāramitā)* and its relationship to "not knowing" *(wuzhi)*.[72] This discussion, and its proximity to the coming

---

70. Hu Shi, *Shenhui*, 277.

71. The *Lidai fabao ji*'s replay of this conversation, which is largely illegible in the *Treatise*, has Shenhui cite the "Lion's Roar Chapter" as the basis for his argument that seeing the buddha-nature is the sine qua non for having the right to lecture on *Nirvana Sūtra*; see T.51.185b.25–29.

72. Hu Shi, *Shenhui*, 280.

discussion of the robe-of-transmission, raises a number of important questions about the interplay of negation and the "thingification of tradition" in the family of truth-fathers. On the one hand, Shenhui is applying a kind of rhetoric very typical of the *Diamond Sutra* and Prajñāpāramitā literature in general. According to Shenhui, in the sphere of Prajñā, there is no attainment, no knowledge, and so on, and yet this dangerous negative language of "the Prajñā of no-knowledge" or "nothing to know" *(banruo wuzhi, or wu suo zhi)* can exist right next to the most precise and exacting kind of lineage claims, claims presented in visible items like Bodhidharma's robe. Thus, "nothing to know" in no way impedes a historical narrative of ownership.

Actually, conjoining these two apparently antithetical elements is altogether traditional since Indian sūtras at times built narratives out of the transmission of "lack." In fact, that was exactly how the *Diamond Sūtra* rewrote the pre-Mahāyana understanding of the exchange between Dīpaṃkara Buddha and Śākyamuni Buddha, a topic that will appear later in these exchanges between Shenhui and Chongyuan.[73] As I will argue below, in Shenhui's writing—and Chan writing in general—dangerous Prajñāpāramitā language is applied in a highly circumscribed manner that reworks status claims and power relations, as it does throughout Mahāyana literature, even as the negativity and violence of the Prajñāpāramitā rhetoric then disappears, allowing for the staid reinstallation of alternative forms of power and closure based on mundane historical claims that are never subject to the negativity of no-knowledge.

In brief, "no knowledge" never turns into "no lineage," or the nihilism of not knowing where to turn to find final authority. In fact, the lineage is defined as those who have the knowledge to rightfully speak of no-knowledge. As with the other exchanges, this Prajñā discussion ends in Chongyuan's silence, which is immediately broken by a return to a related topic regarding Shenhui's phrase, "nothing to know." And yet this, too, fizzles out without much to-do and marks the end of Chongyuan's role as a contestant. Henceforth, Chongyuan will only ask leading questions and never challenge Shenhui in any manner. In fact, even his silences will disappear and not be again noted until one line near the end, apparently because silencing him and dramatizing

---

73. Ibid., 305; for discussion of transmission in the *Diamond Sūtra*, see my *Text as Father*, chap. 4.

his lack of capacity to counter Shenhui is no longer the project of this
section of the text.

After this discussion of no-knowledge there is an involved discussion
of the Bodhidharma lineage, a section that is noticeably longer and
more sustained than the prior conversations in P2045. Also, this section marks a major shift in topics. In the first phase of the Shenhui-
Chongyuan exchange, as read in P3047, Chongyuan's role was defined
as a site of value from which Shenhui could win something, and this
was, in essence, the whole point of the encounter, which ended when
Chongyuan was humiliated and silenced, and Shenhui turned to the
crowd and essentially said, "And you took this sad sack for your
leader?" In those three exchanges, the mode for extracting value from
Chongyuan was limited to replaying sūtra quotes in a sūtra-like setting. Though Dugu Pei had Shenhui present the brief history of the
Bodhidharma lineage in that long offstage whisper at the beginning of
the text, in their "debate" there was no mention of lineage legitimation
or other supposedly historical events in China that would influence
either figure's claims to preeminence. All this is different in this section
of P2045 where legitimation is defined strictly as a function of historical claims regarding the man-to-man inheritance of pure tradition.

In fact, this section of the text is concerned *only* with historical
matters. Dates appear, with great specificity, as do a series of important Chinese personalities. In short, we have left the world of sūtras
and calm dharma discussions and are now knee-deep in controversy
over who did what in the past fifty years. In particular, the historical
questions circle around the claim that the Bodhidharma lineage was
unjustly diverted from Huineng to Shenxiu and then on to Puji. In
establishing Shenhui's historical claims in this lengthy section, many
topics come and go, but I want to focus on four themes that are both
prominent and essential to Shenhui's claims: (1) transmission is singular, and therefore there can only be one master per generation; (2)
transmission occurs with the gift of Bodhidharma's robe, so, no robe,
no legitimacy; (3) Shenxiu didn't get transmission from Hongren,
Huineng did, regardless of what Puji has been saying; and (4) Huineng
gave transmission to Shenhui, though this final point will remain muted
and only comes in a glancing way when Shenhui says things like, "The
teachings of each and everyone of *my* six ancestral masters *(wo liudai*

dashi yi yi jie yan),"[74] or clarifies the content of the lineage, thereby signaling that he is one who knows the substance of the lineage.[75]

ONE, ONLY ONE

Assuming singular transmission within the Bodhidharma lineage had been implicit in Du Fei's and Jingjue's writing, and even in Faru's stele. However, none of these earlier writers explicitly announced this rule or explained its logic. Presumably, in crafting their histories of transmission that sought to move perfect enlightenment from India into contemporary China, they had every reason to keep this transmission singular. Once perfection had been brought up to the recent past, however, this singularity changed in Du Fei's and Jingjue's histories since in both cases multiple transmissions occurred only at the place of trying to fuse their masters into a preexisting lineage. Hence, until Shenhui's writing, claims to inherit a lineage opened up the final link in the "target lineage" and inserted their chosen ancestor as a double to the final recipient; thus, Du Fei put Shenxiu next to Faru, and Jingjue put Xuanze next to Shenxiu. Shenhui's strategy was different because he broke off the final two links of the chain—Shenxiu and Puji—and then snapped his chosen replacements in their place—Huineng and himself.

Shenhui's argument regarding singular inheritance is also key for larger arguments in this book because it shows, rather precisely, how Shenhui's rhetoric of universal buddhahood dovetails with a claim to singular leadership. In fact, in making this argument about the singular inheritance of the lineage back to the Buddha, Shenhui mixes four types of unique leaders: kings, *cakravartins* (the ideal Indian emperors), buddhas, and Chinese masters. All four, we learn, would never have a second version of themselves in their kingdom. Thus, in this section of the text, Shenhui is quoted to say:[76]

---

74. Hu Shi, *Shenhui*, 287. Gernet's translation (*Entretiens*, 92) restarts just here—his translation is based on P3488 (the third relevant manuscript), which begins here. I think, though, Gernet has rather uncharacteristically misread the line. Gernet translated the passage as "le paroles de mon grand maître, le sixième patriarche." And yet to read this passage to be about Huineng's teaching and not the teachings of the six generations of masters, Gernet has to take "six generations" as "sixth generation" and then ignore the three characters that follow "each and every one of them" *(yi yi jie)*, which leave little doubt that Shenhui is talking about the teachings of all six generations.

75. Hu Shi, *Shenhui*, 293.

76. Ibid., 281–82.

[unreadable lines] . . . transmitted to Chan Master Can. During the Sui
Dynasty. . . . [unreadable lines] On Twin Peaks *(shuangfeng)*, Chan Master
[Dao] Xin took the robe and transmitted it to X [unreadable character but
has to be "Ren"] Chan Master. Chan Master [Hong] Ren of the Tang, at
East Mountain, took the robe and gave it to Chan Master [Hui] Neng.
Thus, up till now there have been six generations. Internal transmission
is through dharma accord *(faqi)* and is confirmed by the mind *(yi yin
zhengxin)*. External transmission is with the robe, and it defines the lineage/
essence *(zongzhi)*. From the beginning of the transmission [sequence], one
by one, each of them gave the Bodhidharma robe as the guarantor *(xin)*.
*This robe can now be seen at Shaozhou and will not be given to anyone
anymore.* To speak of the transmission of any other kind of object is simply
ridiculous. Also, from the beginning down to the sixth generation, each
generation has had only one person. Never were there two. *Even when
there are millions of students, only one person is allowed to inherit.*
   Chongyuan asked, "Why is only one person per generation allowed
to inherit?" The monk [Shenhui] answered, "*It is like the way a kingdom
only has one king.* Never is it said that there are two. It is like the way
that there is only one *cakravartin* in the four [directions]. Never is it said
that there are two. It is like the way that in the world, there is only one
buddha who appears. Never is it said that there are two.

What this exchange makes absolutely clear is that Shenhui's version of
Chan, like its precedents, is first and foremost about creating templates
of leadership and not about new doctrines or practices. And when new
doctrines or practices are mentioned, they need to be read under the
umbrella of this more pressing concern for establishing leadership.
Whatever else is mentioned in this text—such as the "nothing to know"
trope or the assertion of universal buddhahood—these items are unde-
niably part of the package of ideology in which Shenhui is fighting to
be something like the ruling king qua buddha of Chinese Buddhism,
and never could those dharma topics trump this basic concern with
defining unique leadership.

No doubt if we read this literature without noting the creation of
this great divide between the masters and the masses, we will have
missed what motivated the entire early-Chan polemic, evident from the
beginning in the Faru stele but brought out here with stark clarity. In
the following exchanges Shenhui develops his position by arguing that
currently there are hundreds of people teaching meditation *(chan)*, and
this "is confusing the true dharma, misleading students of the Way,
and more, is a sign of the end of Buddhadharma *(mie fofa xiang)*."[77]

77. Ibid., 283.

This line not only demonizes the opposition, a trope common in Du Fei and Jingjue, but also implies for the first time that failure to establish the lineage will result in the end of Buddhism. The possibility of demonic input in the current situation is made clearer in a later line from this section that echoes the one just cited above: "today in the world it is obvious that the teachers of meditation *(jiao chan zhe)* are many, and that confusion is extreme among those who study Chan; I fear that Mara *(Tianmo)*, Boxun *(Papiyan)*,[78] and all the other heretics have entered among them [those who teach Chan], and that they are deluding those who study the Way, and are destroying the true dharma."[79] In short, Shenhui is arguing that if his dharmic kingship is not properly established everything will fall apart, and that current leadership is but a diseased heretical front for demons.

At this point in the text, Chongyuan, now ever docile, wants clarification about the one-master rule and first seeks to draw out the difference between receiving transmission and achieving enlightenment. This is a crucial distinction because Shenhui's answer will bring to the surface another key node in the genealogical polemics that created Chan: enlightenment doesn't matter, there is something much more important, and it is transmission:[80]

> Chongyuan asks, "Everyone took Shenxiu to be one who has achieved the fruit of the path *(de daoguo)* and to be an inconceivable person. How come he can't be permitted to be the sixth patriarch?" Shenhui answered, "It is because Chan Master [Hong] Ren didn't transmit to Shenxiu. So even if later he has obtained the fruit of the path, he is still not permitted to be the sixth patriarch. Why? Because Chan Master [Hong] Ren didn't give him a prediction *(yaoshouji)*, so it is not permitted.

In this exchange, enlightenment and the inheritance of "enlightenment" are notably separated. The transmission from Hongren is suddenly distinguishable from "the fruit of the path" and is to be understood as the sole basis for being a patriarch. According to Shenhui, masters aren't enlightened in some generic way that has to do with the standard

---

78. This phrase, "Tianmo Poxun," occurs in the *Nirvana Sūtra*, T.12.408c.18, in the context of all those beings who couldn't harm the internal buddha-nature of all sentient beings *(zhongsheng foxing)*.

79. Hu Shi, *Shenhui*, 291; Gernet, *Entretiens*, 95. Jingjue seems to have created a similar kind of discourse for Daoxin in his *History*, see Cleary, *Zen Dawn*, 55, 61.

80. Hu Shi, *Shenhui*, 283.

Buddhist path, but rather they are endowed through a unique transmission, and one shouldn't confuse the two.

THE RULE OF THE ROBE

Shenhui's kingship model for owning truth goes hand in hand with his creation of the rule of the robe, a development that occurs in this section of the text and which complicates patriarchal ownership of truth in a very interesting manner. The earlier genealogies sought to take possession of truth by writing histories that explained how truth flowed into certain historical persons—a rule about the ownership of truth where truth was oddly turned into something jewel-like that could be given as a gift, even if it wasn't visible. Moreover, in Du Fei's text, though truth is Thing-like, it leaves a lasting residue in the bodies of those who possess it, thus making their relics worth worshiping. Hence, for Du Fei, each master's body still holds a claim to have once owned truth, and this claim to ownership *does not* appear to leave his body when he hands over truth to the next figure in the lineage since his remains are still seen as worthy of worship, and still, notably, produce stupa miracles.

Shenhui's rule of the robe takes the notion of owning total truth in a very different sense. Though one might first think that the rule of the robe is the most natural outcome of lineage arguments—a visible talisman for the lineage—a closer analysis shows that it works at cross purposes with the logic of the prior lineage narratives. Thus, in the Shenhui material one will look in vain for any discussion of the power of relics or the lasting powers of the prior masters. Shenhui will talk about Puji's attacks on the Huineng mummy, but this isn't part of a discussion of the power of Huineng's corpse, an issue that is not mentioned.[81] Similarly, no other relic sites are mentioned, except Puji's Hall of the Seven Patriarchs, and clearly that isn't described as a place where truth would be manifest.[82] In sum, Shenhui's construction of Bodhidharma's robe as the sine qua non of the lineage oddly takes buddhahood *out* of the patriarchs' bodies, and presumably out of their relics as well, so that it can be condensed into the singular robe.

---

81. Ibid., 289. Shenhui uses the term *spirit essence (lingzhi)* for Huineng's corpse but doesn't explore other postmortem powers that his body might have.

82. This hall is mentioned twice in passages that are very parallel; see Hu Shi, *Shenhui*, 284, 289.

Given that the robe condensed transmission into its own fabric, it seems clear that Shenhui doesn't expect truth to leave any residue in each master's body, hence his lack of interest in the relics of the former masters. Truth in the robe, then, is hermetically sealed and doesn't leak out to share it powers with its possessors. With the robe, in fact, Shenhui has "conquered" the other Chinese masters because now they, too, like Puji, lack the Thing that marks sanctity. Thus, six generations of masters essentially equal one robe, and this one robe not only can stand in place of their presence, but seems to void them of their enduring value.[83]

In effect, Shenhui's discourse on the robe, while intent on forging a link back to Bodhidharma, doesn't care about the Bodhidharma lineage per se. No wonder, then, that Shenhui never spends time writing or "talking" about the prior Chinese masters as Du Fei and Jingjue did. He will mention that they transmitted the robe to one another in a sentence or two, but their teachings, their glory, and their narratives don't interest him in the least. With total truth lodged in the Bodhidharma robe, the Chinese masters are downplayed as but possessors of the item that generated the lineage. With content completely lodged in the robe, Shenhui is in a position to dispense with the prior masters and whatever Du Fei or Jingjue had put in their mouths as teachings. Similarly, while Bodhidharma's robe is the essence of the lineage, the robes of the other Chinese masters don't matter. Shenhui is never shown talking about Huineng's robe, or Hongren's robe, and presumably this reflects another of Shenhui's strategies for establishing a more refined notion of patriarchy that further divests the other Chinese masters of relic status.

Arguably, this focus on Bodhidharma and his robe renders the rest of the lineage something like an obstructing matrix that has to be excised for Shenhui to rejoin his most cherished father—Bodhidharma. In this light, it is not too shocking that at the end of P2045 the narrator has the lay and clerical audience exclaim in the wake of the Shenhui dialogues that he is Bodhidharma's reincarnation *(Damo houshen)*.[84] Obviously, this kind of claim only makes sense when Huineng and the other masters have been downgraded to second-rate fathers, with Bodhidharma essentially leapfrogging over them to "become" Shenhui. In short, Bodhidharma's robe does to the Bodhidharma lineage what the Bodhidharma lineage had done to Chinese Buddhism: it essential-

83. For an alternative discussion of Bodhidharma's robe, see Adamek, "Robes Purple and Gold," and *The Mystique of Transmission*, chap. 5.
84. Hu Shi, *Shenhui*, 316.

izes prior sites of truth down to a single form that overcomes those prior forms and then provides the logic for effectively maintaining ownership of this condensed form of prior value.[85]

PRIVATE CLOTHING FOR PUBLIC VERIFICATION

The intended role of the robe-of-truth is made clear as Shenhui explains to Chongyuan that the dharma is not in the robe itself but that the robe is a guarantor of the dharma for *students*.[86] Shenhui explains:[87]

> "Even though the dharma isn't in the robe, it demonstrates *(biao)* the successive transmission [of the dharma] with the transmission of the robe as a guarantor, thereby giving propagators of the dharma proof of inheritance *(bincheng)*. It is also [used] to let students of the Way know that the essence of the lineage *(zongzhi)* wasn't in error."

Here, the robe functions to secure the link between the masters and between the masters and the public, since now the public has a visible marker for who is to be trusted.

In fact, right after this line Shenhui turns to a rather well-known Indian story to support his explanation of the robe as a visible marker of transmission. Shenhui invokes the story of the Buddha giving the robe to Kāśyapa, who, apparently, then entered Chicken Foot Mountain, where he waits for Maitreya's arrival, an arrival that will mark the return of buddhahood in a fully manifest form.[88]

Actually, Shenhui explicitly sets up Kāśyapa's maintenance of the robe as an analogy for the way the six patriarchs in China transmit the robe. Thus, he closes out the comparison saying, "In the past, Śākyamuni's Golden Lan robe was at Chicken Foot Mountain, and now Kāśyapa is there holding it, waiting for Maitreya to come to the world so that he can give him this robe, and this demonstrates that

---

85. In fact, in later texts the power of the robe has so grown that Hongren is made to say to his disciples after transmitting the robe to Huineng, in effect, "I can't teach you anymore because I gave the robe to Huineng and he has left, so I no longer have the Buddha-dharma." See, for instance, *Huineng's Separate Biography*, in Jorgensen's translation in *Inventing Hui-neng*, 684. Thus, the robe as retainer of the lineage, in this slightly later strata, appears to have become bigger than the masters themselves such that even Hongren was nothing once he had ceded the robe.

86. Hu Shi, *Shenhui*, 284.

87. Ibid., 284–85; for an alternative translation, see Adamek, *The Mystique of Transmission*, 157.

88. For discussion of this story and more relevant sources, see Kieschnick, *The Impact of Buddhism on Chinese Material Culture*, 103–4; see also Shinohara, "The Kaṣāya Robe of the Past Buddha"; and Adamek, *The Mystique of Transmission*, 128 ff.

Śākya Tathāgata [the Buddha] transmitted the robe as a guarantor *(chuan yi weixin)*. The six generations of my ancestors *(wo liudai zushi)* also do likewise."[89] Thus, Shenhui is working from a rhyme scheme: truth-fathers in India relied on a robe to hold themselves together, and that is why we do something similar now. This is a perfect case of the mimesis of patriarchy, since the Indian form of constructing patriarchy is, with the simple jump of an analogy, reduplicating itself in another sphere. That is, a template for authority didn't make just more authority; it made another template. Consequently, by relying on this analogy, the form of identity and legitimacy that had been primed to "jump" from Śākyamuni to Maitreya via Kāśyapa and the Buddha's robe, now jumps out of that context and into eighth-century China, where Shenhui can claim it as a sanctifying template. Note, though, that Shenhui is not saying that Bodhidharma's robe is the Buddha's. He is simply saying that the Buddha did it this way and that is why Bodhidharma and the Chinese patriarchs also do it this way *(furushi)*. In Shenhui's argument by analogy, and it is crucial to my argument, this metastasis of patriarchy occurs through reading and textuality. Hence, it was *by reading* about the robe as the supposed core of tradition in India that Shenhui found a precedent for creating a nonlinguistic item like the robe as the mascot for tradition and as "proof" of the invisible and nontextual form of tradition that Shenhui was championing. Thus, whatever tough-sounding terms like *no-thought* or *sudden enlightenment* meant in earlier passages, in a more basic sense, Shenhui would be nowhere without his run-of-the-mill sūtra quotes that he relies on to build his bridge back to the Buddha. In short, Shenhui's actual relationship to tradition is again based on just those traditional texts that he was also claiming to supplant.

HISTORY AS WILL AND REPRESENTATION: SONS MAKING FATHERS

Shenhui's appeal to this Indian story of the Buddha's robe at Chicken Foot Mountain seems congruent with his general interest in things

---

89. Hu Shi, *Shenhui*, 285; for an alternative translation, see Adamek, *The Mystique of Transmission*, 157. I should add that Adamek seems to be mistaken in her rendering of the final line, where she takes *wo liu dai zushi* to mean "our sixth patriarch is also like this." Shenhui uses the cardinal number marker *di* quite often and consistently—three times in the preceding paragraph—so there is no reason not to take the sentence at face value: "The six generations of my ancestors also do likewise."

Indian. In particular, he (and I am using "Shenhui" as shorthand for
the author of this section of the text) will be the first to try to write
the Bodhidharma lineage, man-to-man, back to the Buddha. Whereas
the other lineage writers had been content to leave the world of India
vague, Shenhui wanted to transform it into a zone that was modeled
on the Chinese system of inheritance that he was helping to write into
existence. In metaphoric terms, Shenhui was intent on making the
father look like the son so that the son could look more like the father.
Thus, whereas Du Fei explicitly mentioned that India didn't need a
transmission system, and Jingjue likewise had next to nothing to say
about it, Shenhui insisted that it did have a transmission system and
then cobbled one together to create a very odd theory of how truth got
from the Buddha to himself.

To understand Shenhui's inventions, we need to remember that in
the Faru biography, and then again in Du Fei's *Record,* there was a
gap of about one thousand years between the listing of the handful
of patriarchs that followed the Buddha and then Bodhidharma and
the patriarchs that he supposedly generated in China in the sixth century. The information about the set of patriarchs that descended from
the Buddha—Ānanda, Madhyāntika, and so on—was taken from
Huiyuan's preface to *Dharmatrāta's Meditation Sūtra,* while the Bodhidharma–Huike–Sengcan–Daoxin–Hongren part of the lineage was
stitched together from elements in Daoxuan's *Encyclopedia.* Shenhui's
invention was to hook these two lists together as one continuous conduit running from the Buddha to Bodhidharma and then into China:[90]

> Chongyuan asked, "Who did Bodhidharma inherit from? And how
> many generations were there?" The monk [Shenhui] responded,
> "Bodhidharma, in the Western country [India], inherited from
> Saṇgharakṣa, Saṇgharakṣa from Śubhamitra, Śubhamitra from
> Upagupta, Upagupta inherited from Śaṇavāsa, Śaṇavāsa inherited
> from Madhyāntika, Madhyāntika inherited from Ānanda, and
> Ānanda inherited from Kāśyapa, and Kāśyapa inherited from the
> Tathāgata. China *(Tangguo)* has Bodhidharma at its head. In the
> Western Country [India], Bodhidharma is the eighth patriarch. In
> India, Prajñā Miduolou inherited from Bodhidharma. In China,
> Chan Master Huike inherited from Bodhidharma. Altogether, there
> were thirteen generations.

---

90. Hu Shi, *Shenhui,* 294–95. See Yampolsky, *The Platform Sūtra,* 8–9, for a very
useful display of these various versions of the patriarchy; and 29–30, for an alternative
translation.

This passage is fascinating for several reasons. First, obviously, Shenhui's new form of the patriarchal family has only eight figures to cover roughly the one thousand years from the Buddha's death in the fifth century B.C.E. to the sixth century C.E. when Bodhidharma supposedly lived. Clearly, Shenhui cared much more about making the form look perfect than about adjusting the form to comply with the demands of real history that count the normal human life span to be no more than one hundred years. Second, as Yampolsky and other scholars have noted, Shenhui or the author of this part of the *Treatise,* miscopied one of the patriarchs names from the *Meditation Sūtra,* changing Vasumitra into Śubhamitra.[91] One senses that Shenhui wasn't that worried if he misspelled their names, as long as it looked like a legitimate lineage. In fact, he claims that his source is the preface to the *Meditation Sūtra,* but the list in the preface doesn't match his list (Kāśyapa was left out of the preface's list), and it would seem that his list of patriarchs was drawn from the body of the text, which includes Kāśyapa.[92] Thus, not only is Shenhui careless in citing his sources; his sources are careless in citing their sources, even though the essence of Buddhism, as they have defined it, is supposed to be flowing down this conduit.

Third, by giving Bodhidharma a descendant in India—Prajñā Miduolou—Shenhui is showing us that the one-master-per-generation rule is relative to national spheres, since Bodhidharma of course also transmitted to Huike in China. And thus Shenhui's rule of the robe is, in practice, clearly an argument about national politics and not some larger rule with international applicability. Presumably as long as that other descendant of Bodhidharma, Prajñā Miduolou, stays in India, all is well and good.

In drawing up this single list of patriarchs, Shenhui had to overcome a rather obvious problem. In Du Fei's *Record,* the Indian list of the Buddha's inheritors from Ānanda to Madhyāntika and so on, had been cited via that reference to Huiyuan's preface to the *Meditation Sūtra* simply to prove that there was a lineage system started by the Buddha. Never did Du Fei argue that this lineage poured *directly* into Bodhidharma and then into the Chinese masters. In fact, he said the

91. See Yampolsky, *The Platform Sūtra,* 30.
92. Yampolsky makes this point: *The Platform Sūtra,* 30. *Dharmatrāta's Meditation Sūtra* cites the lineage twice in the front part of the text, T. 15.301a.3 and 301c.6. See also McRae, *The Northern School,* 80–82.

opposite in arguing that in India the bodhisattvas were self-enlightened (see chapter 4). Consequently, Bodhidharma in Du Fei's hands didn't have a master or a lineage, and he didn't need one either.[93] The lineage from Huiyuan's preface was simply there to serve as an analog and no more.

Thus, Shenhui basically had no narrative material to connect the Buddha to Bodhidharma. Besides the thousand-year gap between them, the problem was that *Dharmatrāta's Meditation Sūtra* (referred to as the *Meditation Sūtra*), with its list of the Buddha's eight descendants that rather vaguely led up to master Dharmatrāta, went no further than the first part of the fifth century, when Huiyuan wrote his preface to Dharmatrāta's text. Bodhidharma, on the other hand, according to Daoxuan's *Encyclopedia,* was believed to have entered China roughly one hundred years later, in the middle of the 6th century. Thus, Shenhui had before him Dharmatrāta's vague lineage that was completely unrelated to Chan and/or Bodhidharma, and which anyway couldn't have connected Bodhidharma to the Buddha since it was extinct one hundred years too soon. Shenhui's solution to this textual impasse was to turn Dharmatrāta into Bodhidharma. Following the above passage, Chongyuan asks Shenhui:[94]

> "Based on what can you know that Bodhidharma was the eighth generation in India?" The monk [Shenhui] responded, "[It can be known,] according to the preface to the *Meditation Sūtra* where it clearly explains the number of generations *(daishu)* in India. Moreover, when Huike personally asked Bodhidharma [about this] at Shaolin Monastery on Mount Song, Bodhidharma answered that it was just as it was in [Huiyuan's] preface to the *Meditation Sūtra.*

This quotation clearly shows Shenhui's interest in making his rearrangement of the Buddhist truth-fathers seem factual. Thus, he has Chongyuan ask about evidence for this version of the lineage, and then he has the figures in the lineage—Bodhidharma and Huike—recount Shenhui's version of the "historical facts." Thus, the masters and the historians of the masters are shown to be in agreement about the history of truth and the truth of history, as they must be for this to appear truthful.

---

93. The same could be said for Jingjue's *History,* since even though he wrote Guṇabhadra into the lineage as Bodhidharma's predecessor, Guṇabhadra certainly didn't need an ancestor, and in fact there was no clear connection made between Guṇabhadra and Bodhidharma.

94. Hu Shi, *Shenhui,* 295.

Merging Bodhidharma with Dharmatrāta was aided by the fact that their names share the two characters for "dharma"—*Damo*. Based on a certain similarity in their names, Shenhui merged them into one figure, and the two lineages became one, and what had been but an analogy in the genealogies of Faru and Du Fei now became "factual" and functional, and served to deliver the perfect form of tradition. In sum, by conflating Bodhidharma with Dharmatrāta, Shenhui was able to use these disparate chunks of genealogy to create a much more streamlined lineage claim that, however impossible, appeared useful to him in his attempt to overcome not only the other Chinese genealogists but also the Otherness of India that so haunted Chinese Buddhism.

BAD FAITH TWICE OVER

Noting Shenhui's fusion of Bodhidharma and Dharmatrāta opens up good material for judging the level of bad faith in Shenhui's writing. Hu Shi allows, rather generously, that conflating the two figures could have been, by itself, a simple orthographic slip. But he concludes that when Shenhui then goes on to create the above dialogue between Bodhidharma and Huike in which Bodhidharma confirms "orally" that everything in the *Meditation Sūtra* is as it happened, Shenhui has proved his guilt in the very act of trying to prove his innocence.[95] For my part, I wouldn't have needed the second level of evidence to read the first level as proof of bad faith. Shenhui, who evidently had been reading the earlier Bodhidharma lineage texts by Du Fei and Jingjue, must have known very well that Dharmatrāta was not, and could not have been, Bodhidharma. No one had said they were the same person, and they lived in different centuries; and, there was absolutely no mention of a connection between the two. He saw, however, that this was a weak link in the whole theory of the genealogy of truth since none of the previous genealogies had given Bodhidharma a lineage, and the Indian lineage cited by Du Fei and in the Faru stele drawn from the *Meditation Sūtra* went nowhere. Catching sight of Shenhui's rewriting of the genealogy is particularly telling because this is just the crime that he is going to accuse Puji of committing. I consider his accusation against Puji below, but for the moment I think it fair to say that Shenhui not only knowingly distorted the historical record, but he then

95. For Hu Shi's comments see, *Shenhui,* 296; the Bodhidharma-Huike dialogue starts on p. 295.

charged Puji with just this type of crime—falsification of the past and the overlapping of masters. Thus, Shenhui's bad faith has a second-order component: he charges Puji with a form of bad faith that closely resembles his own.

Recognizing Shenhui's bad faith naturally raises important questions regarding his other statements about truth and authenticity. Chan Studies in general has been very reluctant to open up this discussion of bad faith and what it implies for the entire Chan system of claiming absolute truth and the essence of tradition. Though it has been widely acknowledged by various scholars in the past forty years that the various elements in the Bodhidharma lineages were fabricated, this assessment has not led to addressing the place of duplicity in Chan writing. If we move past this self-imposed politeness, several aspects of the Chan tradition become much more interesting. For instance, in Shenhui's hands, the prior masters who supposedly owned truth appear as puppets to be manipulated as needed. Shenhui, like Du Fei and Jingjue, thought nothing of creating masters from thin air or putting them in different centuries if that was what was required to make a good case for truth in the moment. Similarly, Shenhui didn't hesitate to create dialogues in which these truth-fathers "personally" vouch for his falsifications. And, maybe most startling, he was shameless in putting these fabricated claims out in public in the very act of explaining how this system of inheriting the robe was designed so that the public would know how to trust the right masters. Given this overall authorial deviance, what might we say about Shenhui's notion of truth? And, what kind of ethics permitted this nonchalance in rewriting history and the history of truth, histories that, obviously, were designed to be given to the public?

WHY PUJI IS SO EVIL

While the rule of the robe and the fusion of Bodhidharma and Dharmatrāta certainly show Shenhui (or the author of P2045) as inventive and duplicitous, even more striking is the section of P2045 that vilifies Puji. Shenhui, though saying nothing of Puji in any other text, here details a list of Puji's criminal activities, which range from sending thieves down to Shaozhou to steal the Bodhidharma robe to falsifying lineage evidence to being a bully. Of course, accusing the opposition of dreadful deeds isn't new in genealogical writing—murder was the repeating motif in the *Record,* where Du Fei claimed that Bodhidharma was poisoned many times by his jealous contemporaries. What is altogether different in Shenhui's account of lineage strife is that the criminal now has a name. Du Fei decided to suppress the names of those who had supposedly tried to poison Bodhidharma and, as I argued in chapter 4, seemed to be working up an image of Bodhidharma's past suffering in order to build pressure on current readers, and thus those past acts of violence were more useful as anonymous crimes.[96] Shenhui's accusations work on the opposite premise since he wants everyone to know of Puji's evil deeds. And just as supposedly historical details were supplied for that day of dharma combat between Shenhui and Chongyuan at Great Cloud Monastery, so, too, is Puji accused of specific deeds, committed on specific occasions.

Essentially there are five types of crimes that Shenhui wants to pin on Puji. First, and perhaps most importantly, Puji has claimed to be the seventh patriarch when, according to Shenhui, he isn't. Second, Puji claims to be of the Southern School when he is not, and in fact is supposedly trying to destroy the Southern School. Third, Puji has manufactured several public items that promote a falsified view of the past: a text, Du Fei's *Record,* which Shenhui in his usual haste cites with the slightly abbreviated title *Fabao ji* instead of *Chuan fabao ji,* and a Hall of Seven Patriarchs *(qizutang).*[97] Fourth, he sent, on different occasions, minions to destroy elements of what Shenhui calls the Southern School: these lackeys supposedly erased Huineng's stele (twice), stole the Bodhidharma robe, and, later, attacked Huineng's corpse. Fifth, and repeated three times in formulaic manner, Puji supposedly teaches a bad form of meditation that obstructs the attainment of enlightenment *(puti).* This charge is particularly notable, because until now the specific content of truth had not been clarified in discussions of the ownership of truth. In effect, this is the first time in the early Chan genealogies that a writer seeking to prove his lineage status demonstrates that the other lineage holder is illegimate because he lacks the proper *annunciation of truth.* However, it turns out that what Puji (and his teacher, Shenxiu) really lack, according to Shenhui, is suddenness and not any particular content or teaching.

96. For Du Fei's comment, see McRae, *The Northern School,* 259.
97. For this passage, see Hu Shi, *Shenhui,* 284, and a parallel one, slightly later, 289. The seven patriarchs here probably are Bodhidharma, Huike, Sengcan, Daoxin, Hongren, Faru, and Shenxiu, in which case, though there were seven patriarchs preceding him, Puji would have been only the seventh generation since Faru and Shenxiu were supposedly co-inheritors.

As for the first crime, Shenhui argues that Puji can't be the seventh master since Shenxiu wasn't the sixth. Essentially, then, Shenhui is trying to disenfranchise Puji by disenfranchising Shenxiu. Shenhui develops his case by arguing that Shenxiu, while alive, did not claim to be the sixth patriarch.[98] Actually, this might be true in accordance with my argument in chapter 4 that Shenxiu was created *as a lineage member* after he died, and thus Shenhui may have some historical ground to stand on here. However, he pushes this point much further by creating a dialogue for Shenxiu in which Shenxiu, on the eve of leaving for the Palace Temple in response to an invitation by Empress Wu, is asked by his followers:[99]

> "After the Monk [Shenxiu] goes to the Palace Temple, how will his disciples practice the Way? What will they depend on?" Shenxiu answers, "In Shaozhou, there is a great Spiritual Friend *(da shanzhishi)*, who, from the beginning, received transmission from the Master of East Mountain, [Hong] Ren. The buddha-dharma is completely in that place. All of you, if you have doubts to resolve, should go to that place to settle them—it will surely be inconceivable to come to know the buddha-dharma, the essence of the lineage *(zongzhi)*."

In crafting this scene, which closely parallels how Du Fei constructed Faru's deathbed statement as an endorsement for Shenxiu, Shenhui not only disenfranchises Puji by excluding his father, Shenxiu, from the lineage, but he has rather brazenly enlisted Shenxiu in the task of recommending Shenhui's own supposed master, Huineng. Huineng, in this brief exchange, appears as the complete owner of Buddhism even as Shenxiu goes off to court to serve as the National Teacher, an ironic tension that Shenhui makes use of later. Having read and trusted the historicity of this passage, we would know that only the shell of truth went to the capital with Shenxiu, with the real buddha-dharma far away in Shaozhou.

Seeing the ease with which Shenhui constructs and "relays" self-serving conversations from the long dead, it is noteworthy that he nowhere quotes Huineng. Why not include lines in which Huineng castigates Shenxiu as a second-rate teacher who should have never been confused with the real descendants of the Bodhidharma lineage? I think the answer to this problem has two parts. First, Shenhui might have been reluctant to put specific words in the mouth of the figure that

98. Hu Shi, *Shenhui,* 291.
99. Ibid., 291–92.

he was dressing up as a buddha—Huineng also says next to nothing in Wang Wei's epitaph that was written on Shenhui's urging. Second, and probably much more important, to make Huineng enter into these lineage struggles would ruin his image as one above the fray. Thus, it is much better for Shenhui if he can keep his truth-father clear of these lineage battles; such involvement in status claims clearly suggests a diminution in status.

Given the negative consequences of putting his own master into lineage combat, it is not too surprising that Shenhui relied on the father of the opposition—Shenxiu—to ratify Shenhui's father—Huineng. Just before the above quotation, Shenhui had created another "public" event where Shenxiu is made to say essentially the same thing, though this time the essence of Buddhism is spoken of in the form of the robe. Supposedly, when Shenxiu was at court in 702, having set up a precepts-platform *(jie tan)*,[100] he was asked by the Vinaya master Wang, "I have heard that Bodhidharma had a robe that was transmitted *(xiangchuan fushu)*, is that robe now with the Great Chan Master [Shenxiu] or not?" The Monk [Shen] Xiu responded, "The Great Master of Huangmei, [Hong] Ren, transmitted the robe, and today it can be seen in Shaozhou with Chan Master [Hui] Neng."[101] Assuredly, this is totally self-serving since Shenhui has created this conversation to enlist the prestige of Puji's truth-father, Shenxiu, for the dual task of undermining Puji and legitimizing Huineng, while maintaining the image of Huineng as calm and innocent, far from both the capital and the dubious implications of lineage combat. Of course, too, in this sequence Shenxiu is made to implicitly endorse the rule of the robe, a further gain for Shenhui as now the rule appears "in history" forty-some years before Shenhui spoke of it, and thus Shenhui can seem innocent of its invention.

The second crime that Shenhui wants to pin on Puji, plotting to destroy the Southern School, is more involved and shows how Shenhui ought to be "credited" with the creation of the titles Northern and Southern Schools. As mentioned in the introduction to this chapter, several prior sources had claimed that Bodhidharma was the third son of a Brahman from southern India. Thus, whereas the term *Southern* previously refered generically to Bodhidharma's lineage from south-

---

100. Du Fei had mentioned that Shenxiu was so popular that "students did not consider even ten thousand *li* too far to come to 'take refuge' at his dharma platform." Translation from McRae, *The Northern School*, 265–66.
101. Hu Shi, *Shenhui*, 290–91; see also Yampolsky, *The Platform Sūtra*, 27–28.

ern India, Shenhui made it into a moniker for his own private lineage claims. Then, with southern *China* established as the site of the authentic version of the Bodhidharma lineage, Shenhui could point to figures such as Puji who apparently had called themselves "Southern" with the Indian reference in mind, and accuse them of being outside the true lineage of Bodhidharma because vis-à-vis Huineng's locale in Shaozhou, near modern-day Guangdong, they were northerners. To legitimize this remapping of southern India onto a North/South polarity in China, Shenhui cites a popular saying that supposedly existed at the beginning of the eighth century:[102]

> "Southern Neng, Northern Xiu." Everyone knew this and because of this there came to be the two schools *(zong)*, North and South. Chan Master Puji is definitely a student from Yuquan and has never been to Shaozhou, so that he today falsely claims to be of the Southern School can't be allowed.

In generating a geographic divide to signify the gap between his own legitimacy and Puji's decadence, Shenhui is demonstrating his usual level of inventiveness, but on another level this is a fine example of taking away someone's title in a gesture that simultaneously disenfranchises him and relocates that title in another place that is now set in clear opposition to its former owner. In short, this is another moment of "sudden unenlightenment." Presumably, Shenhui saw that Huineng's geographic southernness—Jingjue's *History* had mentioned that Huineng was from Shaozhou—could be conjoined with that phrase about Bodhidharma's arrival from southern India, as the basis for developing a theory of his exclusive ownership of tradition. Reading Shenhui's creation of the Southern School in this manner seems altogether parallel to the manner in which he rewrote Bodhidharma's identity as Dharmatrāta based on the accidental sameness of their shared name "Dharma." In either case, there is no precedent for the claim, and yet that did not deter Shenhui from taking random historical happenstances and conjoining them into a powerful polemic, based on the thinnest bit of similitude.

The third type of crime that Shenhui charges Puji with is fabricating genealogies. This charge is rather straightforward and warrants discussion only in terms of the historical evidence it offers. Thus, for instance, when Shenhui accuses Puji of writing *(xiu)* the *Record* we

102. Hu Shi, *Shenhui*, p. 288.

gain some measure of confidence in identifying Puji as the instigator who asked Du Fei to compile that text. Then, in a slightly different sphere, Shenhui charges that Puji sent henchmen down to Shaozhou to erase the Huineng stele. This claim, among other things, shows how important stelae were for advancing lineage claims and also, like the loss of the robe, gives Shenhui an alibi for why he cannot produce the content of the stele or the robe.[103]

In trying to unseat Puji's claims to be the seventh patriarch, in addition to enlisting Shenxiu as his number one spokesperson against Puji, Shenhui appears to have expected to win ground by pointing out the way the author of the *Record,* here identified as Puji instead of Du Fei, overlapped Shenxiu with Faru in the sixth slot. Shenhui says to Chongyuan in this latter section of P2045:[104]

> Now Puji erects a stele for Shenxiu in which he calls him the Sixth Patriarch, and then he compiles the *Record (Fabao ji),* in which he makes Faru the Sixth Patriarch. I don't understand how these Great Virtuous Ones *(dade)* can both be the Sixth Patriarch. Which is true and which is false? Let's ask the Chan Master Puji to explain himself in detail.

Here, Shenhui is identifying that tender spot in the *Record* where Du Fei doubled up the final slot so as to steal Faru's lineage for Shenxiu and his descendants (see chapter 4). We shouldn't miss, too, that with the phrase "true and false," the author of this section of the *Treatise* is trying to transpose this problem between Shenhui and Puji back on to the initial problem of Shenhui and Chongyuan, as it had been established in the first part of the *Treatise* and in the title of the work. Shenhui's attack on the *Record* also suggests that Shenhui read it carefully, and this is important for making sense of the way he has constructed Shenxiu as Huineng's cheerleader, a trope that matches closely the way Du Fei constructed Faru as the self-destructing promoter and guarantor of Shenxiu in the *Record.*

The fourth crime, attacking the public sites associated with Huineng, doesn't need to be belabored. This dark underside of Puji's supposed activity is presumably set up to be the inverse of his aboveboard public acts. Thus while Puji "writes" the *Record,* he destroys Huineng's stele; as he sets up an ancestral hall, he destroys Huineng's mummy, and so on.

---

103. Ibid., 289.
104. Ibid., 289–90. This translation, with small changes, is from Yampolsky, *The Platform Sūtra,* 28.

DID YOU SAY "MEDITATION"?

Puji's (and Shenxiu's) fifth crime, the teaching of harmful meditation techniques, is worth considering closely because it requires rethinking our notion of Shenhui's own "teachings" and how he is attempting to construct authority for himself by defining Buddhist truths and practices, including meditation. Unfortunately, thinking through these passages has been thwarted by three modern assumptions: (1) that a discussion about meditation is actually about meditation; (2) that this charge of "bad meditation" has anything to do with Puji or Shenxiu; and (3) that we ought to read these passages in good faith and set them apart from self-aggrandizing lineage claims, an interpretive position, which, given the above evidence, ought to seem unpromising.

Approaching Shenhui's denunciation of Puji's meditation techniques with at least a suspicion that the interests shaping the discussion are complex, we can see right away that there is a certain redundance to the charge of teaching bad meditation. According to Shenhui's logic, if Puji doesn't have transmission and the robe, he doesn't have the right to teach Chan, and that was clearly said several times already in the *Treatise,* in the starkest terms.[105] So, in a strict sense, what Puji actually teaches is a moot point since he is not an heir to the lineage of truth, and therefore his teachings can be presumed, a priori, to be heterodox in some basic manner. However, it would seem that Shenhui wants form and content to match up here: Puji is not an heir to truth (he is in bad form), and thus it is no surprise, and in fact it is veritable proof of this "bad form," that he teaches a harmful kind of meditation (bad content).

As mentioned above, this is the first time in genealogical writing that the specific teaching of the opposition has been "quoted" in a challenging text. Presumably, this is a little dangerous because it shifts the basis of the debate significantly. What had previously been a "history" debate about the flow of truth in a lineage now is a debate about content that could lead in any number of new and uncontainable directions precisely because new grounds of legitimacy are being opened up. That is, the question of the legitimacy of Puji's meditation *program,* on its own terms, potentially could draw in all sorts of nonlineage arguments that would damage Shenhui's claim to be Buddhist "roy-

---

105. See, for instance, Hu Shi, *Shenhui,* 282–84.

alty." The danger of letting content into the discussion, however, is quickly contained since Shenhui's construction of Puji's "content" leads immediately into a zone that Shenhui has shown himself well adapted to—restaged sūtra scenes. Thus, Shenhui's attack on Puji's bad meditation quickly finds its way back into a scene from the *Vimalakīrti* where Shenhui gets to play, as usual, Vimalakīrti's role, while Puji is given Śāriputra's subaltern status.

To contextualize Shenhui's charge against Puji's teaching, let's remember that here in the midst of a very messy and chaotic text, the *Treatise* has not, up to this point, been about meditation. The topics covered in the first and second sections of the text were substantially other than meditation—the thickly dramatized trouncing of Chongyuan with sūtra quotations took up the first section, which then spilled into wandering discussions of Bodhidharma's robe, Buddhist "kingship," and Puji's evils. Clearly, as a discourse claiming total authority for "defining the true and false," outlining a meditation strategy for the populace wasn't at the top of the list of topics to cover. Equally clear, Shenhui has not, prior to this point in the *Treatise,* tried to strengthen his claim to own tradition by advocating proper meditation techniques. Of course, this isn't unusual given that none of the early Chan texts have been that concerned with defining meditation for the masses. Their interests, like Shenhui's, were directed toward establishing historical "evidence" for who should be the leader of Chinese Buddhism. And, in general, it had not been said that meditation was the answer either for the masters or for the masses, with the exception to the rule being one section in Daoxin's biography, as concocted by Jingjue in the *History.*[106] In fact, the trope of suddenness, usually linked with privacy and secrecy, worked to keep at bay the possibility that there were functional techniques for getting into truth and the lineage. Actually, this position will also be upheld by Shenhui who, in the end, argues that one only gets to truth by truth, a position that obviously collapses cause and effect in an exciting and yet forbidding manner.

Shenhui will shift the masters' monopoly on suddenness by offering the masses "sudden-seeing of the buddha-nature" *(dunjian foxing),* though the sudden-seeing for nonlineage members doesn't result in

---

106. In this section, meditation for beginners is explained, though this passage, too, follows statements on the need to find the right person(s) from whom to receive transmission of the "secret essence of this dharma." See Cleary, *Zen Dawn,* 61 ff; Faure, *Le bouddhisme Chan,* 155 ff.

buddhahood or master status, and instead is to be followed by gradual practice.[107] Thus, though exciting for promising some kind of contact with that interior buddha-nature, Shenhui's offer, in the end, looks as intent on regenerating the master-slave dialectic as the prior lineage texts had been, though with a rosier glow around it. Equally important, Shenhui never explains how one is to do the sudden-seeing or the subsequent practice, and thus these topics seem to be potent and important simply on the level of rhetoric. And, obviously, anyone who thought that they were going to learn how to meditate from reading the dossier of the Shenhui-Chongyuan debate would be rather disappointed.

As to the question of whether Shenxiu or Puji ever taught this form of bad meditation, we have to admit that we don't have any evidence to support this assumption. In fact, texts by either of them have yet to be discovered. The regular claim that Shenxiu wrote the *Treatise on the Five Upāya (Wu fangbian)* and/or the *Treatise on Contemplating the Mind (Guanxin lun)* doesn't have convincing evidence behind it.[108] In fact, Jingjue's *History* tells us that Shenxiu didn't write anything at all, and he was presumably closer to Shenxiu in time and would have had no real reasons to suppress Shenxiu's writing if it had existed.[109]

In the first passage in which Shenhui makes this charge against Shenxiu's and Puji's teaching on meditation, a good bit after he has

---

107. Hu Shi, *Shenhui*, 287.

108. As far as I know, there is no reliable evidence establishing Shenxiu as the author of the *Treatise of the Five Upāya*. Literary evidence connecting Shenxiu with the *Treatise on Contemplation of the Mind* comes, at the earliest, in 788 or perhaps later, in 806/7, from Huilin's (750–820), *Yiqie jing yinyi* (see McRae, *The Northern School*, 325 n. 159). Why McRae takes such a late attribution—eighty or one hundred years after Shenxiu's death—to be convincing evidence is hard to understand. He writes, "Evidence from a contemporary T'ang manual [Huilin's] has established beyond question that it was written by Shen-hsiu" (*The Northern School*, 148). In fact, the *Treatise on Contemplation of the Mind* has survived in manuscripts that attribute the work to Bodhidharma—another unlikely author—and so the better assumption ought to be that various Buddhist literati of the eighth century, or later, thought it would be good to give this text an ancestor, as was so often done in China, and some chose Bodhidharma, others Shenxiu. This is hardly solid evidence of Shenxiu's authorship. Also, if Shenxiu had written anything, one would have expected Shenhui to have cited it directly, as he did with Du Fei's *Record*. Faure also bends over backward to make these texts belong to the masters of the "Northern School." In a particularly chaotic and I think fundamentally misguided effort that assumes that early Chan is really about content, Faure works at explaining Shenxiu's doctrinal background and its development in the Northern School, and assumes that he wrote the *Treatise on Contemplation of the Mind*, though again without convincing evidence; see his *The Will to Orthodoxy*, chaps. 2, 4. In fact, Faure even relies on this text by Shenhui, *The Treatise*, to claim that the *Treatise on the Five Upāya* might have been based on one of Shenxiu's lectures; see p. 117.

109. See the line in Shenxiu's brief biography in Cleary, *Zen Dawn*, 72–73.

already listed Puji's other unsavory deeds, he closes out the charge with a "sūtra" quote explaining why, even if Shenxiu and Huineng were "classmates" under Hongren, they taught different things. Shenhui writes:[110]

> The sūtra says, "the mind doesn't abide internally, nor externally, therefore it quietly abides (*yanzuo*). This kind of meditation, the Buddha certified (*yinke*). None of the six patriarchs ever taught [as Shenxiu and Puji supposedly did] that 'one freezes the mind to enter into meditation, stabilizes the mind in viewing purity, awakens the mind so that it shines outward, and concentrates the mind so that it internally confirms [truth.]' Therefore what they [Shenxiu and Puji] taught is different."

This so-called sūtra quotation that Shenhui supplies is actually from the *Vimalakīrti,* and it is our first big hint about what Shenhui is doing here.[111] In the *Vimalakīrti,* and especially in the section from which this line is drawn, basic Buddhist topics such as meditation, ethics, and begging serve as the topics for Vimalakīrti to unseat and humiliate traditionally revered figures like Śāriputra, Maudgalyāyana, and Subhuti, figures who were supposed to be experts in these particular topics and yet are shown to be no match for Vimalakīrti's rhetoric.[112] In this passage, Vimalakīrti has found Śāriputra meditating under a tree and proceeds to ask him a series of challenging questions that "prove" to him, and, more important, to the reader, that tradition was wrong to assume that these stalwart figures actually had the wisdom of tradition. Moreover, the reader is invited to enjoy this turning of the tables and, in particular, to delight in Vimalakīrti's extravagant refiguration of tradition's foundations.

In his assault on Śāriputra's supposed small-mindedness, Vimalakīrti redefines meditation in a series of unthinkable ways that have nothing to do with actual meditation in the sense of a physical practice and instead thrill the reader with unthinkable combinations. Thus, the full passage in the *Vimalakīrti* includes the phrase, "Entering nir-

110. Hu Shi, *Shenhui,* 286.
111. The line is generic enough that it probably could be found in other Māhāyana sūtras, but the rather idiosyncratic term *yanzuo* along with the following phrase "certified by the Buddha," which is also found in the next sentence in the *Vimalakīrti,* leave little doubt that the *Vimalakīrti* is the source for this passage; see T.14.539c.23–27. Shenhui's *Questions and Answers* also draws on this passage; see Hu Shi, *Shenhui,* 97; Gernet, *Entretiens,* 5. For an English translation of this passage, see Watson, *Vimalakīrti Sūtra,* 37.
112. For more discussion of this section of the *Vimalakīrti,* see my *Text as Father,* chap. 6.

vana without having put an end to earthly desires—this is quiet sitting
(anzuo). If you can do this kind of sitting, you will merit the Buddha's
seal of approval *(yinke)*."[113] Clearly, this kind of riddle-like challenge
in *Vimalakīrti* is about undermining confidence in traditional forms
of practice by displaying for the reader the possibility that tradition
missed the essence of Buddhism and that tradition doesn't even warrant
the Buddha's approval because it was unable to achieve this impossible
task of manifesting the end of desire while still having desire. Of course,
just as with the *Lotus Sūtra* and the *Diamond Sūtra*, this passage from
the *Vimalakīrti* threatens the reader, by threatening Śāriputra, that
failure to assent to this redefinition of Buddhism will result in the loss
of one's Buddhist identity. Here, of course, Śāriputra is on the verge
of losing the Buddha's approval for his standard meditation practice
and will for the rest of the *Vimalakīrti* remain a pathetic figure only
slowly realizing that truth is somewhere apart from tradition as he had
understood it.

In a very basic sense, then, we ought to read Shenhui's comments
on the "meditation debate" as a literary effort to slide Vimalakīrti's
humiliation of pre-Māhāyana leaders onto contemporaneous Chinese
figures such that he can do to this caricature of Puji what Vimalakīrti
supposedly did to Śāriputra. Of course, reading this way matches both
the polemical context of the *Treatise* and the fact that Shenhui quotes
again from just this scene in the *Vimalakīrti* the next time Puji's bad
meditation is brought up.[114] In short, Shenhui appears to have seen in
the *Vimalakīrti* a promising template for undoing established tradition
and reestablishing it elsewhere. Thus, it isn't that he wanted to evoke the
"meaning" of the *Vimalakīrti* passage on meditation—whatever that
might be; rather, he wants its *function*. In other words, the "debate"
about meditation is really no more than a technique for moving Shenhui
into the literary space of the *Vimalakīrti* so that he can appear as the
victorious underdog owning tradition; thus, I doubt that this debate
has anything to do with meditation or any kind of practice at all.
Consequently, instead of mining these passages for the supposed differences between Northern and Southern Chan—a twentieth-century
obsession—we ought to focus on Shenhui's literary ingenuity and what
this might tell us about how he was reading tradition and redeploying
it to his own advantage. Or put another way, that Shenhui pulled the

113. Translation from Watson, *Vimalakīrti Sūtra*, 37.
114. Hu Shi, *Shenhui*, 288.

schismatic polemics of the *Vimalakīrti* into Tang-era lineage battles needs to be read as the *transmission of polemical strategies*, not as his definition of some particular new Buddhist meaning or practice. The clear point of this debate is to show Shenhui audaciously playing out these tried and true Mahāyāna roles himself and treating his adversaries as small-minded "Hīnāyānists" who have missed the essence of tradition and aren't even to be ratified as authentically Buddhist. In effect, then, Shenhui's "Chan" is largely the reenactment of earlier *forms of polemics,* and thus we have to understand his writing as deeply involved in the reading of tradition and the reinscribing of prized literary "moments" into new forms of literature that offered new boons. Oddly enough, then, part of making Shenhui look like the recipient of the Bodhidharma transmission—a transmission supposedly beyond language and literature, as Shenhui insists—is to stage, in a new literary space, this kind of literary transmission in which segments of beloved sūtras glimmer through Shenhui's body and verbiage.

This critique of bad meditation is followed immediately by lineage issues. Chongyuan asks, "Did Huineng transmit to anyone?" Shenhui answers, "Yes, later you will know who."[115] If the location of this question about Huineng's transmission isn't accidental, then it proves that a certain logic is in place in the arrangement of this supposed discussion of meditation such that the denunciation of Shenxiu's and Puji's teaching leads into a review of the lineage from the Buddha down to the present. Thus, the meditation discussion is resolved with Shenhui formally declaring knowledge of the continuation of the lineage and tempting Chongyuan with the promise that he, too, will soon know who is the current representative of this line of truth.

Joining the meditation discussion with this short exchange about Huineng's heir gives the distinct impression that the author has guided Chongyuan's gaze, and the reader's, back into India, where the Buddha ratifies one form of meditation that is supposedly the only legitimate form of meditation; and, then, with that singular item established, our gaze is brought up to the six Chinese patriarchs who apparently never taught the erroneous doctrines that Shenxiu and Puji did. Thus, Shenxiu and Puji are doubly outside of the lineage, with neither transmission nor an accurate facsimile of true teachings. Then with our gaze following the conduit of truth into the present, Chongyuan wants to know

---

115. Hu Shi, *Shenhui,* 286.

about Huineng's descendant, because he has now been convinced that Huineng's teachings are legitimate while Shenxiu's are fabricated, and now needs to know where to find the current owner of that legitimate form of tradition. Evidently, though meditation is the ostensible topic, the flow of the conversation is still within the cadre of defining which individual master is the legitimate descendant of this line of truth-fathers.

SUDDENNESS FOR THE MASSES

With that quick interlude establishing the correct gaze following truth from the past into the present, supported by the none-too-subtle hint that Shenhui is the heir to this lineage, Chongyuan again asks why this [bad] form of meditation can't be taught,[116]

> "Why can't this kind of teaching [by Shenxiu and Puji] be buddhadharma? Why can't it be allowed?" The Monk [Shenhui] answered, "All [this] is because sudden and gradual aren't the same *(dun jia butong)*, therefore it is not allowed. Each of *my ancestors* of the past six generations *(wo liudai dashi yi yi jie)* all spoke of directly entering [into truth], like a knife, and directly understood and saw the [buddha]-nature. They didn't speak of steps or gradual [progress]. Those who study the Way must directly see [their] buddha-natures and then gradually cultivate the causes and conditions, and without having left this life, they will achieve liberation. This is just like a mother who suddenly gives birth to a child and breastfeeds it—gradually it is nourished, and the child's wisdom will increase naturally.[117] As for the sudden enlightenment of seeing the buddha-nature, it is just like this. Wisdom will naturally *(ziran)* increase gradually *(jianjian)*. Consequently, [Shenxiu's and Puji's teaching] isn't permitted.

Here the author is clearly advancing a number of new claims. First, he has redistributed sudden and gradual in a tantalizing manner. Up to now suddenness was the special preserve of the masters, even in Faru's biography. And, in a way, Shenhui is replaying that singularity when he says that the masters "never spoke of steps or gradual [progress]." But, even as suddenness seems to remain the special purview of the masters in the lineage, a form of suddenness is being offered to all students of

---

116. Ibid., 287; for an alternative translation and commentary, see Luis O. Gómez, "Purifying Gold," 88–89; P3047 picks up here, and Gernet translates this section in *Entretiens*, 92 ff.

117. Among the various parental motifs in the voluminous *Nirvana Sūtra*, there is an extended metaphor of the Buddha treating his disciples just as a mother raises a son; see T.12.385b.22 ff.

the Way. The difference, though, is that suddenness for the student is but the introduction to the gradual cultivation of wisdom. In short, suddenness for the masters came with sudden completion since they "directly understood and saw the [buddha]-nature." For the student, however, suddenness comes without completion since it designates the beginning of an organic-like progress metaphorized as a child's gradual growth and natural increase of wisdom.

Consequently, though it is undeniable that Shenhui is offering a kind of suddenness to the average person, he has done so only after having constructed two very different kinds of suddenness. Thus, suddenness for the masters seems as effective as ever since it takes them, knifelike, into truth, and this isn't followed by a lingering need to be suckled on truth thereafter. The case of the student's sudden-seeing, however, is altogether different: it promises to confirm the presence of the buddha-nature within the student, and yet it also comes within the confines of a gradualness that affirms the student's distance from truth and the truth-father. Equally clear, this form of sudden-seeing on the part of the student doesn't produce master status, something that Shenhui has, all along in this section of the *Treatise,* been restricting to one kinglike figure. Thus, readers learn to acknowledge the virtuoso's performance even as they agree that they must mimic this basic gesture and find that buddha-nature within, though with the understanding that it will be but a small seeing in comparison to the masters'.

There is something else to appreciate in taking "seeing" as the secret to the master's identity and the students' practice. In the midst of advocating seeing as the answer to Buddhist truth, Shenhui, or the author of this section of the text, has relied on a distinctly hazy mode for transmitting the "fact" that Shenhui is the seventh patriarch. Thus, Shenhui's identity as Huineng's sole descendant has been half-stated in several of the above passages, but each time it has been done on the sly. There is no passage that stands out and says, "Now hear this: Shenhui is Huineng's sole inheritor of the totality of tradition, and everyone else is deluded." Instead, the reader has been given several clear unmistakable hints that Shenhui is the One, and in fact the whole discussion seems designed to make the reader come to this conclusion *without* really knowing what is happening. That is, if my above readings are right about the interplay of Chinese sectarianism with older polemical models in the *Vimalakīrti,* set up to further the basic subtext regarding Shenhui's buddha-identity, then the entire text is an exercise in coming to know of truth in a very blind manner. That is, the reader is only gradually induced into seeing Shenhui as the one who sees all truth, and who can define seeing for all; and this process, when it works, only proceeds when the reader doesn't see what is going on.

SUCCESSFUL SITTING

Right after the line with the mother-child metaphor, Chongyuan again asks about meditation, saying that Puji and Xiangmo (another master who is often associated with Puji) teach people seated meditation (zuochan) in which "one freezes the mind to enter into meditation, stabilizes the mind in viewing purity, awakens the mind so that it shines outward, and concentrates the mind so that it is internally confirming [of truth]. This is what they take to be the [correct] teaching (jiaomen), so why doesn't the Chan Master [Shenhui] now teach seated meditation?"[118] Shenhui repeats this four-phrase summary of Puji's and Xiangmo's instructions and asks rhetorically how this could be seated meditation. Then he repeats the summary yet again, saying that this would obstruct enlightenment (zhang puti), and then turns to redefine the two terms seated and meditation in a manner that shows he is again working from the Vimalakīrti template. Shenhui argues:[119]

> Now when we say "sitting" it means "thinking does not arise" (nian buqi wei zuo). And, when we say "chan" that means "seeing one's nature" (jian benxing wei chan). Therefore, we don't teach people to sit their bodies down (bu jiao ren zuoshen) and hold their mind in concentration (zhu xin ru ding). If this had been taken as the teaching (jiaomen), then Vimalakīrti wouldn't have had to ridicule Śāriputra for his "quiet sitting" (anzuo).

Here Shenhui once again pulls out the Vimalakīrti template to unseat Shenxiu, Puji, and Xiangmo. Clearly, it is this Indian text that is providing Shenhui with the form and content of his position since Shenhui performs like Vimalakīrti as the definer of tradition and practice, and moreover does so in a manner that mixes cause and effect in the explanation of meditation. When Shenhui defines sitting as "thinking does not arise" and chan as "seeing one's nature," it is evident that he has front-loaded the whole enterprise: the effect of the practice is now defined as the practice itself. This kind of confusion of cause and effect

---

118. Hu Shi, Shenhui, 287.
119. Ibid., 288.

is rampant in the *Vimalakīrti*, actually in many Māhāyana discussions, and so Shenhui apparently is drawing on that style of repacking practice *as* perfection, a position that naturally makes the discussion of practice look a whole lot more attractive, even if in that rhetorical ploy one has created a definition for practice that isn't very practical. In terms of form, Shenhui is again adopting Vimalakīrti's role and giving Puji and Xiangmo the dubious distinction of being Śāriputra, and thus warranting a real dressing-down for not knowing what is what with meditation.

With this final quotation, Shenhui closes out the discussion of meditation and returns to cataloging Puji's criminal activity. In the midst of this attack, Chongyuan asks Shenhui why he waited several decades *(shu shi yu nian)* to make these charges, and Shenhui answers that Puji was a bully so no one had the courage to ask about the lineage.[120] This question seems placed here to deal with the obvious problem that Shenhui has waited a long time to make these charges, and this in itself seems suspicious. As usual, Shenhui takes this problem that might be damaging to his program and turns it into an occasion to recount yet another bad thing about Puji: he was a bully.

Soon after, a related point concerning the legitimacy of Shenhui's discourse comes up in the account of Puji's evils. Chongyuan asks:[121]

"In *writing* this treatise, aren't you seeking fame and fortune?" Shenhui answered, "In writing this treatise I didn't care about my life, how could I be concerned with fame and fortune?"

This exchange is as telling as the issue of the lateness of these charges against Puji. Here we have undeniable evidence that this part of the text admitted that it was written and not spoken. Without assuming that Shenhui is the author, even if this passage says as much, this line nonetheless suggests that the production of this part of the discourse was self-consciously a writing event and identified in just those terms—*xiu cilun* can't mean anything but writing out a text and suggests that the whole "conversation"with Chongyuan is no more than an authorial ploy, even as Chongyuan is made to question the writing of this drama as though he were external to it.

120. Ibid., 290.
121. Ibid., 294. Actually, just before this passage we have another in which Shenhui had spoken directly of those who would "read this treatise" *(du cilun zhe)*, making clear that the actors "onstage" are actually the author's creation and thus can "speak" about their coming appearance in book form.

THE *DIAMOND SŪTRA*,
AS READ THROUGH SHENHUI'S BODY

Following this very brief exchange vindicating Shenhui's authorial motivations, the "discussion" turns to the question of Bodhidharma's Indian lineage (as borrowed from Dharmatrāta) that I treated above. Right after explaining Bodhidharma's supposed eight Indian predecessors, and why the robe wasn't transmitted in India, there is another major shift in the text's rhetoric. Chongyuan asks about what Shenhui practices.[122] Of course, the very framing of this question reflects again what the entire *Treatise,* in its various sections, has sought to accomplish: truth and the definition of correct Buddhist practice should be sought, uniquely, in the figure of Shenhui, who, unlike all other spokespersons, actually knows truth and its sources and thus can speak authoritatively for the whole tradition.

In response to Chongyuan's question about his practices, Shenhui launches into a verbose account of the value of the *Diamond Sūtra,* and the Perfection of Wisdom in general. In this response, Chongyuan and the dialogue format completely disappear. Pages go by without any indication of who is speaking and certainly no references back to the supposed setting at Great Cloud Monastery. In effect, this is a fairly dense and autonomous commentary on the *Diamond Sūtra,* though with some rather notable twists and turns that connect Shenhui to truth and legitimacy, and in particular demonstrate his right to define the essence of tradition.

In terms of content, there are four basic points: (1) one needs to read and accept the *Diamond Sūtra* as the essence of Buddhism; (2) the *Diamond Sūtra* is the mother of all buddhas, and the ancestral master *(zushi)* of all dharmas, and it also clears away all sins and is the doorway for transmission between buddhas; (3) no-thinking *(wunian)* is the culmination of the *Diamond Sūtra,* a point that appears late in the discussion but seems important and leads into the ostentatious claim by Shenhui that he has the Tathāgata within him; and (4) Shenhui is the medium through which the current public should access the *Diamond Sūtra,* and thus the *Treatise* explains that Shenhui is currently sacrificing his life to preach so that all sentient beings will take up the *Diamond Sūtra.*[123] Actually, this final point of Shenhui's funnel-like

122. Hu Shi, *Shenhui,* 296.
123. Ibid., 310.

role in reinstituting the centrality of the *Diamond Sūtra* is indicative of the whole section. Suddenly, it is as though the *Diamond Sūtra* couldn't stand on its own but needs to be retaught by a master who claims buddha-status for himself.

In making sense of these four themes, we ought to see that they are all about essentializing and relocating the totality of tradition. Even though the discourse will, at different moments, shift emphasis from the *Diamond Sūtra* to the Perfection of Wisdom to no-thinking to Shenhui's identity, each element will be treated as the singular reservoir of tradition, even if at the end of the discussion it is claimed that, for instance, no-thinking is the same as the *Diamond Sūtra*. Thus, this long train of discourse keeps trying to fold Buddhist value and practice into a series of singular items that are glorified in extravagant terms and fetishized as the essence of tradition. It is, then, no surprise that after pages of this kind of discussion, Shenhui will claim that he himself is no different from the Buddha.

In appreciating how this section works, we shouldn't miss that though it is so full of long sūtra quotes, it still is set up to be a discourse given by Shenhui "live," to Chongyuan, and of course to the shadow assembly at Great Cloud Monastery. This "live" factor is particularly important in considering how the *Diamond Sūtra* is presented as coming out of Shenhui's living body, which, supposedly, is preaching in public and playing the Buddha's part, almost as if the sūtra was being taught for the first time, with Shenhui's voice and the Buddha's voice overlapped and mingled as usual. Equally interesting is the way that the *Diamond Sūtra*'s discussion of its own value will reappear, but this time, instead of directing the total value of tradition to land on the *Diamond Sūtra* as text, it lands on Shenhui's body, an effect clearly consonant with fusing his voice with the sūtra's.

To visualize the way the *Treatise* has installed the *Diamond Sūtra* in Shenhui's person and vice versa, imagine a large fresco of Shenhui on a temple wall, standing ten feet tall and facing the viewer. The perimeter of his body is well defined against the surrounding plaster, but on closer inspection one can see that the colors that make up his body also reproduce recognizable depictions of scenes from the *Diamond Sūtra*. Thus, as we look at the Shenhui fresco, we see both the *Diamond Sūtra* and Shenhui's person, and the two seem inseparable. This arrangement invites one to read the *Diamond Sūtra* through Shenhui's person, and all the exponential value claims that the sūtra had made for itself now seem indistinguishable from the vessel—Shenhui—that holds the sūtra as a kind of outer packaging. Hence, the *Treatise* tries to disappear and give us Shenhui "live," away from textuality, and yet this image of Shenhui is nothing but a new perimeter drawn around selected elements from the *Diamond Sūtra*. Consequently, the *Treatise* has produced a kind of trompe l'oeil, since when we "look" at Shenhui onstage, we see and hear chosen snippets from the *Diamond Sūtra;* or, in the other direction, when we "hear" the *Diamond Sūtra,* we see Shenhui's body.[124]

Skipping over several sections, we come to the important topic of confession where it is argued that confession doesn't erase one's sins; only the *Diamond Sūtra* does.[125] This topic isn't found in the *Diamond Sūtra* and thus represents an extension of the powers of the sūtra. As we will see, working confessions into a public format is a crucial element in other mid- to late-eighth-century Chan texts, such as the *Platform Sermon* and the *Platform Sūtra*.[126] In the *Treatise,* Shenhui first argues that the *Diamond Sūtra* can function as the total purifier of even the gravest sins, just in the way that the magical Mount Meru turns the various colors of all birds to white through it august moral power.

Following this discussion, there is a brief return to the question of the merit gained from trafficking in the *Diamond Sūtra,* but then there is a significant break in the *Treatise* marked by four questions that lead into a discussion of no-thought. This will be the final topic before Shenhui declares that he has the Tathāgata within him. Apparently picking up the theme of the merit won from teaching the *Diamond Sūtra,* Shenhui works to condense teaching and wisdom into the term *no-thought.*

Without clarifying who is speaking, the following exchange appears:[127]

---

124. For a clearer sense of the politics involved in so clearly linking the *Diamond Sūtra* and Shenhui's person/body, one could consider the recent dispute in Mexico over whether the state of Hidalgo could run an ad campaign with images of Mexico's national monuments draped over the body of a popular model (Irán Castillo). Mexico's National Institute for Anthropology and History was upset about "Ms. Castillo wearing Mexico's patrimony on her curvaceous form" (New York Times, May 27, 2008, A6). In a similar vein, one could imagine many Chinese partisans of the *Diamond Sūtra* dismayed to see it, as something like a public national treasure, become so intertwined with Shenhui's private person.

125. Hu Shi, *Shenhui,* 304.

126. For a useful history of public ordination rituals in China, see Paul Groner, "The Ordination Ritual in the *Platform Sūtra.*" For a well-documented discussion of how these ordination rituals were reformulated in early Chan, see Adamek, *The Mystique of Transmission,* chaps. 3, 6.

127. Hu Shi, *Shenhui,* 308.

What is taught? The non-adoption of signs *(bu qu yu xiang)*.
What is the non-adoption of signs? It is what is called "in accordance with thusness *(ruru)*."
What is in accordance with thusness? It is what is called "no-thought."
What is no-thought? It is what is called not thinking of being or non-being. Not thinking of good or evil. Not thinking of borders or no-borders. Not thinking of limits or no-limits. Not thinking of bodhi and not taking bodhi to be something that could be thought *(bu nian puti, bu yi puti wei nian)*. Not thinking of nirvana, not taking nirvana to be something that could be thought. Therefore it is no-thought. Precisely no-thought is the Perfection of Wisdom, and the Perfection of Wisdom is the one-practice samādhi *(yixing sanmei)*.

The odd questions that run through this passage are clearly rhetorical and seem orchestrated as a call-and-response sequence. As the exchange develops, it is evident that the goal of the "questions" is to focus Buddhist meaning and value down into the term *no-thought*, a progression that the following passage will continue. No-thought is supposedly the essence of Buddhism, and thus after the list of negations, Shenhui identifies it with the Perfection of Wisdom and one-practice samādhi, a rather innovative turn since of course this hadn't been said before in the other parts of the *Treatise* or in the sūtra quotations.

Shenhui continues expressing the centrality of no-thought, saying:[128]

Good Friends, if when you are on the level of practice *(xuedi)*, you have thoughts arise in your minds, this is just a conceptual version of insight *(juezhao)*.[129] When the mind that has appeared is extinguished *(qi xin ji mie)*, the conceptual version of insight *(juezhao)* dies on its own and just this is no-thought. This no-thought doesn't have a single sense-field *(jingjie)*. If it had a sense-field, it wouldn't correspond to no-thought. Therefore, Good Friends, if you actually see it *(shi jian)*, you will penetrate to the most profound dharma realm, and just this is one-practice samādhi.

Therefore the *Shorter Perfection of Wisdom Sūtra* says, "Good Sons, the Perfection of Wisdom is what is called 'nothing to think vis-à-vis all dharmas *(yu zhufa wu suo nian)*.' I and the other [buddhas] abide within the dharma of no-thought *(zhu yu wunian fazhong)* and obtain in this way the diamond body, the thirty-two marks, the great brilliance, the inconceivable wisdom, the incomparable samādhi of all buddhas, incomparable wisdom, and go beyond the limit of all merit. The merit of this [is

128. Ibid., 308–9.
129. This term is somewhat unusual and is found in the *Awakening of Faith*, T.32.576c.22.

so great that] even if all the buddhas explained it, they couldn't complete
the explanation. What need is there to mention if the Hearers or Solitary
Realizers could understand it?

"To see no-thought is to purify the six senses. To see no-thought is to
obtain the seeing of the buddha/s *(de xiang fo zhi jian)*. To see no-thought
is called the real sign *(shi xiang)*. To see no-thought is the final truth of
the Middle Way. To see no-thought is to make complete, in a moment,
merits [as numerous as sands] in the Ganges. To see no-thought is to be
able to produce all dharmas. To see no-thought is to be able to collect all
dharmas."[130]

Clearly the work of this passage is to set up no-thought as the fullest
fetishization of Buddhist truth and tradition, even as all these other elements need to be in place to support this claim, including the *Diamond
Sūtra*, the buddhas, the merit system, and so on. This circle of reliance
is obvious enough, but another important aspect of this passage isn't
so evident. I believe that there are good reasons to see that several passages from the above quotation have been taken from the *Awakening
of Faith* and, though modified in some ways, still would have evoked
that source for eighth-century readers.

Finding yet another literary source in Shenhui's supposedly oral discourse raises a number of problems. First, these passages weren't signaled as quotations, but why not? Was it that the *Awakening of Faith*
was seen as too common, in comparison to the *Diamond Sūtra* and
the *Shorter Perfection of Wisdom Sūtra* cited above, or was it that the
Awakening of Faith had already been cited by writers such as Du Fei
and Jingjue and thus couldn't shine in the brilliance of uniqueness that
these passages seem to demand? However we choose to answer these
questions, we have to agree that this section of the *Treatise* is providing
a kind of final commentary on tradition in a way that passes literary
statements from marked and unmarked sources through Shenhui in
order to deliver this commentary as though it represented an integrated
position spoken from a single person who supposedly has *seen* truth
and not simply read about it. In short, once again when we look carefully at how these eighth-century Chan texts were constructed, we
see how deeply traditional and textual they are, even as they try to

---

130. This final line "to collect all dharmas" matches a line in the *Awakening of
Faith,* T.32.576b.10, which, too, is concerned with the end of the arising of mind and
also advocates "seeing no thought" *(guan wunian)* as buddha-knowledge, T.32.576b.27,
and works from this logic of the end of sense-fields, too. The *Lidai fabao ji* cites from
this section of the *Awakening of Faith* to provide explanations for no-thought (see
T.51.185a.24), suggesting that Shenhui's recycling of these passages was recognized.

appear otherwise, and that, arguably, is the art and talent of the Chan authors.

Also, and this ought to hit one like a ton of bricks, content in Shenhui's writing is coming from prior texts and never from Huineng, who, if he existed, doesn't seem to be credited with passing on anything to Shenhui. Apart from supposedly giving Shenhui the right to be the king of Chinese Buddhism, Huineng serves no discernible function in Shenhui's discourse, and Shenhui never looks to him for the content of tradition. This, again, makes it seem like the specific profile of Huineng as an illiterate, rustic truth-father is a formal construct that took shape as the inverted image of the elite monastics with their claims to be Hongren's descendants: he is the opposite of all that had, in the previous generations, been ratified, and he is designed to wreak havoc on these prior structures of authority by claiming authority in new, "natural" and illiterate ways. And, thus, Huineng represents one of those clear cases of religion being about religion in the sense that Shenhui's Huineng doesn't supply Buddhist content or styles of practice, or enlightenment, or human experience of any kind. Instead, he takes form through the force of other religious claims and is designed to get rid of them—a kind of "Little Cat Z" that Shenhui has generated to undermine any other formal claim to Chinese buddhahood.[131]

In the next section, Shenhui claims that seeing no-thought produces the final effects of Buddhist practice: "To see no-thought is to make complete, in a moment, merits [as numerous as sands] in the Ganges."[132] Thus, at this point Shenhui is offering all students of the Way sudden access to completion. How this is to fit inside Shenhui's other statements about one patriarch per generation isn't explained, but in the next line Shenhui, "in a loud voice," proclaims his sameness with the Buddha:[133]

I am, today, able to understand the Tathāgata nature *(wo jin neng liao rulai xing).*
    The Tathāgata is today within my body *(rulai jin zai wo shenzhong).*
    There is no difference between me and the Tathāgata *(wo yu rulai wu chabie).*
    The Tathāgata is just my sea of thusness *(rulai ji wo zhen ruhai).*[134]

131. "Little Cat Z" is found in Dr. Seuss's *The Cat in the Hat.*
132. Hu Shi, *Shenhui,* 309.
133. Ibid., 310.
134. The Tathāgata as the ocean for all sentient beings is a motif found in the *Nirvana Sūtra;* see T.12.381b.25.

Thus, as Shenhui so stridently claims a form of buddhahood for himself, we can see how the overall flow of truth is being organized in this section of the *Treatise*. Shenhui is pouring into his own person all the successes that he had proposed to his students in the prior sections. Those lines about seeing no-thought didn't open up into asking if there weren't others in the audience who similarly saw no-thought. Thus, defining the purest form of truth in tradition, along with the techniques for accessing that truth, end up being inseparable from claiming that one man alone had found it.

If fact, what follows next is a very strange section that lionizes Shenhui as a uniquely self-sacrificing master who takes the following vow before the audience and all the buddhas and bodhisattvas, saying:[135]

> Today I offer my life in order to compose *(xiu)* the "Treatise on Sudden Enlightenment of the Supreme Vehicle" *(dunwu zuishangcheng lun)*, wishing that all sentient beings could hear and praise the Diamond-Like Perfection of Wisdom, finalize their profound faith, and abide in non-reversal.

This statement is then repeated three times with slight shifts, and thus the statement and its formulaic quality suggest that the text is now beginning to orient itself toward a ritual setting, with Shenhui shown speaking to the audience explaining what is needed to fulfill their Buddhist desires, even as he declares that he is prepared to die so that they can reach those goals. The logic of the situation suggests the following chain of signification. Shenhui is set up as a doorway, and as he offers himself to the masses, they are in a position to gain or regain a relationship with the Diamond-Like Perfection of Wisdom as found in the *Diamond Sūtra* and thereby insert themselves into the truth-sphere of Buddhism in a nonreversible manner.

However, in this promise of sudden intimacy with total truth, authority isn't leaking away from Shenhui's singular personhood. The final line in this passage is:

> May I, in the limitless future, unceasingly offer my body and life so that sentient beings may accept and guard the Diamond-Like Perfection of Wisdom and so that all sentient beings will rely on the Perfection of Wisdom and obtain non-obtainment and, eventually, become buddhas.[136]

135. Hu Shi, *Shenhui,* 310.
136. Ibid., 311.

At this point of closure, Shenhui has extracted the essential way to buddhahood: it is obtained through the Diamond Perfection of Wisdom (and the text that houses it) *and* through Shenhui himself, who promises that he will provide all sentient beings in the limitless future access to that point of closure through the repeated gift of his body. Truth and buddhahood, then, flow into the present via Shenhui's body and can be expected to do so for the rest of time.

In a completely anticlimatic way, the next line has Shenhui ask Chongyuan, "Have you ever lectured on the *Nirvana Sūtra?*"[137] This question is an attempt to reintroduce Chongyuan and connect back to the public setting at Great Cloud Monastery, as established at the outset of the *Treatise.*[138] The text repeats a scaled-down version of the conclusion at the end of P3047, but in fact this leads on to another collection of discussions, the first of which has Shenhui playing the Buddha's role of being reluctant to preach because no one will understand him. Instead of pursuing the rather chaotic pieces that follow, I want to turn to Shenhui's *Platform Sermon,* a text that is structured much like this section above where Shenhui put himself forward as the avenue for the future enlightenment of all sentient beings and again replays the trope of offering himself to the masses in a simulacrum of what one buddha would offer another buddha-to-be.

THE *PLATFORM SERMON:* CAUTION, BUDDHA AT WORK

As a final piece of evidence for my argument about the transformation of Buddhist notions of power, privilege, and paternity wrought by genealogical discourse in the eighth century, I am going to present an overview of what is called, for brevity's sake, Shenhui's *Platform Sermon;* the full title is the *Platform Sermon of the Master from Nanyang, the Sudden Teaching Which Leads to Liberation through the Chan Door of Directly Seeing the Nature (Nanyang heshang dunjiao jietuo chanmen zhiliao xing tanyu).*[139] This text is particularly interesting because it seems designed to orchestrate a public "Chan

---

137. Ibid., 311.
138. Gernet notes that this conversation is also found in the "Suzuki" edition of *Questions and Answers;* see Gernet's "Complétement aux *Entretiens du Maître de Dhyāna Chen-houei,*" 462.
139. W. Liebenthal has translated this text in his "The Sermon of Shenhui." Unfortunately, Liebenthal's rendering is often unreliable, and thus, though I have benefited in a number of ways from his translation, I have not followed it.

meeting," with a distinct ritual program embedded in it. I should say from the outset that, like all of the Shenhui material, attributing this text to Shenhui is problematic. There is material in the lecture that is shared, both specifically and generally, with other Shenhui texts, but for reasons that will become evident in a moment, imagining Shenhui as the author of this text doesn't make sense for several reasons.

It has survived in two manuscripts, one in the Pelliot collection, where it is part two of P2045 written in the same hand as part one, which was the *Treatise*.[140] The other manuscript is in the Beijing Dunhuang collection, and I haven't consulted it, though I have relied on Hu Shi's edited version of the text, which makes use of both manuscripts.[141] As for date of composition, it seems that we really only have circumstantial evidence. First, the *Lidai fabao ji,* a text dated to roughly 780, notes that Shenhui used to hold monthly meetings in which he constructed "platform sites" *(zuo tanchang)* and taught the people dharma; this same passage then provides a brief description of Shenhui's teachings that summarizes some of the themes in the *Sermon.*[142] This lets us assume that in 780, roughly two decades after Shenhui's death, content roughly matching this text was known and explained as part of public meetings that Shenhui supposedly held. Given that Shenhui's stele mentions that Shenhui was invited to the capital of Luoyang, we probably are right in assuming that Shenhui was brought to the capital, most likely after Puji's death in 739, and then, once there, held these monthly meetings. Other details from this period of his life are "known" only from sources that come a good bit later and under rather unreliable circumstances.[143]

Despite Shenhui's moniker in the title ("Monk from Nanyang"), the text presents a teaching figure who is left unidentified in the body of the text. The text prescribes a role for this figure that is something like a master of ceremonies who is to lead a Buddhist audience in a blend of a confession service and a dharma lecture dedicated to overcoming their sins and recognizing their innate buddha-natures. This text

---

140. As I was finishing this book, I learned from Adamek's *The Mystique of Transmission* of another manuscript of the *Tanyu.* For more details, see 433 n. 176.

141. For Hu Shi's discussion of these two manuscripts, see *Shenhui,* 223–25.

142. T.51.185b.14. For a translation, see Adamek, *The Mystique of Transmission,* 340–42.

143. For an overview of the material from Zongmi and the *Song Encyclopedia of Eminent Monks,* see Gernet's "Biographie du Maître Chen-houei du Ho-tsö"; see also McRae, "Shenhui as Evangelist."

makes a useful place to conclude my history of early Chan because it is clear that this teaching figure is poised to function as a buddha-like leader and that Chan's rhetoric of the ownership of truth is now being explicitly deployed to organize public Buddhist events that show ritual formats.[144] Thus, what is fascinating about this text is that it is designed to establish a *repeatable framework* for public practice centered on Chan claims to uniquely represent the totality of the Buddhist tradition. In short, "history" has become practice, with private lineage claims installed in public rituals.[145]

The shift toward a ritual template for the master's performance can be found on three levels. First, the *Sermon* lacks a frame to establish and control a reading experience, which all the other accounts of Shenhui's public "oral" performances had included. Thus, there is no preface explaining how and why the live dialogue was transferred into textuality. Similarly, the text never falls away from this position of direct orality, as the *Treatise* did, to talk of itself as a text. Also, there is no explicit admission that the writing of this text was intended to influence the reader in any specific manner as Dugu Pei and Liucheng had given us. In short, the text doesn't explicitly position itself as a piece of propaganda for a reading public.

Second, there is no historical particularity given to this lecture. The sermon isn't set anywhere, nor is there a date for it. Similarly, no specific audience is established, and no effect on the audience is mentioned. Also, there is nothing describing the leader and definitely nothing that would invite specific worship of Shenhui as an individual—there is no mention of who received the robe or transmission

---

144. Adamek, quoting Faure, seems to believe that it was only in aberrant moments that the Chan masters would have been taken as buddhas or buddhalike, but, in fact, generating just that kind of buddha-identity for these masters was clearly the whole point of writing the genealogy of truth-fathers. For her comments, see *The Mystique of Transmission,* 174: "Faure argues that this [rhetoric of immediacy] resulted in various forms of the 'return of the repressed' in which the Chan master, rather than Buddhas and bodhisattvas, became the focus of sometimes bizarre forms of devotion, representation and propitiation." McRae, on the other hand, sees Shenhui's writing intent on making him a buddha substitute; see "Shenhui as Evangelist," 142.

145. In wondering about the genre of this ritual, we shouldn't overlook recent reflections by Barrett on the emergence of ordination-like events in which the public was treated to a number of rituals that weren't ordinations per se and yet would have been taken to be markers of new Buddhist identities. For his discussion, see "Buddhist Precepts in a Lawless World," esp. 115 ff. It is also worth considering that Shenhui's name in the title represents something like a brand-name, akin to a recipe named "Julia Child's Chicken Cordon Bleu." In either case, the name of the master is included to popularize repetition of the ritual/recipe in his or her absence.

from Huineng or what it is that makes the master suitable to play this role for the public. Instead the text works from two forms of address, one for the public, "Friends" (*zhishi*; lit., "those who know"), and one for the master, "Good Spiritual Friend" (*shanzhishi*; Chinese translation of the Sanskrit, *kalyānamitra*, which means something like spiritual adviser—a common term, actually, and already used by Du Fei at the beginning of the *Record*; see chapter 4). Thus, minus the title mentioning Shenhui's moniker, we have an open template structuring a dialogue between a nameless, faceless master and an equally unidentified audience, neither of whom address each other in a manner that would reveal their particular identities or restrict the text's use to certain figures. Similarly, in the one line that mentions the six patriarchs, they, too, are left unnamed and seem poised simply to provide legitimacy to anyone who happens to be leading the service.[146]

In short, even if the text originally was exclusively Shenhui's, once it has been copied into public reading space, as the three surviving manuscripts of it suggest, the discourse represents an open invitation to repetition by other Buddhist leaders. And, obviously, the very fact that Shenhui's "routine" was re-presented in textual form has profound implications for duplicating his own claims to singular authority. Imagining this shift in genre to a ritual format might at first seem inconsequential, but once we remember that part of Shenhui's position was the singularity of one buddha-master per generation, then there is a definite tension here. Reading the text as a ritual manual is supported by the fact that one of manuscripts, P2045(2), has attached to it a cycle of songs that are to be sung during the five watches of the night.[147] These songs clearly are for ritual reenactment and in fact are found attached to several other Chan texts.[148] Evidently, then, the ritual structure in the *Sermon* invited these other ritual additions since the text was seen as organizing a repeatable public Buddhist rite.

This layer of evidence leaves little doubt that the lack of a specific historical setting in the *Sermon* isn't accidental. And, yet, breaking away from recording a historical event to designing a generic ritual text implies all sorts of shifts in the structuring of authority that the

146. Hu Shi, *Shenhui*, 232.
147. Ibid., 253–57.
148. See Demiéville, "Deux documents," 4 nn. 23, 24. Liebenthal has translated the five songs; see his "The Sermon of Shen-hui," 154–55.

text does not try to address. Thus, the text seems designed to allow any other master entrance into the buddhified space that Shenhui had constructed for himself, but in a manner that doesn't rely on a genealogical justification. That is, master status is essentially being offered to anyone who would get hold of a copy of this text and perform in accordance with its dictates.

I will explore this shift in Chan genre below, but for the moment let's clarify that if we agree to read the text as constructing a ritual, then it would seem that the Chan texts written up to this point fall into three categories: genealogies, "live" discussions, and ritual formats. In the first, the genealogy, the history of truth is given to the reader so that the past can serve as proof of truth in the figure of the present master. These texts, such as Du Fei's *Record* or Jingjue's *History* or Wang Wei's epitaph for Huineng, offer no ritual instructions for the reader. Their goal is simply to show the history of truth and to generate in the reader a certain gaze and devotion. The second category of texts, those delivering "live" discourse, may contain some lineage history but focus on demonstrating the ownership of truth through a presentation of a master's articulations. This category, up to this point, has been filled almost exclusively by Shenhui material—the various live conversations in *Questions and Answers* and the dharma combat with Chongyuan in the first part of the *Treatise*. Nonetheless, Jingjue's *History* also has elements of this kind of live discussion as seen in the masters' recitation of chosen sūtra quotes and those supposedly off-the-cuff remarks tacked onto four of the lineage masters. The last category of texts, those defining rituals, are works that establish buddhahood in a figure and then organize contact between that figure and the public.[149] Certainly the final parts of the *Treatise* were headed in this direction with Shenhui "speaking" to the public about his willingness to die over and over so that the public might have the *Diamond Sūtra* for all time. And, obviously, the *Platform Sermon* is even more focused on formally delivering the buddhalike master to the masses. Likewise, it is worth mentioning that with the *Platform Sūtra*, produced soon after Shenhui's death, we have another clear example of a text that includes ritual formats that suggest repeatability. In fact, it would seem that

149. Reading Shenhui's texts in this manner works well with McRae's thoughtful comments about why concerns with vinaya platforms and ordination ritual overlap with various types of lineage claims. For his discussion, see "Daoxuan's Vision of Jetavana," 90–93.

the *Platform Sūtra* incorporates and develops much of what is in the *Platform Sermon*.

Though I believe we are right to read these three examples as marking out the emergence of Chan rituals, it is possible that this budding genre could have been consumed by readers apart from a ritual setting. That is, though the above evidence suggests that several of these texts were designed to be templates for public performance, this doesn't mean that they might not have circulated as reading material, consumed in a reading experience in which one participates in the "ritual" in a kind of as-if manner. Certainly, the *Platform Sūtra* can be read in this fashion where one is transferred back in time to be in the specific historical audience that Huineng addresses, as in a sūtra, but then moves through a complex ritual that suggests repeatability. Given that we have more than one example of texts sitting in this gray area between the onetime sūtra model for Chan discourse and the repeatability of ritual formats, there may be good reasons to keep this possibility open for all these ritual-looking texts.

Two other details are important for understanding the ritual structure of the *Platform Sermon*. First, the leader is shown speaking directly to an audience. An interlocutor such as the hapless master Chongyuan isn't introduced and instead the leader addresses the audience as *zhishi* (Friends), as he did in the section of the *Treatise* dedicated to promoting the *Diamond Sūtra*. In fact, it seems that the *Platform Sermon* is attempting to build a ritual sequence from that section of the *Treatise*. Both presentations of Buddhist leadership are built around condensing Buddhism into the leader who then offers the possibility of perfection to everyone in the audience. The *Platform Sermon* is more developed, though, since it sets that exchange in the context of a basic Mahāyana purification rite and a dharma lecture.[150]

The second detail in the *Platform Sermon* concerns the many phrases that emphasize that *every* member in the audience is to become involved in the search for perfection. Each member of the audience is, in effect, being called to participate in the quest for enlightenment, a quest that is to occur "today" in the very process of this event, even if we aren't told when this event is occurring or why. Hence, there is an avid attempt to make this text touch the interests of every kind of

---

150. There is another connection between the *Platform Sermon* and the latter part of the *Treatise*: both texts contain the same eight-line poem on giving rise to bodhimind; see Hu Shi, *Shenhui*, 313–14, 250–51.

Buddhist. In fact, we probably ought to say that the text represents an attempt to join the elite master, as defined by the text, with the most common Buddhist aspirant. Thus, this discourse, though clearly privileging the leader, is arranged so that this privilege becomes part of a totalizing social structure that leaves no one out.[151]

Arguably, then, in its most basic framing of access to Buddhist truth, the *Platform Sermon* is a perfect example of the key Chan thematic of "enlightenment for the masses" offered by the singular master who, though he promises sudden enlightenment for all, never arranges for this to actually happen. All members of the audience are incited to participate in the recovery of the internal buddha-nature, but this search is led by one who from the beginning positions himself as a rare buddha-like figure and in a key line mentions that there is a whole other kind of transmission of truth—"mind to mind and beyond words"—practiced within the narrow track of the six patriarchs, a form of perfect Buddhism that is obviously *not* being offered to the masses.[152] Thus, it would seem that the text is structured so that the very possibility of offering "enlightenment to the masses" requires that it be previously domesticated and privatized within a unique family whose members, based on their private possession of truth, then have the right to offer it, or at least a facsimile of it, to others. Actually, a similar tension can be found in the *Nirvana Sūtra,* a source that shows up regularly in the *Platform Sermon.* In the *Nirvana Sūtra,* the tension appears in the way the sūtra insists on inherent buddha-nature but insists equally on the need to find a buddha or a Good Spiritual Friend to excavate that buddha-nature.[153]

Though the leader in the *Platform Sermon* will adopt just this title Good Spiritual Friend, and will function in just the way that the *Nirvana Sūtra* explains, we need to see that this engagement between the leader and the commoner in the *Platform Sermon* shifts the logic of the *Nirvana Sūtra* in three ways. First, this dyadic relationship is brought into the present and set in the space between a current Chinese speaker and his audience. The leader, "today," as the text clarifies, is obviously offering himself to the audience as just such a Good Spiritual

151. For McRae's reflections on this aspect of the *Platform Sermon,* see his "Shenhui as Evangelist," 142–44.

152. This line about transmission among the six patriarchs sits right next to an injunction for each listener to believe that he or she has the buddha-nature within; see Hu Shi, *Shenhui,* 232.

153. See T.12.40ba.23. I owe this reference to Gernet.

Friend and refers to himself with that title.[154] Second, midway through
the ritual, the leader explicitly compares his current offering of teaching to the prediction of future buddhahood that Śākyamuni gave to
Maitreya, and claims that they are no different.[155] Thus, there is the
extravagant promise of making available to the public a version of
transmission that had been only found between buddhas, even as
this gesture implies that the leader is in the Śākyamuni position of
owning and sharing out the totality of Buddhist truth to Maitreya-like
descendants.

In short, the *Platform Sermon* can only construct a ritual for offering enlightenment to the masses when it has fully taken possession of
enlightenment from India and installed it in a Chinese spokesperson
who claims to be able to deliver it, today! to all and sundry. What
is not to be missed, though, is that just this gesture was performed
by the *Lotus Sūtra* and the *Vimalakīrti,* which both downgraded
Maitreya's inheritance and offered a facsimile of such a prediction to
anyone who would accept the *Lotus Sūtra* or the *Vimalakīrti* as the
final truth.[156] Thus, the leader in the *Platform Sermon* functions like
other Mahāyāna reconstructions of truth that likewise promised the
audience the most extravagant gifts provided that the audience, in
turn, offers back full faith that this new medium represents the totality of Buddhism.

And, third, the barrier that separates innate buddha-nature from
manifest buddhahood is now made to appear incredibly thin. The
leader tries to convince the audience that even though they came to the
platform with evil thoughts, they can obtain enlightenment even before
they leave their seats on this very day.[157] Thus the audience is told that
it can accomplish all Buddhist goals in a minute, though again nothing
in the *Platform Sermon* prepares either the audience or the leader to act
out these moments of success.[158]

The leader's role in essentializing and redistributing the totality of
Buddhism is made completely obvious a little later when he promises
the audience that the immediate reception of his words will equal the
reception of all of Buddhism:[159]

---

154. Hu Shi, *Shenhui,* 234.
155. Ibid., 231.
156. For more discussion of this issue, see my *Text as Father,* chaps., 2, 3, 6.
157. Hu Shi, *Shenhui,* 232.
158. Ibid., 232.
159. Ibid., 248.

"Today I take the unsurpassed dharma of the Way *(wushang daofa)* and share it with the Friends *(fenfu zhishi)*. If you [the Friends] accept these words, then the Six Perfections [of the Māhāyana], and all the various buddhas [as numerous as] the sands of the Ganges, as well as the 84,000 various doors of samādhi will in one moment *(yishi)* enter into the bodies and minds of the Friends."

The immediacy of this offer is made even clearer in the final line of the text: "If there are any [of you] with doubts come and ask me. Good trip [home]."[160] In sum, the leader in this sequence is designed to own and control the totality of Buddhism—the Six Perfections, all the buddhas, the 84,000 samādhis, and so on—and promises to offer this perfect form of Buddhism to anyone, provided that they accept the whole premise of the arrangement, especially the implicit claim that a local Chinese leader could have the right to make such an audacious offer.

EVIL DESIRE FOR THE GOOD

The relationship of the leader to the participants has another twist to it, a twist around desire and sinfulness that warrants careful reflection. In reading the *Platform Sermon,* and even in the lines just quoted above, one can't miss the way that it is designed to produce an intense desire for Buddhist goals—total Buddhist perfection is seemingly on hand, with not only the promise of overcoming all the long eons of practice that the Hīnayāna figures mistakenly engage in but also the extravagant claim that one is getting just what Śākyamuni gave to Maitreya.[161] What is odd, however, is that the leader also spends considerable time explaining that one can't desire Buddhism—that one should not want enlightenment, or nirvana, or the Buddha.[162]

This conversation begins by not too subtly identifying the members of the audience as sinners, and worse, sinners for desiring to be out of sin. Throughout the discussion, the leader's desires are never spoken of; instead he speaks of the audience's desires and, in a rather direct manner, castigates them for desiring to be where he, supposedly, is—in the sphere of enlightenment. This passage on sin comes in the first third of the text and works around the explanation of two types of desire:[163]

160. Ibid., 252.
161. Ibid., 231.
162. Ibid., 234–35.
163. Ibid., 234.

Friends, listen carefully as I explain deluded mind *(wangxin)* for you.
What is "deluded mind"? Everyone here today came with greed and lust
(tanai) for wealth, sex, men, women, and so on, and was thinking of
gardens, forests, and houses. This is mundane delusion *(chenwang)* and
you must not have this mind. As for subtle desire *(xiwang)*, you all don't
know about it. What is subtle desire? [It is] when your mind hears of
bodhi, and that incites [the desire] to grasp bodhi, or when your mind
hears of nirvana and that incites [the desire] to grasp nirvana. Or, again,
when you hear of emptiness, that incites [the desire] to grasp on to
emptiness [and similarly] for purity and samādhi.

This is delusion *(wangxin)* and is also a dharma fetter *(fafu)* and a
dharma view [in the negative sense of the term]—if one has such desires,
one isn't going to be liberated. This isn't the original quiescence and purity
of mind *(fei benzi jijing xin)*. If you abide in nirvana you are bound *(fu)*
by nirvana. If you abide in purity, you are bound by purity. If you abide
in emptiness, you are bound by emptiness. If you abide in samādhi, you
are bound by samādhi. Proceding with this kind of motivation *(zuo zi
yongxin)* is to block the path to bodhi.

This passage establishes that the leader knows the audience, and he
knows them to be greedy and desirous. They all came to the meeting
with their minds full of desires for the coarsest of items—money,
sex, and property. This accusation presumably wouldn't have shocked
the audience since its generic evil had been broadly exclaimed at the
beginning of the confession sequence, which began: "Friends, the
mouths of commoners *(fanfu)* are filled with limitless evil talk and
their minds are full of limitless evil thoughts, and [thus] they cycle
for a long time in samsara and don't obtain liberation."[164] Hence,
from the outset the text depicts two types of people in the world:
commoners destined to cycle in samsara and those purified of desire
who will win liberation. However, this division in humanity is further
refined by creating the categories of coarse and subtle desire since
the leader accuses the audience of also mistakenly desiring Buddhism
and the positive items in Buddhist discourse, such as nirvana, purity,
and emptiness. Thus, the leader's discourse seems to include a rather
daunting prohibition: if you desire that which is being displayed for
you, and even promised to you, then you will, by definition, fail in
the enterprise.

Thus, if you came to the hall today to hear the *Platform Sermon*,
you are by default in the group of desirous commoners who need to

164. Ibid., 226.

be cleansed and instructed by a Good Spiritual Friend.[165] So, from the beginning, the leader's role as a buddhalike master has been broadcast in the most exciting terms, but it turns out that in accepting the master's perfection in the present, the audience has submitted to a basic master-slave paradigm. And, obviously, the real sticking point here is that the discourse is designed to prohibit anyone from changing sides. The Good Spiritual Friend's status isn't in question, and though the commoners are to be convinced that they have been purified in some measure, they are never allowed to graduate into the master's role, and, in particular, they surely aren't being taught to hold these meetings themselves. Thus, the discourse appears tightly conservative since it reproduces a need for itself even as it prohibits others from learning how to enter into this exchange from the side of the master.

Reading the text in this manner seems to me particularly justified given the form and function of desire-producing rhetoric in the other early Chan works. One notable difference is that the intensity of the double bind has increased. Before, readers of the genealogies were simply called on to recognize total truth in a lineage that they could never have access to. Here, the ritual format invites the participation of average Buddhists in an exchange where they acknowledge an authority figure who castigates them for their sinful attitudes and in particular for their desire for Buddhism, even in the midst of a ritualized discourse designed specifically to incite desire for Buddhism. In short, in taking Chan rhetoric down to this level where supposed perfection is put in contact with its opposite, the *Platform Sermon* fuses the two sides of the spectrum in a tight master-slave relationship. The leader speaks of the universal buddha-nature, and its availability, even as he asserts that wishing for that perfection will keep one from obtaining it.

To get a fuller sense of how desire and identity are constructed here, let's return to the opening lines. The discourse begins with no formal introduction, or placement of the speaker in front of the audience. Instead the leader launches into the lecture by locating this current event as a most unusual and valuable cosmic event—an event during which the public will be offered access to what they had never had before. Clearly the leader is promising in these introductory remarks

165. In a way, this arrangement mirrors the construction of Hongren and Huineng since they were basically only available in literature, and in particular literature designed to create desire for them, but they basked in that zone of freedom from literature and desire, leaving the reader in a rather compromised position of enjoying his opposite via a medium that condemned him from the get-go.

to lead the audience into an encounter with true Buddhism that ought to change their destinies forever—something akin to Methodist tent revivalism.[166] Moreover, it is undeniable that though universal buddhahood is a repeating topic, there is a clear hierarchy within that sameness, with the leader presented as a superior kind of spiritual adviser, in the category of buddhas and bodhisattvas, who is so difficult to meet and who implicitly has the right to lead the audience in this manner when one does chance upon one.

The text opens with the following announcement:[167]

The dharma of unsurpassable bodhi is what all the buddhas profoundly praise as inconceivable.

Friends, now, today you have been able to come, and each of you [will] give rise to unsurpassable bodhi-mind *(wushang puti xin)*.

All the buddhas and bodhisattvas, and true Good Spiritual Friends *(zhenzheng shan zhishi)* are immensely difficult to meet. *What you have not heard in the past, you will have a chance to hear today. Those whom you didn't have a chance to meet in the past, you will have a chance to meet today.*

After underscoring the rarity of the moment and explaining that common people's minds and words are full of evil, the text moves abruptly into the confessional sequence. The two manuscripts differ slightly here, but at the very least it is clear that the master is to lead the congregation in the following recitation:[168]

Everyone [should] worship the Buddha [with the following lines]:

"[I] worship all the buddhas of the past. I worship all the buddhas of the future. I worship all the buddhas of the present. I worship the holy dharma, the wisdom *(prajñā)* sūtras. I worship the various great bodhisattvas and all the virtuous and sagely monks."

Everyone should confess wholeheartedly so that the three [types of] karma in the Friends will be purified:

"The four types of sins of body, mouth, and mind, of the past, present and future, I today *(wo jin)* wholeheartedly confess, and wish that they may be dispersed and never arise again."

"The five perverse sins of body, mouth, and mind . . ."

Without following the full confessional, it should already be clear what is to happen here. Despite the opening promise that the audience was

---

166. For McRae's reflections on the evangelizing quality of the *Platform Sermon,* see his "Shenhui as Evangelist," esp. 142–43.

167. Hu Shi, *Shenhui,* 225; McRae, "Shenhui as Evangelist," 143.

168. Ibid., 226 ff.

to hear what they had never heard before, they are being led through a very standard Māhāyana ritual.[169] In fact, situating this event on a platform *(tan)* implies that this is to be an induction into Buddhism but with the added boon that one is taking refuge now with a Good Spiritual Friend who, from the outset, claims that this moment is terribly unique and fortuitous. In sum, we are very close to the heart of Chan rhetoric: now, via this local Chinese leader, one can receive the purest version of tradition that comes from a buddhalike figure, that bypasses the sūtras (though it relies extensively on them), and that offers to the public an immediacy to truth that seems to mirror its own claim to be immediately in touch with the heart of Buddhism. Thus, the suddenness that the early Chan texts relied on to explain their private ownership of Buddhist truth is now being turned outward in the form of sudden teachings for the masses, teachings that are choreographed to confirm just that divide between the commoner and the Good Friend, the master.

Clearly, these sudden teachings on sudden enlightenment are not designed to confer master status. No surprise, then, that the end of this rite includes advice from the leader for the audience to read widely in the Māhāyana sūtras, an activity that is likened to polishing a mirror so that it can reveal a face.[170] Moreover, it is announced that what is most important is to not doubt the Buddha's words, and to purify the three types of karmic obstruction so as to be able to enter into the Māhāyana. Evidently, by the end, one is back where one began—reading Māhāyana sūtras and trying to figure out how to get in the Big Vehicle. What has changed, though, is that the Māhāyana now has a living spokesperson who is intent on convincing the public of the total presence of Buddhism in his own person, and with that claim taking hold, tries to convince others that they, too, are perfect but in a way that requires them to continue to rely on texts, practices, and the current spokesperson for the whole of tradition—the master speaking in the moment.

In sum, this text and the others associated with Shenhui give us a glimpse of what happened in the hundred-some years of development between Guanding and Shenhui: a new form of Chinese Buddhist leadership was gradually constructed with genealogical claims, and

169. For discussion of Tang-era confessional formats, see Kuo Liying's *Confession et contrition dans le bouddhisme chinois du Ve au Xe siècle.*
170. Hu Shi, *Shenhui,* 252.

this identity—sanctified by the State—was structured to overcome the sūtras and other forms of tradition so that it could be turned outward to be performed "live" in these public situations where "old" tradition was revivified by a living master who could pose as one essentially no different from the Buddha in India. In effect, all this literary and ritual invention was dedicated to proving that nothing was invented and, more important, that there never had been a need to do this kind of inventing.

WIDER REFLECTIONS: IT'S GENRE THAT MATTERS

Standing back from the Shenhui material, it is clear that we have in view several things that are completely at odds with current interpretations of this early phase of Chan. First, it seems impossible to read this material and come away with the sense that the texts reflect the emergence of new patterns or styles for practice, be it meditation or manual labor or master-disciple encounters. Instead, the new elements that have implications for "practice" fall into two categories, and both are quite far from standard interpretations. The first is simply the practice of reading lineage texts, figuring out how they work, and rewriting them for new ends and the benefit of new masters. That is, this cycle of early genealogies reveals the invention of Buddhist historiography in a decidedly rough-and-tumble form. More exactly, on this level of reading and rewriting, the new "Chan" technique that was being practiced was a selfish and duplicitous style of receiving and re-creating tradition: Chan in these works doesn't at all appear to be the result of new forms of meditation and new forms for Buddhist communal living, but rather, it appears as the gradual, and unsteady, development of literary techniques for convincingly owning and redistributing tradition around the central claim that these men were buddha-equivalents and that sūtras and Indian relics could be bypassed in favor of these "local" buddhas.

The second category of practice hinted at in these texts is an active faith-in-the-master—as seen in a growing confidence that the public would accept these papier-mâché Chinese buddhas and respond to them in increasingly ritualized manners. In addition to noting how the texts grew more audacious in their claims to own and distribute tradition to an adoring public—implying that the former claims had in some measure been accepted—we see that the public is increasingly counted on to participate in this reworked form of tradition such that by the period of the Shenhui material, authors scripted full-scale, repeatable rituals with the local buddhas now put directly before the people and primed to offer them the totality of tradition. Of course, way back in the Faru biography this is exactly how Faru was made to perform during that single all-encompassing dharma meeting right before his death. However, in the decades that followed, the logic and structure of that narrative event slowly morphed from a literary account into a ritual sequence that presented a way for the narratively produced Chinese buddhas to be presented to the public in formal and repeatable rituals. In short, there are two "practices" emerging here: the techniques needed to justify leading the public in actual ritual moments and the public's growing knowledge of how to participate in these events. Thus, as the *Platform Sermon,* the late sections of the *Treatise,* and the *Platform Sūtra* suggest, the mid-eighth century was a time in which the general public was steadily expected to participate in the practice of adoring a local buddha.

Conclusion

Assessing the Hole at the Beginning of It All

IN PLACE OF AN ORIGIN, THE ART OF IT ALL

Since my basic conclusions regarding the form and function of Chan genealogies have been slowly generated and thickened in the preceding chapters, I want to end the book by exploring more general questions that have come out of this investigation. For instance, How should we assess someone's claim to having experienced Chan enlightenment, in any era, in the wake of seeing that Chan enlightenment, and the lineages that supposedly delivered it, rest on a large zero—a deep hole of never-happened, over which sits the entire house of cards that promised to maintain the pure essence-of-tradition? What, then, might these experiences of enlightenment be "made of"? That is, do we know how to explain how the fantasy and fabrication of early Chan writing turned into the actual practices of tradition, with the "return" of real human experience mimicking the figments of literature in one way or another?

In thinking about how literature and "creative writing" generated the "experiences of tradition," let's begin by asking about the art of this literature. That is, what should we say about the literary craftsmanship, humor, thematic complexity, intersubjective engagement, character development, and so on that one finds in seventh- and eighth-century genealogies? The most basic answer to the question of the artistic content of the early genealogies has to be that it varies radically. Certainly

Wang Wei's epitaph to Huineng is a tour de force that, while lacking historical content, is an enticing and well-designed smorgasbord, compressing and encapsulating a variety of Chinese literary tastes in a new workable totality. Too, Wang Wei used the upper registers of Chinese literature to create an image of culture's opposite—the bumpkin buddha, who nonetheless now owned these choice literary values. On the other hand, Jingjue's *History* is clumsy in its rushed and inelegant depictions of the masters' supposed speech. Du Fei, for his part, wrote with confidence, making his points and also dramatizing scenes with flair. The Shenhui material is highly mixed, bouncing from the clever setting at Great Cloud Monastery, with its catchy mise-en-scène, to the flat and uninspired commentary on sūtras that made up so much of *Questions and Answers* and the second half of the *Treatise,* which wandered off into repetitive ruminations on the *Diamond Sūtra.*

Even recognizing these differences in skill in presentation, given the sophistication of some of the imported Indian Buddhist literature and the talents of Chinese writers, the genealogical texts seem, by and large, to be rather poor and pinched. They are philosophically shabby, repetitive, uneven, self-contradictory, and weighed down by their realpolitik agendas. Similarly, if one were expecting the perennial problems of life to be addressed, these texts would sorely disappoint. Instead of exploring the intricacies of human experience, they worked to fetishize tradition—that act whereby the complexities of previous forms of tradition are collapsed and condensed into a singular Something—the esoteric transmission from the Buddha to Ānanda and so on, the "dharma-jewel," the *Laṅkāvatāra Sūtra,* Bodhidharma, Bodhidharma's robe, and so on—which is then put forward as the ultimate reservoir of tradition and legitimacy. In short, wisdom, and especially wisdom about human experience, is never explored. The construction and display of content remains focused on convincing one that total content is somewhere: most importantly, in the masters' bodies; but also in a "dumb" form in the reader's innate buddha-nature. However, as seen in the close reading of these texts, this promise of total content slips away until it evaporates into a kind of vapidity of pure being, be it of the buddha-nature, the dharma-body, or the One Mind. And, despite the grandiose claims of total tradition and perfected humanity, the actual content of these items is quite meager since the genealogies present little more than stick-figure masters who say little and lack interiors. In short, Chan discourse appears as a parsimonious symbolic order primarily concerned with its own success and largely uninterested in the realities of human experience.

There are, as argued throughout this book, two main reasons for this outcome. First, the point of the genealogy-of-truth was never to present anything other than the *ownership* of truth and tradition. The content of the genealogy was always only a *claim* about content, not a specific position with substance. Second, since these texts were written in bad faith and without any direct connection to the human experience of the "masters," there was no easy way, even if that had been a goal, to posit the content of the masters since these past figures weren't masters to begin with, and in some cases never existed. What, after all, could a writer say about Bodhidharma's sense of truth or humanity after having read a couple lines about him in Daoxuan's *Encyclopedia,* especially when, as in the case of Du Fei, it was said that verbal accounts of truth and teaching were useless for getting at Truth. Similarly, what did Jingjue know of Guṇabhadra's notion of reality after Jingjue had buddhified Guṇabhadra by hastily tacking him on to the front of the Bodhidharma lineage, having pulled the frame of his biography out of Huijiao's *Encyclopedia* and then rewriting it with details from Bodhidharma's life? Obviously, the goal never was to recover information or knowledge about anybody or anything real, and, worse, whatever historical information was available was liable to be deformed and reworked to make a more convincing demonstration of perfection's presence. In short, once we recognize the early Chan dynamic of fathering one's father, the attempt to retrieve content—about Truth, humanity, and history—from these texts ought to be seen as both impossible and absurd.

Likewise, for all the discussion of consciousness, we never "hear" anyone thinking. Slightly later in the cycle of genealogical combat, in the *Platform Sūtra,* there is an elaborate scene depicting Shenxiu's failure to win transmission from Hongren.[1] It is only at this point that we finally get, via an omniscient narrator writing some seventy years after Shenxiu's death, supposedly direct access to a master's thoughts. It turns out that what we hear is the discourse of the loser—Shenxiu is beating himself up over a basic Chan problem: How am I going to actually get transmission when I know that desiring transmission excludes me from receiving it? Thus, the first direct and purportedly "honest" account of a master's interior is developed around Shenxiu's moments of darkness, a scene developed for the simple purpose of showing his

1. See Yampolsky, *The Platform Sūtra,* 129–31.

illegitimacy and making Huineng look honest and legitimate. In effect, the art of writing human experience into some sort of communicable form was avoided, except in this rare exception when the desire to eviscerate the opposition was strong enough to push a writer toward this more novelesque depiction.

Equally troubling, the presentation of Shenxiu's interior, instead of reflecting Shenxiu's own particular experience of the world, is replaced with an interior generated according to the rules of lineage combat in the ongoing escalation of genealogical polemics; his internal monologue is nothing more than symbolic suicide, designed to make the claim of Huineng's legitimacy appear valid. Arguably, in Chan, human interiors function something like patriotism in General Patton's comment that the point of war isn't to die for one's country but to make the other guy die for his. It is not interiority or patriotism that matter in polemics and war—it's winning. Everything else is secondary and perhaps even debilitating, especially if the order of priorities is confused.

Against these disappointing showings in a range of literary categories, early Chan discourse does appear smart and inventive precisely in the place it needs to be—organizing that triangle of Buddhism, the State, and the populace. On this front, there is plenty of ingenuity found in designing paradigms in which Buddhism is privately held by a lineage figure who engages the State, overshadows other competing Buddhists, and claims to have the right to make this privately held universality available, at least for worship, to all. Also, in arranging these complex agendas, there are several forms of innovation at work in cloaking these power plays: (1) purifying the master of desire in order to render him desirable, either by emphasizing his echolike personality or by describing him in Daoist terms of simplicity and naturalness; (2) shaping and coloring the discourse of the master in modes and models drawn from other genres—the sūtras or the standard funeral epitaph or the Chinese classics—that will make the discourse appear unmotivated and reliable; and (3) refining the master-masses dialectic such that the ownership of enlightenment can be enjoyed by the masses, even as they are instructed to admit that they have no chance to get at truth other than through the newly minted master. In brief, early Chan authors seem to have been quite savvy in producing a public discourse that arranged a full spectrum of ideological agendas, including the need to avoid appearing to have an agenda.

While producing and arranging these public relations coups doesn't seem that complicated to us moderns so used, as we are, to well-honed propaganda politics and high-tech advertisement, in the medieval setting these developments ought to be counted as strikingly innovative since these texts reflect the authors' growing sense of an anthropology of desire. In fact, over the centuries this anthropology of desire in Chan writing became refined and even exquisite. Seen from the longue durée, each author's individual efforts need to be set within the arc of an emerging craft that was dedicated to presenting seductive images of human perfection, in literature. Looked at this way, Chan discourse could be profitably compared to the development of the violin in Western music. The violin went through a slow transformation by which the rougher forms of the Renaissance fiddle and the viol (lira) de braccio were improved to perform better in terms of tonality, volume, ease of playing, and so on. That is, the violin, like Chan rhetoric, underwent a gradual development in which its position at the meeting place between performer and audience was refined to maximize that exchange.

In the case of the violin, its growing sophistication allowed for more complicated and demanding music to be composed and appreciated by audiences, just as Chan writers' gradual mastery of the forms of innocence and authority made a new range of exciting forms of religious fantasy part of audiences' expectations. On another level, this comparison is provocative: the violin, like Chan discourse, spawned a set of parallel instruments—the viola, the cello, and the contrabass—that follow the violin in form but offer differences in register in just such a manner as to create a richer field for the play of the violin. Arguably, Chan literature, too, began to produce knock-off versions of itself in the discourse of judging poetry and art in China—not to mention Neo-Confucianism—discourses that mimicked many elements of Chan but then, in deploying Chan-style discourses in other cultural zones, produced a more resonant background against which Chan discourse could glow more brilliantly and with more "naturalness."[2]

The key difference between the evolution of Chan rhetoric and the violin is that Chan doesn't have a tangible product. The knowledges at play in Chan discourse produce musiclike discourse effects that are as real as anything else; it is just that they aren't secured to anything substantial and instead derive from subjects thinking in a certain way about other subjects (the perfect masters) and then reconceiving their

2. For a discussion of the use of Chan's Northern and Southern categories in Song and later discussions of poetry and painting, see James Cahill, "Tung Ch'i-ch'ang's 'Southern and Northern Schools' in the History and Theory of Painting."

own subjecthood in a new form as a consequence of that fantasy-about-the-master being taken as real. As long as we commit to the game that is essentially defined as "I'm sure the master knows the Real and has, in fact, become that Real, and knows the Real about me, a Real that I can recover from him," there is much to do, say, and desire. But once that figure of the absolute master and his absolute knowledge is revealed as a discourse phenomenon, constructed over the centuries, for a host of reasons, the game loses its foundation and appeal.

Chan's art, then, is quite the opposite of many styles of painting. For instance, a painter might not seek to hide how her figures rest on the uneven surface of the canvas or silk, and might even use the texture of those fabrics to enhance the presentation of the painted scenes. Thus, it would seem that the viewer is invited to appreciate how the medium—the background silk or the brush strokes—is both what it is and also the basis for the created image, be it a windswept tree or a snowscape. In these cases, the artist seems to delight in revealing how art is made: it is that act of rendering not-image—the silk and ink—into image, even as the not-image aspect of the image is still available for observation, with the flickering gap between the two being part of the pleasure of the depiction.

Chan writing works on completely different principles. Its discourse is important and meaningful only insofar as it is able to transcend its literary matrix—its ink and silk. It is only by looking completely *through* the medium of Chan literature that that medium can deliver its content: the supposed orality and isness of these enlightened masters, and other types of proof that will convince the reader that *behind* the literary presentation there is a Real master with Real truth far from the artistic cunning of any particular writer. In short, as an art form, Chan works only when it isn't recognized as art, and that of course is the art of Chan. However, given that one isn't ever supposed to come to this realization about Chan, it could be argued that it isn't really art at all, and this has some profound consequences for how we judge its lasting value, a topic that I will have to leave for another venue.

However we think about Chan as art, it is still true that it was knowingly produced, century after century, by a tradition of author-artisans who were (1) quite aware of the play of form and content in Chan discourse in which both disappear into the fantasy of the absolute master; and (2) quite capable of reproducing these "artistic" effects in more elaborate and effective formats. In other words, throughout this book I have tried to reveal how the "antiart" of Chan was recognized as an art form and practiced as such by the series of Tang authors who wrote their genealogies-of-truth having read previous ones and recognized the art of writing genealogies-of-truth with enough clarity that they could profitably turn to re-create and perpetuate this practice of writing about the ownership of tradition.

At the center of this discussion of Chan-as-art is the problem of what to do with Chan authors' use of intersubjectivity since it seems clear that they practiced a writing in which they thought about how others thought and then wrote in a manner that worked from that understanding of the Other's understanding. The problem is that that circle of intersubjectivity was never admitted or shared back to the Other, which, I think, excludes a basic element in the construction of the artistic experience. That is, part of appreciating art seems to involve recognizing how the artist is moving your sensibilities, even as you also appreciate that the artist knew enough about experience and human sensibility to be able to direct and manipulate those sensibilities. In effect, you are invited to look at the art to see how the artist looks at how you look, and this naturally changes the way you look at yourself and the world. This is clearly a rather full form of intersubjectivity, perhaps the fullest, and fulfills the fundamental charge of art: to find mediums that express human interiors with exterior items in such a way that other humans are not only impressed, literally, but also come to reflect on human experience. On these grounds, Chan, for all its later involvement in the arts, is a very odd cultural figure, based as it is on the self-erasure of the author-artist and the denial of the cycle of intersubjectivity as defined by author, text, and reader.

ACADEMIC MYSTICISM AND THINKING ABOUT THINKING

Among the range of responses that we could pursue once we start looking at "Chan art" *as art,* one response stands out as particularly promising and involves yet another art. This is a kind of intellectual or academic mysticism. This academic mysticism probably doesn't deserve the title "mysticism," but I have chosen this odd phrase to speak of the queasy reverie born of watching meaning systems come into being. It is, in fact, just this commitment to judiciously reviewing the play of signifiers and signifieds within the evolution of a tradition that I posit as an art form, an art form that is the basis of this book's theoretical approach and which seems to me to be simply another way of articulating the full force of the liberal arts' summons: How to learn from watching what everyone else has been doing. Thus, this book has been dedicated to the project of getting more comfortable *thinking about thinking* by watching how thinking was understood and manipulated in the past. Or, in more topical terms, I have tried to investigate human identity by watching how it was so forcefully reinvented in Tang-era China with the lineages of Chinese buddhas.

Admittedly, this approach will annoy the more ardent Chan-for-Chan's-sake reader who, even in light of the Dunhuang findings, hopes to recover something authentic and inspiring here, but I hope such a reader will consider whether if instead of pushing against the wave of disappointment that is clearly the effect of the Dunhuang material, we might do much better to surf forward and think more placidly about the gradual and mediated creation of truth, enlightenment, and perfection from a position that might offer as much philosophic ease and insight as was expected from a more credulous reading of this material. In short, I am arguing that there might be something enlightening about reconsidering the creation of Chan enlightenment.

My point here is not that we need a new, demythologized Chan, one refitted in view of twentieth- and twenty-first-century criticism but rather that the whole promise of Religious Studies as a critical discipline was, from the beginning, headed in this direction in which understanding the "all-too-human" origins of religions could also be grounds for a kind of liberating flexibility vis-à-vis symbolic orders, a flexibility born of recognizing how these orders were created and consumed—something that obviously Nietzsche cared about immensely. That is, understanding the mechanisms by which humans devise systems of desire, belief, and closure requires being both inside them and outside them, and just this flexibility and irony vis-à-vis meaning and truth sets the stage for some rather profound reflections on human being.

Thus, if Nietzsche was right when he argued in the second essay in *On the Genealogy of Morals* that humans became interesting once they invented religion several millennia ago, then it is also true that we became doubly interesting in the nineteenth and twentieth centuries when we discovered how to think about our discovery of religion and our long, and continuing, affair with "the perfect man"—be he the Chinese buddha or, more ironically in Nietzsche's case, the *übermensch*. In sum, it is precisely in not looking away from the fathering of fathers in Chan literature that we regain our kinship with our ancestors and, unavoidably, ourselves.

Chinese Glossary

Anzhou 安州

Baiguwu 柏谷塢
Baiguzhang 柏谷裝
banruo wuzhi 般若無知
Baolin zhuan 寶林傳
benxin 本心
biezhong 別眾
biao 表
bihuaxiang 壁畫像
bincheng 稟承
bing buding 並不定
Blue-robed Master Ming 青布明
Boxun 波旬
Bodhidharma 菩提達磨
bujiao ren zuoshen 不教人坐身
buju huaxia zhi di 不居華夏之地
bujin youwei 不盡有為
buzhong 部眾
buzhu wuwei 不住無為

chanfa 禪法
chanshi 禪師
chanzhi 禪智
chanzong 禪宗
chaowenzhe 朝聞者
chaowu 超悟

chenwang 塵妄
chengken 誠懇
chouwei yu gengsang zhi lu 臭味於耕桑之侶
Chuan fabao ji 傳法寶紀
chuan yi weixin 傳以為信

dade 大德
daishu 代數
Damo 達摩
Damolun 達摩論
Damozu 達摩祖
daoru zhenjing 道入真境
Daoxin 道信
Daoxuan 道宣
Dazhidu lun 大智渡論
de daoguo 得道果
dexiangfo zhijian 得向佛知見
di 第
dichuanfa 遞傳法
didai 帝代
ding 定
Ding shifei lun 定是非論
dishi 帝師
dun 頓
dunjian foxing 頓見佛性
dunjiao 頓教
dunru 頓入
dunwu 頓悟
Dunwu zuishangcheng lun 頓悟最上乘論
duomiu 多謬

Erru sixing lun 二入四行論

fabao 法寶
Fachong 法沖
fafu 法縛
Fahua wenju 法華文句
fajie 法界
fan 梵
fanfu 凡夫
fanseng 梵僧
faqi 法棄
Faru 法如
fatan 法壇
fa wuzhongbian 法無中邊
faxin (dharma guarantor) 法信

fa xin　發心
fei benzi jijing xin　非本自寂淨心
fenfu　分付
fobei　佛碑
fomiyi　佛密義
foxing　佛性
fozong　佛宗
fu　付
furushi　復如是
fuzhu　付囑
Fu fazang yinyuan zhuan　付法藏因緣傳

Gaojiong　高頴
Gasengzhuan　高僧傳
gaozu　高祖
gong'an　公案
Guanding　灌頂
Guanxin lun　觀心論
guobao　國寶
guoqing shi　國清時
Guoqingsi　國清寺
Guoqing bailu　國清百錄
guoshi　國師

Hongren　弘忍
huabi　化畢
huadaozhe　化道者
huafo　化佛
huangdi zhi zhu　黃帝之珠
Huahujing　化胡經
Huadusi　化渡寺
Huataisi　滑臺寺
Huangmei　黃梅
hui　慧
Huike　慧可
Huineng　慧能
Huisi　慧思
Huiwen　慧文
Huiyuan　慧遠

jier michuan fayin　即而密傳法印
jihu　及乎
jishen　機神
jianbenxing wei chan　見本性為禪
jianjian　漸漸
jiaomen　教門

jietan 戒檀
jingjie 境界
jingxin 淨心
Jizang 吉藏
jueding 決定
juezhao 覺照
jun 君

kai fozhijian 開佛知見
kan 龕
Kou Qianzhi 寇謙之
kuxin 刳心

Lao An 老安
Leng qie ren fa zhi 楞伽人法志
Lengqie shizi ji 楞伽師資記
li 離
Lidai fabao ji 曆代法寶記
lingfu 靈府
lingzhi 靈質
Lihuo lun 理惑論
Li Shimin 李世民
Li Zhifei 李知非
lunben 論本

menren 門人
mie fofa xiang 滅佛法相
miyin 密印
miqi 密棄
Mingbaoji 冥報記
Mohezhiguan 摩訶止觀
mofa 末法
Moshuo 魔說

nian buqi wei zuo 念不起為坐

Pan Shizheng 潘師正

Nanyang heshang dunjiao chanmen zhiliaoxing tanyu 南陽和上頓教解脫禪直
    了性檀語
neiyin 內隱

Pei Cui 裴漼
pingdeng 平等
pu 樸
Puji 普寂

Puti Damo nanzong ding shifei lun 菩提達摩南宗定是非論
Puti Damo nanzong yimen 菩提達摩南宗一門

qixin ji mie 起心既滅
Qixin lun 起心論
qizutang 七祖堂
qinshuo 親說
quzheng yuxin 取證於心

rentian 人天
ru cimen 入此門

Sanjiejiao 三階教
Sengcan 僧璨
shanxing 羶行
shanzhishi 善知識
Shaolinsi 少林寺
Shaolinsibei 少林寺碑
Shaozhou 韶州
Shenhui 神會
shenseng 神僧
Shenxiu 神秀
sheng yu ren qi gan 聖與仁豈敢
Shiji 史記
Shijiashipu 釋迦氏譜
shijian 實見
shixiang 實相
shizi 師資
Shizi xuemai zhuan 師資血脈傳
shouchuan 授傳
Shuangfeng 雙峰
Sima Chengzhen 司馬承禎
shouben 守本
shouqidao 授其道
shushiyunian 數十餘年
Songshan 嵩山

tan 檀
tan'ai 貪愛
Tangguo 唐國
Tanglin 唐林
Tanlin 曇林
Tanyu 檀語
tian he yan zai 天何言哉
tibai 稊稗
Tianmo 天魔

tianshi 天師
tongwu 通悟
tuisheng 退省

wangdao 王道
Wang Shichong 王世充
Wang Wei 王維
wang xiang 妄想
wangxin 妄心
weiwang 細妄
Wendaza zhengyi 問答雜證議
wenzhao 文照
wo jin 我今
wo liudai dashi yiyi jie yan 我六代大師一一皆言
wo liudai zushi 我六代祖師
Wu fangbian 五方便
Wu gengzhuansong 五更轉頌
wujinzang 無盡藏
wunian 無念
wushang dabao 無上大寶
wushang daofa 無上道法
wushang zhenzong 無上真宗
wusuo xiuqu 無所委曲
wuwei 無為
wuwenzi 無文子
wuzhi 無知

xianren 仙人
xiangcheng 相承
xiangcheng chuanfa 相承傳法
xiangchuan 相傳
xianji 先機
xiansheng zhi dao 先勝之道
xianyou fuzhu 先有付囑
Xianzongji 顯宗記
xifasi 希法嗣
xindi 心地
xintong rulaixin 心同如來心
xinru foxin 心如佛心
Xinxing 信行
xinyuanxiang 心緣相
xinzhi dude 心知獨得
xingzhuang 行狀
Xiuxi zhiguan zuochan fayao 修習止觀坐禪法要
xiu 脩
xiuji 脩紀
Xuangao 玄高

xuanwang 玄網
Xuanze 玄賾
xuedi 學地
Xugaosengzhuan 續高僧傳

yangxing shanzhong 養性山中
yanlun butong 言論不同
yanshuoxiang 言說像
yanzuo 宴坐
yaoshouji 遙授記
yayang seng 啞羊僧
yibu 異部
Yifu 義福
yijian zhongzhi 一見重之
yinke 印可
yishi 一時
yiyin zhifa 一印之法
yiyin zhengxin (confirmed by mind) 以印證心
Yixing 一行
yixing sanmei 一行三昧
yixun 遺訓
yiyi jie 一一皆
youguan 幽關
youru fumu 有如父母
yougu 幽谷
yuan jiang 元匠

za 雜
zeng buqiyu 曾不起予
zhenjingjie 真境界
zhenru 真如
zhenrumen 真如門
zhenruzang 真如藏
zhenzong 真宗
zhengxin 證心
zhengyi 證義
zhi 之
zhilun 至論
Zhiyi 智顗
zhiru 直入
zhishi 知識
zhongsheng foxing 眾生佛性
zhuan 傳
zhuanshi 轉識
zhuangyan 莊嚴
zhuxin ruding 住心入定
zijue 自覺

ziran 自然
zongji 宗極
zongtong li zongtong 宗通立宗通
zongzhi 宗旨
zufoweishi 祖佛為師
zuochan 坐禪
zuo ciyongxin 作此用心
zuohua 坐化
zushi 祖師
zuotanchang 作檀場
Zuozhuan 左傳

References

Adamek, Wendi. "Imagining the Portrait of a Chan Master." In *Chan Buddhism in Ritual Context*, edited by Bernard Faure, 36–73. London and New York: Routledge Curzon, 2003.

———. *The Mystique of Transmission: On an Early Chan History and Its Contents.* New York: Columbia University Press, 2007.

———. "Robes Purple and Gold: Transmission of the Robe in the *Lidai fabao ji*." *History of Religions* 40, no. 1 (2000): 58–81.

Althusser, Louis. "Ideology and Ideological State Apparatuses." In *Lenin and Philosophy and Other Essays*, 127–86. New York: Monthly Review Press, 1972.

Balkin, J. M. *Cultural Software: A Theory of Ideology.* New Haven: Yale University Press, 1998.

Bambach, Charles. *Heidegger's Roots: Nietzsche, National Socialism and the Greeks.* Ithaca: Cornell University Press, 2003.

Barrett, Timothy H. "Buddhist Precepts in a Lawless World: Some Comments on the Linhuai Ordination Scandal." In *Going Forth: Visions of Buddhist Vinaya*, edited by William Bodiford, 101–23. Honolulu: University of Hawai'i Press, 2005.

———. "The Date of the Leng-chia shih-tzu chi." *Journal of the Royal Asiatic Society*, 3d ser., 1, no. 2 (1991): 255–59.

———. "The Emergence of the Taoist Papacy in the T'ang Dynasty." *Asia Major*, 3d ser., 7 (1994): 89–106.

———. "Kill the Patriarchs!" *Buddhist Forum* 1 (1990): 87–97.

———. *Taoism under the T'ang: Religion and Empire during the Golden Age of Chinese History.* London: WellSweep, 1996.

Barthes, Roland. "The Eiffel Tower." In *A Barthes Reader*, edited by Susan Sontag, 236–50. New York: Hill and Wang, 1983.

Bielefeldt, Carl. "Recarving the Dragon: History and Dogma in the Study of

Dōgen." In *Dōgen Studies,* edited by William LaFleur, 21–53. Honolulu: University of Hawai'i Press, 1985.

———. "Tsung-tse's *Tso-Ch'an I* and the 'Secret' of Zen Meditation." In *Traditions of Meditation in Chinese Buddhism,* edited by Peter Gregory, 129–61. Honolulu: University of Hawai'i Press, 1985.

Bourdieu, Pierre. "The Field of Cultural Production, or: The Economic World Reversed." In *The Field of Cultural Production,* 29–73. New York: Columbia University Press, 1993.

———. *Language and Symbolic Power.* Cambridge, MA: Harvard University Press, 1991.

———. "The Production of Belief: Contribution to an Economy of Symbolic Goods." In *The Field of Cultural Production,* 74–111. New York: Columbia University Press, 1993.

———. *Les règles de l'art: Genèse et structure du champ littéraire.* Paris: Seuil, 1992/1998.

Broughton, Jeffrey. *The Bodhidharma Anthology: The Earliest Records of Zen.* Berkeley: University of California, 1999.

Cahill, James. "Tung Ch'i-ch'ang's 'Southern and Northern Schools' in the History and Theory of Painting: A Reconsideration." In *Sudden and Gradual Approaches to Enlightenment in Chinese Thought,* edited by Peter Gregory, 429–46. Honolulu: University of Hawai'i Press, 1987.

Campany, Robert Ford. *Strange Writing: Anomaly Accounts in Early Medieval China.* Albany: State University of New York Press, 1996.

Chen Jinhua. "A Holy Alliance: The Court-appointed 'Monks of Great Virtue' and Their Religious and Political Role under the Sui Dynasty (581–617)." *Tang Yanjiu* (Journal of Tang Studies) 7 (2001): 19–37.

———. *Making and Remaking History: A Study of Tiantai Sectarian Historiography.* Tokyo: International Institute for Buddhist Studies, 1999.

———. *Monks and Monarchs, Kinship and Kingship: Tanqian in Sui Buddhism and Politics.* Kyoto: Italian School of East Asian Studies, 2002.

Cleary, J. C., trans. *Zen Dawn: Early Zen Texts from Tun Huang.* Boston: Shambhala, 1991.

Cleary, Thomas, trans. "Transmission of Light." In *Classics of Buddhism and Zen,* 4:17–228. Boston: Shambhala, 2001.

Cole, Alan. *Fetishizing Tradition: Desire and Reinvention in Buddhist and Christian Narratives.* Forthcoming.

———. "It's All in the Framing: Desire and Innocence in Early Chan Narratives—A Close Reading of the *Biography of Chan Master Faru.*" Paper presented at the University of California, Berkeley, March 17, 2002.

———. "A Plan for the Past: The Role of Innate Perfection in the *Awakening of Faith's* Sinification of Buddhism." Paper presented at the annual meeting of the American Academy of Religion, Philadelphia, 2005.

———. Review of *Filial Piety in Chinese Thought and History. Journal of Chinese Religions,* 34 (2006): 82–84.

———. Review of Jamie Hubbard, *Absolute Delusion, Perfect Buddhahood: The Rise and Fall of a Chinese Heresy. Journal of Asian Studies* 60, no. 3 (August 2001): 838–40.

————. "Simplicity for the Sophisticated: Rereading the *Daode jing* for the Polemics of Ease and Innocence." *History of Religions* 46 (2006): 1–49.

————. *Text as Father: Paternal Seductions in Early Mahayana Buddhist Literature.* Berkeley: University of California Press, 2005.

————. "Upside Down/Right Side Up: A Revisionist History of Buddhist Funerals in China." *History of Religions* 35, no. 4 (1996): 307–38.

Csikszentmihalyi, Mark, and Michael Nylan. "Constructing Lineages and Inventing Traditions Through Exemplary Figures in Early China." *T'oung Pao* 89 (2003): 59–99.

Dawkins, Richard. *The Selfish Gene.* Oxford: Oxford University Press, 1976.

Demiéville, Paul. *Choix d'études bouddhiques (1929–1970).* Leiden: Brill, 1973.

————. "Deux documents de Touen-houang sur le Dhyāna chinois." In *Essays on the History of Buddhism Presented to Professor Zenryū Tsukamoto,* 1–27. Kyoto: Nagai Shuppansha, 1961. Reprinted in *Choix d'études bouddhiques (1929–1970),* 241–60. Leiden: Brill, 1973.

Donner, Neal, and Daniel B. Stevenson. *The Great Calming and Contemplation.* Honolulu: University of Hawai'i Press, 1993.

Dr. Seuss. *The Cat in the Hat.* Boston: Houghton Mifflin, 1957.

Dubuisson, Daniel. *Impostures et psuedo-science: L'oeuvre de Mircea Eliade.* Paris: Presses Universitaires du Septentrion, 2005.

Faure, Bernard. "Bodhidharma as Textual and Religious Paradigm." *History of Religions* 25, no. 3 (1986): 187–98.

————. *Le bouddhisme Ch'an en mal d'histoire: Genèse d'une tradition religieuse dans le Chine des T'ang.* Paris: École Française d'Extrême-Orient, 1989.

————. *The Rhetoric of Immediacy: A Cultural Critique of Chan/Zen Buddhism.* Princeton: Princeton University Press, 1991.

————. *La volonté d'orthodoxie dans le bouddhisme chinois.* Paris: Editions du CNRS, 1988.

————. *The Will to Orthodoxy: A Critical Genealogy of Northern Chan Buddhism.* Translated by Phyllis Brooks. Stanford: Stanford University Press, 1997.

Fontein, Jan. "The Epitaphs of Two Chan Patriarchs." *Artibus Asiae* 53, nos. 1–2 (1993): 98–110.

Forte, Antonino. *Political Propaganda and Ideology in China at the End of the Seventh Century.* Naples: Istituto Universitario Orientale, 1976.

————. "Daitoku." In *Hōbōgirin: Dictionnaire encyclopédique du bouddhisme d'après les sources chinoises et japonaises,* edited by Jacques Gernet et al., 8:1071–86. Paris: Adrien Maisonneuve, 2003.

Foulk, T. Griffith. "The Koan: The Form and Function of Koan Literature: A Historical Overview." In *The Kōan: Texts and Contexts in Zen Buddhism,* edited by Steve Heine and Dale S. Wright, 15–45. Oxford: Oxford University Press, 2000.

————. "Myth, Ritual, and Monastic Practice in Sung Ch'an Buddhism." In *Religion and Society in T'ang and Sung China,* edited by Patricia Buckley Ebrey and Peter N. Gregory, 147–208. Honolulu: University of Hawai'i Press, 1993.

Foulk, T. Griffith, and Robert H. Sharf. "The Ritual Use of Portraiture in Medieval China." In *Chan Buddhism in Ritual Context*, edited by Bernard Faure, 74–150. London and New York: Routledge Curzon, 2003.

Gernet, Jacques. "Biographie du Maître Chen-houei du Ho-tsö." *Journal Asiatique* 239 (1951): 29–68.

———. "Complétement aux *Entretiens du Maître de Dhyāna Chen-houei*." *Bulletin de l'École Française d'Extrême-Orient* 44, no. 2 (1954): 453–66.

———. *Entretiens du Maître de Dhyāna Chen-houei du Ho-tsö*. Paris: École Française d'Extrême-Orient, 1949.

Gjerston, Donald. *Miraculous Retribution: A Study and Translation of T'anglin's Ming pao chi*. Berkeley: Center for South and Southeast Asia Studies, 1989.

Gómez, Luis O. "Purifying Gold: The Metaphor of Effort and Intuition in Buddhist Thought and Practice." In *Sudden and Gradual Approaches to Enlightenment in Chinese Thought*, edited by Peter Gregory, 67–165. Honolulu: University of Hawai'i Press, 1987.

Groner, Paul. "The Ordination Ritual in the *Platform Sūtra* Within the Context of the East Asian Buddhist Vinaya Tradition." In *Fo Kuang Shan Report of International Conference on Ch'an Buddhism*, 220–50. Gaoxiong, Taiwan: Foguang, 1990.

Guisso, Richard W. L. *Wu Tse-t'ien and the Politics of Legitimation in T'ang China*. Bellingham: Western Washington University, 1978.

Hakeda, Yoshito S. *The Awakening of Faith*. New York: Columbia University Press, 1967.

Hirai Shun'ei. *Hokke mongu no seiritsu ni kansuru kenkyū*. Tokyo: Shunjūsha, 1985.

Hu Shi. "Leng-ch'ieh tsung k'ao." In *Hu Shih wen-ts'un*, 3:194–244. Taipei: Yuan-t'ung t'u shu kung-szu, 1953. Reprinted in Yanagida Seizan, ed., *Ko Teki zengakuan*, 154–95. Kyoto: Chūbun shuppan sha, 1975.

———. *Shenhui heshang yiji*. Shanghai: Oriental Book Company, 1930.

Hubbard, Jamie. *Absolute Delusion, Perfect Buddhahood: The Rise and Fall of a Chinese Heresy*. Honolulu: University of Hawai'i Press, 2001.

———. "Chinese Reliquary Inscriptions and the San-chieh-chiao." *Journal of the International Association of Buddhist Studies* 14 (1991): 253–80.

Jorgensen, John. "The 'Imperial' Lineage of Ch'an Buddhism: The Role of Confucian Ritual and Ancestor Worship in Ch'an's Search for Legitimation in the mid-T'ang Dynasty." *Papers on Far Eastern History* 35 (1987): 89–133.

———. *Inventing Hui-neng, the Sixth Patriarch: Hagiography and Biography in Early Ch'an*. Leiden: Brill, 2005.

Keenan, John P. *How Master Mou Removes Our Doubts*. Albany: State University of New York Press, 1994.

Kieschnick, John. *The Impact of Buddhism on Chinese Material Culture*. Princeton: Princeton University Press, 2003.

Kirkland, Russell. "Ssu-ma-Ch'eng-chen and the Role of Taoism in Medieval Chinese Polity." *Journal of Asian History* 31, no. 2 (1997): 105–38.

———. *Taoism: The Enduring Tradition*. New York and London: Routledge, 2004.

Kohn, Livia, and Russell Kirkland. "Daoism in the Tang (618–907)." In *The Daoist Handbook*, edited by Livia Kohn, 339–83. Leiden: Brill, 2000.

Kuo Li-ying. *Confession et contrition dans le bouddhisme chinois du Ve au Xe siècle*. Paris: École Française d'Extrême-Orient, 1994.

Laignel-Lavastine, Alexandra. *Cioran, Eliade, Ionesco: l'oubli du fascisme*. Paris: PUF, 2002.

Lamotte, Etienne. *History of Indian Buddhism*. Translated by Sara Webb-Boin. Louvain: Institute Orientaliste, [1958] 1988.

Lau, D. C., trans. *Confucius: The Analects*. New York: Penguin, 1979.

Lewis, Mark Edward. "The Suppression of the Three Stages Sect: Apocrypha as a Political Issue." In *Chinese Buddhist Apocrypha*, edited by Robert E. Buswell Jr., 207–38. Honolulu: University of Hawai'i Press, 1990.

Li Ronxi, trans. *The Biographical Scripture of King Aśoka*. Berkeley: Numata Center, 1993.

Liebenthal, W. "The Sermon of Shen-hui." *Asia Major*, n.s., 3, no. 2 (1953): 132–55.

Lusthaus, Dan. *Buddhist Phenomenology: A Philosophical Investigation of Yogācāra Buddhism and the Ch'eng Wei-shih lun*. London and New York: Routledge Curzon, 2002.

Magnin, Paul. *La vie et l'oeuvre de Huisi (515–577)*. Paris: École Française d'Extrême-Orient, 1979.

Maspero, Henri. "Sur la date et l'authenticitè du Fou fa tsang yin yuan tchouan." In *Mélanges de'Indianisme (offerts à S. Lévi par ses élèves)*, 129–49. Paris: E. Leroux, 1911.

Mather, Richard B. "K'ou Ch'ien-chih and the Taoist Theocracy at the Northern Wei Court, 425–451." In *Facets of Taoism: Essays in Chinese Religion*, edited by Holmes Welch and Anna Seidel, 103–22. New Haven: Yale University Press, 1979.

McRae, John R. "The Antecedents of Encounter Dialogue in Chinese Ch'an Buddhism." In *The Kōan: Texts and Contexts in Zen Buddhism,* edited by Steven Heine and Dale S. Wright, 46–74. Oxford: Oxford University Press, 2000.

———. "Daoxuan's Vision of Jetavana: The Ordination Platform Movement in Medieval Chinese Buddhism." In *Going Forth: Visions of Buddhist Vinaya,* edited by William M. Bodiford, 68–100. Honolulu: University of Hawai'i Press, 2005.

———. *The Northern School and the Formation of Early Ch'an Buddhism*. Honolulu: University of Hawai'i Press, 1986.

———. *Seeing through Zen: Encounter, Transformation, and Genealogy in Chinese Chan Buddhism*. Berkeley: University of California Press, 2003.

———. "Shen-hui and the Teaching of Sudden Enlightenment in Early Ch'an Buddhism." In *Sudden and Gradual Approaches to Enlightenment in Chinese Thought,* edited by Peter Gregory, 227–78. Honolulu: University of Hawai'i Press, 1987.

———. "Shenhui as Evangelist: Re-envisioning the Identity of a Chinese Buddhist Monk." *Journal of Chinese Religions* 30 (2002): 123–48.

———. "Shen-hui's Vocation on the Ordination Platform and Our Visualization of Medieval Ch'an Buddhism." *Zenbunka kenkyūjo kiyō* 24 (1998): 43–66.

———. *Zen Evangelist: Shenhui (684–758), Sudden Enlightenment, and the Southern School of Chinese Chan Buddhism*. Honolulu: University of Hawai'i Press, forthcoming.

Morrison, Elizabeth. "Ancestors, Authority, and History: Chan Lineage in the Writings of Qisong (1007–1072)." Ph.D dissertation, Stanford University, 2004.

———. "Contested Visions of the Buddhist Past and the Curious Fate of an Early Medieval Buddhist Text." Seminar paper, Stanford University, 1996.

Nattier, Jan. *Once upon a Future Time: Studies in a Buddhist Philosophy of Decline*. Berkeley: Asian Humanities Press, 1991.

Nietzsche, Friedrich. *On the Genealogy of Morals*. Translated by Walter Kaufman. New York: Vintage, [1887] 1967.

Ogawa Takashi. "Shoki zenshū keiseishi no ichi sokumen: Fujaku to 'Sūzan hōmon.'" *Komazawa Daigaku Bukkyō Gakubu Ronshū* 20 (1989): 310–25.

Owen, Stephen. "The Self's Perfect Mirror: Poetry as Autobiography." In *The Vitality of the Lyric Voice*, edited by Stephen Owen and Lin Shuen-fu, 71–85. Princeton: Princeton University Press, 1986.

Pelliot, Paul. "Notes sur quelques artistes des Six Dynasties et des T'ang." *T'oung Pao* 22 (1923): 215–91.

Penkower, Linda. "In the Beginning . . . Guanding (561–632) and the Creation of Early Tiantai." *Journal of the International Association of Buddhist Studies* 23, no. 2 (2000): 245–96.

Poceski, Mario. "*Mazu yulu* and the Creation of the Chan Records of Sayings." In *The Zen Canon: Understanding the Classic Texts*, edited by Steven Heine and Dale S. Wright, 53–80. Oxford: Oxford University Press, 2004.

Rong Xinjiang. "Dunhuang ben Chanzong dengshi canjuan shiyi." In *Zhou Shaoliang Xiansheng xinkaijiuzhi qingshou wenji*, 231–44. Beijing: Zhonghua shuju, 1997.

———. "Youguan Dunhuangben *Lidai fabo ji* de xin ziliao." *Jiechuang Foxue* 2 (2002): 94–105.

Saso, Michael. *Zen Is for Everyone*. Honolulu: University of Hawai'i Press, 2001.

Shahar, Meir. "Epigraphy, Buddhist Historiography, and Fighting Monks: The Case of The Shaolin Monastery." *Asia Major*, 3d ser., 13, no. 2 (2000): 15–36.

Sharf, Robert H. "Buddhist Modernism and the Rhetoric of Meditative Experience." *Numen* 42, no. 3 (1995): 228–83.

———. *Coming to Terms with Chinese Buddhism: A Reading of the Treasure Store Treatise*. Honolulu: University of Hawai'i Press, 2005.

Shih, Robert. *Biographies des moines éminents (Kao Seng Tchouan) de Houei-kiao. Part I, Biographies des premiers traducteurs*. Louvain: Institut Orientaliste, 1968.

Shinohara Kōichi. "Guanding's Biography of Zhiyi, the Fourth Chinese Patriarch of the Tiantai Tradition." In *Speaking of Monks: Religious Biography in*

India and China, edited by Phyllis Granoff and Kōichi Shinohara, 98–232. Oakville, Ont.: Mosaic Press, 1992.

———. "The Kaṣāya Robe of the Past Buddha Kāśyapa in the Miraculous Instruction Given to the Vinaya Master Daoxuan (596–667)." *Chung-Hwa Buddhist Journal* 13, no. 2 (2000): 299–367.

Strenski, Ivan. *Four Theories of Myth in Twentieth-Century History.* Iowa City: University of Iowa Press, 1988.

Strong, John S. *The Legend of King Aśoka: A Study and Translation of the Aśokāvadāna.* Princeton: Princeton University Press, 1983.

Szonyi, Michael. *Practicing Kinship: Lineage & Descent in Late Imperial China.* Stanford: Stanford University Press, 2002.

Taishō shinshū daizōkyō. 100 vols. Edited by Takakusu Junjirō and Watanabe Kaigyoku. Tokyo: Taishō issaikyō kankōkai, 1924–32.

Tonami Mamoru. *The Shaolin Monastery Stele on Mount Song.* Translated by P. A. Herbert. Kyoto: Italian School of East Asian Studies, 1990.

Turcanu, Florin. *Mircea Eliade: Le prisonnier de l'histoire.* Paris: Découverte, 2003.

Twitchett, Denis. *The Writing of Official History under the Tang.* Cambridge: Cambridge University Press, 1992.

Twitchett, Denis, and Howard J. Wechsler. "Kao-tsung (reign 649–83) and the Empress Wu: The Inheritor and the Usurper." In *The Cambridge History of China: Sui and T'ang China,* edited by Denis Twitchett, 242–89. Cambridge: Cambridge University Press, 1979.

Watson, Burton, trans. *Chuang Tzu: Basic Writings.* New York: Columbia University Press, 1964.

———. *The Complete Works of Chuang Tzu.* New York: Columbia University Press, 1968.

———. *The Vimalakīrti Sūtra.* New York: Columbia University Press, 1997.

Wechsler, Howard J. "The Founding of the T'ang Dynasty: Kao-tsu, reign 618–26." In *The Cambridge History of China: Sui and T'ang China,* edited by Denis Twitchett, 150–87. Cambridge: Cambridge University Press, 1979.

———. *Offerings of Jade and Silk: Ritual and Symbol in the Legitimation of the T'ang Dynasty.* New Haven: Yale University Press, 1985.

———. "T'ai-tsung (reign 626–49) the Consolidator." In *The Cambridge History of China: Sui and T'ang China,* edited by Denis Twitchett, 188–241. Cambridge: Cambridge University Press, 1979.

Weinstein, Stanley. *Buddhism under the T'ang.* Cambridge: Cambridge University Press, 1987.

Welter, Albert. "Lineage and Context in the *Patriarch's Hall Collection* and the *Transmission of the Lamp.*" In *The Zen Canon: Understanding the Classic Texts,* edited by Steve Heine and Dale S. Wright, 137–80. Oxford: Oxford University Press, 2004.

Wen Yucheng. *Shaolin fanggu.* Tianjin: Baihua wenyi, 1999.

———. "Ji xin chu tu de Heze Dashi Shenhui taming." *Shijie zongjiao yanjiu* 2 (1984): 78–79.

Wright, Arthur. "The Formation of Sui Ideology, 581–604." In *Chinese Thought and Institutions,* edited by John K. Fairbank, 71–104. Chicago: University of Chicago Press, 1957.

Wright, Dale S. *Philosophical Meditations on Zen Buddhism.* Cambridge: Cambridge University Press, 1998.

Yampolsky, Philip. *The Platform Sūtra of the Sixth Patriarch.* New York: Columbia University Press, 1967.

Yanagida Seizan. "Passion for Zen: Two Talks by Yanagida Seizan at the San Francisco Zen Center." *Cahiers d'Extrême-Asie* 7 (1993–94): 1–30.

————. *Shoki no zenshi, I: Ryōga shijiki; Denhōbōki.* Tokyo: Chikuma shobō, 1971.

————. *Shoki Zenshū shisho no kenkyū.* Kyoto: Hōzōkan, 1967.

————, ed. *Ko Teki Zengaku an.* Kyoto: Chūbun shuppan sha, 1975.

Yoshikawa Tadao. "Dōkyō no dōkei to zen no hōkei." *Tōyō gakujutsu kenkyū* 27 (1988): 11–34.

Young, Stuart. "Conceiving the Indian Buddhist Patriarchs in China." Ph.D. dissertation, Princeton University, 2008.

Zeuschner, Robert. "The *Hsien Tsung Chi* (An Early Ch'an [Zen] Buddhist Text)." *Journal of Chinese Philosophy* 3 (1976): 253–68.

Zürcher, Erik. *The Buddhist Conquest of China: The Spread and Adaptation of Buddhism in Early Medieval China.* Leiden: Brill, 1959.

Index

Text   10/13 Sabon
Display   Sabon
Compositor   BookMatters, Berkeley
Printer and binder   Maple-Vail Book Manufacturing Group